THE LONG SHADOWS
OF LAMBETH X

"Take heed therefore unto yourselves, and to all the flock, over which the Holy Ghost hath made you overseers, to feed the Church of God, which he hath purchased with his own blood. For I know this, that after my departing shall grievous wolves enter in among you, not sparing the flock. Also of your own selves shall men arise, speaking perverse things, to draw away disciples after them."

Acts 20 : 28–30

The Long Shadows of Lambeth X

A CRITICAL, EYE-WITNESS ACCOUNT OF
THE TENTH DECENNIAL CONFERENCE OF
462 BISHOPS OF THE ANGLICAN COMMUNION

JAMES B. SIMPSON and
EDWARD M. STORY
Priests of the American Episcopal Church

McGraw-Hill Book Company

New York   Toronto   London   Sydney

For

The Order of the Holy Cross
with gratitude for its prayers

and in memory of

James Hazelton Pearson, 1922–1968,
Priest of the Diocese of Springfield

PREFACE

THE OBJECTIVE OF THIS BOOK on the tenth Lambeth Conference is to report the centenary Conference exactly as it was—not
as we wish it might have been or as we wish it had not been.

Throughout the Conference and in the months following we have
held as always to our creedal belief in the One, Holy, Catholic,
Apostolic Church. Some events of Lambeth X reaffirmed that tradition, others seemed to detract from it and to indicate a tendency
toward compromising the ancient principles of catholicity. For that
reason, we were always glad when "the Catholic voice" was heard
at Lambeth. However, it was also our responsibility to report on the
more liberal voices. The latter faction was a strong one, but even
amid radical change we are greatly heartened by Lambeth X. Further, we are enormously encouraged in our belief that Anglicanism
in the future, as in the past—in sacrament, word, and worship—
has perhaps more than ever before its own particular vocation in
the world as part of Christ's Holy Catholic Church.

If this was the last Lambeth Conference, a book about it may
have something of the same value as a scientific report on a disappearing species such as the passenger pigeon—which, we trust,

despite its not inappropriate name, is never mistaken for the symbol of the Holy Spirit!

If Lambeth X was another in an ongoing series of Lambeth Conferences—and we hope and believe that it was—perhaps this work will add some valid footnotes to the continuing history of the Church.

The "Case of the Altered Resolution," a subject of considerable transatlantic correspondence reported in the section on the diaconate, is included with regret but with the belief that, devious or well-intentioned, it is part of the picture of the personalities and issues dominant in Lambeth X.

Whatever the case, it was a high privilege and an unforgettable experience accorded us, as priests of the American Church, to be present at a Lambeth Conference. We are grateful to all who made it possible, especially to those who served in our absence—the Reverend Fathers Sydney Atkinson, OHC; James F. S. Schniepp; and William E. Berger, Canon of Springfield—and to the Rector, Wardens and Vestry of Christ's Church, Rye, Diocese of New York, and Trinity Parish, Lincoln, Diocese of Springfield [Illinois]. We are deeply grateful for the interest and counsel of the Reverend Fathers H. L. Foland, founder and editor of *The Anglican Digest;* Anselm Broburg, Rector of St. Peter's Parish, Port Chester, N.Y.; Dewi Morgan, Rector of St. Bride's, Fleet Street, London; and Peter Harvey, editor of *Anglican World.* For ready help in research we are indebted to the Reverend Fathers Roland Foster and Lawrence Crumb, both of Nashotah House; Powell Dawley and Robert Bosher of General Theological Seminary; and John Macquarrie of Union Theological Seminary.

The diocesan heraldry and other coats-of-arms in our book, *The Hundredth Archbishop of Canterbury,* a biography of the Most Reverend Michael Ramsey published in 1962 by Harper & Row, has been supplemented in this volume by the same skilled artist, Miss Andrea Clark. Our knowledgeable consultant in the sometimes obscure matters of mitres and shields was the Reverend Edward N. West, Sub-Dean and Canon of the Cathedral Church of St. John the Divine, New York City.

We also thank Mr. Lawrence Grow and Mr. Paul Smart, formerly of McGraw-Hill Book Company; Dorothy Mills Parker, journalist and member of St. Columba's Parish, Washington, D.C.; and Mrs. George Gleason and Mrs. F. C. Gardner of Christ's Church, Rye.

We appreciate the use of the libraries of Nashotah House, the 127-year-old Episcopal seminary at Nashotah, Wisconsin; the General Theological Seminary and the Henry Knox Sherrill Library of the Executive Council in New York; the Sisterhood of the Holy Nativity, Fond du Lac, Wisconsin; and the Order of the Holy Cross, West Park, N.Y., of which we are honored to be Priest Associates.

Unlike the prophet Amos, who hated the noise of "solemn assemblies," we found the racket stimulating and interesting, a vibrant reminder of the liveliness of the Church in all times and all places.

JAMES B. SIMPSON
EDWARD M. STORY

Feast of the
Conversion of St. Paul, 1969

CONTENTS

xiii

THE LONG SHADOWS
OF LAMBETH X

CHAPTER 1

"A SYMBOL AND A BOND"

THE VENERABLE CHOIR STALLS OF Canterbury Cathedral fairly bulged with bishops as the tenth Lambeth Conference was officially opened on the afternoon of July 25, 1968, the Feast of St. James the Great.

The ten blocks of seats in the choir, augmented by two long rows of benches, held the largest number of bishops ever seen in the eventful history of the old cathedral town—a total of 462 men, assembled from dioceses throughout the world, for the consultative, nonlegislative meeting of the Anglican episcopate held on the average of every ten years since 1867.

An ecclesiastical checkerboard in their convocation robes of red and black and white, they watched with rapt attention as the Lord Archbishop of Canterbury, whose office they traditionally respected as that of *primus inter pares,* settled into the ancient stone Chair of St. Augustine, which had been placed in front of the high altar.

"Today we have all come to Canterbury with hearts full of thankfulness for a place, a man and a history," said the Archbishop, Arthur Michael Ramsey, hundredth in succession to Augustine, as he began masterfully to bring history and modern concerns into a single focus. "This place means very much to us as we think of St. Augustine and his monks coming here from Thanet with the Cross borne before them, preaching the Gospel to King and people, and inaugurating a history which includes not only the English Church in its continuity through the centuries but a family of Churches of many countries and races which still see in Canterbury a symbol and a bond."

The Archbishop's voice resounded through the vast cathedral as he spoke of thankfulness to God "for all this and for the witness within Christendom of a tradition of ordered liberty and scriptural Catholicity which the name Anglican has been used to describe."

Turning again to the sixth century (Augustine reached the nearby Kentish shore in 597), the Archbishop recalled Pope Gregory's advice to Augustine that the best customs of the Gallican or Roman or any other church should be adopted in England because "things are not to be loved for the sake of places but places for the sake of good things." Once a Cambridge don, the Archbishop carefully repeated the phrase in the original Latin.

"The local, the limited, the particular is to be cherished by Christian people not for any nostalgic attachment to it for its own sake, but always for the *real thing* which it represents and conveys, the thing which is catholic, essential, lasting," he said. "So our love for Canterbury melts into our love for Christ whose shrine Canterbury is; our love for what is Anglican is a little piece of our love for One Holy, Catholic, Apostolic Church; the love of any of us for our own heritage in country, culture, religious experience or theological insight, all subserves the supreme thing—the reality of God who draws men and women and children into union with himself in the fellowship of his Son."

Archbishop Ramsey then began to develop the sermon text from the Epistle to the Hebrews.[1]

---

[1] Hebrews 12 : 26–29: "But now he hath promised, saying, Yet once more I shake not the earth only, but also heaven. This phrase, 'Yet once more,'

" 'Not things for the sake of places, but places for the sake of good things,' " he reiterated; "let that be a guiding principle, and the good things which concern us are what the apostolic writer calls the things which are not shaken."

Swiftly he sketched the themes of the Epistle—which, he said, was expressed "in cadences which seem to roll like thunder." He told how God's voice shook the earth when He gave the divine law on Mount Sinai and again in proclaiming the New Convenant through the events at Bethlehem and on Calvary.

"Today the earth is being shaken, many things are cracking, melting, disappearing . . . and there can be few or none who do not feel the shaking: the rapid onrush of the age of technology with the new secularity which comes with it. . . ."

In his awareness of worldly tumult—warfare, hunger, violence —the Archbishop also alluded without specific mention to the shaking that was being experienced by the Church, the Anglican Communion, and the century-old institution known as the Lambeth Conference.

After developing briefly the theme of Lambeth X—the Renewal of the Church in Faith, Ministry, and Unity—he asked: " '*Quo tendimus?*' ['Where are we going?'] This Lambeth Conference faces big questions about our relations with one another as a world-wide Anglican family and about our role within a Christendom which is being called to unity in the truth.

"Can we do better than take to heart and apply to our tasks the counsel which Pope Gregory gave to St. Augustine, 'Not things for the sake of places, but places for the sake of good things'?

"We shall love our own Anglican family not as something ultimate but because in it and through it we and others have our place in the one Church of Christ."

With that statement he reached the thrust of his message and also the question uppermost in the minds of the bishops who lis-

---

indicates the removal of what is shaken . . . in order that what cannot be shaken may remain. Therefore let us be grateful for receiving a kingdom which cannot be shaken, and thus let us offer to God acceptable worship with reverence and awe, for our God is a consuming fire." (See Appendix for full sermon.)

tened: Would Anglicanism realize the oft-expressed "vocation to disappear"? Would there never be another Lambeth Conference?

"As the work of unity advances there will come into existence United Churches not describably Anglican but in communion with us and sharing with us what we hold to be the unshaken essence of Catholicity," he said. "What then of the future boundaries of our Anglican Communion? We shall face that question without fear, without anxiety, because of our faith in the things which are not shaken." Perhaps the Anglican role in Christendom "may come to be less like a separate encampment and more like a color in the spectrum of a rainbow, a color bright and unself-conscious."

Finally he returned to the writer to the Hebrews "who has his urgent message for us, telling us of the removal of what is shaken in order that what is not shaken may remain."

In the broad prediction that Anglicanism might serve God as a vibrant band in the ecumenical rainbow, Michael Ramsey was further developing some of the themes he had touched on at the initial press briefing two days earlier, July 23, in Lambeth Palace Library.

In the same library, at the final news conference a month later, he expanded on other predictions also voiced in his opening sermon, particularly his belief that Anglicanism would see another Lambeth, although it might meet elsewhere in the world and might include men who would be bishops in a new and different sense, of churches not readily identifiable as Anglican.

There was no man better able than Archbishop Ramsey—neither historian, ecclesiastical politician, nor any of the veterans of the last three Lambeths—to explain Lambeth's background and functions as well as its uniquely different set-up for 1968.

After welcoming the press he had gone immediately to general organization: "The Lambeth Conference which starts on Thursday is the tenth of a series. The first was held in 1867. The Lambeth Conferences have always been on the invitation of the Archbishop of Canterbury to member churches of the Anglican Communion which is a panoply of churches in many countries, all in communion with the Archbishop and with the See of Canterbury. He, of course, has no authority over the other archbishops and bishops. Most of the churches are now provinces except for a few that are rather isolated that are still under the Archbishop of Canterbury's jurisdiction in a colonial sort of way. The Lambeth Conferences are not legislative—a resolution passed is not binding unless adopted by the churches, though resolutions of the Lambeth Conferences have been found subsequently to have effect."

On the unprecedented size of Lambeth X: "This time we have invited not only diocesan bishops but also suffragan bishops and assistant bishops who are working in dioceses. We have done this for two reasons: we feel the important thing is to be a bishop in the Church of God, working, and the distinction of bishops and suffragans and assistants isn't a distinction to be recognized. Secondly, it gives increased representation to the African churches. Because of the size, the Conference will not be here in the Library, where the others have been held, but at Church House, Westminster."

On another innovation for Lambeth X: "A new feature of this year's Conference is the presence of observers from other churches —some fifty from Roman Catholic, Orthodox, and Protestant churches. They are invited to join in the sessions and the committees, to participate and not just to watch. And we hope that they will give an ecumenical tone not only to our appearance but to our actual work as well. Also there will be Anglican observers and experts."

As the Archbishop spoke, the sense of history that pervaded Lambeth was keenly felt by the men and women assembled for the briefing. The library in which they were gathered had seen many colorful events from the time of its construction in 1663 as the dining hall of the archbishops through the mid-1880s, when it became the Library and the scene of all but two of the Lambeth Conferences.

Strolling in the courtyard, before and after the news briefings, reporters and other visitors noted that the Library and the Guard Hall (where two of the Conferences have met) were linked to other buildings that together form Lambeth Palace. Long the focus point of a far-flung communion, it became the archiepiscopal residence in an era of disunity. The central issue was the plan of the archbishops to establish a rival authority to the monks at Canterbury in the form of a collegiate chapel of secular canons. The forty-second primate, Baldwin, acquired a house at Lambeth (originally a royal manor owned by a sister of Edward the Confessor) from the Bishop of Rochester. Thus a residence that passed to the archbishops during a domestic quarrel within the English church was destined in later centuries to become a symbol of unity.

Its name, Lambeth, like much in Anglicanism, was derived from the general and the particular. *Loamhythe* or *hithe* meant a marshy area of harbors or havens along the Thames; the riverbank where Lambeth Palace was to rise was known as Lam-hithe, or Haven of the Lamb. The name eventually stabilized as Lambeth.

Since the time of the forty-third archbishop, Hubert Walter (1193–1205), a total of fifty-seven primates have divided their time between Canterbury and Lambeth. The most recent, Archbishop Ramsey, was in the fifteenth year of his consecration and the seventh of his translation from York when he convened Lambeth X.

Sixty-three, the first Archbishop of Canterbury to be born in the twentieth century, Ramsey brought to the Conference the vigor, warmth, humor, and theological brilliance long attributed to him. The son of a modest, scholarly family (his father was president of Magdalene College, Cambridge; his brother was a noted mathematician; one sister teaches at Oxford, another is a London pediatrician), the Archbishop is essentially quiet and retiring. He and his wife (they have no children) are fond of the fireside, good books, old friends. Nonetheless, they have responded to the demands of the Primatial See and have been deeply loved and respected wherever they have traveled throughout the Anglican Communion.

After his years as a schoolboy at Repton (when Geoffrey Fisher was headmaster there) he went on to a Cambridge undergraduate career as a skilled debater and President of the Union. When he unexpectedly dropped his lively interest in political life to prepare for seminary, his classmates merely observed, as one of them said years later, "that Michael would reach the top as something else besides Prime Minister."

After training at Cuddeston, he was a curate in Liverpool and then an instructor at Lincoln Theological College where his first book *The Gospel and the Catholic Church,* brought him to the attention of William Temple. Successively he was lecturer of Boston Parish Church, a vicar in Cambridge, and a professor for a decade in Durham University. On becoming Regius Professor of Divinity at Cambridge, he thought he was settling down for a lifetime.

But God and men had other plans and in 1952 Michael Ramsey was consecrated Bishop of Durham. He was translated to York in 1956 and to Canterbury in 1961. Of the hundred archbishops, he is the thirtieth incumbent since the beginning of Anglicanism as a separate branch of Christ's Holy Catholic Church. "Where was the Church before the break with Rome?," he asks. "Where was your face before you washed it?"

"Since his appointment to Canterbury, Ramsey's unmistakable presence has suddenly loomed out from television and newspapers," wrote Anthony Sampson in his *Anatomy of Britain.* "He is a big man, with a venerable medieval look, tufts of white hair and big eyebrows, which wobble up and down in a friendly way while he listens."

In an astute profile that views the Archbishop clearly, as only one Englishman can see another, Sampson also noted the immediate impression of unworldliness and compassion, fondness for simple biblical language, and cultivation of the role of theologian and pastor. "He is much less vague than he seems: he takes a close interest in other people's problems, has a good memory for names, and is not unaware of Church politics," Sampson wrote.

In 1958, as Michael Ramsey and Geoffrey Fisher worked with some 300 other bishops at Lambeth IX, a long era in the Church's life was nearing its close. Before the bishops met again, the face of Christianity was to change drastically. The astonishing transformation began with the death of Pius XII only six weeks after Lambeth adjourned. The last agonies of Eugenio Pacelli, morbidly photo-

graphed by his own physician, would in time symbolize the death
throes of a Roman Catholicism the world would never again know.
On the last day of October the plume of white smoke above the Sistine Chapel signaled the choice of a new pontiff and the beginning
of a fabulous chapter in the long history of the Roman Church. A
rotund, kindly old man, openly regarded as a compromise choice,
an interim Pope, known perhaps to a handful of Anglicans who had
worked in Paris or Venice, Angelo Giuseppe Cardinal Roncalli
soon was revered by the whole world as John XXIII.

It was but a short while after the Papal coronation that the evidence of Pope John's folksy humor and pastoral love of souls suggested to Geoffrey Fisher that the pontiff was a man on whom he
could call, at least unofficially, without compromising the Church
of England or the Anglican Communion.

Carefully placed within the larger context of his return from a
trip to the Holy Land, Fisher's visit to the Vatican was the first by
an Archbishop of Canterbury since 1397, when the sixtieth primate, Thomas Arundel, had called on Benedict XII. It was also one
of the things Fisher wanted to do before announcing his retirement
two months later.

The visits to the Vatican by Fisher and by the Presiding Bishop
of the American Church, Arthur Lichtenberger (who had succeeded Henry Knox Sherrill late in 1958), were significant mile-
stones in the growing ecumenical awareness that caused Pope John
to call the Roman Church to a self-examination—a Council, the
first since 1870.

On October 12, 1962, the day Archbishop Ramsey arrived in the
U.S. for his first official visit since his enthronement at Canterbury,
Pope John opened the Vatican Council that was to continue for four
years.

In response to the Pope's invitation, Canterbury (in consultation
with other primates of the Anglican Communion) appointed three
Anglican observers to attend the Council. It was the first in a series
of appointments that brought Lambeth Palace into unprecedented
intimacy with the Vatican and later prompted Archbishop Ramsey
to establish permanent representation in Rome. Both Fisher and

Ramsey maintained a pleasant correspondence with Pope John, occasionally exchanging gifts, including recordings, and one year all the books Ramsey had written (hand-bound and embossed with the arms of Canterbury) were sent to Pope John.

The friendship continued when the former Archbishop of Milan, Giovanni Batista Cardinal Montini, came to the Papal throne as Paul VI in 1963. The following year Lambeth had its first visit from a cardinal since 1558—the German-born Jesuit Augustus Cardinal Bea, a spry and alert octogenarian who had founded the Vatican Secretariat for Christian Unity at Pope John's prompting.

In 1966, despite the protests of evangelical factions, Archbishop Ramsey paid a three-day visit to Paul VI. Their talks were climaxed by an unforgettable service at St. Paul's Outside the Walls when Pope Paul, accompanying Archbishop Ramsey to the door of the basilica, removed his pontifical ring and placed it on Canterbury's finger. It was a scene that would have been unimaginable to Lambeth IX and was to have far-reaching influence on the plans and agenda of Lambeth X, then twenty-eight months away.

As final preparations were being made for the tenth Lambeth, a rumor persisted that the Conference would receive a visit from Paul VI and the Oecumenical Patriarch of Constantinople. It was a startling report, heard from bishops and other sources. It was a rumor that quickened the heart with the thought of closer bonds.[2] It also appealed to common sense and diplomacy: the prospect of the three great leaders of Christendom—Roman, Orthodox, and Anglican—meeting *outside* the Rome of the Popes and the "new Rome" of the Patriarchs. All the preliminaries of protocol were in order since Archbishop Ramsey and the Patriarch had both met with the Pope, and the Patriarch had in turn received the Pope and had been a guest at Lambeth. The next logical step seemed a joint meeting of the three; clinching the argument, the Pope had already

---

[2] In a pastoral letter issued at Easter 1968, the sixth Bishop of California (Kilmer Myers, who succeeded James Pike in 1966) suggested that Lambeth bishops and delegates to the World Council of Churches should reconvene in Rome under Paul VI who would be considered as "first among equals of the Christian Church on earth."

announced a flight to Bogotá that would take him near London while Lambeth X was in session.

A definite warning that the "summit" would not materialize was seen in a major address made by Paul on June 30 as he began the sixth year of his reign. It reiterated a firm stand on the very issues that were barriers to unity—Papal infallibility, transubstantiation, and acceptance of the doctrine of the Immaculate Conception as necessary to salvation.

Asked to comment on the Pope's address, Archbishop Ramsey said: "Since the Vatican Council began to distinguish between the more fundamental dogmas and the less fundamental ones, I was surprised that particular Roman Catholic dogmas . . . were inserted along with the tenets of the Nicene Creed."

The rumor of a visit persisted, however, and prompted a question at the Archbishop's news conference. He tended to dodge the issue, replying simply that the Roman Church had been invited to send observers and had indicated it would do so. Moments later, when a reporter attempted to bring the conversation back to the Pope, the Archbishop replied: "Yes, yes, *that* answer was about the Pope!"

Those who had seized upon the prospect of such a summit meeting were the last to give up hope; it was as if they expected the Pope and the Patriarch to walk into Church House at any moment. Only the import of the Papal encyclical on birth control made it utterly clear to everyone that Paul VI would not visit the Lambeth Conference.

The dreary weather that greeted the bishops as they arrived in London continued in oppressive grayness for most of the Conference. It was what the English newscasters described as "dull"; it persisted day after day and eventually was recorded as the soggiest, coldest summer in at least forty years. ("That which once never set on the British Empire now never rises on its capital," said the Paris edition of the *Herald Tribune*.) But the weather hardly slackened the tempo of the metropolis, in extent the world's largest city. Greatly changed since the last Lambeth, its burgeoning forest of skyscrapers contrasted starkly with Victorian cornices and Dickensian cobbles. London was also enjoying a swing from traditional dowdiness to new acclaim as a capital of fashion and art.

"Would you believe buildings rising higher than St. Paul's!" exclaimed an American woman. "Would you believe those miniskirts?" asked her husband.

London was lushly green, still preparing for visitors even as they arrived—sweeping up, tidying up, delighting in an air-blasting organization called London Stone that scaled away decades of grime from the stately government buildings in Whitehall and from Nelson's Column and New Zealand House in Trafalgar Square. London was its old self as it politely but sternly reminded visitors and residents of The Rules, indicated by a multitude of signs, including a theologically eloquent one guarding a lawn near Westminster Abbey: THIS BEING ST. MARGARET'S CHURCHYARD, IT IS CONSECRATED GROUND.

In the fourth week of July 1968, as Lambeth X opened, London marked the twenty-eighth anniversary of the Battle of Britain. The generation born since that time, especially the long-haired young men and their girls, were seen everywhere—notably in Piccadilly Circus, where they huddled in the rain with the shabby flocks of pigeons.

In the newspapers a quarrel raged over the unofficial designation of sculptor Henry Moore as the greatest living Englishman. "Not one per cent of us understands Moore's works," said a columnist. But even as they quarreled they queued up at Westminster to observe at Evensong the 150th anniversary of the birth of another artist, the novelist Emily Brontë.

London and all England continued to absorb the paeans with which succeeding generations have saluted their land. "This precious stone set in the silver sea," Shakespeare said. "They do think that England is God Almighty," Alice Duer Miller had admitted, and in midsummer 1968 Malcolm Muggeridge wrote in the Sunday *Observer:* "The truth is that a lost Empire, lost power, and lost wealth provide perfect circumstances for living happily and contentedly in our enchanting island."

Such was the mood of London and the nation as the bishops gathered. At Lambeth Palace, the Archbishop of Canterbury indicated his own mood toward the end of the initial press conference. "My personal feelings are the same as those with which I view any approaching event," he said. "I go through a period of funk and trepidation, then take a sort of plunge, and become cheerful ever after!"

CHAPTER 2

PLANNING FOR LAMBETH

Planning for Lambeth X began
while the 1958 Conference was still in session, influenced the date
of Archbishop Fisher's retirement, figured prominently in the
1963 Anglican Congress at Toronto, took definite shape in the
1966 consultations at Jerusalem, and gathered increasing momen-
tum as the hour neared for its opening in Canterbury Cathedral
Church.

The logistics of finances, invitations, and agenda loomed larger
than ever for Lambeth X after the decision to include coadjutors,
suffragans, and assistant bishops and to invite consultants and
observers.

St. George's Cathedral Church, in the modern section of Jerusa-
lem outside the old walled city, was the meeting place chosen by the
Lambeth Consultative Body for its major planning session for
Lambeth X.[1] Its members lived and worked in the cathedral close, a

---

[1] The Lambeth Consultative Body, established in 1897 and reconstituted in
1958, consists essentially of the primates or presiding bishops of the Anglican

cluster of buff-colored Gothic buildings, unmistakably Anglican, completed in the late 1890s.

Prior to the Jerusalem meeting there had been some talk of a Lambeth in 1967 to mark the centenary but the Canadians pointed out that it would conflict with the Dominion's centennial year. In the end, Lambeth X was accepted as the centenary Conference and only the historical purists, usually English clergy, contended that 1967 alone would have constituted a centenary.

Lambeth X's theme and main areas of discussion (The Renewal of the Church in Faith, Unity, and Ministry) was chosen at Jerusalem. The Bishop of Cariboo's remark later that the meeting "decided to restrict the subject matter" (to three major topics) indicated that considerable discipline was necessary to provide a manageable but fluid agenda. Some sessions of Lambeth X were reserved in advance for "non-agenda items."

"I know I am a fall guy, but that is the business of anyone who organizes a gathering of this size," Cariboo said a few months before Lambeth X convened. The structure and committees that were eventually announced bore his stamp more than Canterbury's. Almost from the start, Cariboo appeared to be something of a devil's advocate by making remarks, wherever he happened to alight in his wide travels, that shocked people into defending the need for another Lambeth.

Big, balding Ralph Stanley Dean (or *Ralph : Cariboo,* as he signed himself) had always liked the idea of competitive sport. As a boy, on the Arsenal practice grounds in the Highbury area of London, he had for a time wanted to be a professional in football or cricket. As a young priest, he coached and played both games and continued to do so until his forties.

---

churches (or episcopal alternates designated by them), the chairmen of the two regional councils of South-East Asia and the South Pacific, and episcopal representatives of the extraprovincial dioceses as selected by the Archbishop of Canterbury. In the late 1960s it had twenty-six members. It met every two years and, in the words of the *Church of England Yearbook,* "it is virtually a continuation of the Lambeth Conference acting in an advisory capacity to the Archbishop of Canterbury, and to other bishops or groups of bishops, in a large range of concerns in which matters of faith and order are especially prominent."

The man who ranked with Canterbury as the most familiar figure of Lambeth X was not handsome. His eyes were slightly hooded behind heavy spectacles; he had prominent nostrils and wide, thin lips. Nonetheless he was an affable, impressive personage in magenta cassock (with sash and starched preaching-tabs), his episcopal ring on the last finger of his right hand, and a handkerchief tucked English-style in a widely cuffed sleeve. He was stuffy, he was casual; he was evasive, he was disarmingly direct. Through it all, he appeared to enjoy himself as perhaps no other bishop at Lambeth X. His efficiency seemed prompted by his own personal reaction of surprise that he was managing a conference of nearly 500 bishops—and there was a strong impression that he was everlastingly after himself to rise to the challenge.

Besides athletics, Ralph Dean as a young man was interested in architecture and spent a year or two in a construction firm's office, but the Church's call persisted. Until he went to Canada, his life had been centered in and around London; he was born there in 1913, was at school in nearby Greenwich, matriculated at London University, and did his theological work at London College of Divinity. Among the English-born bishops, who leaned heavily to Oxford or Cambridge, Cariboo's background was decidedly "red brick," as the British say of city or provincial universities.

Ordained in 1939 by the Bishop of Willesden, Suffragan to London, he married within a few months and spent the war years in two London curacies—St. Mary's Islington and St. Luke's Watford. In his spare time he continued graduate study at his old college. By 1945 his interests ran strongly to teaching and he turned away from parish work (he was never a vicar or rector) to become Chaplain and Tutor at London Divinity. For four years he was Vice-Principal under Donald Coggan, the future Archbishop of York, who spoke often of his own years at Wycliffe College, Toronto. The Deans went to Canada in 1951 when he was appointed Principal of Emmanuel College, Saskatoon. During the next six years he received an honorary doctorate from Wycliffe and in 1955 was made an honorary canon of Saskatoon.

On the Feast of the Epiphany, January 6, 1957, in Christ Church Cathedral, Victoria, British Columbia, he was consecrated fifth

Bishop of Cariboo at the hands of the Archbishop of British Columbia and seven others, including the Bishop of Spokane. His new
diocese (founded in 1914, the youngest of six in the province of
British Columbia) had about two dozen parishes and mission stations. The cathedral church was St. Paul's, Kamloops.

During Cariboo's years as the active ordinary of the large,
sparsely populated diocese, he served for a time as Principal of the
Anglican Theological College at Vancouver, published a book (*In
the Light of the Cross,* 1961), and received an honorary degree
from Emmanuel College, Saskatoon. (As Anglicanism's Executive
Officer he was given degrees by the Vancouver college he headed,
as well as by Huron College in 1965 and by Trinity College, Hart-
ford, 1966.)

A year and a half after his consecration, coming to Lambeth IX
as a member of Archbishop Ramsey's Committee on the Holy
Bible, he began moving for the first time outside the academic
world and the Canadian Church. It was his work five years later, as
program chairman for the Anglican Congress at Toronto, that
brought him into serious consideration as a successor a year hence
to the Anglican Executive Officer, Bishop Bayne.

The post of Executive Officer of the Anglican Communion
(Anglicanism's Ambassador Extraordinary, said the *Anglican
World*) was a position Cariboo approached with humility. He paid
tribute to the work of Bishop Bayne, adding that "anyone who was
not scared by this job would have to be declared insane."

He and his wife Irene moved into the town house at 21 Chester
Street, in the Belgravia section of London near Buckingham Palace, which served as a combination residence and headquarters for
the Executive Officer and his staff. There was a direct tie-line with
Lambeth Palace and its cable address, Compasrose, had been suggested by the Anglican Communion's emblem on the front door. On
the Sundays they were in London, the Bishop and his wife attended
St. Peter's, Eaton Square.

In the next four years Cariboo visited fifty-two countries, cir-
cling the globe sixteen times (on sixty-two airlines) for a total
travel record of more than half a million miles. "I'm a sort of

Church 007½," he said. "But some don't know where Cariboo is—the northernmost diocese in British Columbia. I have been introduced as a bishop from Africa and even as the Bishop of Kalamazoo!"

That the task had its frustrations was evidenced by Cariboo's remark that he was the Anglican Communion's strategist without having any opportunity to strategize.

Whereas Stephen Bayne resigned as Bishop of Olympia to become Executive Officer, Cariboo took a five-year leave of absence from his diocese. He handed over its active direction to a Yorkshireman, Tom Greenwood, who had been Bishop of the Yukon for nine years before returning to England as Assistant Bishop of Chester.

Cariboo spoke frequently and affectionately of his distant diocese, addressed its scattered clergy by radio whenever he was in Western Canada, and referred to it as a refuge when he thought an independent decision might jeopardize his job: "Well, I'm still the Bishop of Cariboo!"

Bishop Bayne did the spadework well: he made the post known to the Anglican world and gave it stature. On departing he left behind a long list of sensible recommendations for the future. One of them was that the Anglican Executive Officer should have two assistants. Cariboo got one—Ernest Jackson, a Canadian priest in his sixties,[1] plus a secretarial staff of three women. (A second deputy, to be stationed in Geneva, was promised for 1969.) After a few years in office, Cariboo believed that he could well use four assistants, but that was impossible with an annual budget of £24,300.

Cariboo's reputation for painstaking work and thoughtfulness preceded him at Lambeth X. One story that made the rounds was of his request for a Prayer Book when he arrived in the Diocese of Zululand & Swaziland; he studied it overnight and next day, in a Swazi parish church, he laid hands on sixty-seven African heads

---

[1] Jackson, who had the title of Deputy Executive Officer, announced in October, 1968, that he would return to Canada within a few months to head up a similar office involving world-wide relationships of the Canadian Church.

and over each clearly pronounced the Confirmation Prayer in the Zulu tongue.

Another story was that Cariboo's years as Executive Officer had left him "heartbroken about the state of the Anglican Communion." He was deeply concerned about the frequency with which he encountered immense impoverished dioceses presided over by an exhausted bishop and a few priests.

Whatever the case, Cariboo projected the image of a man who wanted recognition without being placed on a pedestal. He constantly upgraded his office, but said that he personally liked to don a necktie and meet people in the pubs when he was traveling. In that respect, so did Canterbury, at least on his country holidays in England, but actually the two represented quite different brands of Anglicanism. Cariboo, for instance, was always at pains to say that the Anglican desire for unity should include *even* the Church of Rome, but he was inevitably more concerned about nonepiscopal bodies. Moreover, Cariboo contended that the episcopal office was unknown in the New Testament, that it appeared after the Church emerged from a "tunnel" 150 years later and hence unity could not depend on the acceptance of episcopacy as the *esse* of the Church.

Considering that he carried the work of the Executive Officer with the Secretariat of Lambeth X, Cariboo's easy self-control was admirable and the flashes of ego were forgivable. Only once was there an open show of temper, when some of the bishops became impatient for galley proofs of the Draft Report on Unity. When would they be ready? "Not being God, I don't know," Cariboo told them.

It was Cariboo's responsibility to make routine announcements and read aloud Conference messages (such as one addressed "to Her Majesty, the Queen" along with her reply after the Royal Garden Party). He also conducted Lambeth's lost-and-found in which, over a period of several weeks, it appeared that the bishops might rival college professors for a reputation of absent-mindedness; even an episcopal ring was left behind in the washroom of one of the London clubs; another day, Cariboo reported that the Bishop of Zambia had lost his raincoat. ("An easy thing to do," he sympathized, "since all clerical raincoats look much like another.") On still another day he began his announcements solemnly, "Where there is no vision the people perish," adding that a pair of glasses had been found in the lounge.

Cariboo's general approach to his work as Executive Officer, as compared with Bishop Bayne's, was summed up by a senior American bishop who had observed them both in meetings over the years: "Bayne got off to a bad start because Archbishop Fisher wrote letters to many of us, asking for nominations, then before we could reply he announced the appointment of Bayne. That particularly upset the Canadian bishops . . . [but] that is not why the second man in the office happens to be a Canadian. Cariboo is there because he distinguished himself at Toronto. Bayne was a man of ideas, rushing around the world and building up relationships: Cariboo is more of an executive type and had to solidify those relationships. Bayne is a very intelligent man but Cariboo is the more stable of the two."

"Some of the Americans met at Canterbury to hash out the idea of having an Executive Officer," recalled the same bishop in a confidential interview. "Henry [Sherrill] was not too keen on a central administration. We agreed on a secretary for the Anglican Communion after Archbishop Fisher asked us, 'Do you want me to handle all this correspondence?' The idea finally passed the Lambeth Conference after much debate. The job was first offered to Johannesburg, Ambrose Reeves, later expelled [exiled] from his see, but he turned it down. Steve Bayne was then appointed. Why his post was called 'Executive Officer' was something I've never been able to track down. The English don't like 'executive' because it implies too much authority although they use the world 'general.' I think Bayne probably got the title from having been a chaplain on a ship and being the executive officer aboard. There was the same problem with the Council for Missionary Strategy since 'strategy' is always offensive to the Indians as a military term that suggests warfare."

Yet on one of his long trips a year before Lambeth X, in an address to nearly sixty priests and laymen at Tamworth, Australia

(Diocese of Armidale) the man who had been called "the more stable of the two" appeared to damn Lambeth X even as he sought to jell its agenda. As reported piecemeal on the front page of the *Church Times,* which picked up its story from the Australian *Anglican Times,* Cariboo asserted that he could not see much value in the approaching Conference, adding "It is too much like a bishops' club." Further, he suggested, a Conference every ten years was "totally out of touch with swiftly moving modern conditions" and lacked "a real 'lay' voice in its higher deliberations."

When the story broke in England, a spokesman at Lambeth Palace said that any comment from Canterbury would be "unlikely," adding that "we have the paper sent here, and we shall see the report in due time."

The *Church Times* was not willing to let it go at that. "There is something decidedly odd, on the face of it, about the remarks" began its editorial. "Cariboo in his capacity is charged with the unenviable duty of arranging the organization of this vast episcopal gathering. For him to go on public record now as doubting the value of the Conference would seem to put in question the wisdom of carrying on with the plans for holding it, and to call for some comment at least from the highest Anglican quarters if confidence in the arrangements for the Conference is not to be undermined."

Less shrilly the editorial continued: "Things are not always, however, what they seem to be from necessarily abbreviated press reports. Further investigation suggests that what Cariboo had in mind was not outright condemnation of Lambeth Conferences as valueless occasions, but rather a measured assessment of their admittedly limited usefulness. On the occasion in Australia, he was being questioned about the machinery, or the lack of it, for establishing proper representative government of the Anglican Communion as a whole. It was in this context that he cast doubt on the value of a Lambeth Conference on the reasonable ground that this purely episcopal meeting is certainly not truly representative of the whole Communion—how could it be when not a single lay representative is included?—and that its occurrence at ten-year intervals is far too infrequent to provide the Communion with that instrument of responsible government which many other critics . . . desire to see created."

The editorial gave obvious support to Cariboo. "If the Anglican Communion's Executive Officer did not firmly believe the Lambeth Conference to have *some* value, we may be sure that he would not have consented to devote most of the next eight months to organizing it."

There was nevertheless a negative note to many of Cariboo's comments right up to the time of Lambeth X. One diocesan newspaper quoted him as saying that "if we are serious about our ecumenical enterprises, in ten years' time there ought not to be much left of the Anglican Communion as we know it, and I myself belong to the school of thought that it may well be the last Lambeth Conference." In mid-July he was quoted as telling a clergy meeting at St. Mary's Cathedral, Limerick, that an exception to "the winding up of Anglicanism" might be that it would continue to exist in the West Indies.

If Cariboo was openly prejudiced about future Conferences, Canterbury maintained more of a wait-and-see attitude. "Much will depend on the prayers of Christian people, and in that spirit I commend it to you," Canterbury wrote in one of his first public statements about Lambeth X. A short while later, he observed in the magazine *Pan-Anglican* that "the Lambeth Conference of 1968 is an exciting prospect, and if you ask me what I expect from it I must answer that what is exciting is its unpredictability. . . . The very nature of the Conference will therefore compel a process of searching thought through confrontation, a process which *may* prove creative, and shame upon us if it does not!"

At the Convocation of Canterbury in May, he devoted his entire address to Lambeth X, declaring that the Conferences had become "both an ear listening to the Anglican Churches and a voice speaking to them and beyond them"; but long before they began making public statements in anticipation of the Conference, both the Archbishop and the Episcopal Secretary were engaged in a steadily mounting volume of correspondence with the bishops.

One of the letters from Canterbury to the bishops concerned the acceptable style of episcopal dress. "I am myself not anxious that you should go to the possible expense of buying or carrying with you a suit of gaiters and frock-coat for the period of the Conference," he wrote.[2] "There will be a note of informality at all of our social gatherings, in my own home and in the few that are arranged elsewhere."

As early as October 1966 Cariboo wrote all members of the Episcopate in regard to the proposed structure of thirty-two committees. (The final total was thirty-three, after one of the committees was divided.) He asked the bishops to list three preferences and to do so in consultation with their Metropolitans so as "to make sure that your membership in one or the other of the committees provides the greatest impact of your Province as a whole on the total deliberations of the Conference."

Regarding the leadership of the various groups, Cariboo wrote, "His Grace will shortly be asking a number of bishops to accept responsibility as Chairman, Vice-Chairman, and Secretary of a number of the various committees; and if perchance you are one of those, it may mean going outside the committee of your present choice and I can only hope that you will be willing to cooperate in whatever adjustments may be necessary."

Weeks turned into months as the committees were structured. Meanwhile it was announced that the Steering Committee for Lambeth X would include both Cariboo and Bayne as well as Simms of Dublin, Stopford of London, Mortimer of Exeter, and Eley of Gibraltar. It was also disclosed that the three major sections (Faith, Ministry, and Unity) would be headed by Clark of Canada, Coggan of York, and de Mel of India.

In those announcements, even the most casual reader saw that the non-English were in a minority of leadership but it was also

---

[2] Gaiters, originally designed for horseback riding, incorporate a knee-length cassock worn with knee-britches (knickers) and long stockings. They eventually became the identifying habit of the Anglican Episcopate. The debonair Bishop of Chester turned up in gaiters at registration and Lord Fisher wore gaiters at the Lambeth Palace garden party but otherwise the newspapers were correct in referring to Lambeth X as "the first gaiterless Lambeth Conference."

clear that Lambeth X was drawing wisely on the experience of men who had been at the center of previous Conferences: Eley had been Assistant Secretary of Lambeth VIII (while serving as Fisher's Senior Chaplain), Stopford had been Episcopal Secretary of Lambeth IX, Bayne had bridged the years from the last Lambeth to the start of Cariboo's term.

When the committee appointments were made public, ecclesiastical politicians busied themselves with box scores and charts to see if the makeup of the committees gave any hint of leadership or resolutions that might emerge from Lambeth X. They found that the average size of the thirty-two committees was fourteen members, although they ranged in size from two committees with nine members to three groups with seventeen men each.

For those who viewed the Anglican Communion as a "microcosm of Christian unity"—as Canterbury once described it—the committees represented an interesting exercise in episcopal dispersement. More important was the implied potential of their varied memberships: the possibility of each committee reflecting many points of view, nationally, culturally, theologically. Americans were in the majority on more than half of the thirty-two committees and English bishops were in the majority on eleven others.

Some bishops reportedly stayed away because of distaste at English domination at other Lambeths, and an analysis of the committees showed something of the same tendency. The Church of England episcopate was represented, as was no other Anglican body, on all levels from the highest through the section chairmen, committee chairmen, vice-chairmen, and secretaries.

Only among the committee secretaries did the Church of England fail to predominate. It had four as compared with six given the U.S., three each to Australia and South Africa, and two each to Scotland, Canada, India, New Zealand, Central Africa, and extra-provincial dioceses. The smallness of the Asian episcopate was seen in the presence of Asian bishops on only seventeen of the thirty-two committees.

The over-all tally of committee officers showed that approximately a fourth of the bishops had been given definite responsibility

—twenty-eight out of one hundred and ten Englishmen, seventeen out of one hundred and twenty-five Americans, ten out of thirty-eight Canadians. Every church of the Anglican Communion had at least one officer, and effort obviously was made to give the Africans and Asians stronger representation: eight of eighteen bishops from the Church of India, Pakistan, Burma and Ceylon, and seven of the eighteen East Africans, were committee officers.[3]

Anyone familiar with Lambeth Conferences knew, of course, that for years the Americans had dominated in number and the English in leadership. In fairness, however, it was pointed out that four American chairmen (the Presiding Bishop, New York, Michigan, and North Dakota) had asked to be replaced and two others, Stokes of Massachusetts and Corrigan of the Executive Council, had relinquished appointment as secretaries. Only two were replaced by Englishmen.

Bishops with special interests were matched with committees that were to deal with their areas of concern. The important Committee on Urbanization and the Metropolis included, for instance, the former Industrial Chaplain to Coventry, Phipps of Horsham, Suffragan to Chichester; diocesans of large population centers such as New York and Tokyo; as well as bishops of areas of population growth such as Long Island.

In individual appointments to committees there was common sense right down the line—Westall of Crediton, Suffragan to Exeter, a strong Catholic voice, served on "Dialogue with Other Faiths" with bishops from such widely scattered areas that it easily became one of the best-balanced groups; Robinson of Woolwich, Suffragan to Southwark, famed for his book *Honest to God,* was wisely placed on the Committee on Confessing the Faith Today. Other excellent appointments were Coventry to the Ministry of the Laity; such diverse churchmen as Brady of Fond du Lac and Chilton, Suffragan of Virginia, to the Nature of the Anglican Episcopate;

---

[3] Other committee offices: eight, Australia; six, South Africa; four each to West Africa, New Zealand, and extraprovincial dioceses; three each to Scotland, Ireland, and Uganda; two each to Wales and Central Africa; and one each to Brazil, China, Japan, and Jerusalem.

California and Guatemala to Christian Unity and Human Unity; Hallock of Milwaukee, a member of the permanent Anglican-Roman Commission, to chair the Papacy and the Episcopate; and Scaife of Western New York, a pioneer in inter-Church relationships, as chairman of Relations with the Eastern Orthodox.

Shortly after the committees were announced the bishops received a 407-page paperback book, *Preparatory Essays,* a well-conceived theological study guide for their work. It was published by SPCK with the imprint CONFIDENTIAL: *Printed for circulation to members of the Lambeth Conference only.* The volume of thirty-two essays with its striking orange, white, and magenta cover indicated to the bishops as little else had that hard-chair reading was expected of them in preparation for their work in committees.[3a]

The essayists, like the officers of the committees, were predominantly English. The group included top theologians of Oxford and Cambridge; canons of Birmingham, Southwark, and Ely; among the laity Sir Kenneth Grubb and Mollie Batten; and from the United States, John Macquarrie of Union Seminary, Charles West of Princeton, and Gibson Winter of the University of Chicago.

A companion volume, *Preparatory Information,* was also sent to the bishops. Slimmer and not classified as confidential, its objective was to present in essays, charts, and tables a profile of the Anglican Communion as it existed on the eve of Lambeth X. This book's unique contribution was a series of long and informative accounts on liturgical revision in Anglicanism since 1958. It also traced the development of various plans for Christian reunion in all their multifarious forms.

As a supplement to the two preparatory volumes, some bishops also received reading lists from committee chairmen.

"The Lambeth Conference is going to be five weeks of hard work," wrote the Bishop of Springfield (Illinois) in his diocesan magazine. "I have a stack of books and reports about ten inches high that I must get through before I get to the Conference."

[3a] *Preparatory Essays* was made available to the public by SPCK early in 1969 in three paperbacks, *Lambeth Essays on Faith, Lambeth Essays on Ministry,* and *Lambeth Essays on Unity.*

Of the thirty-two contributors to *Preparatory Essays,* twenty-five were among the consultants appointed for Lambeth X. It was the announcement that consultants would be present, freely circulating among the committees and recognized as speakers in the plenary sessions, that added another serious and stimulating dimension to preparations for Lambeth X.

The consultants' group, in addition to the essayists, included lecturers and missionaries and two Anglican religious, M. Jarrett-Kerr, C.R., and a monk-bishop, Robert Roseveare, S.S.M., for twelve years the Bishop of Accra. Two of three lay consultants were Americans—Paul Anderson, a veteran officer of the International YMCA, and Peter Day, ecumenical officer for the American Church. The third, and the only woman, was Mollie Batten, for sixteen years principal of a theological college. A brain-trust, collectively they had written some four dozen books and had acquired an even larger number of degrees.

A much larger group, also new to the Lambeth scene, was the observers. It numbered seventy-five men from twenty-four religious bodies, ranging alphabetically from two divisions of the Armenian Church (the Catholicossates of Etchmiadzin and of Cilicia) to the World Presbyterian Alliance. They were given places in the Processional Order for Lambeth X, beginning with the Rev. Dr. Ake Andren of the Church of Sweden (No. 600) and ending with the Very Rev. Dom Philibert Zobel, O.S.B., Prior of Le Bec, Helluin, France (No. 675).[4]

The diverse representation was reflected by the presence of Monsignor Jean-François Arrighi of the Vatican Secretariat for Promoting Christian Unity; Dom Christopher Butler of England's Downside Abbey; Fred Pierce Corson, an American Methodist bishop; Commissioner Herbert Westcott of the Salvation Army's William Booth Training College; and Dr. Thomas Zimmerman, Superintendent of the General Council of the Assemblies of God.

Observers from some of the larger churches were accompanied

---

[4] Consultants and observers are listed in the Appendix.

by alternate observers and special guest observers. The most sizable, a group of a dozen Roman Catholics, included two archbishops and four bishops as well as two Jesuits and two Benedictine abbots. The delegations from the Lutheran World Federation and the World Methodist Council were almost as large.

As Lambeth X began to develop a distinctive profile, it was increasingly the subject of study, discussion, and prayer throughout the world.

In mid-June, thirty-one American bishops referred often to the approaching Conference during a week-long study session at the new Trinity Institute on New York's upper West Side. One of their principal speakers was a young English priest whose name was beginning to be heard frequently in theological circles, A. M. Allchin, Librarian of Pusey House, Oxford. Already known for his book *The Silent Rebellion,* he won added acclaim for his paper "Faith and Spirituality," one of the outstanding studies in *Preparatory Essays.*

In some areas the anticipation of Lambeth X even penetrated church-school study groups. They used *Lambeth Link-Up,* a two-shilling packet designed by the Bishop of Rangoon and distributed by SPG or *Lambeth Tours Unlimited Guidebook,* a packet of pictures and other study materials originated in the Diocese of Newcastle.

After the publication of the Conference theme and agenda, Lambeth X, no less than any other international conference, was not spared a plethora of suggestions on subjects it should consider. It was open game for every clergy conference or newsletter. Some were serious: the Vicar of Islington (where York and Cariboo began their first curacies) voiced a serious plea that Lambeth X should open the way for non-Anglicans to receive Holy Communion. Some were curiously inverse: a priest in Essex wrote in a diocesan monthly review that the Lambeth fathers should take on the problems of population explosion and homosexuality. Some were obtuse: the Equestrian League petitioned Cariboo for time to address the Conference on cruelty to horses.

The two most widely discussed issues appeared by their very natures to be in conflict: the need for a more centralized Anglican authority and plans for uniting with other Christian bodies.

While the Anglican world debated the agenda for Lambeth X, the work of planning had to continue without let-up. It was known, well in advance, that the Conference would cost in excess of a million dollars. The cost would fall partially to the churches (transporting more than 400 bishops to London and maintaining them for five weeks), and the general expenses to Canterbury with assistance when necessary to some bishops.

"It's really his houseparty," said a seasoned American bishop. "He extends the invitations and he picks up the bill." That was literally true, said Cariboo's administrative assistant, Ernest Jackson. "We're told to send our Conference expenses to Lambeth Palace and they would be paid from there." Obviously, Canterbury had funds from which he was able to draw, but it was hoped that English parishes would help as much as possible.

The initial appeal was made in mid-September 1967 by the Church Assembly's Missionary and Ecumenical Council. It sent a letter to every parish in the Church of England asking "for prayers, thought and gifts" for the Uppsala Assembly of the World Council of Churches and for Lambeth X.

For Uppsala, the English Church had been asked to subscribe £7500. A further £12,500 was asked to assist in paying the high travel costs of bishops coming to Lambeth from Asia, Latin America, and the South Pacific. The letter suggested that the necessary £20,000 would be raised if each parish contributed £3. Apparently it was not expected that every parish would contribute, since £3 from the 14,397 parishes listed in the *Church of England Yearbook* would have yielded more than twice the amount requested. (A total of £6500 had been received by January 15, 1968, many sending more than £3, but 80 per cent of the needed amount remained to be raised.)

While the Church of England slowly inched toward its goal, other member churches began raising money for their bishops. For most it was a project that had appeared every ten years or so as long as the Conferences had existed. A few, like the Diocese of Louisiana, whose bishops have gone to Lambeth for a hundred years, had made the Conference expenses a regular part of their economic planning. Acknowledging the foresight, Jones of Louisiana wrote in his diocesan magazine with obvious relief, "There is no need for any 'passing of the hat' as was done ten years ago."

Another consideration before departing for London was, as one bishop put it, "the need to find somebody to mind the store." In South Florida and other areas, bishops living in retirement took over episcopal functions. (In Chicago the retired suffragan, Charles Street, died while the diocesan and coadjutor were in London.) In less populous areas there was nothing bishops could do but suspend most of their work for six weeks or longer. A Cowley father in Ontario said bluntly, "We shall be bishopless for most of the summer!" *The Canadian Churchman* seemed to agree, observing editorially that "an episcopal hush has descended over the Anglican Church of Canada."

The stewardship of money and time, always critical issues, came in for a new whaling with the appearance of a slickly produced magazine, *Lambeth '68,* from the Church Information Office. The cover featured the Bishop of Masasi, Trevor Huddleston, C.R., pectoral cross dangling on a white sports shirt, as he stood in the midst of black African children holding one of them in his arms. It was a pleasant-enough picture, but since Lambeth's missionary work was minimal it had little relationship to the Conference; more regretably, the photograph reeked of the paternalism that white bishops go to great lengths to avoid. Moreover, it presented Bishop Huddleston, an energetic, respected, outspoken man, as if he were a benevolent old monsignor modeling for the annual report of Boys' Town.

The cover picture was the first but lesser blooper of the booklet. The other was the widely denounced guide to sightseeing and dining that came at the end. In between were twenty pages of serious presentation of the hopes and plans for Lambeth X as envisioned by Canterbury and Cariboo along with an article on the Conference program, a historical sketch of previous Lambeth Conferences and committees. Much of it was reprinted in diocesan newspapers throughout the world.

Only Canterbury's introduction and the committee listings were spared whimsical presentation. The other material was bordered with line drawings of various ecclesiastical types (running mainly to small, stout bishops in suits, gaiters, or cassocks) supposedly representing all the levels or persuasions of churchmanship and ego attracted by Lambeth.

As the booklet moved on to three final sections (General Information, Places to See, Places to Eat) the drawings grew more imaginative. They featured a bald, paunchy, placid hen-shaped bishop happily exploring London as he juggled the English currency, sipped a foamy brew during the proper licensing hours with a beaming barmaid, tipped for his umbrella, undertipped a frowning taxi driver, photographed a Guardsman, went sightseeing at the Tower of London and the Planetarium and the Design Center, listened to a buxom soprano, sniffed a giant sunflower at Kew Gardens, and dined to violin music. The general impression was that bishops were mostly naïve, bourgeois little men with time to kill in London.

The mood changed with the last page, on restaurants, when the self-conscious writing style became even more imitative of *Punch* or *The New Yorker* at their most pompous. It assumed that the bishops were gourmets on the prowl for the choice, chic cafes either famous or hidden away.

The original printing of 14,000 copies of *Lambeth '68* was exhausted within ten days. As another printing tumbled from the presses, New Zealand asked for a bulk order of a thousand and the American Church cabled for 750 copies to be sent by air.

The London Sunday *Observer* identified the man behind the booklet as Michael De-la-Noy, who for less than a year had held the title of Assistant Information Officer (of the Church Information Office) and Press Officer for the Archbishop of Canterbury. It quoted his prose about restaurants (on Chez Solange in Cranbourn Street, "Very, very French. Ludicrously large helpings, noisy French neighbors and good carafe wine...") and it asked De-la-Noy for his own comments.

"A few of the more conservative seem to think the bishops are caricatured in the drawings, but I think that's really rather stuffy," he said. "It's quite absurd to pretend they'll all go to Lyons every day—they won't. We are catering for them at the Conference as well, of course. They don't have to go to Claridges—they can get lunch with us for five shillings, sixpence."

A few days later a *Church Times* columnist wrote that "maybe some of the restaurants mentioned in that glorious glossy, *Lambeth '68, are* dear, as a correspondent complains this week, but one of them cannot be as I have been going to it myself for many a year."

The letter the newspaper mentioned was only the advance guard of vast dissatisfaction that swiftly overflowed from the church press into the columns of daily newspapers.

"If there are some visiting bishops who can afford to turn their spare time into an expensive spree, they could have been left to find out for themselves how to do it," wrote the Bishop of Bristol, Oliver Tomkins.

A series of letters to *The Times* of London was typified by one from the Provost of Southwell, Hugh Heywood: "We shall not support this scale for the expenses of our episcopate." It drew a reply, again typical, from a woman in Nottinghamshire: "I defend the right of our bishops to have a slap-up meal if they want to. Even our Lord did not disdain a feast occasionally."

The strongest criticism of the booklet and the Conference came on BBC radio on the Sunday evening before Lambeth X began its work. The program's title, "To Hell With the Bishops," indicated the public's attitude, the producers said, toward the purple-vests which were turning up with increasing frequency in the London streets. Noting that it was the last of the season's *Subject for Sunday* programs on Radio Four, the *Evening Standard* wrote with prophetic gentleness that it had "a clear, provocative ring about it."

The program idea had originated with a former prison chaplain, the Rev. Roy Trevivian, who had become a producer in BBC religious broadcasting. Incensed by De-la-Noy's glossy *Lambeth '68,* he planned a confrontation between three prominent bishops and the fiery novelist George Target, who had engaged in a public de-

bate with evangelist Billy Graham (and had later roasted the
Graham movement in a hostile book, *Evangelism Inc.*). The bishops were Trevor Huddleston, always popular and articulate and at
that moment in a state of transition from being Bishop of Masasi to
becoming Suffragan Bishop of Stepney; Coggan, ever the school-
masterish Archbishop of York; and Reindorp, the Bishop of Guildford, least known of the three.

At the taping session in a small, out-of-the way studio forty-eight
hours before the program was aired, Trevivian was such a quiet,
unobstrusive host that most listeners hardly recalled his presence.
But Target came on strong, his husky voice reinforcing his public
image as a sharp-tongued iconoclast.

Target plunged in with an attack on the De-la-Noy booklet, questioning the inconsistency and integrity of "a Conference which
showed to the world the face of a missionary bishop among children
(the cover picture of Masasi) and ended up guiding its bishops to
costly restaurants that serve 'ludicrously large helpings of wood-
pigeons in wine' while dead rats are being sold in the market places
for human consumption in Biafra."

He continued with a devastating characterization of the Lambeth
fathers as too many, too old, too inexperienced in the world, and too
secretive: "They are here to talk for a month but it is all top secret,
like a James Bond movie."

As for the visiting bishops, they were denounced as an "ecclesiastical jet-set that must be costing somebody a packet." Its middle-
class taste, he said, is betrayed by its fondness for a garden party.

The novelist claimed that the agenda was totally unrelated to a
hungry, needy world. With mocking sarcasm he read aloud some of
the topics. "Listen to this: 'The Nature of Theological Language,'
—that's offering a stale crust instead of the bread of life."

Target concluded his diatribe by asking the bishops "Why aren't
you doing a better public relations job? Is all this talking an excuse
for belching in the face of hunger? You are not a very radiant success at the moment!"

In the babble of voices that replied to Target's onslaught, valuable time was lost while the bishops spoke out in confusion. It was a

momentary gaggle of geese to which Target tossed a few more barbs like a handful of peppery grain.

York's voice was the first that was heard clearly. He conceded that De-la-Noy's booklet had been "a major public relations brick and I happen to know that the Archbishop of Canterbury was very, very angry about it." York said, too, that he had protested the bottles of wine that the waiters had been kept busy opening on the train to Canterbury. Perhaps bishops should be younger, but there were some men who gave their best quite late in life, York said.

Masasi made several reasoned replies in an obvious refusal to participate in Target's tango of vituperativeness. Lambeth's agenda, he said, would provide worthwhile dialogue among men who were grappling with serious problems throughout the world.

Taking up Target's challenge that bishops should be "living epistles," Guildford advanced the belief that the theological discussions of Lambeth would help the bishops to be men who *knew* God, not men who only knew *about* Him.

"You are attacking what you *think* the Conference is about," said York, but Target shrilled at the last: "The people don't care twopence about you or your Conference!"

Not a few critics and churchmen described the program as "savage" and within a few days a new rash of letters broke out in the newspapers. One, an ineffectual letter from Cariboo, ignored all the charges except that allegation that the Conference was secretive. "Extremely misleading," he said.

At the BBC offices in Portman Place, Trevivian described audience reaction as "pretty mixed." He added, thoughtfully, that "those who criticized George Target for being aggressive also praised the bishops for the answers they gave without apparently realizing that it was his kind of questioning that produced their kind of answering. Some of the letters did seem to indicate that people aren't expecting much from this assembly of bishops. One hopes that such people will be surprised."

The charge that the Lambeth fathers were "living it up in posh hotels" was easily refuted by the registration lists. They indicated that while five Americans were at luxury hotels more than half of the 462 bishops were staying in private homes and vicarages or in economy quarters at Westfield College in North London.

As the bishops settled in, it was often recalled that during the early Lambeth Conferences some of the English bishops still maintained private town houses in London. Londoners liked to point out a nearby building that had been the residence of the Bishops of Ely, its chapel later leased to a Roman Catholic mission. In 1968 the Bishop of Ely stayed at his club, Brooks's, in St. James's Street, and his suffragan was at the Strand Palace.

The problem of lodgings for the unprecedented number of bishops, arriving in London in midsummer at the height of the tourist season, had been a concern for many months. "Over the last two years not less than five bishops, including a metropolitan, have asked for a bed here during the Lambeth Conference," wrote one priest to an American friend who had also asked him for a room. "I have not yet said 'yes' to anyone of them though I know for certain that at least four of them are still hoping to be here. Since we only have one spare bed it would be an awful crush if it were to happen!"

All during the last feverish days of locating living space for all of the bishops (as well as some of the observers and consultants, whom the Conference assisted) the formal registration procedure continued in the main lounge at Church House.

It was known in advance that a few of the bishops from 1948 would be present along with a sixth of the bishops from 1958. For most of the others, Church House was a new experience.

A bastion of officialdom if not ecclesiastical bureaucracy, it seemed a marvelously honeycombed building of offices, lounges, libraries, and a magnificent chapel. Most of the newer bishops thought it worth an hour's exploring. They found that the five-story structure was also five-sided, ingeniously designed to fit snugly into the tangle of narrow, curving streets and lanes—Tufton, Cowley, Little Smith, and Great Smith—that crisscross at the back of Dean's Yard, Westminster, where once the monks of the Abbey tended their orchards.

The dowager Queen Mary laid the cornerstone for Church House in 1937. It was dedicated on a June day three years later when the bombing of London was so intense that it seemed an act of faith to speak of any building serving the future. After the heavy damage inflicted on the Houses of Parliament, it sheltered the Commons and the Lords and was the scene of some of Churchill's most memorable speeches.[5]

The entrance to Dean's Yard, the broad quadrangle of which Church House formed one side, was an archway marked with a warning signal for motorists, CAUTION: DEAD SLOW. More than one wag said the motto was one that the Conference might well adopt. Indeed, in the final plenary session of Lambeth X, Gray of Connecticut said the sign never failed to remind him of the progress of the Wider Episcopal Fellowship: suggested in '48, recommended in '58, and convened in '64.

Bordering Dean's Yard, the buildings of the old Abbey were a mellow jumble of everything from ancient stone to Victorian brick and plaster. Inside the various archways could be glimpsed other buildings of Westminster School and a few Georgian houses. Westminster's chimes pealed frequently over the quiet scene and at times it seemed possible that the black-robed Benedictines of old might still be keeping a daily round of Offices in the Abbey Church.

Through the Yard, past clergy houses and classrooms lined with schoolchildren's drawings, the bishops walked to the neo-Georgian pile that was Church House.

As the administration headquarters of the Church of England, Church House was known variously as the Little Vatican, the London Pentagon, and, after the American counterpart, the Cave of the Winds.

Church House was a building planned with obvious attention to detail and symbolism. Beyond its wide terrace, the rough-stone

---

[5] Late in 1940, the Assembly Hall was damaged by a bomb and six people were killed. The remainder of the building was requisitioned by the government and for the duration of the war it became the alternative meeting place of Parliament, the Lords occupying Convocation Hall and the Commons in Hoare Memorial Hall. By October 1946 some administrative offices of the Church Assembly had returned to Church House and the Church Assembly was able to occupy it for the autumn session of 1950.

wainscoting of the first story was encrusted with the heraldic shields of all of the English dioceses (with a few spots left blank for growth). Above the triple-arched portico stood a majestic figure suggested by Michaelangelo's painting of David on the ceiling of the Sistine Chapel.

Inside Church House, on the second floor, activities centered in Hoare Memorial Hall, named for a prominent banker and church-man of the last century. Ringed with tables for registration, it was not unlike a hotel ballroom converted to the use of a convention. At the rear of the hall stood tiers of gray metal mailboxes—one for every three Bishops, numbered according to the Conference's offi-cial processional order. Many of the men were accustomed to a number that dictated their places in processions in their own na-tional Churches as well as their seats in an assembly of bishops. All that was momentarily changed: the Bishop of Springfield [Illinois], for instance, ordinarily No. 588, became No. 271. One of his col-leagues remarked, "I'm in the 300s—don't know if I feel like a convict or a hymn."

Behind the registration desks were other tables bearing long rows of plastic briefcases issued for all Conference participants. Lightweight and practical, the bags zipped across the top and had *Lambeth Conference 1968* discreetly embossed in gold letters in the right corner.

The bright blue cases contained tickets to the official services, invitations to the parties, *Who's Who at Lambeth '68,* and several other booklets including lists by processional order, official ob-servers, official consultants, and constitution of committees. The most immediately important items were the badges, small white cards encased in clear plastic with the color of the printing denoting the rank of its bearer—purple for bishops, gold for wives, blue for observers, black for consultants, green for staff, red for press.

The first bishop to sign in on Monday morning, three days before the Conference opened, was the urbane, pipe-smoking Bishop of Arizona, Joseph Harte. Canterbury sauntered in at noon the same day and was given his kit by Miss Peggy Drake, secretary to the Archbishop of Cape Town.

By Thursday, when the bishops departed for the opening service in Canterbury Cathedral, the registration appeared to total 462; of that number, fifteen had been present at Lambeth VIII and forty-nine had attended Lambeth IX.

Inevitably, there were some gaps in the ranks. Among the American diocesans who did not attend or send a bishop to represent them were Craine of Indianapolis, Hall of New Hampshire, Blanchard of Southern Ohio, Hatch of Western Massachusetts, and Minnis of Colorado. (The latter was awaiting trial by a committee of fellow bishops who, two months later, stripped him of power and removed him from office.) Three other U.S. dioceses not represented—Maine, Montana, and San Joaquin—had bishops-elect still awaiting consecration.[6]

A prominent name absent from the roster was Moore, Suffragan of Washington, often suggested as the next Bishop of New York, who was on leave of absence to direct Operation Connection, a national inter-religious coalition to support minority groups.

Others notably missing were DeWitt of Pennsylvania, consecrated in 1964; two veterans of other Lambeths, Stokes of Massachusetts and Emrich of Michigan; and Cole, Coadjutor of Western New York. Banyard of New Jersey had attended only one General Convention since taking office in 1955 and had declined invitations to Lambeth in both 1958 and 1968.

Even with these absences, an editorial in *The Living Church* was less than accurate in declaring that "every Right Reverend Father in God of the Anglican Communion will be out of the country."

Replying to the editorial, Bishop Bayne wrote that in the U.S. "a systematic and arduous approach to this whole matter was undertaken by the Presiding Bishop and our bishops as a whole, beginning last autumn and that (in some instances) decisions have deliberately been taken to arrange and balance attendance so that critical areas at home will be covered. . . ." Bayne referred by name to only two

---

[6] Conversely, Walters of San Joaquin was the only one of four U.S. bishops shortly to retire who did not accept an invitation to Lambeth X. In attendance were Pardue of Pittsburgh, who retired August 31; Barton of Eastern Oregon, October 31; and Carpenter of Alabama, December 31.

of the absent Americans, Michigan and Massachusetts, both of whom were bishops of metropolitan areas of racial unrest and both of whom had suffragans present at Lambeth X.

The prospect of "the long, hot summer" and its threat of racial violence figured in many of the decisions about going to Lambeth. New York's Horace Donegan told his diocesan convention in May that he had asked Canterbury to relieve him of the chairmanship of the Committee on Urbanization and the Metropolis because of the possibility that he might be called home suddenly. The Presiding Bishop of the American Church also requested that he be replaced as head of the Committee on Faith and Society; he remained, like Bishop Donegan, a member of his original committee. It was understood that for the same reason Michigan was also excused as a committee chairman.

As it turned out, the scattered racial incidents in Cincinnati, Little Rock, and a few other cities did not necessitate a return home of any of the American bishops.

The registration of bishops continued steadily in Hoare Memorial Hall for three and a half days, although the Church Information Office's failure to keep a running tally made it impossible to report which day saw the heaviest number.

As the bishops checked in, picked up their mail, and became acquainted or renewed old friendships, they found scattered about the Hall a small avalanche of material for their perusal. It was as varied as it was plentiful: a small white card of prayers authorized by Canterbury for the success of Lambeth X; brochures describing the Anglican Center in Rome, the Westminster Theatre Restaurant, the new Retreat House of the Sisters of St. Peter, the National Evangelical Anglican Congress, the Bible Churchmen's Missionary Society, the Crowhurst Home of Healing, and the Ecclesiastical Insurance Office Ltd. [motto: *"Pro Ecclesia"*].

There were invitations for a special bus trip to Dorchester Cathedral, to the Westminster Theatre Restaurant, to the Southark Festival of Flowers, to the 1970 Pilgrimage to Canterbury, and to the Abbey service for the International Congress of Mental Health (which coincided with Missionary Weekend). There were stacks of hard-cover green books, *Y Cymun Bendigaid,* the Holy Eucharist of the Church in Wales; of blue leaflets on "Lusitanian and Spanish Reformed Episcopal Churches," and orange leaflets entitled "Faith & Order of the Philippine Independent Church."

There were also copies of *The Anglican Digest,* catalogues from several publishing houses, booklets on grants made by the American Church's General Convention, and a newsletter from the British Council of Churches.

Scattered about among the bulk of material were odd pieces, fewer in number: an expensive, glossy magazine, *Twice in a Lifetime,* raising money for displaced Arabs; an architectural folder, *Newly-built Churches in England and Scotland,* and a plainly printed *Appeal to Lambeth on Drugs and Liquor* from the United Kingdom Alliance.

Elsewhere in Church House some rather homey touches began to appear. There was, for instance, the St. John Ambulance Brigade, which established a first-aid post to be maintained for the duration of the Conference. Within a few hours after it opened it received its first casualty, a bishop who had cut his nose while shaving and could not stop the bleeding.

A more serious problem was posed by an American observer who did not have a hotel reservation. He was accommodated by members of the Mothers' Union, who quickly found him a place to stay and loaned him ten shillings to get there.

More members of the Mothers' Union were busy on the top floor of Church House where, in cooperation with the Association of Church Fellowships, they had established a club for bishops' wives.

In a small adjoining room, Mrs. John Burgess, wife of the Suffragan of Massachusetts, was busy ironing a rochet in preparation for her husband's trip to Canterbury. "At home he usually irons it himself," she said.

CHAPTER 3

LAMBETH IN SESSION

The LAMBETH CONFERENCE OF 1968 meets at a critical moment in the history of Christendom," declared Pope Paul in the first message ever sent to Anglican bishops by a Roman Pontiff. "Its overriding theme may be expressed like that of the great assembly just concluded at Uppsala, in the words of Revelation XXI : 5, 'Behold I make all things new'; it is in the forefront of all Christian thinking today."

The Lambeth fathers listened intently as Paul VI's address was read aloud by a member of the Vatican Secretariat for Promoting Christian Unity.

An hour earlier a small incident in the balcony of Church House had almost started the bishops off on the wrong episcopal foot. One report said that the observers were not being admitted for the opening prayers, another that the observers had been asked to leave. Whatever the case, the stories swept Church House and soon reached Canterbury. He instantly decreed that the observers should be present, and a few minutes later, after the opening prayers, his welcoming remarks gave first attention to the observers. "You are here so generously because we need you," he said, "and your participation will assuredly help the Conference to work with greater knowledge and wisdom and in closer touch with all Christendom than would otherwise be possible."

The Papal message followed, read by the Dutch-born titular Archbishop of Mauriana, Jan Willebrands, destined to be named a Cardinal eight months later. An old friend who had often been a guest of the Ramseys and several years earlier had helped arrange Cardinal Bea's visit to Lambeth Palace, he kissed the Primate's ring as he reached the podium.

Next came Britain's highest-ranking Orthodox prelate, Athenagoras II, with whom Canterbury exchanged the traditional brotherly embrace.

The third speaker was an American Presbyterian, Eugene Carson Blake, who shook hands with Canterbury and then began reading a message of greetings from the World Council of Churches, of which he was Secretary General.

Thus a kiss, an embrace, and a handshake symbolized Christendom's interest in Lambeth's deliberations. After the three addresses, the morning was devoted to the development of the Conference themes by the chairmen of the Sections on Faith, Ministry, and Unity.

First to speak was the Faith Section's chairman, Howard Clark, Archbishop of Rupert's Land and Primate of All Canada. He expressed belief that Anglicanism (while not in danger of losing its Scriptures, Creed, and "the other foundations of the Catholic and Apostolic Church") might "be called upon to use them more adventurously, no longer attempting to hold men in check so that the journey will be safe, but releasing them to follow the dangerous Christ."

The second speaker, Frederick Donald Coggan, Archbishop of York, chairman of the Ministry Section, plunged immediately into the controversial question of ordination of women.

The last speaker, Lakdasa de Mel, Bishop of Calcutta and Metropolitan of India, placed his dark hands together in a graceful salaam to Canterbury before beginning his discussion of the work of the Unity Section. Although it was the longest in the morning of talks, de Mel's was well received because of the characteristic humor that enlivened it.

"Sometimes people ask if it is not better to deal with Rome with its vast population, and leave the other Churches alone," he said. "But we must not embarrass Rome by failing to go on with our dialogue with these churches now ready for unity. Do not let us be more papalistic than the Pope! Rome is great enough to stop being a dealer satisfied with the pickings of somebody else's flock. Let us unite and then do some wholesale business!"

Slightly more than two hours after convening, the initial plenary session of Lambeth X adjourned. Departing, Canterbury waved to friends on the terrace of Church House—and narrowly missed a fall down the steps. Caught by his chaplain, he sank heavily into the confines of the small Morris that he preferred to the luxury of the archiepiscopal limousine. As it pulled away, the tiny automobile tilted to one side under the weight of the Archbishop and the newly articulated challenges he bore home to Lambeth Palace.

This Conference has taken note of the Papal Encyclical Letter *"Humanae Vitae"* recently issued by His Holiness Pope Paul VI. The Conference records its appreciation of the Pope's deep concern for the institution of marriage and the integrity of married life. Nevertheless, the Conference finds itself unable to agree with the Pope's conclusion that all methods of conception control other than abstinence from sexual intercourse or its confinement to the periods of infecundity are contrary to the "order established by God." It reaffirms the findings of the Lambeth Conference of 1958. . . .

Acting swiftly but with caution, the Lambeth bishops drafted and unanimously approved a carefully worded Resolution on the Papal Encyclical in less than forty-eight hours after the long-awaited edict from Rome burst with bombastic force on the world and the Conference.[1]

---

[1] In a long article, "Catholic Freedom vs. Authority," nearly four months after the encyclical's promulgation, *Time* on November 22, 1968, declared

For two days it dominated long sessions of debate, obscuring all other discussion and provoking a flurry of statements—including one from Canterbury that became the nucleus of the formal resolution.

The thinking behind the brief resolution that eventually emerged was the belief, advanced by the Bishop of Exeter, that the newly convened Conference should not sit in judgment on a stand the Pope had reached after prolonged study; also there was a strong opinion that the Conference was not speaking to the Pope but to all mankind, because the encyclical was addressed not just to Roman Catholics but to the world. That was the tenor of Canterbury's preliminary statement (issued after consultation with the Steering Committee) as well as of the statements given to the press by the Presiding Bishop of the American Church and by the Canadian primate. All three men had met with a group that included the members of the Steering Committee (except for Bishop Bayne, called home by his mother's death) as well as Beecher of East Africa, Simon of Wales, Ramsey of Durham, and Brown of Warrington, Suffragan to Liverpool.

Interviewed in the corridors of Church House, the Metropolitan of India pointed out that Paul VI had seen fit to uphold the ruling against contraception even though, ironically, he was the first Pope who had visited India and personally observed the starving hordes.

In midafternoon of the day the encyclical was issued, the secular press, its interest sharpened by the news from Rome, flocked to a news conference at Church House. Together they scanned Canterbury's 193-word statement characterizing the encyclical as "widely different" from the opinion of the last Lambeth Conference, which had declared that "means adopted to limit the number of children in a family are a matter for the consciences of each husband and wife."

(In a second paragraph Canterbury said: "The changes in human

that "July 29, 1968, may prove to be a major landmark in the long history of the Roman Catholic Church—as significant, perhaps, as the moment when Martin Luther decided to post his theses on indulgences at Wittenberg Castle Church."

society and world population, as well as the development in the means available for contraception, which have occurred since 1958, seem to me to reinforce rather than to challenge the argument employed and the conclusions reached at the Lambeth Conference of 1958.")

Under the hot glare of television floodlights, Cariboo sat facing four microphones with the statement before him on a table covered with navy-blue felt. In the next twenty minutes he skillfully fielded thirty-two questions on the encyclical's impact, its effect on the ecumenical movement, and its chances for mitigation. The questioning also brought to light that while Lambeth VII was the first major Christian body to give qualified approval to birth control, no official stand had ever been taken on abortion.[2]

"The case has been closed by the laity, anyway," Cariboo said with a shrug.

Cariboo said he did not think the encyclical would effect the holding of meetings on unity but that discussions on mixed marriages would be more difficult. "If the Anglican partner of a marriage asked us about birth control, we would refer him to the 1958 Lambeth Report," he said.

Anticipating a rebellion of Roman clergy, the final questioner asked what the attitude would be toward those who wished to become Anglican priests. "Anglican bishops will have to search their consciences as to what they do with a Roman priest who makes application on this particular issue," Cariboo replied, "because, as I have said, it is not the *only* difference between the Roman Church and the Anglican."

Despite the statements of the three bishops who represented the majority of Anglicans—Canterbury, Hines of the American Church, and Clark of Canada—the Conference still took its time in wording a resolution that would command complete assent of all the bishops.

----

[2] In 1920, Lambeth VI had approved contraception "in abnormal cases." Ten years later its reports and resolutions stated that intercourse has also "a secondary end within the sacrament of marriage, i.e., as an expression or bond of married love."

By noon of the second day it had become known that Sherrill of Central Brazil, with the support of Welles of West Missouri, was endeavoring to persuade the Conference to agree to a reaffirmation of the 1958 decision and to make it even stronger. In seconding Sherrill's motion Welles made a statement, later disclosed in a news briefing, that the press immediately seized upon as the viewpoint most sympathetic with public opinion: the frank admission of the Bishop of West Missouri—sixty-one, married thirty-seven years, father of four—that he had personally found that the practice of contraception enhanced his marriage.[3]

Sherrill urged the bishops to register their belief that the rational and disciplined use of artificial means of birth control did not necessarily lead to "moral degradation," but rather toward a "maturity" of marriage. Such a view was contrary to the Pope's stated conviction that artificial means of birth control would open a wide and easy road to "conjugal infidelity and the general lowering of morality."

A third section of Sherrill's resolution asked that the Anglican–Roman Catholic Commission give closer attention to the whole theology of marriage and its application to mixed marriages.[4]

There were numerous speeches urging caution: like Exeter, Green-Wilkinson of Central Africa warned of "fishing in troubled waters" and that any resolution on such a highly controversial issue should be passed in a spirit of charity; Polynesia's John Vockler,

---

[3] The charge that Vatican rulings were sometimes lacking in understanding because they were handed down by "a group of elderly bachelors" could not be lodged against the Lambeth bishops. Of the 462, fewer than 50 were unmarried and but a handful were widowers. Biographical data indicated that the married bishops had a total of 1101 children. Largest families among the episcopate: ten children each in the households of the Bishop of Kobe (Japan) and the Bishop of Nuku'alofa, Suffragan to Polynesia.

[4] Chisholm of Melanesia, a jolly Australian, reported that one idea used by Roman Catholics on one of the islands in his scattered realm was for young couples between fifteen and twenty-two to "organize trial marriages." "They are merely excommunicated during time of Trial," he said. "Standing Orders suspended, so to speak." *The Guardian* quoted the Bishop under the headline STANDING DISORDER and added its tongue-in-cheek belief that the idea might be "a definite thought for the Isle of Man."

Bishop Hines, and Archbishop Beecher said population control should not be mentioned in a resolution on birth control. His view evidently prevailed; after the Steering Committee's two meetings to consider drafting procedure, all references to "moral degradation" were abandoned.

The resolution that was finally approved was, indeed, so conservatively expressed that one newspaper wrote it off as "a cautious exercise in ecumenical diplomacy." Some bishops said they did not recall that unity was mentioned, but "it was very much in everyone's mind not to injure new friendships by rushing into an offensive statement." [5]

The Manchester Guardian openly reproached the Conference for "refusing to give any aid or comfort to [Roman] Catholic dissidents in developing countries by citing the value of contraception in controlling populations."

It is possible to go considerably further than the *Guardian*'s criticism since the Lambeth fathers did consciously reject the opportunity to interpret the teachings of Christ and the Church in new and fresh ways for thousands who were perplexed and troubled—at a time when those inside and outside Anglican churches needed a strong dissenting voice and positive leadership. Had Lambeth X intended to render such witness and counsel it would not have said that it was "unable to agree" but rather that it disagreed outright —and why. It would not have felt reticence but an obligation to answer the Pope; as one bishop put it, "Five minutes of enlightened thinking *can* be equated with five years of logic mired in the quicksands of 'infallibility.' "

If it is true that references to the thoughtfully worded resolutions

---

[5] "The Lambeth Conference quite properly made its comment and made it in moderate terms," said John Cardinal Heenan, Archbishop of Westminster, to a crowd of 4000 assembled in St. Paul's Cathedral on the night of January 22, 1969, for the Octave of Christian Unity. "The Anglican bishops made no attempt to criticize or to condemn. Our community, embarrassed by attacks on the Pope by some of its own members, was grateful beyond measure for the forbearance and compassion shown by the Anglicans. I have deliberately awaited this opportunity of speaking in St. Paul's to express our thanks . . . for that great act of friendship."

of 1958 indicate a consistency of thought and loyalty to Anglican principles, it is also true that such references rely on reasoning of ten years ago as the basis and almost the whole text of the new resolution. In a sense, it was stale bread handed to hungry people. On the other hand, could 462 men answer one man, Paul VI?

The Lambeth fathers, no strangers to the frontiers of fine-line distinctions, may well have practiced subtle restraint as well as charity, reminding themselves that condemnation could fall on deaf ears at the Vatican but that a resolution set forth with good will might be studied there.

Lambeth's resolution served the Church well in unearthing the brilliantly written paper of 1958, "The Family in Contemporary Society," which, like most Conference reports, has rarely sifted down to the man in the pew.

Moreover, the Anglican Communion may have enhanced itself in the eyes of the world—an achievement not to be prized for the value of public image but for its witness to Anglicanism open to those who seek a position between Romanism and Protestantism.

The bishops put aside their deliberations on birth control and moved on to another nonagenda item, the Bishop of Norwich's resolution urging the U.N. to protect undersea lands from international competition.

As the resolution passed unanimously, the gloom of lengthy debate was finally lifted with one bishop's observation that he was pleased to see that his brothers "favor policing of the sea bed, if not the marriage bed."

A significant result of the debate on the Papal encyclical was the bishops' decision to open plenary sessions to the press, a move that grew out of the candid disclosure by Welles of West Missouri that the use of contraceptives had enhanced his own marriage. It was mentioned in the late afternoon press briefing almost as an aside in transmitting Bishop Welles' thesis that, contrary to the encyclical, the use of contraceptives did not constitute "moral degradation."

Within the next few hours Bishop Welles' highly personal statement was picked up in the evening news broadcasts. Taken out of context, it had a certain sensationalism that was carried over to the front pages of the next morning's newspapers—LAMBETH BISHOP ADMITS TO USE OF CONTRACEPTIVES.

Nobody was more surprised than Bishop Welles himself, but when reporters questioned him he stood by what he had said, adding only that he hadn't known he was going to be quoted. After the completion of morning prayers, he rose to what he later called "a point of personal privilege." Recognized by Canterbury, he said he regretted that his remarks, quoted out of context, might overshadow his respect for the Pope's witness to the sanctity of marriage. In order that distortions or misunderstandings would not arise in the future, he proposed that plenary sessions be opened to the press.

There was no immediate second to West Missouri's motion. Instead, the Archbishop of York pointed out the Lambeth tradition of closed meetings as well as the possibility that the presence of journalists might cause some bishops to speak less and others to speak more frequently. Also, he said, material that would be under study —drafts of the reports and resolutions—should not be made public.

After York was seated, three prominent bishops threw support to West Missouri's motion—the Primate of All Canada, the Presiding Bishop of the American Church, and the senior Australian diocesan, J. A. G. Housden of Newcastle. The consensus was that there was always a risk of news being distorted when it was relayed through a press briefing. The point was also made that the process and reasoning by which the Conference reached its decisions was a matter of public interest.

As the meeting broke for lunch, Canterbury asked the bishops to consider carefully how they would vote that afternoon. When they reassembled the show of hands was in favor of admitting the press —a landmark decision in the history of the Lambeth Conferences.

By the time the resolution on birth control had become a part of the record and the decision had been made to throw open the doors to the press, Lambeth X was thinking of itself as a seasoned Conference. The initial deliberations had been an excellent workout, a lively indication of how the bishops could work together on the huge mass of material concerned with Faith, Ministry, and Unity. The immensity of the themes no longer seemed unmanageable: the birth-control resolution had given them relevance and urgency.

By nature and by necessity accustomed to running their own shows, the bishops conformed with admirable obedience to the exacting schedule of plenary sessions, section conferences, and committee meetings. There were also innumerable luncheons, dinners, informal get-togethers, and occasional meetings of the entire episcopate of individual churches.

The two prelates at the center, Canterbury and Cariboo, may have been astonished at times—perhaps more surprised than anyone—at the workability of a program that enabled such a large group to study so many topics within a few weeks.

Although Lambeth I had lasted only four days in the fall of 1867, some of the other conferences had stretched to over six weeks. The thirty-two-day schedule for the tenth Lambeth Conference judiciously placed the initial plenary session on a Saturday, followed by two more plenary meetings on Monday morning and Friday afternoon of the opening week. The three intervening days of the first week were reserved for committee work.

The second week of the Conference again saw the bishops in full session for two days devoted to nonagenda items [6]—a designation of time that providentially coincided with the Papal encyclical. The remainder of the week was given over to plenary sessions on each of the three major themes.

In the third week, the bishops dispersed for sectional work and committee meetings on the revisions the full Conference had suggested. In the concluding week, they came together again for the final reports and resolutions. It was a crowded week, revealing that even bishops are not exempt from the necessity of crowding in a lot of business at the last minute.

---

[6] At the opening press conference Canterbury explained that special provision had been made whereby, giving three days' notice, any bishop would be able to raise a particular matter, either of a sacred or secular nature, he felt to be of importance.

As they trooped into Church House the first week, the Lambeth fathers seemed far more commonplace than they did in procession at Canterbury or Westminster. They were noticeably free of papers, at least for a few days, indicative of the attitude that they had come to work and be worked, but as mimeographs, Xeroxes, and printers worked overtime to produce a blizzard of minutiae, the bishops began turning up with battered brief cases or the bright-blue plastic "envelopes" that had been issued to everyone.

For the most part, they wore ordinary business suits with clerical collars, rain-slickers or dark overcoats, and old, dark hats. The English held to their fondness for collars a half-size too large—"dog collars" the newspapers called them. The Africans favored sweaters against the London chill that prevailed during the first three weeks. As with any group, there were always standouts in attire— such as Fond du Lac and a few others who favored purple socks to match their shirts.

The bishops, surveyed from the gallery of the assembly hall, came across as an alert, impressive group. Their ages ranged from thirty-seven to eighty, with the Canadian Church boasting the youngest and oldest—John Frame of the Yukon, born in December 1930,[7] consecrated in 1968; and Harold Sexton of British Columbia, born in 1888 in Australia, educated in Ireland and England, consecrated in Canada in 1935.

With an average age of fifty-eight and a half, the general appearance of Lambeth X was little different from that of any group of executives in an international assembly: balding, inclined to heaviness, some getting past their prime but together representing a

---

[7] Two others born in 1930 were William Frey, who at thirty-eight had recently been consecrated first Bishop of Guatemala, and Leonard Romero, one of the two suffragans of Mexico. Some Africans and others did not list birth dates, but it was obvious that younger churches had younger bishops. The average age of the Africans was in the low fifties; the bishops of England, Wales, Ireland, and Scotland, was in the sixties; the Americans and Canadians averaged fifty-eight. Surprisingly, the inclusion of coadjutors, suffragans, and assistants did not lower the average age. In the latter group, the English were older than the diocesans, possibly a result of the large number of them who were originally consecrated for foreign sees.

laudable length of service. If there was one factor that distinguished the episcopate from its contemporaries, it was a tendency to extremes in sternness or gregariousness.

There were, of course, as many varieties as there were bishops present, and each one had his own individual experience and judgment to contribute. As national groups, their characteristics were predictable: the English, frosty or properly friendly; Australians, New Zealanders, and Canadians in their reserve revealing degrees of their Englishness; Americans, gregarious and organization-minded; the Africans, genuinely gracious but shy.

The final registration was fixed at 462, but the number of bishops eligible was in doubt: *The Church of England Yearbook* listed 740; *Preparatory Information,* published for Lambeth X, listed 536 diocesans, coadjutors, suffragans, or assistants. Part of the disparity was accounted for by the bishops who were engaged in administrative, academic, or parochial work. Those eligible for Lambeth ("bishops working in dioceses," as Canterbury was fond of saying) was nearer 600.

Taken as a group, they had a resemblance to Lambeth I closer than the intervening Conferences. There were only a few bearded faces at the first Conference and but a sprinkling of them in 1968, but in between the episcopate reached heights of sartorial splendor with bristling sideburns, luxurious mustaches, and beards that would make Orthodox bishops blush.

In Church House, Westminster, the Lambeth fathers found their most comfortable home in the 101 years of the Conferences.[8] Instead of turning Lambeth Palace Library into an improvised meeting room, the bishops had the assembly hall of Church House; for a lounge, where they picked up mail and messages, they exchanged Lambeth's Guards Room (which once housed the archbishops' private guards) for Hoare Memorial Hall at Church House; and the drafty tent that provided shelter for lunch and tea in the Lambeth

---

[8] Management is vested in the Corporation of Church House, which has a council of thirty members: ten ex-officio, nine elected, six nominated by the Church Assembly, and five "co-opted" by the Council. Canterbury is president and York vice-president.

Gardens was replaced by Westminster School's refectory and scores of private restaurants within walking distance. The result was that London saw more bishops abroad at noon time than ever before and became more interested in the Conference.

Inside Church House, the Conference resembled the U.S. Congress, as it occupied ten tiers of seats that rose in gradual elevation around the circular room known as the Assembly Hall. At previous Lambeths the bishops had been crowded in so closely that there was, literally, almost no elbow room, but at Lambeth X they enjoyed upholstered theatre seats.[9] ("At Lambeth Palace, the English bishops were always opening the windows and the Americans were always closing them," recalled Crittenden of Erie.)

The bishops' purple stocks dotting the hall gave it an august dignity even if the scene did not approach the pictures of the mitred Roman episcopate in grandstands lining the nave of St. Peter's for Vatican II.[10] But, like the Romans, the Anglican bishops gathered beneath a dome. It was not encircled with Biblical verses in Greek or Latin but with words in English spelled out in great golden letters: "Holy is the true light and passing wonderful, lending radiance to them that endureth the heat of the conflict: from Christ they inherit a home of unfailing splendor, wherein they rejoice with gladness evermore."

The cream-colored walls of the chamber, decorated with heraldic symbols of the Empire and the provinces of Canterbury and York, were interspersed by eight evenly spaced exits that suggested a gladiators' arena.[11]

---

[9] In 1930, the bishops were allowed to buy the chairs they occupied. The custom was discontinued by later Conferences but cropped up again in 1953 after the coronation of Elizabeth II, when guests were allowed to keep the chairs that had been custom upholstered in blue-and-gold fabric bearing the royal cipher.

[10] One of the Americans, well known for his low-church loyalties, decided to buy his first purple stock or rabat to wear at Lambeth X and promptly mailed his order to a clerical supplier in New York: "Please send me two purple rabbits."

[11] Archbishop Fisher may have observed the similarity when he came to Church House early in 1961 to announce his plans to retire: "My feelings are those of a schoolboy getting in sight of the holidays. Or more seriously, my

Name tags designated where the primates were to be seated on both sides of the podium; the front row, left to right, was for Scotland, Armagh, York, Wales, Dublin, and the U.S.; the second row was reserved for Perth, Brisbane, New Westminster, Algoma, Frederickton, the Metropolitan of India, and Melbourne; the third row was given over to Jerusalem, West Africa, West Indies, New Zealand, Sydney, Cape Town, Central Africa, and East Africa; in the fourth row were Brazil, Southeast Asia, and Uganda.[12]

At the center of the podium desk, flanked by two secretaries, sat Canterbury and Cariboo. Listening to discussion from the floor, Canterbury slouched in the great oaken presidential chair, its high back surmounted by the arms of Canterbury. The azure blue of the shield, flanked by large gold and silver keys, offered the only focus of color in the restrained decor. Above the podium a rectangular frame of paneling carried a quotation from Isaiah: "The spirit of the Lord shall rest upon him, the spirit of wisdom and understanding, the spirit of courage and might, the spirit of knowledge and of the fear of the Lord."

The meandering corridors of Church House and all of the excellent features tucked away in its layered intricacies became as familiar to the bishops as their own diocesan offices, but no part of it was more familiar than the Assembly Hall where they spent approximately sixty hours in plenary session during the weeks of Lambeth X.

---

feelings are perhaps those of a matador who has decided not to enter the bullring."

[12] The American church had only its Presiding Bishop seated among the metropolitans and primates at Church House and marching with them in processions, a lonely representation that seemed out of proportion to the presence of three Irish bishops, four Australians, and four Canadians. When questioned, the Episcopal Secretary said that the precedent of other years had been followed and that the heads of the nine U.S. provinces did not have the authority of metropolitans in the usual sense of one who has other bishops within his jurisdictional authority. Expressing disappointment, one of the American bishops said they had "rather expected to be included . . . technically we should be." Had they been so regarded, the ranks of the metropolitans would have included, by order of consecration, Connecticut, Western New York, Pittsburgh, Georgia, Minnesota, New Mexico & Southwest Texas, Spokane, Puerto Rico, and Indianapolis if he had been present at Lambeth X.

In a building designed and operated on a grand scale, a small arrangement of flowers, snugly enshrined and regularly replenished in a glass case in the central lobby, seemed a curious concession to cordiality. Except for the uniformed guards who were always courteous, the staff of Church House sometimes seemed as brusque as a hostess who found guests a wearing experience for a whole month—which, indeed, was the situation they obviously "endured."

In contrast, the Mothers' Union [13] and other volunteers from London parishes cheerfully took turns sorting mail and running the information desk. They brought bushels of flowers and they brought conscientiousness and if they were inclined to gushy overhelpfulness they still were unfailingly friendly.

There was hospitality, too, in the adjoining buildings of Westminster School, where cafeteria-style lunch was available for sixty cents. The bishops were served in monkish College Hall, once the state dining room of the abbots of Westminster. Afterward, weather permitting, they strolled in a small interior courtyard.

In the Assembly Hall, at the beginning of the final week, hand-lettered signs were posted above the doors that flanked the dais—"Ayes" to the left and "Noes" to the right—to facilitate the counting of votes. [14] Following the procedure (of clergy and laity) of the Church Assembly, the bishops were counted as they filed out through the door of their choice. The "voting doors," as they came to be known, went unused the first day the signs were up because

---

[13] Founded in 1876 "to strengthen, safeguard and promote Christian family life on the basis of the life-long nature of the marriage vows as taught by the Church," the Mothers' Union flourishes throughout most of the British Commonwealth but has never caught on in the U.S. It maintains Mary Sumner House, a headquarters building and bookstore, in Tufton Street near Westminster Abbey. In recent years it has been increasingly controversial for its refusal to admit divorced women to membership.

[14] As Lambeth X entered its last week, Canterbury drew this distinction between the resolutions of the Conference and the reports of the Sections on Faith, Ministry, and Unity: "Reports are on the authority of the Sections and carry only authority of Sections and the Conference does not endorse the reports and is not committed. On the other hand, the Conference does endorse its resolutions and is committed to them."

nothing more than a count of hands seemed necessary, but on the second day the more controversial resolutions on intercommunion made exact tallies necessary; almost always a few bishops remained in their seats, undecided or uncommitted.[15]

"If it is necessary to count a show of hands, it is easier for four people to do so, each pair taking the left or right segment of the hall as the case may be," said a memorandum given the bishops. "The senior of the four should be responsible for counting the votes of those on the platform, including the Chairman if he wishes to vote. Each pair should compare notes and take the average of the totals at which they arrive unless there is too great a discrepancy, when it may be necessary to ask the Chairman to request a further show of hands."

The instructions for voting "by division" were more detailed: "The Episcopal Secretary details the bishops sitting on either side of the 'Ayes' and 'Noes' doors respectively as tellers; the Episcopal Secretary selects from those sitting on either side of the remaining doors of the hall a bishop to act as doorkeeper; tellers and doorkeepers will take up their position and the division bell will be rung in the corridors; two minutes after the bell has ceased to ring the Episcopal Secretary orders the doors to be shut; the Chairman then formally puts the motion and requests the members to divide; members do so by filing through the 'Aye' or 'No' door as they wish to vote; the tellers count them as they go through; when the hall is empty the tellers and doorkeepers record their votes at the appropriate door and then return to their post, allowing no one to return to the hall until instructed to do so by the Episcopal Secretary; the tellers compare notes and hand, in writing, an agreed total to the Episcopal Secretary; the Episcopal Secretary then orders the doors to be opened; when all are seated the Chairman calls for order and

---

[15] "I save my fire for the right time: the real place to speak is for the resolutions," said an American bishop who had attended two previous Lambeths. "In preliminaries, many bishops talk themselves out of steam or, as Angus Dun [fourth Bishop of Washington, 1944–1962] once said from the floor, 'I regret the necessity of taking the time of regular speakers.' "

announces the result of the division; those who wish to abstain remain seated in their places."

Tedious and complicated as the directions were, the same attention to the discussion of the lengthy drafts of the Report and resolutions could have saved the Conference from floundering for almost an hour at the start of its third week. As it was, the bishops spent valuable time devising a procedure for dealing with the long printers' galleys of material from the committees.

Cyril Kenneth Sansbury, Assistant Bishop of London and General Secretary of the British Council of Churches, thumbed through five galleys of the first proofs that reached the Conference floor, then rose to ask, "Do we discuss the whole of it and *then* take it piece by piece?"

Warming to Sansbury's suggestion, a bishop in the back of the hall called out a request that the Draft Report be read aloud before it was discussed. He was shouted down with loud "noes."

North Carolina's Fraser asked in frank bewilderment, "Is it our task to come up with a theological statement or a pastoral letter, a reference book or what? We need a frame of reference."

In answer to the questions, Canterbury suggested that the bishops take about ten minutes to look over the Draft (the preliminary Report for the Section on Faith) and then begin discussion. Adopting that procedure, the Conference thereafter allowed time for the bishops to peruse the drafts, a scene that invariably made the fathers with their fluttering galleys look like a convention of paperhangers.

It was during the painstaking revisions that Canterbury's abilities as a chairman became more apparent than they had been at the outset of the Conference; it was neither passivity nor directness from the Chair, however, that disturbed the bishops so much as the autocratic fashion in which business was sometimes handled.

"In our talks about birth control, Canterbury's manner of presiding was not the most refreshing change from the overbearing reputations that the archbishops have had in Lambeth Conferences, nor from the condescending schoolmaster ways of Geoffrey Fisher that bothered so many of us in '48 and '58," said an American bishop.

"When we saw how things went with the birth control resolution we decided parlimentary procedure might be more strictly observed if all the sessions were opened up to the Press."

Another American, also a veteran of two Lambeths, said, "There's always a difference of opinion between the overseas bishops—especially Americans, Canadians, and Australians—and the English about how to conduct a meeting. It no longer surprises me because I've learned that the English, when the Archbishop of Canterbury is presiding, never question the ruling of the Chair. The Bishop of Erie was angered the other day and I feel that the Archbishop ignored him and was rude to him; however, there's a solidarity among the bishops that keeps that sort of thing down."

The incident with Erie came, ironically, the first day that the press was admitted to the sessions. Within a half-hour after the draft resolutions were distributed, short, staunch William Crittenden, for sixteen years Bishop of Erie in northwestern Pennsylvania, took the floor to criticize the indefinite method of handling the drafts.

"The comments so far illustrate very clearly that there is something wrong with our process," he said. "I do not agree with the consultant who just spoke [J. Mbiti, a native of Uganda, an Anglican priest educated in the U.S. and at Cambridge, most recently a lecturer at Hamburg] because all of us could go through and pick this Draft apart. We must get down to business, but not in a group of this kind discussing a document of this length. There is a lot of good stuff in it, but I believe it ought to be rewritten right now to take out all of the—well, I was going to use a very strong word, but I won't—but it ought to be referred to a small committee to be worked out. It is a ridiculous process at the moment. I don't know what the answer is but we should do something about the procedure of approaching Draft Reports."

Erie's comments were supported by Hayden of Northern California. Then seven more speakers were heard (four bishops, an observer, and two consultants), giving a variety of comments on the Draft, before Campbell of West Virginia was recognized. "I move that the Draft be referred to Section 1," he began.

Canterbury replied, "I don't wish to accept the motion," and West Virginia countered, "That's just what I want to test," but his microphone apparently was cut off so that only those nearby heard the last of his sentence, "—to test that we are not being treated like a bunch of schoolboys."

Some seated near the dais quoted Canterbury as having said of West Virginia's motion, "What an odious suggestion!" but the Conference heard him declare only, "Of course the Draft should go back to the Section where it originated. No motion is needed, but for the present the discussion should continue."

Canterbury then called on an observer, the Roman Catholic Bishop of Poona, India, who made an inconsequential point, and Baker of Hong Kong, who asked a technical question: "Whom do they mean when they say *we* in the resolutions?"

At that moment, the Bishop of Erie rose to a point of order.

"We are again deteriorating by picking at the draft," he barked. "The motion of West Virginia to return the draft to committee was disregarded and—"

Canterbury cut him short, replying that, in his opinion, the discussion was not "deteriorating" and that, after a brief recess, the Conference would hear another Consultant, John Macquarrie, an Anglican priest of Union Seminary in New York.

"If we are going to have consultants, we are going to hear them!" Canterbury declared, adjourning the session for the customary midmorning break.

In the cloakroom, feelings ran high and there were comments such as "Hasn't he heard of parliamentary procedure? It started over here!" and suggestions that Canterbury should be given a copy of *Robert's Rules of Order*. After the break, the morning session continued without incident and tempers seemed at least momentarily calmed. Later in the day, Erie, chancing to meet Canterbury in a corridor of Church House, expressed his regret at the clash on the floor.

"Will you forgive me?" the Archbishop asked, shaking hands. "So sorry! But I think the bishops enjoyed it!"

Canterbury's brilliance as an articulate theologian maintained the Conference's personal respect for him beyond the regard it accorded his office. After his brief address of welcome and some comments during the debate on birth control, he generally refrained from speaking until the discussions narrowed down to such topics as the integrity of the Church and preservation of Catholic doctrine. He thrice addressed the bishops, taking them by surprise as he rose and spoke extemporaneously for five to ten minutes. Invariably, he was warmly applauded and on one occasion the Conference asked for and received the text of his remarks.[16]

Supplementing his quiet forcefulness was a sense of humor and a rather quaint, courtly manner of presiding. Canterbury was at first slow, then later somewhat too hasty in calling for a vote, but eventually he struck an even course in which he gently nudged the Conference to its decisions. Instead of a formal request to place a matter before the House for a vote, he would ask tentatively, "May I *put* that?" (The way to withdraw a question was to ask that it be "not put.") Then, leaning back in the presidential chair, he would look over the floor and observe the obvious "The motion is carried" or, sometimes with resignation, "The motion is lost." On other occasions he would look at the show of hands with the comment "That is to the contrary" or, more definitely, "That is rejected."

A ripple of laughter often greeted the bland comments from the Chair, substantiating what Geoffrey Fisher had once said about people regarding anyone who held the ancient title Archbishop of Canterbury as "some kind of prehistoric fish who needs poking at to seem real."

One late afternoon, as the talks droned on, Canterbury said, "The Revolution is, uh, ah, I mean the Resolution . . . it is carried! I must be becoming incompetent!"

Canterbury's craggy face "was a map that could easily be read by those before him," Luxton of Huron wrote a few months later. "When a timid or retrogressive viewpoint was being presented, he

---

[16] Reprinted in Appendix.

was blank and heavy with boredom. When the scholastic boys turned the House into a senior common-room debate, he warmed up to the familiar scene. When someone voiced an opinion which he himself held, he almost smacked his lips in great glee, and when the debate became swamped in dullness and irrelevancies, he stood up and intervened with telling force. . . ."

Canterbury was successful, almost without fail, in beginning and ending the sessions precisely on time. On the few days that it was possible to take a longer than average break before discussion of a new subject, he asked for and readily received the bishops' permission to adjourn early.

After the Conference voted to restrict speeches to seven minutes instead of fifteen, Canterbury was especially vigilant in reminding speakers when they had gone beyond the warning bell.[17] Those who had seen him presiding in Convocation or the Church Assembly knew that he would not hesitate to cut off a speaker who disregarded the bell. (They gleefully recalled an afternoon in 1962 when he silenced one long-winded speaker just as the man was boasting of a family lineage of "three Archbishops *de luxe*.") On only a few occasions at Lambeth X did Canterbury have to insist on the speaker stopping. One was the Bishop of Fulham, who made a detailed report of his responsibility for chaplaincies in Europe and on asking for longer time was told "The Bishop has had considerable latitude!" Another was Donald Campbell of Episcopal Theological School (formerly Suffragan of Los Angeles), who spoke for so long on intercommunion that Canterbury was forced to say sharply "Your allotted time is up!"

Perhaps the give and take of the Conference and Chair was

---

[17] The motion to reduce a speaker's time was made on August 8 as the Lambeth fathers restlessly began the discussion of the Draft Report on Ministry. Rising to a point of order, B. I. Chiu of Singapore & Malaya, a lawyer for several years before ordination to the priesthood, suggested that speakers submit their names in advance to the Chair. "We would at least substitute the Bingo method for the Jack-in-the-Box method," he said. "Some of the speeches have reminded me of the peace and mercy of God—they passeth all understanding and endure forever! May I suggest speeches be limited not to fifteen minutes but to seven minutes?"

mainly a matter of growing accustomed to each other. The bishops laughed aloud, whereas earlier in the Conference they might have frowned, when Canterbury refused an amendment articulated directly from the floor with the explanation, "I deal with amendments that are *drafted* and *presented* to me."

The comfortable atmosphere that eventually evolved was seen in a speaker's question about a ruling of Lambeth VIII. "I don't know what they said in 1930, but if somebody else will make a speech I'll take time to look it up," Canterbury said. Instantly, Welles of West Missouri rose obligingly to his feet, was recognized, and began to speak.

The plenary sessions quickly fell into a pattern, the bishops assembling at 9:30 A.M. for twenty to thirty minutes of silent meditation and prayer. Latecomers edged quietly into their places and then, a few minutes before ten, Canterbury led them in the recitation of the Lord's Prayer followed by a few other familiar prayers. He usually ended with the special prayer for the work of the Conference, repeated from memory, after which the bishops said in unison the Grace and began their day's work.[18]

In coming and going from the Assembly Hall, most of the British observed the custom of respecting the Chair by nodding reverently to it when they entered or left the room, much as they might reverence an altar. Everyone stood as Canterbury arrived or departed.

The absence of a rollcall, at the first sessions or in the voting, was conspicuous. It was probably purposeful, however, as a reminder that the Conference was traditionally a meeting of bishops who attended voluntarily, framed their resolutions as a consulting group rather than an authoritarian one, and usually were not bound by advance instructions or promises.

---

[18] SPCK published a white card of prayers authorized by Canterbury "for use in connection with the Lambeth Conference." Prayers for each of the three Sections were preceded by one for the Conference: "Almighty and everlasting Father, we pray thee to guide with the light of thy divine wisdom the Bishops in the Lambeth Conference that all their deliberations may be for thy glory, the good of thy Church, and the spread of thy gospel; through Jesus Christ our Lord. Amen."

Lacking a rollcall, the absences from the group went unrecorded except for critical illness such as the cerebral hemorrhage suffered by Munn of Caledonia (Canada) during the first weekend of the Conference.

Attendance had sometimes lagged at Lambeth Conferences, but in 1968 the presence of nearly 500 bishops meant that there was always a goodly number on the floor. Occasionally, in the early voting, the number who participated fell below 400, and there was a definite drop in daily attendance during the final week, but when important matters arose, such as the resolution on intercommunion or women in the ministry, nearly all were present.

The presentation of a motion and its seconding was carefully arranged behind the scenes. For instance, the Bishop of Erie agreed a week in advance to second the Resolution on Ordination of Women because its proposer wished to indicate a certain comprehensiveness of support that would be indicated by a seconder from outside the Church of England. ("Of course we all hope it doesn't happen in our lifetimes," said Erie even as he agreed to be the seconder.)

There were, of course, many bishops who chose to use their influence in private discussions or in committees. As Pittsburgh's newly consecrated coadjutor, apple-cheeked Robert Appleyard, put it, "Some of us spoke often in the committees and left the floor of the Conference to the older ones."

Bishop Appleyard denied, however, that there had been an advance agreement among the American coadjutors and suffragans to remain silent in deference to a diocesan. One of the suffragans of South Florida was among the few who did speak, but that was not until the Conference was drawing to a close. On the other hand, the frequency with which the Conference heard from coadjutors, suffragans, and assistant bishops from countries other than the U.S. could be attributed partially to their greater familiarity with topics under discussion (because of their responsibility for definite order of a diocese). Also, it was only natural that some of the less well known among the younger assistants spoke often because they wanted recognition that might lead to advancement to diocesans.

As for the consultants and observers, for several days they

rivaled the bishops for recognition from the Chair. "Never have so few observers made so many observations," said Schlingensiepen of the Evangelical Church in Germany. Reflecting their academic backgrounds, the consultants were inclined to scholarly arguments delivered in a lecture-room manner.

"Probably no two consultants would tell the same story about their work," wrote Howard Root, Professor of Theology at the University of Southampton. "Some were used very extensively by a particular committee. Some tried to give time to several different committees. It is just a fact that there were more committees than consultants and so not enough of us to go round. Also, our own interests inevitably overlapped. One day, two or three consultants might be found sitting with the same committee and therefore none, presumably, in a number of others. Perhaps we ought to have been given a definite assignment, because at times one felt very torn, even frustrated, in having to spread one's self so thinly."

The observers were a more varied lot and, as expected, they gave the Lambeth fathers a wide cross-section of international, interdenominational opinion. Throughout the Conference they were regarded as living symbols of Lambeth's ecumenical consciousness.[19]

The observers and consultants had separate sections in the gallery of the Assembly Hall, from which they spoke at microphones placed around the railing. A procedure by which they usually sent their names to the Chairman in advance of being recognized meant that they spoke with less spontaneity but more preparation. Some bishops thought that the presence of an observer or consultant, waiting at the railing to speak, was distracting to the floor. Other bishops, failing to obtain recognition from the Chair, sank back with the comment that Lambeth X seemed all too often to be a

---

[19] Of seventy-five observers, eighteen addressed the Conference, eight of whom spoke on more than one topic and one of whom, Athenagoras, spoke on all three. Six observers were heard on Faith, nine on Ministry, and twelve on Unity. Of the twenty-six consultants, sixteen were heard, six of them on more than one topic. Four of the consultants spoke on Faith, six on Ministry, and nine on Unity.

Conference of consultants and observers rather than bishops.

In the end, it was clear that the consultants and observers had but a momentary time in the spotlight; when the time came to approve reports and resolutions they refrained from speaking and hence did not directly influence the voting.

A new policy of openness pervaded Lambeth X in its relationships with the press.

Significantly, for its success, the Archbishop of Canterbury endorsed the new procedure by twice meeting the press in cordial, informative conferences in the Lambeth Palace Library (Tuesday morning, July 23, and Monday morning, August 26)—at the start and close of the Conference. The new philosophy was also furthered by the Bishop of Cariboo's willingness to hold press briefings and by the advance announcement that the press would be permitted to attend the opening plenary session and the final week of meetings. As events turned out, after the Papal encyclical on birth control, the press was allowed to attend the subsequent plenary sessions—a decision immeasurably helped by the door already being ajar.

"The rule of 'dead secrecy' will not exist, as [before]," Canterbury explained in his short address to the press. "We have felt that kind of secrecy is not in keeping with the way we do things nowadays."

Cariboo reiterated the Archbishop's view. "We are anxious to keep in touch with the press," he said later in the press conference. "If we have 'dead secrecy' you will wind up with something dead."

Such unprecedented openness—the free-wheeling press conferences at Lambeth, admission of accredited journalists to Church House, and their presence in the gallery—represented a vast stride beyond the previous Conference, which had been strictly closed.

Nonetheless, there was a disparity between the new philosophy and its actual practice. The chill hand of bureaucracy, which many had feared in the transition of the Conference from Lambeth Palace across the Thames to Church House, was more apparent in the area of press relations than almost anywhere else.

"The spirit is willing but the flesh is weak," was the explanation of one veteran newsman. "The people in Church House can't quite believe that they're not supposed to keep everything under wraps."

Moreover, the Church Information Office had much to learn in implementing the new policy of openness and cooperation. The staff, sensitive to having spent little, if any, time in secular journalism, was naïve and defensive. Understandably, then, there was a great scraping of gears as the CIO attempted the transition from its slow, Dickensian operation to the new concept of a streamlined service that helped the press. The change was impeded by the open disapproval of many at Church House plus the uncertainty that the bishops, if offended, might reverse the policy.

Another complication was the nature of Church journalism with bishops, priests, and professional theologians "covering" the Conference.[20] A further difficulty was the desire of some publications, notably the *American Church News,* to have three or more accredited representatives working independently and sometimes at odds with each other. A few theologians-turned-journalists posed a special problem in their tendency to convert press briefings to argumentative seminars. All of it meant that Lambeth X was not an easy Conference to cover.

The information program, however conscientiously administered, suffered from an absence of what public relations professionals call "road-mapping." If there were clearly enunciated goals that the CIO hoped to achieve, they were not apparent; nor did there seem to be any timetable or vision of working with editors far in advance to develop positive coverage and exclusive explanatory articles. (The broadcasting media, radio and television, got what it wanted on its own initiative and that was not always what Lambeth wanted or needed.) Little was done to "set the stage" and prepare

---

[20] The Bishop of Taejon's "Report from Lambeth" (*The Living Church,* August and September 1968) carried his signature († Richard Rutt) but otherwise he came near being Lambeth's pseudo-named Xavier Rynne (of Vatican II). Dee Barrett, wife of the Bishop of Rochester, N.Y., was constantly on the job. Also accredited was Edward Welles, son of the Bishop of West Missouri.

the public. Thus Lambeth X was regarded as a "happening" in a world that immediately grew disinterested.

On the whole, the CIO gave the impression that it was doing journalists a favor by listening, impatiently and with obvious disapproval, to requests it usually refused. It implied that its ministrations constituted a generous gift. It was as if it said, "Here's the Archbishop's present labeléd 'Away with Deep Secrecy'—now just *try* to open it!"

The situation represented a sad lack of expertise. Haughty and bungling, the CIO achieved little rapport with writers and demonstrated only slight understanding of how to reach the public through communications media. At best, the CIO coped with the press as a necessary evil, and functioned far more as an impersonal secretariat than as an adviser and interpreter of events.

During the opening days of the Conference, when the weekly recipe column of the *Church Times* featured a mouth-watering dish called Curried Tripe, the CIO spewed forth its first press releases.

It was difficult to know to whom the releases, well intended and laboriously prepared, were directed. If used by diocesan newspapers and magazines, they would be hopelessly outdated by the time of publication; as for the secular press (the London newspapers, wire services, and foreign correspondents) its stories were in print before the CIO releases appeared. If offered as "background," the diocesan press would have been better served with summaries or commentaries and the secular press with straightforward fact sheets.

At least the CIO releases permitted reporters to see the Conference through semi-official eyes. By following the flow of releases, newsmen and columnists easily noted what issues were emphasized and what was played down, but even so the releases were superficial and often in error—the opening Evensong, for instance, was called a Eucharist and, as the Conference progressed, some of the releases talked around a resolution without telling what the resolution proposed.

The dateline of the Xeroxed releases distributed at Church House (and of the mimeographed duplicates mailed out from New

York) was inevitably "London, England," although no self-respecting newspaper would carry any dateline beyond simply "London." It was a typically provincial and unprofessional touch: nobody thought the Conference was in session in London, Ontario. After a few days, the releases, generally disregarded, accumulated in large stacks in most of the reporters' mailboxes.

Meanwhile, the CIO concentrated, if that is the word, on the dissemination of a poorly edited, error-riddled *Who's Who at Lambeth* [21] and the imaginative but disastrously received guide, *Lambeth '68*.

The Church Information Office had a staff of five. It was directed by Major General Adam Block, a bristling, hawk-nosed former artillery officer, far more familiar with the ways of the military than the needs of the press. After him came a pair which may best be described as a right-hand man and a left-hand man, the suave, dapper Michael De-la-Noy, appointed in September 1967 as Assistant Information Officer and Press Officer to the Archbishop of Canterbury; and Edgar Holt, a plump, elderly Englishman who planned to retire from his post as Chief Press Officer at the close of Lambeth X. They were assisted by a tweedy, long-haired young man from Warwickshire, Robert Whyte, and a young male secretary, Michael Jacob.

Auxiliary help was given by the Radio and Television Officer, an English priest named Michael Saward, and a press officer from the Anglican Church in Canada and two from the American Church.

Adam Johnstone Cheyne Block, CB, CBE, OBE, DSO, a colonel's son who married a colonel's daughter, perched at the peak of his British Army career from 1959 to 1962 when he was military commander of Malta. Six years later he continued to operate as the major-domo of an island—the CIO. After taking early retirement at fifty-seven, he gained his appointment at Church House in

---

[21] It contained only bishops' biographies, ignoring consultants, observers, and key staff members. When, after a few weeks, the biographical sketches of the consultants were mimeographed, the distribution was limited to bishops—but, as usual, they discarded them so carelessly that the press, scampering in the episcopate's path, was well supplied with information.

time to accompany Canterbury to Rome, acquiring large pictures of the Papal visit for his office walls.

General Block soon became known as the Adam of Dean's Yard who regarded Church information as a forbidden fruit.[22] He never conducted a news conference, preferring to remain on the sidelines, but when he had a personal conversation with a writer he was known to tap him on the chest to make his point.

If Adam Block was the military personified, thirty-four-year-old Michael De-la-Noy was Saville Row come to Westminster. His well-tailored suits were usually set off, however, with a silk-print handkerchief trailing from a pocket just beneath a wilting rose in the lapel.

There was more than a hint of the egoist and courtier in his first remarks to the press. "It seems strange here in England to introduce myself," he said. "I am Michael De-la-Noy, Press Officer to the Archbishop of Canterbury. Obviously more important is that in a few minutes I shall introduce the Archbishop of Canterbury and the Anglican Executive Officer. There is no restriction at all or rules for the press except that we ask you to observe the no-smoking rules here. To burn down Lambeth Palace on the first day of the Conference would be going too far to make the front page!"

Unpredictable and given to fawning over favorites among the reporters, the ubiquitous De-la-Noy was nonetheless crisply efficient. His experience as a journalist (*National Christian News, Outlook, Prism*) and as a member of the Church Assembly and the Liturgical Revision Steering Committee, made him familiar with both press and Church. He handled the Archbishop's press confer-

---

[22] When the Conference spotlight shifted away from Dean's Yard, the CIO lost its effectiveness almost completely. That was apparent from the first day of Lambeth X, when a clerk at Canterbury—P. J. Norris, the Chapter Agent—was uncooperative and insulting to writers and priest-journalists, refusing them even the use of a typewriter. De-la-Noy arrived in a huff, listened briefly to Norris' whining complaints, and then compounded the rudeness by turning out the writers. Some days later, when the bishops went to the Guildhall, General Block did nothing more than give the City public relations officers a list of "acceptable" reporters; Block then referred reporters he didn't like to the Guildhall, where they learned for the first time that they had not made the list.

ences and the Bishop of Cariboo's news briefings with assurance and order. ("We've a *queue* of questions here," he often reminded newsmen.) Throughout the Conference he labored under the criticism of *Lambeth '68* for it obviously bore his personal mark as a connoisseur and gourmet. To his discredit, he replied sharply to bishops' comments about it and confided to *The New York Times* that a speech by the Assistant Bishop of Zanzibar & Tanga (about the booklet and the world's image of bishops) was "pious rubbish."

General Block's other helper was as reticent as De-la-Noy was flamboyant. Close-mouthed Edgar Holt, pale and puffy of face, kept journalists at a distance, balefully regarding reporters through a window in his office. His advisories ended with the prim request "Please write if you require further elucidation on any of these points."

Officially the CIO *tried* to be cordial, but never quite warmed up. Its RSVP invitations to Cariboo's press reception were included unceremoniously (and easily overlooked) in the press kit given writers at registration. At the reception, De-la-Noy made introductions as Cariboo and his wife greeted guests at the door of the Chichester Room, a nondescript, rented hall at Dolphin Square where they had a temporary apartment. The small, cramped room quickly grew smoky as waitresses pushed through the crowd offering sherry— and, surprisingly for *hors d'oeuvres,* trays of plump chicken legs or pork chops! Graciously intended, it was lacking in any real hospitality for the international press, which thereafter had to remain on the sidelines while the bishops they chronicled were feted in palaces, halls of state, and walled gardens. The evening with Cariboo (the press afterward referred to it as the Drumsticks & Pork Chops Night) said a great deal about the condescending attitude toward anyone who deigned to take up pen or typewriter about the Lambeth Conference.

Four weeks later, the unpretentious sherry party given the press by the Ramseys restored good taste and good will to proper perspective.

Like Cariboo's reception, the idea of news briefings was good in theory and painful in execution. It was impossible to say if the bishops would have become so quickly dissatisfied with it had not the birth-control edict plunged them into the world spotlight.

The decision to admit the press was surprising because only a few days earlier Cariboo had rejected a request that one of the journalists should cover the Conference on a pool basis and then report back to his colleagues. Cariboo told the press he could be as tough as his Roman counterpart at Vatican II, Cardinal Felici. It was an unendearing boast to which he added, less sternly, that the Conference and the bishops were like husbands and wives. "They don't mind having company but they'd like to have some conversations in private," he said. "Lambeth is the same; it doesn't want reporters present *all* the time."

Cariboo was thinking of matters far more routine than Lambeth's reaction to the Papal encyclical. In the wake of its appearance, the *Church Times* reported that "more than one journalist has managed to get into the press gallery during closed debates. Even more annoying to the authorities has been the 'leaking' of stories by indiscreet bishops to even more indiscreet reporters, with titillating snippets which are considered to give an unbalanced picture of the Conference."

So the press was allowed in—a decision that was an anticlimax since, after the birth-control furor quieted, there was no news of similar interest to the world. CIO reacted with characteristic officiousness: it militantly barred journalists from entering the gallery until after the conclusion of the bishops' prayers but could not explain why prayers were confidential. Another blooper was assigning seats to journalists, then holding them even when the journalists failed to appear. It was noted that choice seats were reserved for the CIO staff although they were almost never there at the same time; meanwhile, some writers went without suitable working space.

In an effort to amend botched relationships, General Block scheduled a series of luncheons in his office, but instead of announcing his policy he issued individual invitations that implied that the uninvited were under a journalistic excommunication. Lunch in the General's lair was not the most prized invitation in London, however, and a score of his bids, unheeded, remained pinned to the press-room bulletin board. Quiet meals with bishops proved more enlightening.

The awkward handling of the press reception and luncheons, multiplying ill will even as it sought improvement, was typical of the CIO's fumbling secretiveness. Its refusal to release a list of where the bishops were staying in London was greeted by the discovery that the list was already posted in the press room. Some days later the CIO denied any knowledge of the cost of the Anglican Consultative Council, then left a copy of the entire projected budget fluttering about the floor of the Xerox room. Ironically, the week the Conference ended, the same column that had offered Curried Tripe came up with a recipe for Home-Made Jams. "The addition of a good squeeze of lemon-juice to all jams is a good thing," the recipe declared. "It helps the setting."

Like an ecclesiastical cheering section at a football match, the Lambeth fathers lined up in a grandstand erected in Dean's Yard for the Conference's official photograph. For the first time in the ten days they had been in session the timid English summer gave way to an afternoon of brilliant sunshine that warmed the colorful scene.

The official photograph was almost the only feature that had remained common to every Lambeth Conference. Even more than the long processions, it showed that Lambeth X was six times as large as Lambeth I. It was also the first made outside the courtyard of Lambeth Palace and the only one for which the bishops wore their convocation robes. The huge block of bishops frowning in the sunlight far differed from the tired, rather shabby group of seventy-six bishops who faced the camera (most in gaiters and carrying hats and umbrellas) following the adjournment of the four days of Lambeth I in September 1867. The man who made that historic picture (the original was displayed in Lambeth Palace Library during the 1968 Conference) became the official court photographer to Queen Victoria and to Edward VII; his great-grandson, T. H. Everitt, came to photograph Lambeth X.

During the morning a blue trailer truck pulled into the grassy confines of Dean's Yard bearing the rough boards for the ten tiers of the grandstand. The bishops ignored a memorandum suggesting they vest in the committee rooms and, instead, arrived from all directions and used the terrace of Church House to scramble into cassocks, rochets, tippets, and hoods. The stone porch became a sea of billowing white cloth and flapping scarves—an undignified preparation for an ultimately dignified photograph.

Several charts posted on the grounds directed the primates to be seated on each side of Canterbury and added succinctly, "The remaining bishops may sit anywhere they wish." Unfortunately, the bishops were not divided by churches—making it extremely difficult to identify individuals in the sea of episcopal faces. A plan for the bishops to be seated by Section (Faith, Ministry, Unity) was abandoned at the last moment. Canterbury himself, wandering over to consider one of the directives, was told by an American priest, "It isn't hard to spot your position—you're in the center."

"Yes, yes," replied Canterbury, "but sometimes it's hard to *find* the center, yes, yes!"

The chains bordering the yard were let down shortly before three o'clock and the bishops flooded onto the field. Barton of Eastern Oregon, one of the few without a convocation robe, had already claimed a seat in the uppermost right corner of the bleachers. "I'm about ready to retire," he said. "I think I'll just stay here until they bump me off next month."

A New Zealander, crossing the road to the yard, asked, "Where's the nearest pulpit? Probably an awful queue around it this afternoon!"

In front of the grandstand, Horstick of Eau Clair (Wisconsin) cameras dangling from each hand, posed for his wife. "Hurry up, hurry up!" he said.

The last to take a picture before all the prelates found a place was Hallock of Milwaukee. One of the suffragans of New York, James Stuart Wetmore, was able to photograph the group from the left end of the first row without moving out of place. Finally, General Block used a bullhorn to ask the bishops in the back row to stand—a signal that the photographer was ready.

"Now, gentlemen, please!" cried the photographer, ducking under a black cloth and peering through the lens of his old-fashioned camera. He made several close-ups, retreated for a wider view, and was succeeded by television crewmen who moved in for close-ups of the bishops.

Canterbury and his two chaplains, one holding the new primatial cross, were seated in the middle of the first rows, the Archbishop's convocation robes trailing the ground.

The background for the memorable scene was itself a panorama of English history—the massive tower of Parliament, the conical roof of the Abbey's chapter house with its Latin cross, and the blackened, bomb-scarred buildings of Westminster School topped at one side with a colony of television aerials.

In a few minutes, when the photographing was over and the Lambeth fathers broke rank, the Bishop of Jamaica hurried to a far corner of Dean's Yard to make a picture of his national flag—a banner of purple, green, and black, crisscrossed with golden bars —as it flew from one of the Abbey towers in observance of the sixth anniversary of Jamaican independence.

Canterbury, wandering about among the bishops, was asked whether his visit to Pope Paul, or his presidency of Lambeth X, was the high point of his life.

His magnificent eyebrows came together like the twin sections of Tower Bridge, but he paused only a moment, then replied, "Well, one thing follows another, yes, yes, *one* thing follows *another*."

CHAPTER 4

LAMBETH AT WORSHIP

THE SUPREME MOMENTS OF THE Lambeth Conferences traditionally have been the great services in great churches of Anglicanism—Canterbury, Westminster, St. Paul's. So it remained at Lambeth X, with the addition of an evening Eucharist in a London stadium at which 15,000 people received Holy Communion "in thanksgiving for the progress of the Gospel."

The mark of Lambeth's worship, distinguishing it from all other great occasions, was always the long procession of bishops with the names of their far-flung countries borne high on banners of scarlet, orange, olive, black, gold, purple. Nothing else so emphasized the international scope of Anglicanism as the sight of its twenty-seven primates and metropolitans followed by more than 400 of its bishops; it was a representation that began with the newest province, Cuba, and ended with the oldest, Canterbury and York.[1]

[1] At earlier Lambeths, the absence of the Church in China (*Chung Hua Sheng Kung Hui*) had been dramatically emphasized by a standard-bearer

The pilgrimage to the Cathedral Church of Christ, Canterbury, to "the wellsprings of Anglicanism," was a cherished feature as it has been at all Lambeth Conferences since 1878. It was a return, even for those who had never been there, to the hallowed place where Augustine revived holy religion among the English, where Becket was slain, and where Archbishops of Canterbury have been enthroned for more than a thousand years.

Most of the bishops traveled down to Kent by special train from Victoria Station, the bleak towns of Rochester, Chatham, Sitting-bourne, and Faversham flashing swiftly past, interspersed with the green orchards of Kent.

Twenty years earlier, at the first Lambeth Conference after World War II, the bishops offered special thanks that the ancient cathedral church had been spared destruction in the heavy bombing of the old market town. On the tenth Lambeth's opening day, they met for the first time the new Dean of Canterbury, the Very Rev. Ian White-Thompson (successor to the infamous "Red Dean," Hewlett Johnson, who had finally retired, after more than thirty years of controversy, and had died since the previous Lambeth). As the cathedral church's giant bells pealed across the countryside, the pale, gaunt Dean in splendid golden cope performed the extraordinary duty of welcoming at the West Doors the Holy See's apostolic delegate to Britain.[2]

---

walking alone. That poignant touch was omitted at Lambeth X but the presence of the Bishop of Cuba, walking unaccompanied, had much the same effect. After him came the seven extraprovincial bishops; eight bishops of South-East Asia; two from Brazil; sixty-five from the African churches; five from the Jerusalem archbishopric; three from Japan; eight from the West Indies; thirty-four New Zealanders and Australians; sixteen from India, Pakistan, Burma & Ceylon; thirty-four Canadians; 121 Americans; six Scots; a dozen Irish bishops; five from Wales, thirty from York; and seventy-eight from Canterbury.

[2] The Most Rev. Hyginus Eugene Cardinale was born near Rome in 1916 after his father returned from the U.S. to Italy to fight with Allied forces in World War I. Aged two when his family went back to America, he attended nonparochial schools before being sent to Rome for his seminary education. He was ordained in 1941, consecrated to the titular See of Nepte in 1961, and served in the Near East and at the Vatican (under John XXIII) just prior to

After Evensong and a reception on the grounds of the Old Palace, Canterbury, the bishops returned to London in early evening and next morning settled down to a Day of Recollection at the parish church of St. Mary at Lambeth, just outside the walls of Lambeth Palace. Since the small gray-stone church barely accommodated the bishops, a separate service was held simultaneously for observers and consultants at St. Dunstan's-in-the-West, appropriately chosen because its Vicar, Fr. John Satterthwaite, was Secretary of the Church of England Council for Foreign Relations.

At St. Mary's, a parish that traces its history as far back as the Domesday Book of 1085, the Archbishop of Canterbury conducted a series of three meditations on the Transfiguration, Christ as servant, and the presence of Christ in prayer.

Not until three days after the journey to Canterbury did the Lambeth fathers come together for their first Eucharist. As they converged on Westminster in the Sunday-morning quiet of London, the old Abbey once again came into focus as the parish church of all English-speaking peoples which, belonging to no diocese, belongs to all.

From one of the massive towers added by Sir Christopher Wren in 1732, the Abbey's own flag [3] whipped the breezes of a day for which the BBC had promised "bright spots in some places."

Surely the Dean's Yard, Westminster, was one of the brightest spots of all as the bishops in their convocation robes gathered around a blackboard chart that indicated where they were to be seated in choir.

---

his appointment to Britain in 1963. His name has been among those frequently mentioned as candidates for the Papacy following the reign of Paul VI. In May, 1969, he became Papal Nuncio to Belgium and the Netherlands.

[3] The Abbey flag is reserved for occasions significant to the Abbey's role in national and international life: the Lambeth Conferences, royal birthdays, elections at Westminster School, and the feast day of its patrons, St. Peter and St. Edward. More often seen is the Union Jack or flags of the Commonwealth. The royal standard is flown on the feasts of the "national saints"— George, Andrew, David, and Patrick—and also when the Sovereign is opening Parliament or visiting within the Abbey precincts.

Inside the Abbey, television crews finished setting up camera positions atop the choir screen, a formidable Victorian pile embellished with heavily gabled mosaics and panoramic statuary. The crews' powerful floodlights augmented the Abbey's new crystal chandeliers, while tall candles cast flickering shadows over the ruby velvet frontal adorning the high altar. Meanwhile, some 3000 persons trod reverently past the tomb of Britain's Unknown Warrior to find seats in the nave.

As the service began, it was obvious that most of the Abbey treasures were on display for Lambeth X [4]—an ironic contrast to the summer day in 1867 when the Abbey's use was refused for Lambeth I and its Dean was warned by the Dean of St. Paul's to "leave London before September or you will be in danger of being hunted to death by wild bishops."

The music and the processions at Westminster were grander than at Canterbury. Although the Armenian bishop left at home the jeweled mitre he had previously worn (it had been the only one besides Archbishop Ramsey's) its absence was more than compensated for by Athenagoras, highest-ranking Orthodox prelate in Britain, whose long train, sewn with tinkling bells, was borne by a page. Among the observers, saffron stoles denoted the Church of South India and the ruffled collars of the Old Catholics gave them the appearance of a Rembrandt portrait.

Another unique feature of the Westminster procession was the presence of five elderly priests—"Primates Now Retired," the official program described them—the former occupants of the sees of Canterbury, Quebec, Sydney, West Africa, and London. Geoffrey Fisher walked last, heavier and slightly lame but otherwise lit-

---

[4] The Westminster Cross carried in procession was given by the American merchant Rodman Wanamaker and is made of gold, silver-gilt and ivory, studded with sapphires (as well as seventy-two diamonds added by his descendant, John Wanamaker, on the Abbey's nine-hundredth anniversary). The Ivory Cross was carved from an elephant tusk sent in 1944 by the Emperor of Ethiopia, Haile Selassie, in thanksgiving for the restoration of his country. In 1388 the Abbey's treasures included 307 copes, but by 1553 all had been stolen or burned; not until the nineteenth century did it begin restoring its magnificent wardrobe.

tle changed in appearance since completing his seventeen years as
the ninety-ninth successor to Augustine.

The most impressive of all the groups in the procession was that
of the Westminster Chapter and its associates: canons, stewards,
students, and the vergers and the banners—moss green, mauve,
and blue—of St. Peter, St. Edward, St. Oswald, St. Martin, and the
Blessed Virgin.

As the Chapter passed beneath the choir screen, the Abbey resounded to the fanfare and brass interlude of music composed by
Sir Arthur Bliss for Princess Margaret's wedding there in 1960.

Removing his golden mitre, Canterbury stood before the high
altar in a magenta cope to begin the Lord's Prayer in a Eucharist
offered with the special intention for the guidance of the Holy
Spirit. The preacher was the Archbishop of East Africa.

During the Communions in the nave, administered by four
Abbey priests in surplices, red cassocks, and stoles, the long queues
approaching the altar were as diverse as the national churches they
represented—Englishmen in morning coats and matrons in
flowered hats, tourists with camera cases over their shoulders,
smartly dressed American women, clergymen on holiday, army
officers, two nurses in uniform, women in saris of silver and gray,
an East African woman walking barefoot on the Abbey pavement;
and, most colorful of all, the West African bishops' wives wearing
yards of boldly patterned cloth with matching high-swirled turbans.

In the recessional, the banners of the churches were for the first
time borne together in one group, their juxtaposition—Cuba with
Jerusalem, Central Africa with the West Indies—dramatically
illustrating the global expanse of the Anglican Communion.

After the Westminster Eucharist, the bishops spent two succes-
sive Sundays celebrating and preaching in cathedral churches and
parishes throughout the Diocese of London and much of Britain.
Several preached before the royal family, including the Bishop of
New York, the Bishop of Singapore & Malaya, and the Suffragan of
Lesotho.

The third Sunday was part of the traditional Missionary Weekend—"the Lambeth Walk" the bishops called it, after a dance fad of the 1920s. During that weekend the Presiding Bishop of the American church preached in Canterbury's cathedral church; the Diocese of Bath and Wells welcomed Matabeleland, Bombay, James Bay, and Soroti for choral Evensong in the ruins of Glastonbury Abbey; Ripon and his suffragan, Knaresborough, and the retired suffragan were hosts to Antigua, Maseno, and Bendigo; the grounds of the recently completed cathedral church at Guildford were the scene of a picnic honoring three West Africans (Niger, Benin, and Gambia) as well as the North American bishops of Saskatoon and Atlanta; at Bishopthorpe, the archiepiscopal residence near York, four members of the episcopate—Cape Town, Andaman & Nicobar Islands, Mount Kenya, and Bethlehem, Pa.—were treated to a barbecue, rock-and-roll music, and a "happening" in the form of tableaux about their home dioceses.

In Northumbria, during the same weekend, a crowd of 3000 followed seven Lambeth bishops on a pilgrimage to the Holy Island of Lindisfarne.[5] Shepherd's crook in hand, Ashdown of Newcastle (England) led a procession that included Springfield (Illinois), Haiti, Lebombo, the Assistant Bishop of Malawi, and Trevor Huddleston. Some 3000 people took part in the Eucharist celebrated in the ruins of the twelfth-century Benedictine abbey and later in the day there was solemn Evensong in the parish church.

On the Monday evening following Missionary Weekend, attention turned to White City Stadium, on the outskirts of London. The roads were clogged and the Underground trains jammed by 15,000 people who had responded to boldly printed circulars posted for several weeks on countless parish bulletin boards: GIVE THANKS/ with Lambeth Bishops/at Holy Communion/White City/19th

---

[5] It was from Lindisfarne, that tiny haven of history and natural beauty, that St. Aidan first sighted the shoreline of England on his missionary voyage from Iona in 634. For the next two centuries it was the seat of the bishops of Northumbria (including St. Cuthbert, 685–687). It was also the home of a Celtic monastery that was destroyed in a Danish invasion of 875 and later rebuilt by Benedictines.

August 1968/write for tickets to/ARCHBISHOP'S SECRETARY/157 WATERLOO ROAD/LONDON SE 1.

Twilight in the vast stadium (dedicated in 1908 by Edward VII) marked the start of an evening etched in memory by the spectacle of the bishops processing across a vast green playing field, their convocation robes of red and white billowing in the cool winds of a waning summer day.

Two weeks earlier during a television interview, Canterbury had foreseen "a great altar, very reverently erected." It awaited the bishops, a white pavilion with cone-shaped top sheltering a broad altar. Beneath its traditional "fair linen cloth," the orange-painted altar sat on a wine-colored carpeting that spread out across the grass to the lectern. Devoid of candles, flowers, cross, or credence table, the spacious platform and altar gave the effect of massive simplicity best described in the opening hymn that spoke of the Lord Himself "pavilioned in splendor and girded with praise."

The timetable for the processions from the grandstands and field, usually the scene of dog races, was immediately tucked in cassock pockets as a collector's item.[6] It reflected the careful planning necessary for a ceremonial that combined the complexities of the Feeding of the Multitude with D-Day landings in Normandy.

The congregation rose to its feet as the processions came into view, swelled in number by the dozens of deacons chosen to assist at the Eucharist. Red stoles sashed across their snowy surplices, the deacons carried chalices, patens, and ciboria that dated back to the 1400s and had been especially removed from sacristy safes all over London for use at the White City Eucharist.

The celebrant was the Archbishop in Jerusalem, white-haired Angus Campbell MacIness. He had reminded many Americans of

---

[6] The schedule's first two columns designated the two groups of bishops as "red" and "blue," then gave successive columns to the sacred ministers, choir, and Royal Air Force Band. The ingenuity required to identify assembly points usually dedicated to dog races and holiday crowds resulted in some highly unusual directions: "6:49, bishops reach tunnel steps; 6:51, bishops reach track from entry 14; 6:55, ministers leave American Bar; 6:59, ministers leave tote; 7:00, ministers arrive at grass." ("Did all those dog-collars," asked the *Daily Telegraph,* "subsequently return to their kennels?")

the poet Carl Sandburg, but at White City he was transformed into a medieval abbot by the most magnificent vestments seen at Lambeth X: a flowing cope of yellow-gold with a magenta hood and a tall, glittering mitre.[6a]

After the sermon by the Bishop in Iran the Eucharist continued and by a few minutes after eight o'clock the first of sixty pairs of bishops were moving toward the railings to administer Communion.

Afterward, as the last notes of the Royal Air Force Band faded into the dusk, the bishops approached the grandstands to greet the congregation. It was Lambeth's finest moment of fellowship with its people who, even in the extraordinary setting of a summer night on a playing field, felt something of the same intimacy of a greeting at the door of a parish church.

On the Eleventh Sunday After Trinity, exactly a month to the day since Evensong at Canterbury, a sung Eucharist at St. Paul's on Ludgate Hill in London climaxed the worship of Lambeth X and marked the end of the Conference.[7]

A dramatic innovation for the closing service of Lambeth X was the placement of a free-standing altar directly beneath the dome. It made possible an intimate trinity of sacrament, episcopate, and people and, when viewed from the doors of St. Paul's, it emphasized the broad sweep of the nave toward the high altar and the towering

---

[6a] The cope, owned by the Suffragan of California, had recently been exhibited in London by its manufacturer, the firm of Louis Grosse; the mitre had been sent Archbishop MacIness by a group of Dallas Episcopalians known as "the sewing grandmothers."

[7] St. Paul's, the fifth cathedral church to stand on the summit during thirteen and a half centuries of Christian worship, has been the scene of one of the major services in every Lambeth Conference. In the decade since the Lambeth fathers had last worshiped there the whole neighborhood had undergone considerable rebuilding and the exterior walls of the cathedral church had received their most thorough cleaning in 260 years. It had been the scene of the national memorial service for President Kennedy and of the funeral of Winston Churchill; its pulpit had been occupied for the first time by a woman and a few weeks later by a Roman Catholic priest; and to the stalls in its choir had come a new Bishop of London and a new Dean, the first since 1934.

baldachino crowned with the golden figure of Christ in Triumph.

Processing together for the last time, the bishops moved down the long nave as the crashing organ music sounded the notes of the first hymn, "To the Name of Our Salvation." After the sermon by the Metropolitan of India, Canterbury continued the Eucharist as the other primates and metropolitans concelebrated with him from the railings on all four sides of the altar.

No other hour during Lambeth X rivaled in color or depth of feeling the concluding moments under Wren's great dome as the Anglican bishops and the huge congregation raised with one voice *Te Deum,* "We praise thee, O God: we acknowledge thee to be the Lord. . . ."

Like all its predecessors, Lambeth X was liturgically dominated by the Church of England. That was inevitable, of course, and not without value. For one thing, the 1662 edition of the Book of Common Prayer furnished the basic guidelines. For another, the English were the hosts and hence they were not only free to do as they pleased but, as the chief administrators of the splendid places thrown open for Lambeth worship, they were expected to give liturgical guidance.

The task that fell to them carried more than just the responsibility of arranging an Evensong and three Eucharists. In an age of liturgical revision that in many places was synonomous with liturgical confusion, the English had the opportunity—if not the obligation—of encouraging the churches of the Anglican Communion to hold fast to the traditional dignity and careful pacing of its services. If the bishops were drawn to what they saw at Lambeth, their influence would go far toward charting a steady course in liturgical changes in their own dioceses. Unfortunately, what was served up was a curious combination of habit, happenstance, and direct intention—a conglomerate of liturgical fare that was both appropriate and nostalgic, new and familiar, traditional and modern. It left a good deal to be sorted out.

Evensong at Canterbury was almost entirely traditional, since it is an office that lends itself to experimentation far less than does the

Eucharist. The few who disapproved included a young, recently consecrated bishop who found it "a long and tiring service during which everybody was kept standing for an inordinate length of time."

In retrospect, there was a definite contrast to be drawn between the services at Canterbury and Westminster and the later services at White City and St. Paul's. The first two were almost out of sight of, if not out of touch with, the congregations, while the others were not obscured. Short of demolishing the great old choir screens, however, nothing could be done to better integrate the congregations with the services. Moreover, it should be remembered that the services were for the bishops attending the Lambeth Conference and the spectators were admitted as guests. If the major intention was to give the bishops a ringside seat for the liturgy as the Church of England interprets it, that was done superbly.

The services were further enhanced by Archbishop Ramsey's specific request that the John Merbecke setting be used at Westminster and at St. Paul's and that the congregation join in the singing of the Creed. From the time that he began the Collect for Purity until he took the ablutions in Westminster's Chapel of St. Edward, the Archbishop's celebration of the Holy Communion was a model of reverence that any priest would do well to write on his heart. Even so, it had its critics. One of them, a man in Essex who had watched a telecast from Westminster, wrote to the *Church of England Newspaper* to ask why the Communion Service had "to be adulterated with prayers for the faithful departed, and the order changed after the Prayer of Consecration?" He was sharply critical of the Archbishop, writing that while he appreciated that "the celebrant was an 'Anglo-Catholic,' surely he as the leader of the Anglican Communion should have adhered to one of the official services."

A missionary bishop, himself an Englishman, was also critical of Westminster as "another very long service, full of English pageantry." He wrote that "the tired pomp of the Church of England made perhaps a splendid tourists' occasion, but it was a great opportunity missed. Liturgically and musically it was a hodgepodge, showing the Church of England as she used to be. Neither the order of the

service nor the management of the ceremonial reflected the new
vigor of the worship of the Church. . . . In contemporary jargon it
was magnificently irrelevant, and quite out of tune with the adventurous attitudes being talked of in the Conference chamber the day
before."

The service in Canterbury had remained, selfishly, perhaps, a
cathedral affair, but beginning with Westminster, the primates,
metropolitans, and other bishops, were given increasingly prominent roles in the services. At Westminster, White City, and St.
Paul's, the epistlers were, respectively, Brazil, Singapore & Malaya,
and New Zealand; the gospelers were Brisbane, Zululand, and
Uganda; and the preachers were East Africa, Iran, and the Metropolitan of India.

Those chosen to administer the chalice to the bishops at Westminster included York, Cape Town, India, and the Presiding Bishop
of the American church. There would have been a stronger link
with the congregation had bishops also been sent to the nave to administer Communion.

At White City there was concelebration for the first time at a
Lambeth Conference: Jerusalem, Tokyo, Nagpur, Taiwan,
Uganda; Dunedin, New Zealand; and the American Presiding Bishop, and each of them took a separate part of the long prayer of
intercession.

The participation of all the primates and metropolitans was best
observed around the dome altar at St. Paul's. Indeed, the use of the
free-standing altars at White City and St. Paul's was the single
greatest liturgical innovation since Lambeth IX.

A frequently heard criticism of White City was that the stadium
was far too large (it had accommodated as many as 60,000 for a
Billy Graham rally) in contrast to Toronto's Maple Leaf Arena,
which had been grandly filled right up to the top during the Anglican Congress.

The communions at White City were carefully planned but ill
managed. A missionary bishop reported that in a half-hour he
communicated fewer than fifty people. "That was less than
efficient," he said. "It was a chilly evening and the whole thing
never warmed up."

As the bishops returned to the altar at White City it was obvious that even experimental liturgy can be staid. *Alternative Service, First Series, 1966,* was used but one of the more liturgically conscious bishops described it as "the most conservative possible form of the Eucharist in a sort of semi-concelebrated Low Mass form." He added that "Cranmer sounded very prim over the public-address system. . . . It was hardly the splendor of a great act of worship."

The failure straightforwardly to follow one of the revised liturgies was completed at St. Paul's. The furniture was shifted drastically but the rite was basically that of 1662.

The major disappointment at St. Paul's stemmed from the program note, "It is requested that only bishops, consultants, observers, wives and conference staff shall receive the Holy Communion." A few outsiders crept to the altar railings, but in the press gallery, from which it would have been difficult to reach the altar, the consensus was that things might have been too prolonged had everyone been communicated. That, however, would not have been the case had those in charge utilized even a dozen of the 462 bishops by placing them at the other altars or at temporary stations throughout the cathedral.

There was hardly a shortage of bishops, priests or deacons—or altars. The beloved Eucharistic hymns were sung, but the faithful were not fed and for them the otherwise glorious service remained less than complete, or in a favorite word of Lambeth X, it was left "open-ended."

While the liturgical experimentation was timid and the pastoral theology less than vigorous, everyone admired the precision with which the English handled the services. The instruction sheets for each service were carefully detailed and the rehearsals were exacting. Rarely in the future would a diocesan witness a festive Eucharist or ceremonial—from confirmations to ordinations to institutions to consecrations—without consciously measuring them by the standards of Lambeth X.

Other strong influences were the parish and cathedral churches that the bishops visited, especially Coventry. Its brilliantly conceived new building was expected to be avant-garde, and did not disappoint. That it attracted so many Conference visitors testified to the effectiveness of a superb public relations program. Coventry's striking sense of community was apparent in the participation of the laity, men and women, bearing the alms and the elements to the high altar and momentarily remaining there in a way that seemed to enfold them as an integral part of the Eucharistic action.

There were many special touches at Coventry: the beige Anglican cassocks worn by the vergers (with white turtleneck sweaters!) and by some of the Cathedral Chapter, the modern vestments of the Bishop and his clergy, the use of the Confirmation Prayer when dismissing the children for Sunday School, the services in the Industrial Chapel and the Chapel of Unity, and the friendly, well-informed guides. Coventry's imaginative contrast of the new and the old was best seen in the display of modern sculpture in the bombed-out shell of the old cathedral.

For the Catholic factions, since there had already been a pilgrimage to Walsingham, the place to go in London was, of course, that staunch and famous parish, All Saints', Margaret Street. Kenneth Ross was still the Rector, the hanging Pyx and the high altar remained in place (firmly against the wall) with its six enormously tall candles, but the ceremony was radically changed. In an apparent effort at renewal, much had been trimmed from the High Mass and little poured into the void. Gone were processions, birettas, choir robes, and most of the incense; the people were seated for both the *Gloria* and the Creed, but surprisingly, they stood at the end of the Mass for the *Angelus* said in full. Where visitors might have hoped to find change—at All Souls', Langham Place— (close by All Saints' but miles away liturgically) there was no change at all. At All Souls', renowned for its round porch, high spire, and low-churchmanship, the celebrant continued the awkward custom of standing at the north end of the Holy Table.

Homiletically, the Archbishop of Canterbury was the only outstanding preacher at Lambeth X.

As for the other Lambeth fathers, in their speeches and extemporaneous talks in the plenary sessions, it was plain that many

were able and effective in the pulpit, but the three invited to preach
—the Archbishop of East Africa at Westminster; the Bishop in
Iran at White City; and the Metropolitan of India at St. Paul's—
were lamentably ponderous and old-fashioned. The choices, made
by Cariboo in consultation with Canterbury, were an obvious effort
to be imaginative and charitable, but the effect was patronizing.

The invitation to Iran, for instance, was apparently prompted by
a desire to give recognition to a remote diocese (628,000 square
miles and two thousand Anglicans amid 25 million Muslims),
whose Bishop often spoke of the loneliness of his post. The same
desire to grant recognition was inherent, in some degree, in the
choice of East Africa and India although, in both cases, the invitation also honored "elder statesmen" of Anglicanism. Thus while the
motivations were admirable and understandable, the same purpose
could have been served by the conferring of a Lambeth Degree or
the Cross of St. Augustine. As it was, the bishops failed to see that
the major rule for choosing a preacher for a Lambeth Conference
should be a man's ability to speak to the times in a compelling and
forceful way. A bid to preach at a major service of Lambeth is an
invitation to address the world if the speaker recognizes the opportunity and is able to project his message.

Ideally, the Lambeth preachers should be the most brilliant,
energetic, articulate of all the bishops. Only then would they be
most likely to write and speak with an effectiveness that would
catch the imagination of the press and spread their messages in
widening circles far beyond Lambeth pulpits.

Perhaps it is difficult for an Anglican Executive Officer, even in
his extensive travels, to know who are the most able speakers, and
doubtless it would be a new approach to choose a man on the basis
of his preaching ability rather than his see or years of service; but
until such an approach is made, great Church assemblies will continue to miss the opportunity really to be heard by the world and to
inspire people everywhere.

The most widely quoted of the lot, Archbishop Ramsey's sermon
at Canterbury, was, for all its brilliance, not necessarily a homiletical
model. It was effective because of its comprehensive grasp of many

situations, its deep theological insights, and its simplicity of delivery
—all characteristics of a great Archbishop.

Canterbury finished with the familiar poetic Prayer of St. Richard of Chichester, so commonplace that from anyone else it would
have seemed almost trite, but it was recited with a humility and
deep feeling that made St. Richard's Prayer the Archbishop's own.[8]

Three days later, the Archbishop of East Africa, Leonard
Beecher, ended his sermon with a poem, "Who Is Thy Neighbor?"
It was also well presented, but it failed to carry a conviction that
matched the text, from II Corinthians, exhorting men to be "am-
bassadors on behalf of Christ."

Although anyone's preaching might suffer alongside the skill of
Canterbury's, men and women who had so recently heard the Archbishop could not help placing his sermon next to East Africa's.
Many were aware that a more agreeable or approachable man than
Archbishop Beecher of East Africa would be difficult to find, especially among Anglican bishops, and those qualities were apparent
in his sermon. At the same time it was prosaic and mildly pedantic.
Of the four Lambeth sermons it was shortest (fourteen minutes),
but it was adequate more than admirable. Delivered with conviction, it was obviously the sermon of a man whose greater skills lay
in the pastoral warmth of loving souls rather than in preaching to
them.

In a radio interview, the Bishop in Iran, Hassan Dehqani-
Tafti, came across well despite his accent. But at White City, that
accent was more definite, the microphones failed to carry his voice to
most areas of the grandstand beside him, and he read his sermon

---

[8] Without identifying the prayer, Canterbury used this version: "Thanks be
to Thee, O Lord Jesus Christ/for all the benefits Thou hast won for me,/for
all the pains and insults Thou hast borne for me./O most merciful Redeemer,
Friend, and Brother,/ May I know Thee more clearly,/ Love Thee more
dearly/and follow Thee more nearly." It is attributed to Richard of Wych,
Bishop of Chichester 1245–1253, who was a homeless wanderer in his own
diocese during the two years that Henry III held the temporalities of the see.
Beloved by the Sussex people and considered an exemplary bishop, St. Richard was canonized in 1262 and is commemorated in the English Calendar on
April 3.

with the obvious effort of one not quite at home in a second language. In many ways it was the most relevant of the Lambeth sermons, with cogent references to transplanting of human organs and to space explorations, yet it lacked the touch that inspires a crowd.

Finally there was the Metropolitan of India in the pulpit of St. Paul's on the last day of Lambeth X. It was a good choice for a valedictorian address from a man notably articulate and greatly loved. It was a poor choice because the Conference had already heard him in a keynote address and several subsequent talks; the honor of St. Paul's might well have gone to some likely leader of future Lambeths. There was one other factor: Lakdasa de Mel's keynote address had been written off as a highly entertaining "after-dinner speech" in which he said very little but said it with persuasive oratorical skill. He was vague, but at least he made the bishops laugh, and when that bubbling humor was taken away in favor of a serious, sometimes sentimental sermon, it did not seem to be coming from Archbishop de Mel.

The final sermon at St. Paul's, like the Conference's message read aloud by the Bishop of London the preceding day, was hastily written: neither was ready for the press until a few minutes before it was delivered, and even the prepared texts showed hurried changes and substitutions.

(A few weeks later the Bishop of Taejon offered a footnote on some of the underlying factors surrounding de Mel's presence in the pulpit: "The Metropolitan of India preached a sermon that asserted the great truths of the Faith. Some of the bishops, deeply distressed by his bad behavior in the assembly during the previous week, had tendered their regrets to the Archbishop and intended to stay away from the final service. But some of them had received handsome replies and they turned up, so some wounds at least had been healed.")

Whatever his own misgivings, the Metropolitan's sermon was flawed in that his desire for thoroughness sometimes made his remarks seem contrived. It was, sadly, something of a swan song from a man of conviction who had seen three Lambeths and was passing on his way. As he lingered near the front door of St. Paul's, talking to an Indian woman and her child, he appeared reluctant to turn away even as the vergers were loudly disassembling the dome altar.

Taken as a whole, the preaching at Lambeth X was Biblical, graphic, sincere, faithful, rarely uninteresting, but it was almost never eloquent or imaginative. The impression as the Conference closed was that better preaching might have truly inspired the deliberations.

Coincidental with Lambeth X, *The Times* of London printed a thoughtful article, "Parsons Who Are Unable to Preach," that provoked a series of letters. One of them, from a Londoner, said that Anglicans needed to follow the Eastern Orthodox's lead in developing teams of skilled speakers whose tours of dioceses "make preaching a red-letter day." And the correspondent added, to no avail, that "a simple ruling from the Lambeth Conference would leave the way open to bishops to take such steps. . . ." Another letter, from a vicar in Lancashire, pointed out that "the number of good preachers may have decreased *but so has the number of good listeners.*" That perhaps is as good a commentary as any on the state of Anglican preaching as observed at Lambeth X.

CHAPTER 5

LAMBETH AT LEISURE

As FAITHFULLY AS THEY PRO-
cessed through great churches the bishops marched through a series
of social events both stimulating and stultifying during the opening
days of Lambeth X.

Bishops and their wives who were still recuperating from journeys to London that had been long and exhausting (or short and
tiring, as the fatigue of jet-age travel might best be described) did
not always relish the prospect of dressing, arranging transportation,
standing in receiving lines, remembering names, making small
talk, almost invariably getting rained on, and of finding a late bit of
supper someplace on the way home. For many, the pace was all too
reminiscent of the official functions back home in their own
dioceses.

Each of the events was characterized by warm hospitality—and
occasionally a sense of adventure as the bishops taxied through
strange streets and found themselves honored guests in great houses
or splendid gardens.

The entertaining began simply with the traditional garden party following the Evensong at Canterbury. As rain threatened but never materialized from the pewter skies, the colorful line of guests was greeted by Archbishop Ramsey and his wife at the end of a broad expanse of lawn.

The "alumni" groups that are commonplace at Lambeth Conferences (bishops who have attended the same seminaries, worked together, or shared committee assignments) were seen again in the gardens of the Old Palace at Canterbury. In 1968 there were other groups as well, including the bishops and observers who had been together at Vatican II. One of the groups that sat down to talk over their days in Rome included Moorman of Ripon, DeSoysa of Colombo, both Anglican, and a bishop from the Armenian Church and another from the Syrian Orthodox.

Generally the scene was a tapestry of purple-on-green, the robes and vests of the bishops contrasting with the dewy grass. The Dean of Canterbury was a stand-out in a crisp scarlet cassock, the traditional dress of those who have held appointment as Chaplain to the Sovereign.

Forty-eight hours later, at Lambeth, the guests exchanged the folksy, country atmosphere of the garden party at Canterbury for what was obviously a more formal, cosmopolitan affair. It was the only occasion of Lambeth X when all the bishops and their wives were together within the grounds of Lambeth Palace.

Lord Fisher's effusive greetings in the receiving line of other Lambeth Conferences were remembered with amusement—"My word, here comes California!" "Bless my soul, it's Bombay!" The Ramseys, also hospitable and good at names, gave more time to moving freely among the guests. Those who had grown accustomed in the last week to seeing Canterbury always in purple cassock began to think him less predictable when he appeared at Lambeth in the scarlet academic gown of a Doctor of Divinity.

In a sense, the parties of the first week were good training for the Queen's garden party. Advance word was given the bishops at the opening of one of the plenary sessions.

"My Chaplain, the Reverend John Andrew, has an announcement," Canterbury said from the Chair.

The Chaplain, a slender, balding Yorkshireman in his late thirties who swept along as if there were skates beneath his cassock, rolled into place at the podium.

"There have been some questions about the Queen's reception," he said. "This morning the Palace has informed us that if the bishops would care to wear their cassocks, the Queen would be delighted to see the bishops."

Such recent word from the royal court and the remote world of pomp and correctness, delivered with the inference that it was the ultimate in majestic preferences, left the bishops laughing aloud, but even as they laughed, they took mental inventory of their wardrobes. Within the next few hours there was a new onslaught of business at Wippell's [1] and at Buckingham Palace a good two-thirds of the Lambeth fathers turned up in cassocks that ranged in color through the entire spectrum of blue and red. There was considerable bluish-purple, as well as mauve, maroon, and magenta. Most of the horticultural tints were identifiable—mulberry, peony, petunia, poppy, heliotrope, lilac, violet, geranium, begonia, and rose, plus a sprinkling of crimson, carmine, wine, and heraldic murrey. "The magnificent green lawns appeared to have been sprinkled with giant petunia petals," wrote the Bishop of Taejon.

A few did it up completely: preaching tabs with their collars, cincture bands with tassels, shoes with buckles, and sashes of contrasting colors.

There were some surprises: the observer from the World Methodist Council chose a black cassock, but the Bishop of Milwaukee dressed in a business suit and gray topcoat. One of the Japanese bishops wore a pinkish cassock with a discernible flower pattern and slit at the side in the style of the Far East. African bishops had

---

[1] No fewer than 273 of the 462 bishops at Lambeth X (including sixty-three from the U.S.) placed orders with the Westminster branch of Wippell's, the leading ecclesiastical outfitter. A bishop from the Pacific, while buying a pair of shoes, remarked that at home he rarely wore them.

floppy-brimmed businessmen's hats and long overcoats that contrasted oddly with their cassocks. One bishop turned up wearing a mortarboard.

The most striking costume among the women was the kimono of pale green and gold worn by the wife of the Bishop of Tokyo.

As for the Queen, she assuredly was not startled by the prospect of that colorful afternoon when almost the entire Anglican episcopate came to tea. She had already completed a round of early-summer garden parties involving several thousand guests and earlier that day she had received the President of Pakistan who, in the words of the Court Circular, "remained to lunch."

Whatever the bishops' proclivities to tardiness, Buckingham Palace was an occasion at which nearly all of them, prodded by their wives, came early and stayed late. Nearly forty years earlier, at Lambeth VII, Elizabeth's grandfather, George V, received the bishops in the Throne Room (marks on the parquet floor told them exactly where to stand) and later joined the wives in the garden. The royal style in 1968 was to receive them all together, outside — so they came, in pairs, like an ecclesiastical procession to Noah's Ark.

As they arrived at the Palace, the deep chimes of Westminster could be heard across St. James's Park above the hum of late-afternoon traffic. The weather was bright, the mood was high.

In the Palace gardens, the Band of the Welsh Guards played "God Save the Queen" as members of the royal family appeared on the terrace. Elizabeth, at forty-two, mother of four, great-great-granddaughter of Victoria, looked youthful and fresh. With her were the Duke of Edinburgh, the Prince Consort; Princess Margaret, Countess of Snowden; and Princess Alice, Countess of Athlone, one of the last surviving granddaughters of Queen Victoria.

After being introduced to the metropolitans on the terrace, the royal personages walked across the lawn to greet their guests. The crowd parted like the Red Sea to make a broad path for the Queen as she approached them with Canterbury [2] and with his Chaplain,

---

[2] The Queen's party provided an opportunity to observe Canterbury's own traditional role as ex-officio parish priest to the royal family. Most of his

who made introductions ("Ma'am, may I present the Bishop of Upper South Carolina?") To each she extended her hand for a tight grip of the fingers. Almost all of the women, Americans included, curtsied to the Queen and the Duke.

A few of the guests said later that the Queen concentrated her attentions on the Commonwealth bishops, but most thought that she succeeded admirably in making everyone feel personally welcome. "She asked a lot of questions about Chicago," recalled Bishop Montgomery.

By 5:30 P.M., when people began leaving, streaming out the archways at the front of the Palace and across the paved yard toward the gates, it became plain that the Americans had not forgotten their cameras. (At Lambeth IX they had been chided for hiding cameras beneath their convocation robes in the cathedral processions.) Several took pictures of the Presiding Bishop as the wind whipped his cassock. Chicago's coadjutor hurried around to the other side of the tall iron fence, carrying two cameras given him by other Americans who wanted their pictures made as they left the Palace. Near one of the gates, the Bishop of Newark made a snapshot of the Bishop of Springfield wearing a long black frock coat, the formal dress of a bishop but described by Bishop Chambers as "my Abraham Lincoln coat."

Occasionally the guests had to step quickly aside for automobiles or trucks entering or leaving the Palace grounds: a camera crew, a mail van, and a taxi bearing a late-arriving bishop, two children, and a wife who flashed the pink card of admission for the bobby on duty.

On the curb ringing the great stone statue of Victoria Regina, the

---

predecessors had maintained close relationships—including Lord Fisher, who solemnized Elizabeth's marriage, baptized her first son, buried the body of her father, and crowned her Queen. Ramsey, who as Bishop of Durham stood at the Queen's right hand throughout the Coronation ceremony, has continued the pastoral friendship, baptizing the Queen's two youngest sons and serving as a member of a small commission that plans the education of the Prince of Wales. At Buckingham Palace, his fellow bishops saw him in a new role: a respectful Englishman standing with his sovereign as the bishops were presented to her.

Orthodox Archbishop of Bulgaria in a wide-sleeved black cassock waited for a gap in the traffic.

At six o'clock two large buses of the Hawthron Acorn Coach Company rolled out, bearing the contingent of bishops and wives quartered at Westfield College.

For many of the guests, especially the British, an invitation to Buckingham Palace was recognition gratefully received for years of service—often in obscure parishes with minute incomes. Others regarded it as the epitome of having arrived at a peak of social eminence. For everyone, for a few hours at least, it disputed the shrinking confines and power of the once-great, world-wide Empire of Her Britannic Majesty.

The other royal occasion at Lambeth X was the Queen Mother's reception "for some bishops and their wives."

Some meant about half of the bishops and their wives. It caused a social flap, especially among the wives, as the people who had not been invited wondered who *had* been asked. As it turned out, or at least as it was explained away by those who felt any comment at all was necessary, Buckingham Palace was regarded as official entertainment; the Queen Mother, with a much smaller London residence, was merely having a private party. The result was an aura of exclusiveness that surpassed everything else.

In addition to their afternoons at Canterbury, Lambeth, and Buckingham Palace, the bishops had an evening with the Lord Mayor of London, Sir Gilbert Inglefield. With members of the City Corporation he received them in the Guildhall, the center of civic life in the City, the oldest part of London, a mile-square area marked off by Roman legions centuries ago.

As a layman deeply involved with the Church, the reception for the bishops may easily have been his most interesting among the 800 banquets attended annually by a Lord Mayor. It was an occassion that outshone even the royal parties in elegance, hospitality, and histrionics.

There was also an element of mild surprise in the evening: at its height, Canterbury arose to thank the Lord Mayor and to ask the bishops to forego their noon meal a week hence and instead contribute the money to the Mayor's "War on Want." [3]

The announcement was the only departure from an otherwise strictly planned evening in the venerable Guildhall a few blocks from Mansion House. As the center of London's civic government for more than a thousand years, Guildhall was what its name implied—a banquet hall for the guilds of the City.

London's official reception for the bishops was the only formal evening of the Conference; a good many wives turned up in long dresses; most of the bishops wore cassocks but one came in the odd eighteenth-century outfit owned by some English bishops, a violet suit with gold braid, lace, and knee breeches.

The guests walked from the Underground station at Mansion House or arrived by automobile. Their first sight of Guildhall was a long red-and-white striped canopy that ran along one side of the building. A stone's throw away stood the seventeenth-century Wren Church, St. Lawrence Jewry, named for its prominence in the Jewish community that once flourished in the City.

Guildhall presented an aura of polish and careful preparation. Beyond the carved doors and massive floral arrangements stretched a wide corridor hung with colorfully detailed portraits of great events in Guildhall and the City: royal luncheons and banquets as well as a panoramic painting of Victoria's Diamond Jubilee in front of St. Paul's.

At the top of a short flight of stairs, pikemen in scarlet medieval uniforms, their helmets and breastplates flashing, formed double rows through which the great mace of the City was carried. As the evening began, Sir Gilbert and his wife took their places at the

---

[3] The first foreign newsmen had heard of the "War on Want" (it reminded Americans of President Johnson's "war on poverty") was a brief reference that Canterbury had made to it at the end of his initial news conference and in a memo asking the bishops not to present him with a gift. A confidential announcement of the plans for fasting was made to newsmen by the Bishop of Cariboo a few hours before the Guildhall reception; it was perhaps a small bit of news but nonetheless surprising to those who thought of Canterbury as shrinking from anything so spontaneous. Cariboo said the idea had been advanced "by many" and that Canterbury had decided to go along with it.

head of the receiving line with the Sheriffs and members of the City Corporation. As the bishops moved through the receiving line they turned to behold the lofty hall where Lady Jane Grey was tried and where Thomas Cranmer was sentenced for high treason— grim events difficult to imagine in a room so lavishly garnished with flowers and light. Gradually it filled with the bishops and their ladies, the clergy of the City churches, and the representatives of the City Livery Companies and the Court of Common Council.

Above the guests soared the great Gothic roof (restored after the bombing of 1940 that left standing only the walls of Guildhall and St. Lawrence Jewry) studded with the eighty-four shields of the guilds of the City and with banners of the twelve principal livery companies. Watching from the music gallery were the giant figures of Gog and Magog, household gods representing the conflict between the ancient inhabitants of Britain and the Trojan invaders.

In that splendid, history-laden setting the Lambeth fathers and their hosts sipped sherry and sat down to dinner. Afterward they descended to the crypt for cheese and wine, and saw a film on the devastating bombing raids on the same area in which they were spending such a comfortable evening.

Three weeks later the bishops returned to the neighborhood of Guildhall to attend a special matinee performance of a provocative new play, *Hadrian VII*.

Even during the midsummer doldrums it had been difficult to obtain a seat for the play (a "hard ticket" as some called it) in its out-of-the-way home far from the theatrical district of London's West End. The few overseas bishops who had heard of the play despaired of seeing it until one of the consultants, the Rev. John Taylor, urged the Bishop of Cariboo to consider the possibility of arranging a special performance for the Lambeth fathers.

It was perhaps extraordinary that the rich fantasy of *Hadrian VII* should catch the serious interest of Canon Taylor, who had been in missionary work for most of the thirty years since his ordination. After Cambridge and Wycliffe Hall, he served curacies in London and Lancashire, went to Ugànda in 1943 for the Church Missionary Society, became its African Secretary in 1959 and its General Secretary in 1963. He was, however, convinced that *Hadrian VII* should be seen by the Lambeth fathers, and Cariboo agreed, commenting that "the play has a great message for the Anglican Church as it gets the priorities of the Church right—that of people before property."

Hadrian VII had opened in London in mid-April, the surprise smash hit of the season, as it was to be in New York six months later. It was based on a semi-biographical work of eccentric brilliance in which an Englishman, long rejected for the priesthood, was suddenly accepted and by a fluke of circumstances elected Pope.

The author, Frederick Rolfe, was an Anglican who became a Roman and an unsuccessful candidate for the priesthood. Rolfe died in Venice in 1913 without realizing a shilling from *Hadrian VII* and little from his other works. Gradually through the years he became a legend (the banners he did for the Shrine of St. Winefride, Holywell, are greatly prized) and in 1967 a modern dramatist, Peter Luke, made the novel into a play.

Rolfe's shabby road to prominence was paralleled by the history of the Mermaid Theatre, which the Lambeth bishops visited.[4] Built in the rough brick shell of a Victorian warehouse that was blitzed in the great fire raid of 1941, the Mermaid was given a festive opening on a May evening in 1959. The bells of St. Paul's pealed out over the City to announce the only new theatre opened in the area in three centuries and the first in London in thirty years.

Nestled among the wharves and warehouses of the City and hugging the north bank of the busy Thames just below Blackfriars

---

[4] The Mermaid's address was Puddle Dock, although Puddle Dock itself no longer existed. In the postwar years it lay along the west side of the Thames, muddied and littered, the last vestige of London's watergates. A disused tradesman's entrance into the City, it finally vanished in 1963 as a part of the Blackfriars Road Development Scheme. Its name lives on in a street sign and in the poetry and literature of the sixteenth and seventeenth centuries.

Bridge, the little 500-seat Mermaid awaited the bishops. They filled it to capacity, the choice front "stalls" going to Canterbury, York, Cariboo, and the Roman Pontiff's Apostolic Delegate to Britain, Archbishop Cardinali.

The play's climax with Hadrian's assassination was an uncomfortable scene in the wake of the Kennedy shootings and the uneasiness about Paul VI's visit to Colombia. Yet there was a sadness among the Lambeth bishops as poor Rolfe awakened from his dream to find a bailiff carting away his few belongings, including the manuscript of *Hadrian VII*. Obviously, the bishops relished the play and all its barbs about episcopal dignity; they all but applauded the prelude to Rolfe's acceptance of the triple-crown when a long line of pseudo-Cardinals paraded down the aisles of the Mermaid Theatre accompanied by chanting acolytes and clouds of incense.

In veering from comedy to devotion and then back to comedy, the play proved, as one of the Lambeth fathers put it, that "bishops still laugh loudest at seminarians' jokes." It was, he said, "a strange revenge of the outlawed Rolfe that his life should become a spiritual message to so many bishops, because *he hated bishops!*"

At the intermission (the "interval"), the Apostolic Delegate told an interviewer that he was enjoying it "even though the election scene is a bit different from the ones I've observed."

Alec McCowen, the man who held the title role, recalled his initial dismay on being asked to perform for the bishops. He described himself as "a fallen-away Congregationalist from the Midlands" who was as astonished as Rolfe in the Vatican at the thought of the Lambeth fathers beyond the footlights, but they were, he said, the most responsive audience he had ever known. Certainly it was a rare theatrical occasion for both actors and audience to be outfitted by the same supplier—Wippell's.

Before the intermission was over McCowen was presented to the Archbishop of Canterbury.

"Yes, yes," said Canterbury, taking the actor's hand. "Haven't we met before? Or are you the *second* Pope I've met?"

The social schedule of Lambeth X was regarded as excessive by the world at large but by Londoners as rather inconsequential entertainment. Both judgments were wrong: the parties were held to a minimum but, in their austerity, they served well to acquaint the Conference's participants and give them recognition by the highest figures of Church, State, and City.

The advance program of four garden parties and an evening reception was lessened by one when the Westminster Abbey garden party was canceled because of rain. The invitation was not renewed —nor was it especially missed, the feeling being that the bishops and their wives were by then thoroughly saturated with tea and receiving lines.

Months earlier, Canterbury had expressed hope that "mercifully, in the weeks of the Conference, the organized social distractions will be at an absolute minimum, and the bishops will have—if they wish—some quietness for their concentrated task."

Canterbury kept his own official entertaining simple. Instead of continuing the custom of inviting bishops and their wives to spend a night at Lambeth, the Ramseys restricted their entertaining to small sherry parties and dinners at Lambeth Palace and weekend parties at the Old Palace in Canterbury; even that amounted to a heavy load of entertaining, but it was warmly hospitable. Four evenings a week, guests came for Evensong in Lambeth Palace Chapel and remained for dinner. Coffee followed in the drawing room, and by nine o'clock the guests were departing through the Tudor gateway.

Underlining the international character of the evenings at Lambeth was the confrontation of Federal Nigerian and Biafran bishops at a time when tribal rivalries had provoked a state of war. "We get along very well," said one of the Biafrans. "We treat each other like Christian brothers."

A highlight of one of the Lambeth evenings was a recital of sacred music in modern style by the Retreat Singers, a group of teenagers of Trinity Cathedral Church, Little Rock. Canterbury had heard them the preceding October, during a visit to the Diocese of

Arkansas, and had expressed hope that they could sing for his guests during Lambeth X.

Another center of social life in London was the residence of the Bishop of Southwark, 38 Tooting Bec Gardens. A bachelor of elegant taste, Southwark gave numerous parties and small dinners. In fact he threw himself into the preparations so heartily that he injured his back while cutting the grass and had to use a cane for the remainder of the Conference.

If the bishops had packed themselves off to a monastery, leaving behind wives and city life, the Conference might has been shorter, more serene or thoughtful, and less criticized for its social schedule, but the scene was London and a certain amount of socializing was not only unavoidable but desirable; its conviviality facilitated business on the floor, and its free exchange of ideas ran as much to serious debate as it did to frivolities.

For all the graciousness, the garden parties, as an English institution, were still as misunderstood when the last was over as they had been at the outset. Damned as outmoded, wasteful, precious, irrelevant, even effeminate, garden parties went undefended for their simplicity; nor did anyone point out that they have always been a part of the Lambeth Conferences and probably always will be as long as Englishmen and their ladies are doing the planning. Cocktail parties might have been better understood even while provoking a different kind of criticism.

Although hardly an international incident, it was the Queen's garden party that took the worst beating. A part of the objection was the view from overseas that any association with the British crown was suspect, yet an invitation to Buckingham Palace remained the most prestigious honor Britain could tender.

The sovereign's position as Defender of the Faith and the Church of England's role as the last body in the Anglican Communion that continued to be established by law gave Buckingham Palace significance in the bishops' eyes. Within that tradition, in her sixteen-year reign Elizabeth II had appointed most of the bishops then in office as well as various deans, canons, and chaplains.

The garden party issue was forgotten after the deliberations of the Conference gave serious critics some formidable material for comment; it was a matter of exchanging a teacup for a more meaty portion. But since editorials draw replies, the issue of garden parties dragged on. One exchange centered around the criticism of a young American priest who was a staff member of *The Living Church*. He declared that money desperately needed elsewhere had been foolishly spent, so that "the diocesan and the coadjutor and the suffragan, and their wives, can go to England for high tea with the Queen." In challenging the editorial, Bishop Bayne pointed out that five or six social events at Lambeth X constituted a trim schedule compared with the thirty official gatherings at the two preceding Conferences. His letter was published alongside one from Earl Honaman, Suffragan of Harrisburg, who wrote: ". . . You may count me in the U.S. for the summer so that the *whole* episcopate will not be absent. I know exactly what you mean in that editorial and I was determined that it wouldn't happen to me."

The truth was that Lambeth's social life was sedate and sometimes bordered on dullness. The criticism showed that the world and the press only pretended to believe that bishops should be more like other people: the image of the Church was shaken when its hierarchy appeared to behave in anything approaching the manner of a group of executives involved in a month-long summer meeting in a major city.

Outspoken criticism of a different nature came from a group of young people, self-described as "Christian radicals," led by the bearded assistant curate of St. Michael's, Highgate, the Rev. David Hart. They handed their leaflets to the bishops arriving for the opening service at Canterbury ("We got plenty of this at Uppsala," said one bishop) and they turned up again carrying wooden begging-bowls in a picket line at Guildhall. Their disapproval of almost every aspect of Lambeth X was so general that they tended to be written off as overly critical or youthfully unrealistic, but their objections lingered on in the pamphlets they continued to distribute after the last of the parties was over.

"Jesus said this about garden parties," wrote the young curate and his friends, "When you give a lunch or dinner party, do not invite your friends, your brothers or other relations, or your rich neighbors; they will only ask you back again and so will you be repaid. But when you give a party, ask the poor, the crippled, the lame, and the blind; and so, find happiness.' We suggest that you give away your garden party tickets to such people as Jesus talks about."

CHAPTER 6
LAMBETH AND FAITH

The week Lambeth X con-vened, Archbishop Ramsey said that its Section on Faith would be dealing with "perplexities of the modern world." He expressed hope it would "be able to say things that are strong and reassuring as well as things about the difficulties of faith." Also, he said, its task would be "to show how Christian faith must take its form in action —peace and the relationships of nations."

If the final Faith Report fell short of the Archbishop's hopes, or seemed unable to find a focus in the areas he mentioned, it was because the bishops grappled with more issues than could be handled by any group of men in four short weeks—to name a few: war, racism, justice and freedom, poverty, discontent of youth, urbanization, international morality, technology, problems of contemporary theology, and order challenged by violence.

The recitation of the moral, social, and economic problems of the world left little time for any definitive clarification of the basic precepts of Christianity. The Report made no reference to the

Church's worship or appraisal of its doctrine except for a ponderous attempt to consign honorably and respectfully the Thirty-Nine
Articles to some sort of official limbo. There was no reaffirmation
of the necessity or nature of the Sacraments, only two passing references to the Holy Eucharist; and except for an obscure paragraph
on prayer and contemplation there was scarce mention of an
ordered and disciplined spiritual life.

Anyone who read the Report to find some hope or encouragement in personal faith was predestined to disappointment, if not
disheartenment and confusion. Even with its primarily Western
thought, much of the Report suggested a United Nations survey of
the problems of humanity; most of it was just a repetition of what
the World Council of Churches had to say in greater depth (and
tonnage of paper) at Uppsala.

The complexities of significant reflection were analyzed in advance by the Section Chairman, the Archbishop of Rupert's Land,
Howard Clark. His address to the opening plenary session on July
27, regarded as the most sincere and thoughtful in a long morning
of speeches, was totally realistic in its warning against trying to say
something about everything, yet that appeared to be the appointed
task of the fourteen committees of the Faith Section.

"We seek renewal because the Church always needs renewal," he
said. "The times when she was forgotten have been the times of
her greatest peril. We seek renewal for our Lord's sake and for the
world's sake. We seek renewal in the Church's believing life, in her
intellectual life, in her worship, in her fellowship, in her service, in
order that through Christ, Servant and Lord, dying and rising from
the dead, all men 'might have life, life in all its fulness.' "

Clark said that he could not claim a disciplined, scholarly background that equipped him to treat authoritatively the deep theological questions of the day, but he nonetheless realized his pastoral
responsibility. "I *am* a bishop," he declared, "and even in a day
when the work of a bishop may undergo great and necessary
change, all bishops must recognize their inescapable responsibility
to the Christian faith. . . . The theologian explores the implications
of the primal revelation and the developing understanding of it, and

this is not the first time that the result has been unsettling. The bishop's task is to judge those explorations, not chiefly in terms of intellectual brilliance but in terms of saying and liberating truth lest it be said again, 'the hungry sheep look up, and are not fed.' " [1]

Clark pointed out that he and his colleagues were aware that their preparatory work on faith was recognizably, unavoidably Western. "We decided to wait until all our bishops, from all over the world, were together, before beginning to work on whatever reports or resolutions seem necessary."

Even as he acknowledged the inherent difficulties of the task, Clark's hope for the Section was that somehow it might produce a moving proclamation of the Gospel, a message that would reaffirm the triumph of faith over doubt. His yearning for strong assent was clear in an article he wrote for *The Canadian Churchman* in early summer: "Christian faith has always meant faith in the Gospel, in the story of what God did through the life and death of Jesus Christ. But one of the burning questions of our day is whether today we can believe the Gospel in the way men used to believe. They used to sing the hymn 'Tell Me the Old, Old Story,' but do we want to hear 'old stories' today? That is a question the bishops will have to face honestly, for now we see that we must *never pretend*. We can say only what we believe to be true. We could not be renewed by a Gospel in which we only half believed."

As Clark foresaw, the Report was destined to run into difficulty. Ten days later he returned apologetically to the podium as the bishops thumbed through galley proofs of the Draft.

"In the space of twenty-seven hours the work of the committees had to be brought together and consolidated by the drafting committee," he said. "We are asking for your criticism, and we are fairly certain we will receive it."

Immediately the barrage began. The first question came from one of the three black bishops of the American Church, Mills of the Virgin Islands, who asked for assurance that some comment would

---

[1] In Milton's poem, Lycidas is a shepherd whose tendance of his flock is contrasted with that of "our corrupted Clergy, then in their height," as the poet puts it in a headnote.

be made on racism beyond the fleeting reference that he noted in the Draft.

After Clark replied, expressing his own hope that a final resolution would be brought in on racism, the bishops began general criticism of the weak, uncertain character of the draft. In a memorable Welsh accent, Williams of Bangor stated bluntly, "There is nothing at all about the renewal of faith in the draft. It is a disappointing document. I should expect the report to point to Christ as the source of renewal, to point to the Holy Spirit as the means of renewal, and to point to the fact that the Holy Spirit takes us to the Scriptures for renewal and reveals to us the mind of Christ. There does not seem to be any connection between this Report and what is coming out of the Faith and Order Commission of the World Council of Churches. It sometimes seems that all we are interested in, in Faith and Order, is the necessity of episcopal ordination."

Housden of Newcastle (Australia) added cryptically, "There are gems and pearls within a mass of verbiage."

Among the few speeches praising the draft was one by Myers of California, who regarded it as at least "beginning to move the Anglican Communion into this half of the twentieth century."

One of Clark's countrymen, O'Neil of Fredericton, also lauded the Report ("Excellent!"), but for the most part the long morning session was monopolized by negative speakers—not only bishops but also many of the observers and consultants who, from their special sections in the gallery, were experiencing their first opportunity to join in the floor debates.

The first of the consultants to speak was the Anglican priest-professor from Uganda, John Mbiti, whose white teeth flashed in his dark face. He began with great courtesy to take the draft apart for its stuffiness. He read a portion aloud as the bishops tittered nervously, and mitigated his criticism only partially: "Perhaps it is because English is my third language."

Bishops rose one by one to be recognized by Canterbury and to lament omissions—a few vital, others only pet subjects. Some attacked the theological language—among them Hallis, Assistant

Bishop of St. Edmundsbury & Ipswich, who said "The word *God* is an English word which has many meanings. The whole Draft is far too Westernized and English in that respect."

Wani, Northern Uganda, thought the Draft "too intellectual to be understood by the majority of us from developing countries."

He was followed by his primate, the Archbishop of Uganda, Erica Sabiti, who was to be one of the men most frequently heard at Lambeth X; he stood time and again with old-fashioned evangelical zeal to draw back the Conference to the concepts of "sin" and "forgiveness" and other basic terms. "Renewal means going back to where things are at their best—or at least it does in my country," he said in a slow, direct voice that always seemed tinged with sadness. "In all of our technological process, the sinful mind is still the same. There is no mention of 'sin,' yet the Lord's Prayer still mentions it. And there is no reference to the Cross, although we know there can be no renewal unless we are driven to the Cross."

In the same tenor, an observer from the Church of South India, the Rev. Dr. Joshua Russell Chandran, noted the omission of "forgiveness of sins."

One of the English consultants, John Taylor, General Secretary of the Church Missionary Society, cautioned the bishops that the draft might not, even in revision, go beyond two subjects, theological debate and the Christian appraisal of the secular society. "We need room in the draft for more affirmation of faith, yet we must be careful that we are not just 'beating an antique drum.' "

The most thorough criticism was offered, not surprisingly, by a Jesuit among the observers. From the gallery he identified himself in a clear voice: "Father Herbert Ryan, Society of Jesus, Professor of Historical Theology, Woodstock College, Maryland, U.S.A." He politely prefaced his remarks with the judgment that the document was a "notable achievement," but he said that it did not carry a theology of revelation. He noted that a sort of "cryptographic unitarianism" ran through the Draft which at the same time seemed to miss the point that "Faith, existing in the Trinitarian concept, does not take place in isolation but is an act of the Ecclesia which brings forward the Church." Finally, he said, the true nature of faith "is not a psychological experience but a gift of God which all we as Christians have in common."

The morning ended with the preliminary draft being returned to its section for restudy and the final writing. It was a scheduled procedure but it was obvious that the plenary session had not been pleased by the committees' work. One of the American consultants, John Macquarrie, saw the task clearly when he asked the Conference "What does it matter to the modern world if God is real?" [2]

Whether Professor Macquarrie's question was answered in the final Report, submitted a fortnight later, remains unclear, but the Report improved on the Draft in being more concisely written and less spotted with errors and omissions. [3]

The revision began with two questions: "What has the Church to say, in this time of turmoil and upheaval? What does the Church's faith, deeply rooted in history and tradition, enable it to affirm in an age when all that it stands for is being challenged, and its long-established beliefs are being widely rejected?"

Once again a note of apology crept in as Clark presented the Report: "Circumstances did not allow us the time we have wished to consider or amend a number of drafts, or to gain unanimous approval for every phrase, but we are hoping that this Report taken as a whole may succeed in portraying an attitude and an approach that combine Christian assurance with a bold exploration of theology and society; that unite Christian confidence and intellectual and social risk."

---

[2] After winning his doctorate at Glasgow and teaching there several years, John Macquarrie in 1962 was appointed Professor of Systematic Theology at Union Seminary in New York, became a convert from Presbyterianism, and in 1965 was ordained priest. He is one of the foremost spokesmen of the Anglo-Catholic wing of the American Church, lectures widely, and functions as a parish priest on the staff of St. Mary's, Manhattanville, in New York City.

[3] "The Report could not have been presented to the world in the form in which you first saw it," Archbishop Clark told the Conference. "As it now stands, it is 90 per cent the work of the committees and the Bishop of Durham has pulled it all together and has written the preamble." He also thanked Noel Davey of SPCK for editing the Report.

A philosophy that lingered in the Report had been spelled out in the Draft: "It is not in accord with the ethos of Anglicanism to draw up particular statements of faith, after the manner of some contemporary statements of the [various] Churches. We consider, however, that doctrinal commissions in the various provinces, acting with liaison between themselves, should address themselves to examining questions of faith and of the interaction between faith and, it may well be, such problems as race, war, and poverty."

The first section of the Report centered on the theme "Affirmations of Faith in the Living God."

"Renewal in faith must begin with an affirmation of faith," it declared. "Our faith is in Jesus Christ, through whom, by the Spirit, we have been brought into a relationship with God our Father."

The report also asserted: "We see . . . the goodness and love of God. . . . We acknowledge that the completion of God's purpose for the world has not yet been attained . . . and that the goodness of man is frequently spoiled by men's sin.[4] . . . We are confident that God . . . works in every man to make him perfect. . . . We believe that . . . all men can respond to God's goodness. . . . We look forward in hope to the completion in Christ of God's purpose for the whole created universe."

Perhaps as a gesture to tradition, the Report said that "This faith, which is set forth uniquely in the Scriptures and is summed up in the Catholic creeds, develops and grows under the guidance of

---

[4] The phrase came under considerable discussion. Ramsey said it could make the bishops "a laughing stock" and Wickham of Middleton called it "a slight understatement." It was revised in the published Report to read ". . . because of sin, evil has entered the world and man constantly needs God's forgiveness."

Those who spoke from the floor at the plenary session on the draft of the Report on Faith, August 7, included Oregon, Virgin Islands, Bangor, California, Peterborough, Utah, Fredericton, Newcastle (Australia), Arkansas, Erie, Northern California, Northern Uganda, Wangaratta, Perth, Mashonaland, West Virginia, Hong Kong, Gambia, Nelson, Winchester, Nuku'alofa, Crediton, Willesden, Uganda, Horsham, Chicago, Leicester, Woolwich, Iran, Huron, North Carolina, the Suffragan of Toronto, and the Assistants of London, St. Edmundsbury, Polynesia, and Guildford (Usher-Wilson); consultants were Mbiti, Jenkins, Macquarrie, Taylor; observers were Athenagoras, Chandran, Gomes, Payne, Ryan, Stewart.

the Holy Spirit within the Life of the Church, the Body of Christ. The mission of the Church is to bear witness to Jesus Christ as Lord and Saviour of the world, who offers all men the true fulfillment of their longings and their hopes."

On the implications of renewal for the Church, the Report observed that "renewal entails radical change. . . . At the heart of all such renewal in the Church is the necessity of dying and rising again with Christ. Here alone is the source of the renewal that leads to reform according to God's purpose."

The Report declared that "renewal entails identification with Christ . . . in Christian baptism—understood not merely as the rite of a moment but the principle of a lifetime; and in the Eucharist—understood not merely as an occasional act of worship but as the focus of a constant, reciprocal relationship with God and our fellow men. Renewal entails identification with our neighbor. . . . We cannot know Christ, or be one with him in his Church and sacraments, unless we are also prepared to know and serve him in the least of his brethren in the world."

It remained for the bishops' message at the end of the Conference to give the strongest affirmation of faith: ". . . The faith of the Church that God reigns and loves and speaks is sustained and renewed in its members by constant prayer. Its life is in Christ and its life is vigorous as its members try to live in and with Christ. . . ."

Resolution No. 2 on Affirmation of Faith, approved by the Lambeth fathers as the Conference drew to a close, stated that "the Conference . . . calls the Church to a faith in the living God which is adventurous, expectant, calm, and confident, and to faith in the standards of Christ, who was, and is, and is to come, as the criterion of what is to be welcomed and what is to be resisted in contemporary society."

Canterbury expressed considerable satisfaction with the Faith Report. "I believe that when this is read it will be bound to fulfill my own hope that the Conference would say something reassuring about Christian faith in real depth while being really sensitive to the perplexities about faith," he said. "I believe that some of the pages in this Report really do that and the reading of them should bring help to many people, both helping them to a deeper and also to a bit more understanding and sensitivity about intellectual changes of the times."

Canterbury also voiced his conviction that "this Report will help the members of the Churches to know that their faith must urgently be expressed in life in the service of mankind in their trials, terrible things—lack, want, avarice."

"It's splendid to note," he said, "that this sort of involvement in the world is balanced by a keeping alive of the other-worldly strain of Christianity."

THE LANGUAGE OF FAITH

After reading the Draft, consultant David Jenkins warned the bishops that they should be less concerned with defining God. "Let God establish his own existence," said the brilliant young English priest who had been a theological adviser to the British Council of Churches, the World Council, and the Archbishops' Doctrinal Commission. "I do not believe [that] all the bishops from all the hierarchies in the world could establish that. . . . God is as much at work in the world as in the Church and sometimes more."

At the same session the Lambeth fathers listened again to Professor Macquarrie, who had written the preparatory essay for the committee. He criticized them for falling into an old trap—a dichotomy in their thinking and language about "matters theological and those that refer to the secular society. It is symptomatic of the state of the Church. . . . If God is only a piece of metaphysical furniture, then perhaps it doesn't mean very much whether there is a God."

Similar counsel was offered by Allison of Winchester. He said that the Draft's admonition that "we must not think of God as if he were an individual person" could be quite misleading to the "ordinary people who are entrusted to our pastoral care."

"We may be able to distinguish," he added, "but it is a very 'nice' distinction . . . for we do preach a personal God."

The ebullient consultant from Uganda, John Mbiti, was heard

from again when the Draft, appealing for the presentation of the faith in imaginative ways, described the speech of Jesus Christ as "concrete, simple, poetic, evocative." Not so, said Mbiti, "If Christ's language had been simple, the Gospels would long ago be exhausted." The result was that the word "direct" was substituted for "simple."

Resolution No. 3, based on the work of the Committee on the Language of Faith, was moved by Arden of Malawi. It recommended "that theologians be encouraged to continue to explore fresh ways of understanding God's revelation of himself in Christ, expressed in language that makes sense in our time . . . [and] that requires of the theologian respect for tradition and, of the Church, respect for freedom of inquiry."

THE DEBATE ABOUT GOD

The shock value of the "debate about God" and the "death of God" was already declining as the bishops chose their committee assignments. At an earlier date it might have been one of the livelier groups, but the few references to it on the floor of Lambeth X indicated that the subject had become almost passé.

Dwindling interest in a once-hot controversy was perhaps predictable, but it was also surprising in that world attention had centered on a book, *Honest to God,* by a Lambeth bishop, John A. T. Robinson of Woolwich, Suffragan to Southwark. He turned up on the Confessing the Faith Today Committee and was heard several times on the floor. A prominent name, he was often sought for interviews by the press, but somehow his presence did not match his book.[5] Perhaps he wanted it that way—a suffragan who did not wish to overstep or have the other bishops resent his prominence. (It was rumored that Canterbury had written off *Honest to God* as

---

[5] Published by SCM (Student Christian Movement) Press, where the Rev. David Edwards was managing director and chief editor, its sale of 350,000 copies was a record for a theological book. After Robinson's sequel, *The Honest to God Debate,* sales of the two books totaled more than a million. In April 1969, he resigned as Suffragan to become Dean of Trinity College, Cambridge.

"quite muddled.") Whatever the case, the lanky black-haired bishop seemed a stranger to the image of a debunking author.

On the other hand, the relatively unknown David Jenkins, who had been lecturing at Oxford for most of his fifteen years since ordination, established himself as one of the keenest intellects among the observers. His preparatory essay "The Debate About God" was written with the same fresh and direct approach that characterized his speeches. He diagnosed the debate as "a sign of the times," and added that it was "up to the leaders of the Church to make a reasonable and, if God wills, a prophetic discernment of the significance of that sign."

Jenkins wrote that "Western atheism has much to teach us both about the liveliness of the world and about the deadliness of the Church, and thence about God . . . [but] a God who requires defending is hopeless as God and useless to man. His existence is not even debatable, it is merely contemptible."

Pondering Jenkins' paper and the negativism that had raged since the last Lambeth, the bishops recorded their recognition "that recent theological discussion, while it has been liberating to some, has been thought by others to be destructive of faith."

They found "grounds for hope and encouragement in this 'debate about God,' and optimistically added that beneficial reformulations of the Christian faith have often arisen out of conflicts, and we are confident that out of this present travail new understandings of the Christian faith will similarly be born."

Resolution No. 2 (c) on the subject said that the Conference "welcomed . . . the searching inquiries of theologians." Thus the Lambeth fathers assumed a new image, at least in one area, of tolerance and liberal open-mindedness. They were all those things and, at the same time, they were reacting calmly to a theology that was no longer startling. If a suggestion of the death of God had burst on the world for the first time from the floor of the Lambeth Conference the bishops might have been fiery, but since the curious holocaust appeared to have died down, the bishops were not of a mind to fan it.

THE FINALITY OF CHRIST

The pendulum of the discussions on faith swung swiftly from the "Debate about God" to "The Finality of Christ." The latter subject was regarded as a question for discussion rather than resolution.

The committee was given a singular honor when Canterbury cited a section of its Report at his final press conference twenty-four hours after the closing Eucharist at St. Paul's. "I value greatly a remark like this," he said, and read aloud: "We may rightly say that there is no finality in science, in metaphysics, or in ethics, but we must also say there is no finality in our expressions of Christian thought and life. There is finality in Jesus Christ as Lord"; then he added in his own words: "And finality in him as a Person in which we find the truth about God and about men."

The preparatory paper, which urged a progressive reformulation of doctrine, was written by the Rev. Henry Chadwick, for nearly a decade Regius Professor of Divinity at Oxford, and with his fellow consultant, David Jenkins, a member of the Archbishops' Commission on Doctrine.

"To believe in the 'finality' of the Gospel is none other than to believe that Christ is the Word of God," Chadwick wrote. "Nevertheless, the modern term 'finality' should not lead to misunderstandings. The New Testament contains important warnings against the assumption that the task of adequate theological statements consists only in an accurate repetition of the original words of holy Scripture without putting the message in relation to an ever-changing situation."

When Chadwick wrote that "contemporary understanding of doctrinal development must include not merely the idea of an organic growth and enlargement, but also that of some occasional pruning of the tree" most bishops readily agreed that they should bring their pruning-hooks (some wanted to use them on the Thirty-Nine Articles), but no strong voice suggested that they also bring a watering can.

The relatively brief paragraphs that emerged under the chairmanship of Brown of St. Edmundsbury & Ipswich carried extraordinary impact. "Every generation needs fresh affirmations and expressions of faith in the living Christ at work in the Church and in the world . . . offering the world, through the Church, the love which will never come to an end (I Corinthians 13 : 8) and which is the foretaste of his own finality."

OTHER FAITHS AND UNBELIEFS

Striding beyond the ecumenical outreach that had been a feature of every Lambeth Conference since 1888, the bishops expressed a desire for talks and cooperation with non-Christian religions and also with nonbelievers, including Marxists. They bore out Canterbury's prediction that "the Conference will be meeting with deep awareness of how the world is questioning religion."

The chairman of the Committee on Dialogue With Other Faiths, Appleton of Perth (Australia), submitted the Draft of his group's work with strong urging that the Conference support "an emphasis on the necessity of dialogue with those in other faiths."

He pointed out the necessity of taking other religions seriously "if we hope to present Christ to other faiths as the convergent point of all faiths." Also, he said, "we have got to work in partnership with them wherever it is possible without in any way soft-pedaling our faith in Jesus Christ."

A path, if not a program, had been charted for both Committee and Conference in the preparatory essay written by Kenneth Cragg, an authority on Islamic culture who, while Warden of St. Augustine's College, Canterbury, worked with scholars from all over the world. "Faiths must be met in their integrity, not their compromise, in their strength, not their failure," he wrote, "and the discovery of what is due for reproach carried into the diagnosis of man rather than the discomfiture of opponents."

Canon Cragg wrote also that "men must be helped to the recognition of truth by the truth-evoking quality of the relationships we bring them. These relations embrace the whole of life and not alone the theses or dogmas by which the Gospel is credally housed and stated."

He posed a question from Albert Camus, "Mighn't it be better for God if we refused to believe in Him?," and added one of his own: "Could it be in the end that we so pathetically discourse with the world because we so feebly discourse within our own souls and thus in turn have so little converse with the living Spirit?"

When the Draft was submitted it gained significant support from an observer, William Gomes, Roman Catholic Bishop of Poona, India, and from Westall of Crediton, Suffragan to Exeter.

The suggestion for a mission to Marxism came from the former Industrial Chaplain of Coventry, the recently consecrated Phipps of Horsham, Suffragan to London. "I have been a bishop only three months and I am learning a certain bit of episcopal subtlety," he said. "If the word 'included' is too strong, then I suggest 'not excluding Marxism.' "

Phipps' suggestion stuck, as evidenced by Resolution No. 12, adopted several weeks later when the Conference commended "similar assistance for dialogue with Marxists and those who profess no religious faith." (It also urged "increased Anglican support" in personnel and financing.)

In introducing Resolution No. 12, Perth expressed belief that the world's sympathies toward the Czechoslovakian Communists indicated that "there are some Marxists with whom we can have fruitful relations."

In the discussion that followed, opposition came from Chandu Ray, Bishop of Karachi, West Pakistan, himself the son of a non-Christian family. "We drain away our energies and manpower so that evangelism goes overboard," he warned. "Dialogue with other faiths is of value, but our support must be given to evangelism."

Welles of West Missouri saw the matter as a far larger issue, commenting that "the unity of mankind should take a place above all other things."

In addition to supporting inter-religious dialogue, the bishops approved the long, comprehensive Resolution No. 11, which recorded their conviction that "in their obedience to Christ's mission and command" Christian churches should encourage the common unity of mankind as well as cooperation economically, socially, and morally. The Resolution concluded with a call to Christians "not only to study other faiths in their own seriousness, but also to study unbelief in its real quality."

PRAYER AND CONTEMPLATION

"The Christian is one who all his life will arise and start out afresh on the journey to the Father," wrote one of England's most promising young theologians, A. M. Allchin, in the preparatory paper for the Committee on Faith and Spirituality. "Seen in that light, there can be no separation between Christian faith and Christian spirituality: both are God-centered."

Aware of the trend toward liturgical renewal as well as spiritual renewal, Allchin wrote that "we must never separate them [for] man responds not in isolation but in community: all our prayer is rooted in our baptism and flowers in the great Thanksgiving."

The final Report distinctly echoed much of Allchin's thinking. "Man's instinct for prayer corresponds to God's fatherly care for his creation, even though man does not always recognize that it is so," it said. "Deep concern and gratitude are the raw material of prayer; and every man has a capacity for silence and contemplation, although that capacity may be unknown to him and will always need cultivation."

The bishops' awareness of "all sorts and conditions" of men was shown in the Report's statement that the vocation to prayer and contemplation may not be the exclusive province of religious communities. "Old age and sickness may provide special opportunities for responding to that vocation," it declared. "The clergy need to be able to help each individual to find his own way of prayer and contemplation. . . ."

In the floor discussion, Bryan of Barrackpore (India) said that the reports should not seem partial to any particular book or author by mentioning them specifically (as it did in referring to *Prayers of Life* by Abbé Michael Quoist). His point was well taken, but the

Report and Resolution nonetheless included a recommendation to "new and modern methods [of prayer], such as those of Michael Quoist."

In Resolution No. 4, the Lambeth fathers affirmed "that the primary task of the Church is to glorify God by leading all mankind into life in Christ, and that this always involves a continuous advance in the practice of prayer in the Spirit; and therefore calls upon the clergy and laity of the whole Anglican Communion . . . to deepen and strengthen their life of prayer. . . ."

At his final press conference, Canterbury commended the committee's work. "There is a meaningful section on prayer and contemplation," he said, a broad smile spreading across his face. "At long last we have got the word 'contemplation' into an ecclesiastical pronouncement, for which I feel very thankful, indeed, though none will accuse me of being an escapist from the world's problems around us."

Because of his deep interest in those who give themselves to a life of vows as well as his friendship with and personal encouragement to both Roman and Anglican monastic life, Canterbury must also have been gladdened by Resolution No. 5 on Religious Communities. Some of the orders had passed their centennial in the years since the last Lambeth and, in looking back, it was proudly noted that as early as 1897, Lambeth IV had stated that it "recognizes with thankfulness the revival alike of Brotherhoods and Sisterhoods and of the Office of Deaconess. . . ."

At Lambeth X, the bishops again gave grateful recognition to "the contribution of religious communities, both men and women, to the life of the Church" and it spoke especially to the trend of renewal that the orders were experiencing. The Lambeth fathers counseled religious orders "to renew themselves according to the priorities of the Gospel and the original intention of their foundation." Cognizant of the difficulties that some aspects of renewal had brought to community life, the bishops asked that close cooperation be maintained and developed between themselves and the communities.

ECONOMIC AND SOCIAL PROBLEMS
IN THE SECULAR WORLD

The Lambeth fathers seemed possessed with references to urbanization, technology, and the secular. It was almost as if they were apologetic for still hanging on in the modern world, yet their anxiety about being "relevant" was well ministered to by an American and an Englishman, neither of them consultants, who wrote preparatory papers.

"The basic change in a technological society is the transformation in the character of human dignity," declared Gibson Winter, an Episcopal priest and Professor of Ethics and Society in the Divinity School of the University of Chicago. "Personal dignity was something to be gained through the exercise of individual initiative in our earlier period; personal dignity in a technological society is ascribed by the inclusion of the individual within the technical capacities of the society."

The Rev. R. S. O. Stevens, Bishop's Adviser on Industry in the Diocese of Birmingham (England), observed that some "consequences of family mobility" are to be seen "in loose sexual attitudes and more seriously in the various escapist trends of which drug-taking is at present the most prominent." (Canon Stevens was among the few who made any mention of drug addiction among young adults.)

More hopeful than many, Stevens said the technological society was beginning "to rediscover the New Testament doctrine of the Church—that the Church is a chosen body appointed to do God's work in the world, a work of healing and reconciling and redeeming."

Further, he said, an essential prerequisite of the full acceptance of the task of service "is a recognition and acceptance of the secular as the field of God's activity, and perhaps the biggest step the Church must take before it can fully assume its contemporary role is wholeheartedly to rejoice in the secular."

"The secular society," a phrase popularized by Harvard professor Harvey Cox's book of that title, was taken up in the Report with the comment that "the growth of technological change and urbanization has altered man's basic assumptions about himself and the world. He finds himself more and more in control of his environment and less and less in need of God, whom he has come to regard as, at the most, a 'God of the gaps' who will supply—or remedy—his deficiencies."

The Report labeled modern man "secular" and applied the term to "the society that is emerging from contemporary changes." A secular society, it said, is "a society chiefly concerned with this present age (*saeculum*)—and with man's mastery of his own environment. Such a society rejects an authoritarianism claiming a religious or metaphysical basis."

In a lengthy lament of what it called "the sickness of the contemporary world," the Report itemized the symptoms but offered little in the way of remedies; it went on record, however, as being painfully conscious of "the tensions between men of different races and the pressures of, and upon, minority groups; the increasing use of drugs; the spread of violence so that it seems everywhere to be becoming endemic."

The Church, it said, whose members are part of the society, shares in the sickness.

The recitation of global sickness ended in anticlimax if not confusion: "To such a world as this, the Church has to offer the Gospel with understanding and relevance." What did that mean? Was it a cliché or a startling insight?

The Report did, however, adhere to the truths the Church has always proclaimed. It was not ashamed in a sophisticated culture to speak of sin as the Archbishop of Uganda and some of the evangelicals had repeatedly urged the Conference to do. "In all these problems we recognize that factor of rebellion, conscious or unconscious, against God's laws, which we call sin," it declared. "These human problems are caused, or increased and aggravated, by the pride, greed, and lust of men and communities. The gospel of God's redemption is addressed to sinful men inside as well as outside the

Church, for the sins we see in the world are evident also in the life of the Church and her members."

Although the Report might be found eloquent and discerning in its approach to some of the world's economic and social problems, it failed to make any practical application in the plethora of resolutions.

There was, for instance, a lengthy Resolution on the Church's role in "agrarian forms of society." It was presented by Trevor Huddleston (speaking for the first time as Bishop of Stepney), whose sincerity no one doubted. Yet another suffragan, Wickham of Middleton, himself a specialist in sociological problems, was correct in calling the Resolution "a grab-bag." Bryan of Barrackpore added that he detected a "trend to write essays first and then append a resolution to it." As for Middleton's "grab-bag" comment, what he wished to do was to replace the Resolution under fire with one recommending study of the World Council of Churches' 1966 paper "Church and Society." Generous to a fault, the bishops approved the Resolution on agrarian society as well as Middleton's Resolution No. 20.

Not everything went through so smoothly, and the bishops were entirely capable of vigorous objection even when they seemed drowsy or restless. There was, for example, a spirited reaction when Luxton of Huron submitted an amendment that asked every Anglican diocese to raise a special fund to avert world poverty and hunger, a fund that would be initiated "through commitment of at least two per cent of the bishops' own stipends for the balance of 1968 and the full year of 1969." (The motion had been presented earlier as the first nonagenda item by the Irish Bishop Buchanan of Clogher, but was tabled.)

Canterbury, too, in his sermon from Augustine's Chair, had pointed the way to teaching by example when he reminded the Lambeth fathers that "our faith will be tested in our actions, not least in our actions concerning peace, concerning race, concerning poverty."

Not only tested but judged, Canterbury might have added, and the bishops were mindful of that when they wrote in the Faith Section's Report that "for the Christian, aid must neither be patronizing benevolence nor a safeguard for security, but the sharing with others of what has been given of God."

In calling the bishops again to personal witness, Huron stated, "Most of us here haven't obviously sacrificed. We continue to fight 'the battle of the bulge'. . . . If we pass this motion it will show the Anglican world that the old boys mean business."

Huron said such a contribution would mean doubling what he was already giving. He told of a gift of nearly $50 from a Baptist, the wife of a laborer, "who speaks of the posh parishes she sees around her and feels it is time for the Baptists to act in direct help to others."

The proposed Resolution was seconded by Girard, Assistant Bishop of Sheffield, and adoption was urged by Sambell, Coadjutor of Melbourne, who said the bishops should follow the lead of the popular song lyrics, "If you love me, show me. . . ." He suggested, however, that no fixed percentage be stated in the wording.

After that the dissent began. Dehqani-Tafti of Iran found the motion ambiguous. Barron of George (South Africa) denounced it as moral blackmail. "It is difficult to vote 'no' because that will be misunderstood," he said. "Giving should be a private decision for some and as for bishops who are married, they may want to consult their families."

It was Allison of Winchester who settled the waters by urging that the bishops resolve to further *all* aid through central organizations that were already set up for that purpose instead of fostering exclusively Anglican endeavors.

"For many of us it would be no sacrifice," Winchester said, "but for many of our brethren outside the U.S., Canada, and Britain, we should not mention a percentage. Besides, many of us give quietly, unseen, and without publishing what is given."

Wilson, the bearded Bishop of Birmingham,[5a] spoke of his years

---

[5a] John Leonard Wilson, Knight Commander of the Order of St. Michael and St. George, returned from Singapore to be Dean of Manchester in 1949, became Bishop of Birmingham in 1953 (he claimed the automobile license SOB-1), announced in March, 1969, that he would retire the following September 30.

as a prisoner of the Japanese. (Consecrated Bishop of Singapore in 1941 a few months before the fall of Malaya, he was beaten and tortured as a prisoner of war in the dreaded Changi Prison.) "As one who knows what hunger is, what it means to make grass and cockroaches palatable, I believe most of us are giving to world hunger," he said, "and I am concerned that we should be too mindful of our public image. 'Your Father who seeth in secret, rewardeth openly.' We are to do our alms secretly."

The complications that arose as amendments were proposed to the Resolution on giving caused Welles of West Missouri to agree with an earlier speaker, the Bishop of George, that the matter should be referred to committee until, as West Missouri put it, "we have the whole ball of wax."

Canterbury, who appeared to have been writing one of the many notes and letters he often dispatched from the Chair, sat boldly upright. "What was that, what was that?," he asked. Turning to the Bishop of Cariboo, whom he considered his consultant on North American slang, he received a whispered explanation.

Eyebrows furrowing, the Archbishop listened intently to Cariboo; then, brightening noticeably, he responded, "It seems to me that we have *three* balls of wax!" He rolled off the expression with relish as the bishops joined in the laughter, and often in the tedious hours that remained of the Conference, Canterbury lightened the moment with a quizzical smile and a plea "for the whole ball of wax." Happily, it seemed to compensate for his puzzlement and later dislike of the American custom of calling "Question! Question!" when a vote was sought.

The Lambeth fathers were called back to the seriousness of the issue by Strutt of Stockport, Suffragan to Chester: "I hope we will put the motion in the wastebasket. If we are committed to stewardship of our money we are committed forever, nor by percentages which tell the world what we are giving and thus create the wrong impression."

After a few more speeches—from Polynesia, Wales, once again from West Missouri, and from Grimsby, Suffragan to Lincoln —the bishops voted to refer the Resolution not to its origin but the

Steering Committee. No more was heard of contributions from the bishops.[6]

The next Resolution that came before the House ("The Conference welcomes the deep concern about the economic and social frustrations of developing countries. . . .") also was given considerable discussion. It was presented by Vaughan of British Honduras and seconded by Reed of Ottawa.

Throughout the Conference the bishops' attention had been called to "the Third World"—a designation (popularized by the World Council of Churches) which referred to the Asian and African, Far Eastern, and South American peoples. Too often in the past, Lambeth Conferences had thought in terms of only the European "Old World" and the North American "New World," but 1968 had brought a third force to prominence both in politics and in the Church, and Lambeth X did not miss the opportunity of encouraging the developing nations.

Immediately, Temple of South Carolina questioned the financial implications of the Resolution, specifically the minimum net amount of 1 per cent of gross national product to be officially transferred, exclusive of private investment, to developing countries, echoing the recommendations of the World Council of Churches. He said he would be reluctant to ask people to give eight and a half billion dollars to developing nations without guidelines or restraints. Moreover, he said, he would be at a loss to explain to responsible businessmen why the Conference had approved such sums. "What am I to say? That I voted for it because it was recommended? In my part of the world, the World Council of Churches is looked upon with a great deal of suspicion."

Bishop Temple, whose diocese is a textile center, was especially aroused by a section of the Resolution that called for "agreements

---

6 "The English debaters rose in wrath and demolished my simple suggestion," the Bishop of Huron recalled in frank admiration of British forensic skill. "They found a dozen chinks in my sketchy armor. . . . The assembly clouds were heavy with storm and fury until that supreme interventionalist, Ed Welles, cleared the air. . . . He explained to me later, 'I just saved you from being completely clobbered!' "

stabilizing and supporting at an acceptable level the prices of vulnerable primary products and providing preferential access to developed markets for the manufactured products of developing countries."

Another American, Crittenden of Erie, rose to answer South Carolina. He pointed out that the 1 per cent was already a policy of the American government. Secondly, he said, preferential treatment in prices for manufactured products of developing countries had recently been made part of the platform of the Republican Party which, he said, "is hardly considered a liberal party."

The Resolution, No. 21, passed, but with South Carolina and a few others dissenting.

LAW AND ORDER

The terrifying incidence of world-wide violence in recent years hovered ominously over the deliberations of Lambeth X. The flames and bloodshed of race riots loomed large; the term of office of the man who succeeded John Kennedy was drawing to a close —a poignant reminder of the young President's death; the assassination of his Senator brother was not yet three months past; and the murder of Martin Luther King, Jr., was almost as recent.

American tragedies, combined with other instances of violence throughout the world, had an effect on the bishops—as they did on every group, and several times Lambeth officially proclaimed its shock and concern. Indeed, some of the committees on Renewal in Faith spoke so liberally on civil disobedience that the other bishops could not approve: "The kingdom of God is often advanced by revolutionary change following on a change of heart," said a Draft Report. "Here the Christian Church must be ready to support individual Christians as they search for justice even by means which sometimes seem extreme, for example, by civil disobedience."

The statement was not included in the final Report, but it did receive far less discussion than the substitution of "justice" for a reference to "law and order." As the last full day of work began, Mills of the Virgin Islands drew attention to a sentence which declared that "the Christian commitment is generally to the maintenance of law and order, so that society may achieve its wholeness under God."

For a moment the bishops may have had a that-is-where-we-came-in feeling, for the Bishop of the Virgin Islands had been the first, days earlier, to question the Draft of the Faith Report. It seemed full-circle at the end of the Conference as they listened again to the black American bishop. "I should like 'justice' instead of references to 'law and order.' We have law and order in Czechoslovakia, Rhodesia, in South Africa, but we don't have justice," he said. "In America, twenty million black people are crying for justice."

He drew support, significantly, from Stark of Newark, whose see city (Newark, New Jersey, a large industrial metropolis) had been ravaged by one of the worst racial episodes of 1967.

Realizing that feelings were being aroused because of the substitution of one word for others—albeit a vital bit of editing—Canterbury warned humorously, "The Sections are very sensitive to legislative direction. . . ."

The Faith Section's chairman, Clark of Rupert's Land, agreed, however, that the Committee would be quite willing to see that changes were made. It was Cariboo who suggested the phrasing "just law and order," and that stood in the published Report.

There was one more opinion to be heard on the matter; it came from Brown of Arkansas, who in identifying himself pointedly added "See City: Little Rock." Then he recalled to the bishops the grim days of September 1957, when U.S. troops had to force the integration of Little Rock High School. "There is a complicity here which should not be voted on hastily," he told them. "As Martin Luther King said, 'Law cannot make you love me, but it can keep you from killing me.' Before the spirit of love, there has to be law."

The Conference's feelings on violence figured prominently in a part of the commentary on "The Sickness of the Contemporary World," in the Faith Report: "The contemporary world is a world so acquainted with social revolution that men are beginning to accept the idea that violence of any kind is inevitable and even good for its own sake."

It was, of course, a statement of what the bishops saw as fact, but later in the Report they added another opinion: "There is a widespread revolt against current systems of power in most parts of the world. This revolt, often violent in its nature, is frequently a response to the less spectacular but equally destructive violence of social injustice. . . . Christians need to understand the causes of those social upheavals and the reasons that lead men to seek to change the existing order in their countries by violent means. In specific situations, circumstances of such extreme oppression may arise that some justice-loving Christians may conclude that the lesser of two evils is to join in armed revolt."

Proceeding further, the bishops offered an alternative: "Christians who are unable to endorse such action must find non-violent ways of changing the existing order. We commend in particular the non-violent approach so ably embodied in recent times by the late Dr. Martin Luther King."

After all the talk, Resolution No. 17 on "The Study of Social and Political Change" seemed to be the usual timid episcopal suggestion: "The Conference recommends that the Provinces should set up study groups, Anglican and ecumenical, to study the documents on all aspects of violent and non-violent social and political change."

It carried an amendment, added in the dwindling hours of the final plenary session, declaring that "In view of the urgent nature of this matter, it further recommends that those groups promptly report their findings and recommendations to the Anglican Consultative Council or Lambeth Consultative Body, which will make them generally available to the Anglican Communion."

In the end, the process called for in Resolution and amendment sounded slow, cumbersome, and academic. As often before, it remained for concerned men and women throughout the Anglican provinces to be the medium of the Holy Spirit for counsel that would calm a restless, disordered world.

RACE

It was a bitter, shocking scandal of Lambeth X that the black bishops had to demand a resolution on racism.

When the final Report offered a scant two paragraphs on race and failed to provide a resolution, the black bishops became a strong, united voice insisting that the Conference declare itself on the subject which, in the words of the black Suffragan of Massachusetts,[7] "seems to be troubling every sector of society except the Church."

"Your Grace, I would like to express my dissatisfaction and disappointment on the statement in the Faith Report," began Bishop Burgess in an address from the floor. "It is bland and it is dull. It contributes nothing new to our Christian understanding of racism, and makes no new proposals for dealing with it as a Church."

When the bishops located the statement to which he referred, many of them readily agreed that it was so cautious and cliché-ridden as to be almost totally ineffective. It started off with the obvious: "Racism asserts a separation and even a rejection one of another." It concluded with the mundane observation that "the major responsibility and final decision remains with the individual in the person-to-person relationship demanded by Christian discipleship."

The disappointment and anger of the blacks and others was summarized by Bishop Burgess when he likened the statement to the platform of American political parties: "It says nothing to which we could not agree, and proposes nothing that would come to cause embarassment or sacrifice on the part of anyone."

It was, he said, foolish to say that the Church had to educate itself when it was simply "lacking in will."

As for the failure to provide a resolution, Burgess decried the

---

[7] Fifty-nine-year-old John Melville Burgess, a native of Michigan, spent a decade as Episcopal chaplain at Howard University, Washington, D.C. (for years the largest exclusively Negro U.S. campus), before becoming Archdeacon of Boston in 1956 and Suffragan of Massachusetts in 1962. On June 7, 1969, he was elected Bishop of Massachusetts.

lack of a directive "that we can look to as we return home to scenes of hatred, violence and death." He added with obvious bitterness, "It is hard enough in these days for a black Christian to remain faithful to a Church that is predominantly white in its leadership and power. There is little in this statement that gives encouragement to maintain our loyalty or to equip us to face the gainsayers."

There was agreement from Garnsey of Gippsland (Australia) and then, from Davis of Nova Scotia, came the question that was most pertinent: Would it be possible for Bishop Burgess to work with Wilson of Chichester, chairman of the Faith Section Committee on International Morality, in framing a Resolution that could be presented to the Conference?

Chichester's Roger Wilson faced the task realistically. It was possible, he said, "if we can find a Resolution which can say something and have some teeth in it." He went on, "Our committee was asked to include something on international morality in a Section dealing primarily with Faith. It was addressing itself to Christians and not to the world."

A typically blunt statement was made by Trevor Huddleston, who had spent most of the last twenty-five years in South Africa and had recently accepted appointment as an English suffragan to make way for a native bishop. "I have become cynical about such resolutions, not that I don't agree," he said. "I would say that if you are convinced that racism in any form is a sin, then be prepared to be misunderstood far more often than you are understood—and go through life as someone who is ultimately bound to pay the price for it."

One of the blacks, Swaby of Jamaica, expressed disappointment that there was no resolution, and then an Irishman, Moore of Kilmore, turned the bishops' attention from what had not been written to what was proposed in the Report. He took exception to a reference that condemned opposition to interracial marriage.

"Does this mean that if a parent objected to an interracial marriage of a child under twenty-one he should be prosecuted?" Kilmore asked, referring to the statement that all forms of discrimination should be dealt with and enforced by law if necessary. "This

Conference does not know everything," he added. "Some feel that interracial marriages are not always right."

Momentarily the issue of racism became yet more detailed when Brown of Albany said he hoped that a resolution would refer to the Church's own employment practices. Then Makhetha, Suffragan of Lesotho, the black bishop who had recently preached before the royal family, returned the discussion to the over-all subject. "Racism is not a thing we can brush away in one day, but one must go on and on saying it is a sin," he declared. "I should be happy if we could have from this Conference a word of hope and encouragement to those countries troubled with racism."

Once the bishops had spoken up for a Resolution on Racism, it was written and approved before the day was out. Chichester proposed the Resolution and the Suffragan of Massachusetts seconded it. The swift framing of Resolution No. 16 was due, in part, to its dependence on quoting from a similar statement which the World Council of Churches had approved the previous month at Uppsala: "Racism is a blatant denial of the Christian faith. (1) It denies the effectiveness of the reconciling work of Jesus Christ, through whose love all human diversities lose their divisive significance; (2) It denies our common humanity in creation and our belief that all men are made in God's image; (3) It falsely asserts that we find our significance in terms of racial identity rather than in Jesus Christ."

After endorsing that statement, the Resolution declared that "The Conference acknowledges in penitence that the Churches of the Anglican Communion have failed to accept the cost of corporate witness to their unity in Christ and calls upon them to re-examine their life and structures in order to give expression to the demands of the Gospel (a) by the inclusiveness of their worship; (b) by the creation of a climate of acceptance in their common life; and (c) by justice in placing and appointment."

It concluded with a call for the member churches of the Anglican Communion "to press upon Governments and communities their duty to promote fundamental human rights and freedoms among all their peoples."

On the whole, the black bishops had been fighting for a principle rather than the declaration, which in itself was rather hollow. Instead of speaking out of conviction, they played it safe, in their haste, by falling back on the words already hammered out at Uppsala. It was, however, to their credit that they did not rely on the resolution of 1958 as they had in replying to the Pope's encyclical on birth control. It was not that Lambeth IX's statement was lacking, affirming as it did "the natural dignity and value of every man, of whatever color or race," but rather that the approach of the 1970s demanded more. The bishops realized all of that, but realization was one thing and the articulation of a statement was another.

For whatever it was worth, Lambeth X went on record about racism, but it was doubtful that the resolution provided the kind of directive that the Suffragan of Massachusetts longed for when he spoke of returning to a world of hatred, violence, and death.

There were more references to racism (and to war and poverty) in discussions of the Unity Section; eventually the work was combined to appear under Faith in the final report.

In the plenary session on Unity, Burnett, Assistant Bishop of Johannesburg (for nine years Bishop of Bloemfontein until he resigned to become Secretary of the Council of Churches of South Africa), drew the biggest hand of the morning when he said "Racism is denying the Gospel. We need more said about racism and more than pious resolutions."

Bishop Huddeston again spoke on the subject: "Words about race are getting exceedingly dangerous to the Church. I have heard pronouncements about it at synod after synod in Africa and nothing really happened. I would plead with all the passion that I can summon to stop talking and call upon Christians in South Africa and Rhodesia to bear their witness and, if necessary, let congregations die if they are not prepared to do so."

Brown of Arkansas agreed, adding, "I, for one, am not convinced of salvation by resolution!"

YOUTH

The enthusiasm for youth that characterized the Draft—and, to a lesser extent, the Report—came to nought. The Resolution was so patronizing that it died aborning.

Considering how often the subject of youth arose, the proposal to kill the Resolution was a surprising turn. Many of the bishops had come to Lambeth keenly aware of the restlessness of young people and they had only to walk in London streets to see more evidence of it. Like racism, it was much on their lips but less apparent in the Drafts from the committees. Brown of Arkansas pointed out the failure to articulate any clear statements about youth, especially the absence of strong emphasis on youth's obedience to the law of God. He said his experience had been that "they are not young enough, long enough, to do enough, before they become old fogies like me."

Burrill of Chicago, one of the most skilled of the extemporaneous speakers, also expressed concern that the Conference should "speak in a strong and positive and helpful way to the young people of our Church." The short, graying, ruddy-faced Chicagoan noted the swing from the "silent generation," as the young people of 1958 had been called, to the rebellious, outspoken young people of the late sixties. "It hardly seems possible, but now things are quite different. We seem to say we hope youth will come and help, but that is a negative approach. We should say that we rejoice that youth is awake and alive and receptive to God the Holy Ghost."

It was therefore ironic that statements of the tenor the bishops were asking for were included in the Draft but dropped from the Report. There was, for instance, a line perhaps too strong for the bishops to retain: "The apparent hesitations of society at large, and the Church in particular . . . account, far more than we are willing to admit, for much of the violence of our times, particularly among the young."

It was that same Draft that carried the declaration, also later deleted, that "the Church needs the participation of youth, with its foresight, its hopefulness, courage, and flexibility, and with its capacity for mistakes. . . . This participation is unlikely to be won unless the Church is ready to live much more dangerously and sacrificially than it has so far seemed ready to do. Failure of this kind makes it difficult, particularly for the young, to recognize in the preaching of the Church the reflection of the gospel of sacrificial love."

An excellent statement that did survive in the Report declared that "in such a world as ours it is natural that youth should be consciously preoccupied with the areas of social and political disorder, impatient with adult apathy and prejudice, and in revolt against the perpetuation of things as they are; so that in many nations, youth protests and revolts are becoming familiar occurrences. The Church must recognize that, even when confused and strident, the protest of youth against existing conventions and institutions often comes from a sincere desire for a well-ordered society where justice, love, and service will be found. Such protests sound an authentic note of criticism recalling Christians to obedience to the Gospel."

The Report also affirmed that "the Church must be ready to deal pastorally with a younger generation often deeply affected by having to live in two worlds—a world represented by home and a world represented by school and places of higher education . . . [and] tensions become acute."

Having well expressed itself in the Report, it was unfortunate that the same spirit did not carry over to a Resolution. It was not that the bishops did not have empathy with youth nor that youth lacked spokesmen among the bishops. Three U.S. bishops were especially concerned—Arkansas, Chicago, and the Presiding Bishop, who himself was accused of being unable to speak without making some reference to the rights of youth or of women. Two others who spoke often of youth were Myers of California and Frey of Guatemala.

The latter, consecrated less than a year earlier as the first bishop of the American Missionary District of Guatemala & El Salvador, proposed that the bishops should pass over the Resolution on youth. Bishop Frey, a one-time Texas disk jockey and sportscaster, was at

thirty-eight one of the youngest men present and the father of four
sons and a daughter: he certainly was not out of touch with the
younger generation. Precisely because of that he was chosen to talk
with the delegation from the Fourth British Conference of Youth
which had met in Edinburgh while Lambeth X was in session. Out of
that meeting came a few lines of a proposed Resolution, "the Conference records its thankfulness for the willingness of these young
men and women to share with it our common Christian concern for
social justice and the reordering of societies in the interest of the
fuller development of human personality."

When Bishop Frey had an opportunity to reflect on the proposed
Resolution he felt that it was lacking. As he waited his turn to address his fellow bishops on the last morning of Lambeth X, three
young women and a young man burst into the conference hall carrying a crudely lettered banner, NOT CHARITY BUT JUSTICE.

Silently, they advanced to the center of the room, holding aloft
their banner as the bishops strained to read it. Momentarily the
final plenary session came to a halt. Canterbury seemed to ignore
the intruders, but Welles of West Missouri rose to say that the bishops had seen the banner and that the group should retire. They did
so quickly, and dropped the sign at the feet of the Bishop of California, who had an aisle seat near the door. As they left, the bishops gave them a flutter of applause and one of the girls confided
afterward that a bishop had leaned over and said "We are glad to
see you."

After the interruption—a quiet demonstration, but unprecedented in the history of Lambeths—Guatemala was recognized by
the Chair. The group he had met with was pleasant and courteous,
he said, "but the way the youth paragraph reads in the Report
seems like a paternalistic, supercilious, and condescending statement—a nice pat on the head. Since it has been cut down so much,
I feel that we should be accused of having been asked for bread and
having given a stone. So I ask that the Resolution not be put." The
Conference agreed.

Guatemala was no doubt also disappointed with the concern for
youth shown in the Ministry Section's report the previous day. Al-

though the Section's final Report remained silent on the subject, the three committees dealing with the laity did submit two resolutions adopted by the Conference. One, No. 28, stated that the Conference "values the initiative shown by young people in witnessing to their faith in Christ; and urges that they should be encouraged to do this in their own way. . . ." The second Resolution recorded that the Conference, "thankful for the intensified interest of young people in human welfare . . . request Provinces, Dioceses, and Parishes to promote this involvement in every way possible." Lambeth X did summon youth to the Church's side, but ever so mildly.

THE ACHIEVEMENT OF PEACE

The closing days of Lambeth X witnessed the dramatic coincidence of Russian troops marching on Czechoslovakia at the precise moment that the bishops were framing their statements on war and peace.

The Conference was sadly aware of the fighting in Vietnam and Biafra, but it was the threatening rumble of Soviet tanks, heard by short wave from Czechoslovakian villages, that heavily underlined Lambeth's opposition to war as "incompatible with the teachings and example of our Lord Jesus Christ."

With the use of that phrase Lambeth X reaffirmed the statement of Lambeth VII nearly forty years earlier. Meanwhile, a great war had shaken the very building in which the bishops were sitting, had reshuffled their decennial meeting dates, and had vastly changed the lives of countless people, yet the bishops knew that the dictates of the Gospel remained the same and that, in the words of the 1968 Report, "The killing of man by his brother man is agonizingly incompatible with the ethic of our Lord Jesus Christ."

Besides reiterating the declaration of 1930, the bishops reaffirmed their position of 1958, which called for governments "to work for the control and abolition of all weapons of indiscriminate destructive power, atomic, biological, and chemical, as a condition of human survival." Again the Conference declared, "Nothing less than the abolition of war itself should be the goal of the nations, their leaders, and all citizens."

The report was keenly conscious of events since the last Lambeth: "While progress has been made in limiting the nuclear arms race, especially in the partial test-ban treaty and the nonproliferation treaty, a real threat to humanity has arisen in the repeated outbreaks of non-nuclear wars using highly sophisticated conventional weapons. They cause terrible suffering to civilian populations, aggravate the refugee problems, and bring the danger of escalation. It is an international scandal that such wars are being encouraged by proxy through the competitive delivery of arms."

In a sweeping look at the international situation the Report observed that "the revolutionary ferment of our day, as it is seen in the emerging nations of Africa, in the developing nations of Latin America, and in the Black Power movement, and in the Vietnamese conflict, reflects, whatever else its motives, the primary basic human longing for dignity and freedom." [8]

The task of the Church, the Report said, "is to interpret the Gospel in terms that speak to man's prevailing sense of need, and to his thirst for meaning and hope."

Whatever the sympathy, eloquence, and comprehensiveness, the Report was cloaked in a certain anonymity. Hence the resolutions contributed a significant counterbalance in giving the bishops the opportunity to express themselves forcefully on vital issues of war and peace.

Resolution No. 8, which reaffirmed the condemnation of war, was presented by Allison of Winchester. It also condemned the use of nuclear and bacteriological weapons, upheld the right of conscientious objection, opposed the claim that total war or ruthless weapons are "justified by results," and urged support of the United Nations.

Myers of California seconded the Resolution but faulted it for showing "a lack of courage on the part of this Conference" to condemn specific acts of violence. "We seem afraid to do this and I

---

[8] The reference to "and in the Vietnamese conflict" was deleted from the bound Report.

think the world is going to condemn us for it," he said. "We seem reluctant to mention Vietnam, to condemn acts of violence in Nigeria, and we have not spoken of Czechoslovakia."

The Resolution also failed, said Myers even as he moved for its approval, "to face up to the problem that leads to war—power, the wrong use of power. Perhaps the time has come when we Christians will have to disassociate ourselves from centers of national power and associate ourselves in supranational structures of Christians around the world."

Sadiq of Nagpur went further in faulting the Resolution. He denounced it as "toothless" and proposed an amendment calling for stronger language and also for the simplicity of reaffirming "that participation in war or preparation for war is against our Lord's will and his teaching about love for our neighbors."

The Indian's amendment set off a lively discussion during which Canterbury remarked from the Chair that he had read the statement "as being completely a pacifist resolution." Nagpur agreed.

Fraser of North Carolina cautioned the bishops against running into the danger of "an absolute ethic in one area of life, war and peace, and not in others." He expressed belief the Conference could not say that all power and violence was evil because "there are some Christians who believe that a war of containment may be the only hope of peace." He pointed out that "we have spoken for conscientious objectors, but we must also speak with admiration for those who have shown their love by giving their lives for their brothers."

A Canadian, Norris of Brandon,[8a] said that Nagpur's amendment indicated "that we are saying that anyone who serves in any force is doing it against the Lord's will." He was supported by Hunt, Suffragan of Toronto.

Hargrave, one of the Suffragans of South Florida, warned that the amendment "would be misinterpreted throughout the world." He added that "If this is the pacifist point of view, let's say so. If we were not under the protection of flags, we wouldn't sit here." He in

---

[8a] Ivor Arthur Norris, consecrated in 1950 and simultaneously since 1952 Bishop-in-Ordinary to the Canadian Forces, died at his desk in the synod office at Brandon, Ontario on January 24, 1969.

turn was supported by another American, Stark of Newark, who said that such a statement on unconditional condemnation of war would be ridiculous.

An amendment that fared better on the floor was the one that pressed for the specific reference against the use of nuclear and bacteriological weapons. It was presented by a veteran crusader for peace, Greer of Manchester, Senior Bishop of the York Convocation, who offered an interesting sidelight on the alignment of an established church with the government. "At the last Lambeth Conference I proposed a resolution condemning nuclear weapons and it was not passed," he recalled. "Archbishop Fisher, who was presiding, said that if it had passed, he didn't know what he should have said to the Prime Minister. I believe we should say that in no circumstances will we use any nuclear weapons for we believe it morally wrong, and that no nation should place citizens in the position where they might have to use them."

Manchester's stand a decade earlier was also recalled by Baines of Wellington, who at that time was Bishop of Singapore. "I admired what Manchester had to say then and now," he said, "but I ask the question, 'If I were Prime Minister, would I be helped by such a resolution in the time of crisis?' In a time of political crisis, one should pray for leaders, those with their finger on the trigger, that they may choose the right. So, with the resolution, would the Prime Minister be helped? I am inclined to answer no."

Having thrashed it out, the bishops approved the specific condemnation of nuclear and bacteriological weapons but voted down an amendment, proposed by Mize of Damaraland, asking for a reexamination of the doctrine of "just war."

In considering the conscientious objector, the resolution held that it was a concern of the Church "to uphold and extend the right" of those who morally object to being a member of the armed forces. The Report went further in stating that it recognized "anew the vital contribution to the Christian Church made by many of those who in conscience cannot participate in any war or in particular conflicts."

It was the Report's reference to conscientious objectors that es-

pecially caught the ear of the American bishops, who knew of
growing numbers of young men appealing to the clergy for advice
and sometimes fleeing the U.S. to live abroad. One of the Americans, Mosely of Delaware, failed to clarify the reference but at the
same time he effectively stated the objectors' position.

"There is no provision of law that recognizes their right not to
participate," Delaware lamented. "They end up in jail. They end up
in flight, humiliated by being called draft-dodgers and deserters
whereas in truth many of them are refugees in good conscience,
refugees for conscience' sake. Their consciences have been formed
and sharpened by the Church and I should like us to make clear that
those people have our understanding and that they do make, in our
opinion, a vital contribution to the Church."

The Conference passed on to Resolution No. 9, which stated a
great deal but stated it so broadly that it lost much of its meaning:
"The Conference affirms that human unity can be achieved only if
all governments are willing to work towards a form of world government designed to serve the interests of all mankind."

It was typical of the generalized expressions that resulted when
the bishops took the long way around an issue—particularly Vietnam. The majority of Americans and Australians and some others
wished to keep any notice of it out of the reports and resolutions,
and Gowing of Auckland (New Zealand) went so far as to say so.

Ray of Karachi came to America's defense when he said that "we
in Asia feel if no stand is taken against communism our countries
will be overrun in a short time."

The Lambeth fathers' conservatism in commenting on current
conflicts may have spilled over into Resolution No. 31 on world
peace; otherwise it is difficult to see how at least some drama did
not mark the presentation of the Resolution that called for a consultation of Canterbury, the Pope, the Ecumenical Patriarch, and
the Presidium of the World Council of Churches. It was a Resolution of originality and bold vision, approaching what many thought
that Lambeth X was going to amount to in the first place—a meeting of Primate, Pope, and Patriarch. In the words of the Resolution
approved by the bishops, the Conference invited the distinguished

religious leaders to consult together "on the possibility of approaching leaders of the other world religions with a view to convening a conference at which in concert they would speak in the interests of humanity on behalf of world peace." The Resolution was little noticed but the fact that Lambeth X went on record with such a recommendation left the door open for bold interpretation in the future.

The vision of such a meeting to call for world peace moved Burt of Ohio to observe in addressing the bishops that "there is a sovereignty of man that is more important than the sovereignty of nations."

POLYGAMY

The conflict of polygamy and Christianity had concerned the Lambeth Conferences for at least eighty years, and at Lambeth X it remained unresolved.

As early as 1888, a Resolution of Lambeth III that carried by a vote of 83 to 21, said that persons living in polygamy should not be admitted to baptism but should be "accepted as candidates and kept under Christian instruction until such time as they shall be in a position to accept the law of Christ." (Another Resolution of Lambeth III, passed by a much slimmer margin, held that "the wives of polygamists may, in the opinion of this Conference, be admitted in some cases to baptism, but that it must be left to the local authorities of the Church to decide under what circumstances they may be baptised.")

In 1968, with polygamy still very much a part of some areas of the Anglican Communion, the Archbishop of West Africa, C. J. Patterson, said prior to the opening of Lambeth X that his province was hoping "for something more practically helpful than a statement that the introduction of monogamy into a polygamous society raises problems which have not yet been solved."

Another West African bishop said he longed for some fresh thinking beyond the usual viewpoint that whereas African society permitted what he called "simultaneous polygamy," Western society permitted "consecutive polygamy," and that one should be no more condemned than the other.

Chisolm of Melanesia asked for a Resolution that might encourage the relaxing of the rules that forced women in some cultures to accept economic destitution as a result of baptism.

The original Resolution, while proclaiming "monogamous lifelong marriage as God's will for mankind," did offer some help to those churches troubled by the strict stand of prior Lambeths, but the African evangelicals (mainly through the strong objection voiced by their archbishop, Erica Sabiti) succeeded in eliminating a sentence that recognized "that polygamy is a fact in some countries and that the abrupt termination of polygamous marriages may cause great suffering and great disruption to many."

The result was the watered-down Resolution No. 23 and the continuing lack of a strong directive from Lambeth. Considering the predominance of Western bishops, a clear-cut resolution might have been regarded as unpalatable dictation from men unfamiliar with the problem. On the other hand, little progress was seen in the Resolution's recommendation that each province "re-examine its discipline in such problems in consultation with other provinces in a similar situation." Perhaps it took the unwritten authority of a Lambeth to help the provinces toward fuller discussion and united action, but the tragedy was that many African priests were left floundering in their anxiety to bring souls to baptism.

Resolution No. 23 as finally approved at least had a different title —"Marriage Discipline" instead of "Polygamy." In it, the Conference recognized "that polygamy poses one of the sharpest conflicts between the Faith and particular cultures." It also stated that "the Church seeks to proclaim the will of God in setting out the clear implications of our Lord's teaching about marriage. Hence it bears witness to monogamous lifelong marriage as God's will for mankind. The Conference believes that such marriage alone bears adequate witness to the equal sanctity of all human beings which lies at the heart of the Christian revelation; yet recognizes that in every place many problems concerning marriage confront the Church."

THE THIRTY-NINE ARTICLES

The Lambeth fathers approached the Thirty-nine Articles as men who were going to clean out an attic but ended up by deciding not to throw anything away.[9]

The relevance of the Articles has been questioned many times from Lambeth III in 1888 through the mid-1960s when James Pike, then Bishop of California, lumped them with the doctrine of Trinity and other creedal beliefs as "excess baggage" that were stumblingblocks for people who might otherwise embrace the Church.

In a separate move, the Diocese of Maryland had asked the 1967 General Convention of the American church to remove the Articles from the Prayer Book; no action was taken, but the matter was referred to the Lambeth Conference.

Meanwhile, the Archbishop of Canterbury and the Archbishop of York appointed a doctrinal commission to study numerous issues, including the Articles. Its seventeen members included top English theologians, many of whom were official consultants to Lambeth X.

When it was found that the commission's first report would concern the Articles and would be ready by the start of Lambeth X, Canterbury made an optimistic announcement at his initial news conference. He said their findings constituted "an important document" for the Conference and that the Section on Faith would decide "what place the Thirty-nine Articles has."

During the question-period at Canterbury's news conference, John Redfern, the small, leathery, highly knowledgeable reporter for the *Daily Telegraph,* was incredulous at Lambeth's supposed in-

---

[9] The Thirty-nine Articles, a revision of Archbishop Cranmer's Forty-two Articles of 1553 as finally amended by Convocation in 1571, reflect sixteenth-century anti-Roman thinking colored by Calvinistic theology. They appear in most of the Prayer Books except for Scotland, India, South Africa, East Africa, Japan, and the Arabic version of the book used by the Archbishopric in Jerusalem. In East Africa the Articles are printed in the Swahili and English versions but not in most vernaculars.

terest in placing the Articles on its crowded agenda. "The Thirty-nine Articles are such a dead duck that for the Conference to consider it when so much else is happening in the world—it is astonishing!"

Unmoved by surprise or criticism, Canterbury calmly replied, "The Articles have differing degrees of importance to the different Churches."

The report was released six days later at a special news conference at St. Bride's Church, Fleet Street. It declined to propose any drastic alteration in the place of the Articles in Church life. In explanation the commission said that "the most practicable method of avoiding distress to those who are happy to assent to the Articles as they stand while at the same time easing the conscience of those who cannot at present make the required subscriptions without mental reservations, is to modify the formula of assent."

Instead of requiring assent to the Articles by ordinands and clergy, the commission suggested a new form: "I profess my firm and sincere belief in the faith set forth in the Scriptures and in the catholic Creeds and my allegiance to the doctrine of the Church. . . ." (In England, there would follow a preface which would include the Articles, and His Majesty's Declaration of 1628 would not be used.) The commission said its purpose was "to devise a form of assent which can be made with a good conscience."

The chairman, Ramsey of Durham, a stout North-Countryman, formerly Nolloth Professor of the Philosophy of the Christian Religion at Oxford, explained that the Articles had been under study "because the Church of England is concerned for truth and intellectual honesty."

In his distinctive accent ("miracle" became "merhel"), Durham concluded that "the Articles should be set squarely in historical context and the form of assent should be modified." Further, he said that he did not believe that retention of the Articles was a hindrance to unity since "the anti-Roman feeling is anti-Roman only to Rome of 1571."

The news conference ended in laughter when Durham commented, "We do not want to sweep the Thirty-nine Articles under the carpet but to send them to a stately home in England where we can visit them from time to time." [10]

The Church Times characterized the commission's report as "one of those ingenious compromises traditionally dear to the Anglican heart." The Articles were not revised and were still to be mentioned, albeit as a part of "the inheritance of faith." [11]

The bishops accepted the commission's report, adding to it (in Resolution No. 43) a suggestion that each church consider whether the Articles need to be bound up with its Prayer Book. The Conference also suggested that when subscription to the Articles is required it should be asked "only in the context of a statement which gives the full range of our inheritance of faith and sets the Articles in their historical context."

During the floor discussion the bishops appeared divided and curiously ill at ease: some were plainly bored; several evangelicals and others were obviously agitated, and at least a handful were deeply anxious that the Conference, with but an hour or so to remain in session, might take hasty, regrettable action.

Luxton of Huron, expressing fear the discussion should not be cut short in favor of accepting the commission's report, thought that ordinands would consider it "doubletalk" and that he would be hard put to explain to them such middle-of-the-road action. He concluded his brief speech with a proposal that the Conference suggest that assent to the Thirty-nine Articles be no longer required of ordinands.

---

[10] Looking back on the Commission's work, the Bishop of Durham pointed out in a letter to James B. Simpson in March, 1969, that "there has been an alternative suggestion, which I aired during the debate in the Church Assembly, that if the Articles ever cease to be bound up with the Prayer Book they might well form part of a manual containing certain historical documents not only of Anglicanism but of the Christian Church, to be a kind of doctrinal handbook of general interest."

[11] New interest in the Articles reminded the English to explain to visiting bishops that the word *article* once referred to a chamberpot. The explanation led to the revival of a story of Archbishop Fisher's complaint to Winston Churchill that there was insufficient furniture for the many bedrooms at Lambeth Palace. "Well," replied Churchill, "you have Thirty-nine Articles!"

The import of Huron's words was about the same as if he had suggested the Articles be abandoned altogether: there were protests from Brown of Quebec and Taylor of Cape Town, but Huron's motion passed. A count of votes on Resolution No. 43, demanded by Cape Town, disclosed thirty-seven dissenters, mainly English evangelicals.

At his final news conference the following week, Canterbury commented that, in his opinion, the plenary session had given too little thought to the subject. "I said at the beginning that I hoped the Conference would tackle the Thirty-nine Articles," he explained. "It did so, but I was very sorry it came right at the end of the Conference. That wasn't my fault. I pleaded that we should tackle it on the previous day, but some of the Conference thought it more important to tackle polygamy. [Laughter] I was very happy that the Conference endorsed the findings of the valuable Report on the Articles produced under the Bishop of Durham's chairmanship, and, indeed, took a rather more radical line than the [Durham] Report did, rather more radical though rather clumsy, last-moment line."

NATURE AND CREATION

"Nobody argued with nature!" an American reporter observed with relief after Resolution No. 6 on "responsible stewardship" of natural resources, glided through a plenary session with unanimous approval. It urged all Christians to act "in obedience to the doctrine of creation," to preserve natural resources and animal life. It also spoke of soil conservation and the prevention of pollution of air, soil, and water.

A related Resolution, No. 7, concerned the conservation of the ocean floor—"seabeds"—beyond the present national jurisdictions. As one of the nonagenda items, it received more time than some vital issues at the opening of Lambeth X.

The consensus of the resolution on seabeds was to give encouragement to the United Nations in establishing international jurisdiction of the ocean floor. The measure had a knowledgeable and articulate proponent in its proposer, Fleming of Norwich.

Many of the American bishops had as young men studied in England, but William Launcelot Scott Fleming was one of the few Englishmen who had gone to the U.S. for graduate work (he was a Commonwealth Fellow at Yale). Like a Jesuit scholar who excels in a nonreligious field of knowledge, Norwich was conversant with oceanography because of his experience as chaplain and geologist with the British Graham Land Expedition to the Antarctic (1934–1937), four years as a Navy chaplain, and two years as director of the Scott Polar Research Institute at Cambridge. Against that background he was able to word the Resolution with conviction right up to the closing line, which asked that the ocean floor "be conserved exclusively for peaceful purposes in perpetuity."

INTERNATIONAL TENSIONS

True to tradition, Lambeth X conveyed concern about troubled areas of the world without allowing any feelings of nationalism to intervene.

Like the Popes of Rome, the Lambeth fathers' need to witness to their beliefs was disciplined by a wisdom of restraint. As in past Lambeth Conferences, the bishops avoided offending governments of areas where the Church wished to work and felt that they should not make pronouncements that might seem to reflect the dominance of nationalities within the episcopate. As a result, the fighting in Vietnam was not the subject of a Resolution, nor was it directly mentioned in the reports. Rhodesia escaped any direct notice as did apartheid in South Africa, and no attempt was made to advise the U.S. on its racial and urban problems, or Britain on its rising influx of emigrants from India and the West Indies.

Similarly, no resolution was made on the Soviet invasion of Czechoslovakia, although the bishops expressed their prayerful concern for it as well as Biafra in special services at the Abbey and at St. Margaret's, Westminster.

On the matter of the Southern Sudan, a troubled area for more than a decade, the bishops afforded themselves the mildly worded Resolution No. 13 of sympathy and assurance of prayer for Christians who had persevered "during the past years of testing of the Church." It was proposed by Allison of the Sudan after a moving address in which he read aloud from a smudged and tattered letter written in pencil by one of his priests "from deep in the jungle forest" on the day that Lambeth X convened. The priest, who had not been heard from in three years, encouraged the bishops as much as himself in quoting Jesus' words in the Gospel of Matthew, "Go ye therefore and teach all nations. . . ."

The Resolution was readily seconded by Wani of Northern Uganda, whose diocese had aided many of the refugee Sudanese.

The comments from the floor were opened by Stuart of Georgia, who represented a diocese in the heart of America's Southland, and objected to a reference to "southern problems," reminding the bishops that "there are other southern worlds where there are other problems."

Mwang'ombe of Mombasa (Province of East Africa) warned that "the mention of one government in this Conference will spoil what we have done." Instead, he suggested, "Let us pray for Africa and for England, where there are many color bars. There are also many problems in America. Leave out the Sudan." Mombasa was answered by Welles of West Missouri, who suggested that the reference to the Sudan government be changed to "responsible authorities" and that "southern problems" should be changed to "existing problems." Once that was done, he said, his own deep conviction was that "God knows all our problems and we are grateful when others help us recognize them. I think that when the saintly Bishop in the Sudan asks us for a resolution we ought to uphold it." The amendment was seconded by Brown of St. Edmundsbury & Ipswich, for fifteen years a missionary priest in India and later the first Archbishop of Uganda. It became part of Resolution No. 13.

Careful maneuvering of legislation also saved the bishops from international offense in Resolution No. 14 on the war between Nigeria and the breakaway state of Biafra. It was a complicated problem made more sensitive by the predominance of the British within the Anglican Communion.

The decision to call a special Saturday-morning plenary session to deal with the matter was reached after the bishops had seen demonstrations in London streets and in many other ways felt the pressures of warfare and the thousands starving in Biafra. They were poignantly reminded of it by the presence of a Lambeth delegation of nineteen West Africans and by the position of bishops of the Church of England who, as men holding office in an established church, owed allegiance to the government that was allowing the sale of arms to Nigeria, its former colony.

To their great credit, the West African bishops themselves, who might easily have been a tragically split group, came forth with a statement for the Conference's consideration. The group, meeting for the first time since the outbreak of the war, included six bishops from dioceses within the new state of Biafra and five from the areas loyal to the Nigerian Military Government,[12] along with others from the province of the Church of West Africa whose areas were not directly concerned in the war.

Their first action, shortly after Lambeth convened, was to cable a message of encouragement to Addis Ababa where the Emperor of Ethiopia was attempting to negotiate peace.

The principal figures at the plenary session on August 16 were Archbishop Patterson and C. K. Sansbury, Assistant Bishop of London, who had been asked by Canterbury to make a special study of the situation.

London-born Cecil Patterson, who went to the Diocese of Niger as a missionary in 1934, was introduced by Canterbury. Speaking from the dais, Patterson prefaced his remarks by saying that the bishops of West Africa had decided among themselves that they would remain silent during debate from the floor. At the Lambeth Conference, he said, they had renewed friendships as well as a common fellowship in Christ "and we don't want to spoil it by having the type of situation that arose at Uppsala where, despite a balanced and wise statement, an unedifying wrangle nevertheless took

---

[12] From Biafra: Cecil Patterson, Bishop of Niger, who also was Archbishop of West Africa, and his assistant bishop; Niger Delta and assistant; Cwerri and assistant. From Nigeria: the bishops of Benin, Ekiti, and Lagos, and Ibadan and his assistant.

place." Moreover, he said, "This is no place where the tangled story of Nigeria should be rehashed. If one brought out an inflammatory remark, another might feel that a retort should be made."

Patterson said that he and his fellow bishops were "seeking the advice of the Lambeth Conference for the road we should take . . . so we as bishops can exercise a reconciling ministry." Finally, before going to the prepared statement of the bishops,[13] he disclosed that Emperor Haile Selassie had cabled a reply asserting his belief "that the present talks in Addis Ababa can bear fruitful results only if Almighty God guides our deliberations. Remember us in your prayers."

In reply, Bishop Sansbury read a proposed Resolution that, he said, had been worked out with the West Africans' statement close at hand. Skillfully avoiding any hint of partisanship, it expressed gratitude for the efforts of the Church and others to promote peace and reconciliation.

In seconding the Resolution, Wilson of Chichester reminded the Conference that it should "make the world see that we are a reconciling body."

A consultant, the Rev. John Taylor, CMS General Secretary, said he found the Resolution overly complacent. The same reaction was expressed by the newly consecrated Bishop of Mashonaland, Paul Burrough, formerly chaplain to immigrants in Birmingham, who said, "I could not sit here, having sat in the dust and tears of Nigerians and Biafrans, and give assent to anything which does not call directly on Her Majesty's Government to cease sending arms to either side."

The only African who spoke was the Bishop of Burundi (of the province of Uganda, Rwanda, and Burundi) who appealed to Canterbury to designate one Sunday when the whole Church could pray for West Africa. "God is the only one who can stop this war," he said.

Before the morning was out, Resolution No. 14 passed with no

---

[13] The statement of the West African bishops was later printed in full in the Conference Report in reference to Resolution No. 14.

objections.[14] It gave thanks for the compassion and reconciliation of the West African bishops, urged prayer and work for peace,
and in its strongest recommendation said that the Lambeth Conference would welcome "any agreement between the belligerent parties to provide channels for the supply of goods, medicine, and
clothing to those in need." Secondly, it called on governments "to
engage in a massive intergovernmental relief operation on both
sides of the conflict. . . ."

An offstage drama that failed to make the headlines which its
sponsors had hoped for was the arrival of a nine-year-old American
girl, Melanie Nix of Perth Amboy, N.J., bearing a letter from the
American Committee to Keep Biafra Alive. The child flew from
New York to London with a Roman Catholic missionary priest to
bring the messages addressed to the Archbishop of Canterbury and
to Pope Paul. She did not see the Archbishop but instead was given
an informal conference with the Bishop of Cariboo and photographed exchanging the letter for the Conference's statement on
Nigeria and Biafra.

---

[14] In another Resolution on international matters, No. 15, Lambeth X expressed its concern for "the continuing tensions . . . [and] tragic plight of
hundreds of thousands of Arab refugees." Feeling no need to go into detail, it
merely endorsed the stand taken by the World Council of Churches and urged
"men of good will to use their influence in each nation and in the United
Nations toward the finding of a just solution."

CHAPTER 7

LAMBETH AND MINISTRY

THE MAJOR ISSUES CENTERING around the renewal of the Church in Ministry were flagged long before the bells of Westminster rang out for the convening of Lambeth X. They included an evaluation of the diaconate and its potentialities, clarification of the status of deaconesses, and the possibility of women's ordination to the priesthood—subjects that triggered intense reactions, although it is doubtful if the prolonged debates really changed many minds.

The topics were, in the words of the Archbishop of York, "as plentiful as buttercups in an English field in springtime." He was referring to an agenda that, among other matters, called for a thorough examination of the role of the laity and a study of the nature of the Anglican episcopate.

As head of the Ministry Section, York obviously had the top job in the area where his principal interests lay. His opinions came through strongly in numerous speeches, sermons, and papers all during the months preceding Lambeth X. His address to the opening plenary session set the pattern for the Ministry Section's work and, to a great extent, pointed the way to many of the conclusions eventually drawn in the Ministry Report.

Above all else, York was intent on furthering the ordination of women; his determination to force his convictions on the Conference led some bishops to characterize his efforts as heavy-handed and his resolutions as loaded. In the end, he undertook to "clarify" the Resolution by adding key words the bishops had not approved. Early in the Conference, Shevill of North Queensland objected to York's directiveness, but York persisted undeterred and in the final session of Lambeth X some bishops, notably Trevor Huddleston and the Assistant of Zanzibar & Tanga, were still objecting loudly.

At fifty-nine, Donald Coggan looked far younger than his years; his straw-colored hair, schoolmaster manner, and preoccupation with intricacies of the New Testament, belied his aggressiveness; but behind his rimless glasses and cautious smile lay an iron will devoted to the domination of evangelical low-churchmanship.

York's position at the head of England's second most prestigious see had been determined, like so many other ecclesiastical appointments, by the Prime Minister who, legally, is not required to be an Anglican—nor a Christian. Fortunately for the choice of top leadership, "the P.M." in 1961 was Harold Macmillan, himself an active churchman and an admirer of Michael Ramsey, then Archbishop of York. Macmillan passed over Fisher's choice, rumored to be Robert Stopford, then Bishop of Peterborough, in favor of Ramsey, but as a concession to the low-church faction, Macmillan permitted Coggan, then Bishop of Bradford, to be recommended for appointment as ninety-third Archbishop of York.

By the time Lambeth X came along, Ramsey and Coggan had settled comfortably into their archiepiscopal roles: in a relaxed fashion they maintained the counterbalance of churchmanship that has existed before between Canterbury and York. It was no surprise therefore that York's chairmanship of the Ministry Section meant that it would be a voice of low churchmanship, with far-reaching consequences for clergy and laity alike. Had Michael Ramsey or a man of similar tradition still been at York and at the head of the Ministry Section, the reports and resolutions might have taken an entirely different turn.

York was Lecturer in Semitic Languages and Literature at Manchester University prior to his ordination and, after three years as a curate of a London parish, he went back to the academic life as Professor of New Testament Studies at Wycliffe College, Toronto. He returned to England in 1944 as Principal of the London College of Divinity, a post he retained until consecration as third Bishop of Bradford in 1956.

Out of his own scholarly pursuits as well as his years as professor and bishop, York drew a reasoned approach to the ministry in his address to Lambeth's opening session.

He spoke first of the ministers of God as persons " 'apprehended by Christ Jesus my Lord.' " And "that 'apprehension,' that domination by such a Lord," he said, "is the very essence of his ministry."

"What is the authority for his ministry?" York asked. "It is the strand of the authority which is *inherent in the word we proclaim.* The mighty acts of God in Christ, wrought out on the plane of human history, the stuff of which the Gospel is made, have an authority of their own into which their minister enters as he does his work."

York touched briefly on his interest in seeing restoration of deacons as a distinctive order in the Church, as Lambeth IX had recommended. He spoke out strongly for the need to clarify the status of deaconesses. Then he turned to the major portion of his address and interest—the ordination of women:

"Here in England we are suffering desperately because of our timidity and disastrous ambivalence of attitude. We are losing our most able women and losing them in great numbers from the recognized spheres of service in the Church. . . . The social services are the richer—very much the richer—for our folly; but that is small excuse for our failure. . . . Too long have we allowed women of ability and experience to be inferior in status, in general estimation, and in security of tenure of office, to the raw curate who comes to his parish straight from college at the age of twenty-three; too long have we grudgingly allowed her to inch her way into the ministry of the Church instead of welcoming her with gratitude for the gifts and insights which only a woman can bring."

York moved swiftly to the challenge. "Let us think hard and speak clearly on the question of women and the priesthood, but let us not get bogged down in it, for the matter is far wider and more far-reaching even than this. And one further parting shot before I leave this subject: is it not strange that, in an age which, as I believe rightly, is producing ecumenical theological colleges, so very little is being done in training men and women *together* for the ministry of Christ's Church?"

Twelve days later, in presenting the Draft Report of his Section, York did not go immediately to prime topics; he first mentioned what he considered to be a less than adequate reference to the work of suffragans and assistant bishops. "There has been some distilling that will need expansion by those who distilled it," he said.

Knapp-Fisher of Pretoria (South Africa), one of the members of the highly articulate Committee on Priesthood, did not agree, commenting later in the morning that at one point the Draft was four times as long as the one in the bishops' hands.

Vaughan of British Hondurus faulted the Draft's generalized approach, and reminded the Lambeth Fathers that the purpose of renewal was neither repair nor renovation. "What we should be doing here is seeing whether God is about some new thing," he said. "It is a problem of perception—like the American bishop watching a test match who sees but does not understand it." Vaughan went on to say that there was too much in the Draft "about parochial structure and not enough about global structure, nothing about the missionary structure of congregations or the spiritual life of clergy."

Urging that a thoughtful revision be undertaken, Hondurus said, tongue-in-cheek, "I take it you do not want essays from retired bishops or letters from retired archbishops!" [1]

---

[1] He was obviously referring to Lord Fisher's endless stream of letters to the Church and secular press, typified by a letter that had appeared that day in *The Times*. The bishops burst into laughter, and Canterbury was almost bent double.

Canterbury had foreseen the general outlines of the Ministry Section's work, if not what York was promoting, when he told his news conference that the ministry committees would be "concerned with the many varieties of Christian ministry both ordained and lay, including the services Christians give when they immerse themselves in the communities about them." Whatever his dissatisfactions with the Report, he was able to say at the end of the Conference that "there's some good stuff within the Report, in my humble judgment . . ." [2]

THE LAITY

"We begin with a consideration of the renewal of the ministry of the laity because we believe that it is here that the greatest spiritual and human resources of the ministry of the whole Church reside," declared the final Report of the Ministry Section.

---

[2] *Those who spoke from the floor at the plenary session on Ministry, August 8, included:*

Dublin, Hines (USA), Sydney, Central Africa, Uganda, Hong Kong, Singapore, Seoul, Jesselton, Iran, British Honduras, Jamaica, Pretoria, Polynesia, Gippsland, Armidale, North Queensland, St. Andrews, New Guinea, Kurunagala, Nagpur, Barrackpore, James Bay, Calgary, Ottawa, Huron, Suffragan of Oregon, California, Rochester (USA), Fond du Lac, West Missouri, Ossory, Moray, Kilmore, Stockport, Woolwich, Knaresborough, Middleton, Wakefield, Bradford, Chester, Trapp of USPG, Woolwich, Barking, Stafford, Croydon, Colchester, Salisbury, St. Edmundsbury, Leicester, Peterborough, Winchester, and the Assistant Bishops of Zanzibar, Sheffield, and London.

Observers were Athenagoras, Beazley, Coventry, Chandran, Huxtable, Ignatiew, Parthenios, Purdy, Ryan, Toumayan, Schlingensiepen, Van Kleef.

Consultants were Batten, Green, Jenkins, Macquarrie, Luwum, Nineham.

At the final plenary session on Ministry, August 22: East Africa, Sydney, Durham, Coventry, Southwark, Chelmsford, Lexington, Lichfield, Dacca, Pretoria, Exeter, Hong Kong, Grafton, Nassau, Chester, Derby, Limerick, Kurunagala, Swansea, Gibraltar, Canberra, Minnesota, Milwaukee, Mbale, Gippsland, Ottawa, George, Montreal, Polynesia, Barrackpore, Killaloe, St. Johns, Adelaide, Oxford, Malawi, Nova Scotia, Ely, Nelson, Gloucester, Masasi, Calgary, Peterborough, Birmingham, Iran, Western Michigan, Leicester, Johannesburg, Riverina, Wellington, St. Albans, Portsmouth, Whitby, Minnesota, Oklahoma, Zanzibar, Colchester, Lynn, Guildford, Alabama, and Bishop Bayne.

Such a comprehensive conclusion had been a long time in the making: its development at Lambeth IX had been encouraged by four assemblies of the World Council of Churches (two of them since Lambeth IX), and had been the subject of the Vatican II Decree on the Apostolate of the Laity.

"Too sharp a distinction has been made between clergy and laity," one of the Lambeth reports had asserted in 1958. "There is a ministry for every member of Christ; every man and woman who is confirmed is commissioned to that ministry in the Church, the home, the community, the world of business, and social life."

Lambeth X took up the theme, doubtful perhaps that it would be able to contribute much that was new, but still eager to remind itself and the faithful that "the whole people of God exists as the Church for God and for the world, not for the sake of the Church."

In his preparatory essay, "Laymen in Mission," Canon Webster,[3] Professor of Missions at Shelley Oak College, Birmingham, caught the imagination of many when he wrote, "The porch of every church building throughout the world opens onto a missionary situation. . . . To support 'foreign' missions—or to depend on them—while neglecting missions on one's doorstep is to deny the very nature and purpose of the Church. The front line of the local or neighborhood mission is the laity."

Another excellent essay in the same area was contributed by James Mark, a member of the staff of the Ministry of Overseas Development. In a paper entitled "Laymen in Ministry," he spoke out for "more opportunity in the pulpit to laymen who have the necessary theological insight to be able to speak from their experience of the world and who will speak not merely as substitutes for the clergy."

Mark's thesis was that there were many jobs that a layman could

---

[3] The evangelical influence of the London College of Divinity was well represented in the Ministry Section through Douglas Webster, a faculty member during Coggan's administration; the Rev. J. Luwum from Uganda, one of Coggan's former students; and the Rev. Michael Green, lecturer in New Testament. The Bishop of Cariboo followed Coggan in his first London curacy, did graduate work under him, and later joined the faculty.

perform, sometimes more effectively, even though there was a presumption ("but not, alas, a certainty") that the priest can perform them best. "A peculiar responsibility rests upon the clergy," he said. "They have to encourage the laity to recognize the problems (in the Church's structure and life) and to consider how their responsibilities may be changing."

In looking over the Draft Report, some of the bishops thought that the Ministry Section had picked up an eloquent definition of the Church in a statement made by the Fourth Assembly of the World Council of Churches,[4] but Michael Green, an Anglican priest among the observers, brought them up short with the comment that he was astounded "that we have to look to the World Council of Churches to see what the Church is to be." As a result, the rather flowery definition was deleted from the Report.

James Bay, Suffragan of Moosonee (Canada) said the listing of lay ministries should include the office of catechist, "a word and function which has a real meaning to our African brethren and also in the Indian work in Northern Canada." He added that "the work of the catechist is the seeding-ground for the indigenous ministry."

Another consultant who was also heard and heeded—very widely heeded, indeed—was the only woman among the group, buxom, gray-haired, plainly dressed Mollie Batten.[5] Her major contribution concerned the diaconate and priesthood, but her comments on laity were praised by Canterbury in his final news conference. "There are some good things [in the Report] about the role of laymen in society," he said. "Although personally I valued immensely the utterance of Miss Mollie Batten from the gallery, a

---

[4] The Church, it said, is "a community of joyous people who have a hope and a message for the world, who are capable of forgiving, who fight for economic justice and human dignity, who are concerned for the sick and the despised, who support and defend the responsible freedom of scientific research and the arts."

[5] The Bishop of Coventry, Chairman of the Subcommittee on Laymen in Mission, publicly thanked Canon Webster and Miss Batten when he presented his group's findings. "Miss Batten was the only laity around when we discussed laity," he said, "but one ounce of Batten is worth ten stones of non-Batten laity!"

warning about having high hopes of an extended diaconate, and she warned us against turning laymen into pseudo-clergymen. We want laymen to serve God and the Church without an additional laying on of hands and a kind of half-clerical collar before they start doing so. But that's just personal judgment, and my personal judgment has never been excluded or resented in the course of the Conference." There was laughter and Canterbury added, amid more laughter, "I don't see why it should be reputed altogether!"

The Report on the Laity, in the Ministry Section, represented considerable coordination, including, as it did, laymen in mission, headed by Coventry; laymen in society, with Natal as chairman; and laymen in ministry, with Southwark as chariman.

The Report, as finally accepted, acknowledged the need to "reflect in contemporary forms, the abiding truth that 'there are differences of ministries, but the same Lord.' "

The Report called the laity to mission and vocation, to a program of action in the congregation and in the life of the world. It urged the laity to action which would bring Christian insights to bear on decisions that the layman and others may make in the world. Most of all it called on laymen to give Christian witness by "sharing with others the experience of God's love."

The spirit of the Report was borne out in four resolutions. "The Conference recommends that no major issue in the life of the Church should be decided without the full participation of the laity in discussion and in decision," said Resolution No. 24, setting forth the thrust of the thinking.

CHRISTIAN INITIATION

Lambeth X found itself probing the very foundations of the Faith when two committees of the Ministry Section raised serious questions about "the apparent ineffectiveness in certain parts of the Anglican Communion of the present practice of Christian initiation —baptism, confirmation, and first communion."

It was suggested in the Draft Report that the churches might want to follow an experimental scheme that had been used in East Africa and in two English dioceses, Chelmsford and Southwark: the blessing of a child at a service of thanksgiving, with baptism and confirmation delayed until the individual could make his own mature decision for confessing the Faith.

The proposal came under sharp attack from the bishops when Stockwood of Southwark proposed it as a Resolution. The first to question it was Ramsey of Durham: "What is the theology implied in the service? How do we relate it to the theology of grace? I should like to know what has happened to the view that without baptismal grace, children are lost. That is an old doctrine, if not one of the most cheerful, and it was one of great effect. I'd like a better map at this theological junction. I can't vote in favor of it at the present time, at least until clarifications are made."

Seemingly taken aback, Southwark replied, "Well, there's no intention of foisting it upon the whole Anglican Communion." He said its need was deeply felt by "some members of the clergy in some parts of England who are concerned about indiscriminate baptism of infants."

The other diocesan who had permitted the use of the service, Tiarks of Chelmsford, explained that "when parents are not ready to make promises, the service is designed to show the love of God for all children. The attempt is to make infant baptism more relevant—not just a social custom, but a religious service."

Durham, however, had already won supporters, among them Moody of Lexington (Kentucky), who said, "I have been watching Baptists do this kind of service for twenty years. They have been forced to it by our baptism of infants. It has only a vague meaning for parents. . . . At ordination, a priest is given power to bless in God's name. Do we need to pass a Resolution to enable a priest to do that?"

Reeve of Lichfield cautioned the bishops: "If we pass the Resolution, we will be giving the whole Communion the impression that the service is being advocated. There is no guarantee that the child will be brought to baptism later."

Southwark continued his defense: "It is no denial of infant baptism, but it now appears that either way we vote on the Resolution it will be an embarrassment."

The motion that no vote be taken was made by Blair of Dacca

(still called East Bengal by some of the bishops who had known him at Lambeth IX before his diocese changed its name after its separation from the Diocese of Calcutta).

Although the Resolution was killed, two alternatives remained in the Ministry Report. One plan was for baptized children to be admitted to the Holy Communion and their confirmation delayed until later. The other plan was for simultaneous baptism and confirmation for infants who would be admitted to the Holy Communion at an early age and then, much later, would appear before a bishop when "capable of making a responsible commitment."

Both plans were flawed in their inability to keep track of large numbers of people well enough to shepherd them through the vaguely defined processes. Objections had also been registered by some of the observers. One of them, Athenagoras, the ranking Greek Orthodox prelate in Britain, said bluntly, "When we depart from the apostolic experience we do not contribute to the unity of Christianity." Another, an American, George Beazley of the Churches of Christ, whose church baptizes only adults, pointed out that admission to the Holy Communion before confirmation "becomes a problem in the ecumenical scheme because we have always considered confirmation as the Anglican churches' confession of Faith, which is what other churches require before people can receive Holy Communion."

Dr. Beazley's caution caused a last-minute change in the printed Report, in which the recommendation was extended to read: "Experiment along the first of these alternative lines should include careful examination of the bearing of this separation in ecumenical dialogue with (a) those holding to believers' baptism and (b) the Orthodox churches. In both instances, the intimate relationship of baptism and confirmation with admission to the Holy Communion is a matter of major importance."

FELLOWSHIPS FOR CHURCHWOMEN

Lambeth's concern for women centered around the movement to integrate them with the whole of the laity and, some hoped, with the priesthood. It was not an "in" thing to be much concerned with women's organizations as such; from the summit of Lambeth they seemed irrelevant, although many bishops knew such organizations to be powerful achievers and fund-raisers; indeed, the Lambeth fathers appeared to sit through the discussion of fellowships for churchwomen with a definite look of forbearance.

That being the mood of the Conference, no one envied Gordon Strutt of Stockport, Suffragan to Chester, as he presented Resolution No. 30 drawn up by the Subcommittee on Ministry of the Laity. He began by reminding his listeners that women and their work had been much in evidence at Lambeth X through the hospitality extended to bishops and their wives, especially the clubs and lounges "at the top of this house, Your Grace." When he commended the Fellowships of Churchwomen for being wide open to all women of the Church ("as wide open as the church door") he was obviously referring to the Mothers' Union and its stand against admitting divorcees to membership.[6] He said, however, that fellowships were "not set up in opposition to the Mothers' Union, which has its own standards [and] is prepared to stand by them and remain a force within the Church."

The Resolution was seconded by a Canadian, Steer of Saskatoon. "I cannot claim, Your Grace, to have the intimate knowledge of churchwomen that the Bishop of Stockport has," he said, provoking Lambeth's single burst of bawdy laughter. "But we must be careful not to suggest that women are peculiar creatures who do not otherwise have a place in the life of the Church. For that reason I am glad that we call it a fellowship and not an organization: we should be sorry to see another organization grow up in the Church!"

After a seconding speech by Housden of Newcastle (New South Wales), the Resolution passed unanimously. A tidy statement, it

---

[6] At Canterbury's first news conference, a woman who identified herself as "a member of the Mothers' Union as well as the press" asked if Lambeth X would give further direction on the Church's stand on divorce. Pointedly avoiding the term *divorce*, Canterbury said: "The Churches [of the Anglican Communion] have their own rules about marriage . . . and those rules are partially influenced by the Lambeth Conference, but since it is a nonlegislative body it cannot give a directive to the Mothers' Union."

declared that "The Conference welcomes the appearance of Fellowships for Churchwomen in various parts of the Anglican Communion and commends the development and extension of those
associations for an increase of devotion and neighborliness and for
witness to the faith of Jesus Christ."

PRIESTHOOD

The possibility of ordaining women, and of granting laymen
many of the priestly functions, somewhat overshadowed the efforts
of Lambeth X to speak directly to the traditional office of the priest.
For that reason, the preparatory paper by Leslie Houlden, Fellow
and Chaplain of Trinity College, Oxford, took on added meaning.
"The priest is to be a priest, whole and integrated, not a layman
doing priestly tasks," he wrote. "The priest is to take hold of his
whole personality, so that he lives what he is. It should be meaning-
less to ask of any of his significant thoughts or actions whether he is
acting as a priest or as himself."

A similar theme ran through the Ministry Report. "The understanding of the ministry of the whole people of God (the *laos*)
means that the special function of the priest is all the more emphasized," it declared. "He is the representative of the whole Church,
ordained by the bishop to preside at the Eucharist and to pronounce
in the name of the Church the reconciling and renewing forgiveness
of God. . . . He has to stand for God to the people of God who are
going out to serve God and find God in the world. A clearer understanding of the ministry of the laity demands a corresponding
clarity about the special ministry of the priest and bishop."

The Committee on the Priesthood, headed by Reindorp of Guildford, a wartime chaplain and keen skier, pointed out varying
aspects.

On the priesthood of Christ: "Christ offers his perfect obedience to the Father on behalf of mankind, and so He perfectly ful-
fills the priestly vocation of all men."

On the priesthood of the Church: "*All* Christians share in the
priesthood of their Lord. This is the primary order of ministry in

the Church to which *all* Christians are consecrated by baptism, and which in union with Christ they fulfill by offering the diversity of their lives, abilities, and work to God."

On the ordained ministry: "In order that all the members of the Church may grow up into the fullness of that priesthood, Christ calls and empowers some to be priests of the priestly people. . . . In presiding at the Eucharist a priest is seen as an agent of Christ, of the Church, and of the bishop; for a priest as well as a bishop is a focus and symbol of the unity in Christ of all his people. That unity of bishop, priest, and people is obscured unless the relationship between them is seen to be a continuing reality."

A section on vocation was added to the Report at the urging of an observer, the Rev. John Coventry, S.J., Secretary of the Roman Catholic Ecumenical Commission for England and Wales. "It is not sufficiently brought out in the preliminary Report," he said, "that within the priesthood itself there are various ways of being a priest. For instance, it seems to exclude contemplative vocations. It would be a pity if the Conference lost sight of that. Then there are also the priest-scholars, serving the needs of God's Church, yet not in a pastoral ministry. What separates a priest from any other ministry is his devotion to the Eucharist. . . ."

Also as a result of the Jesuit's prompting, the expanded Report declared: "God calls to the ordained ministry people of various gifts in a variety of ways, and their ministry must be exercised in a wide variety of circumstances. Some, for example, are called to a parochial ministry, some to a ministry of scholarship or teaching, some to community life. Others may fulfill their ministry in the context of professional, business, or industrial life, but whatever the circumstances priesthood always involves pastoral responsibility within a particular community."

In developing a commentary on vocations, the Ministry Report gave added attention to seminaries. "Many of those engaged in training men for the ministry today are showing courage and vision in their readiness to experiment with new methods," it said. "Any period of training is also essentially a time when vocation is tested. Called by God to serve a world in turmoil, priests must be helped in their training both before and after ordination to that faithfulness in prayer and study which is the indispensable foundation of their ministry."

In a section headed "The Work of a Priest," the Report spoke of the ordained man in a multiple role as priest, pastor, and prophet: "As *priest* he serves by faithful obedience in prayer and worship, in ministering the sacraments and in absolving sinners. As *pastor* he serves in gladly accepting the discipline imposed upon his time, his energy, and his compassion. . . . As *prophet* he serves in proclaiming God's word, not only in preaching but in pronouncing God's judgment on sin and His mercy in forgiveness, and in equipping and renewing God's people for mission."

The description of the priest as prophet was questioned by Mortimer of Exeter. "These words are so general they would describe the prophet Isaiah!" he told his fellow bishops, adding that it might be improved upon and that his objection would be heard beyond the confines of the conference room. The Report, however, was not changed.

Other objections were registered by Knapp-Fisher of Pretoria (South Africa), who said he found no mention of "the power of penance," and by Sansbury, Assistant Bishop of London, who thought the report lacked recognition of "those ordained to the priesthood in the context of the royal priesthood of the whole Church."

Treacy of Wakefield pleaded for emphatic reference to the indelible character of the priesthood. He said that "any other ways of speaking of it other than irrevocable and indelible would be mistaken, and even if that concept should result in fewer men being ordained, it would not worry me." Although the Draft had described the priesthood as "no merely temporary or functional office" and had declared that "ordination, no less than baptism, is irrevocable," those admirable references were lost in the preparation of the final Report. It was not certain that the Report intended to refer to indelibility when it made a passing reference to contemporary perplexity about the meaning "of a ministry which calls for sanctity, lifelong commitment, and constant renewal."

(The "sure foundation" of such a Ministry, the Report said, "is the calling and abiding faithfulness of God, and it is in that assurance that every priest can find fulfillment and joy.")

One of the consultants, D. E. Nineham, Regius Professor of Divinity at Cambridge, expressed considerable disappointment in the Draft Report:

"The question in the mind of many young people is, 'What good can I do for the Gospel and humanity as a priest that I could not do as a teacher or social worker on a full-time basis?' Many struggle with that question. What is it that bishops and priests do for and in the Church of God? What sort of people do we need? How do we train them? And how should the structure be organized to help them do their work as well as possible? Those questions are not answered in the lines on the priesthood."

Nineham also questioned the indelibility of priesthood, adding, "Can men at the age of twenty-three irrevocably commit themselves?"

The Draft Report ran into more trouble when it tackled the terms *priest* and *presbyter*.

"Even though philologically ... identical, and indeed interchangeable, the complete abandonment of the term 'priest' would mean impoverishment, since it is associated with sacrifice, which is an essential mark of the life of a minister of the crucified and risen Lord," the Draft declared.

"Cromwell said, 'Presbyter is priest writ large,' consultant John Macquarrie reminded the bishops.[7] "But I am for one-syllable rather than three-syllable words."

---

[7] Dr. Macquarrie's reference was to a poem, "On the New Forcers of Conscience Under the Long Parliament," written by John Milton in defense of Cromwell in 1646: "Because you have thrown off your Prelate Lord,/ And with stiff Vows renounc'd his Liturgy/ To seize the widow'd whore Plurality/ From them whose sin ye envied, not abhorr'd,/ Dare ye for this adjure the Civil Sword/ To force our Consciences that Christ set free,/ And ride us with a classic Hierarchy/... Men whose Life, Learning, Faith and pure intent/ Would have been held in high esteem with Paul/ Must now be nam'd and printed Heretics/... But we do hope to find out all your tricks,/ Your plots and packing worse than those of Trent,/ That so the Parliament/ May with their wholesome and preventive Shears/ Clip your Phylacteries, though

Another point of view was expressed by consultant Michael Green, who said that "the word 'presbyter' refers to lay ministers in the New Testament; 'presbyter' is not the same as a priest." He charged that the Draft offered many different priestly references without definition "and, in turn, many different meanings were given to priesthood—meanings that change as swiftly as the lights in Piccadilly and are as different."

The upshot was that the portions where the controversial words were used were rewritten, and in accomplishing the task the previous mention of sacrifice was lost to the Report. The rewording, however, enabled the Report to reach an intensity of religious eloquence it might otherwise have missed: "Only as a priest remains close to Christ and all his members by daily persevering in personal prayer and by taking his proper part in the Church's worship, can he grow in his ministry of service to God and man. A priest, himself a sinful man, is set apart by Christ in ordination to minister to Christians living within the tension between nature and grace—a tension which he shares—in order that he and they may be transformed into Christ's likeness. It is immaterial whether in his office he be described as priest or presbyter, provided it is recognized that his ministry is both ordained by Christ Himself and acknowledged by God's people."

In a brief explanation, if not apology, the Archbishop of York assured the Conference that the Ministry Section had "used care in choice of language." York said that it had "arrived at a language which would not be offensive to or misunderstood by people of cultural backgrounds different from those of us who have had the Faith for many centuries."

In conclusion the Report returned to its orientation, the preparatory paper by Leslie Houlden, by asserting that the priest who perseveres faithfully in his vocation will discover that "the work which he has undertaken and the skills which he acquires, far from being a superficial layer on top of his 'real personality,' becomes wholly in-

---

baulk your Ears,/ and su:cour our just Fears,/ When they shall read this clearly in your charge:/ *New Presbyter* is but *Old Priest* writ Large."

tegrated with himself. If a man becomes a priestly man, he can never cease to be what he is."

As Resolution No. 31, passed with but a few dissents, it said, "The Conference commends the study of the paragraphs on 'Priesthood' in the Report of Section II as an Anglican contribution towards an understanding of the nature of priesthood in the present ecumenical situation."

A WIDER ORDAINED MINISTRY

A realistic evaluation of the "great gulf" between theoretical recognition and real recognition of every member of the Church as a minister of Christ—as well as its threatening aspects for ordained clergymen—was offered by Eric James, Canon Residentiary of Southwark, in his preparatory paper for the Committee on Voluntary and Part-time Ministries.

"It is one thing to be doing this and that because 'the Vicar asked me'—or even to see what one is doing and being asked to do as part of ministry in general," he wrote. "It is quite another for each local church to know itself deeply responsible for recruiting the supplying part of the commissioned and empowered ministry and for there to be organic and objective ways of calling such a ministry into being."

Further, wrote Canon James, "it will not be easy to knit into a team those who are on Church pay and those who are on secular pay, those who have university qualifications and those who are not so equipped intellectually: it never has been, but here is another opportunity for the Church's words on fellowship to be more than words."

Moreover, he foresaw that "the ordination of self-supporting laymen to sacramental functions could go a long way to destroy the stranglehold of clerical bureaucracy. . . . [It] may be for this and for many other reasons one of the Church's great advances in our time."

A more specific view was taken in the Report. Acknowledging that in a wider ordained ministry "the Church may be continually renewed for mission," it said that "in this variety of ministry the part-time nonstipendiary priest is in no way inferior to his full-time stipendiary brother." It predicted that "the need for priests who will earn their living wholly or in part in some nonecclesiastical occupation" would arise where clergymen are grossly overworked, where communities have not been evangelized, and where finances are severely limited.

In short, Lambeth X was attempting to outline diversification in ministries to fit the diversification of need.

"Because of the particular demands which the part-time ministry will make on a man's character and faith, as much care should be taken in his selection as with any candidate for the full-time ministry," cautioned the Report. "Candidates must be experienced Christians, mature in outlook, acceptable alike to Church authority and to the community they are to serve. No considerations of urgency or expediency should be accepted as excuses for ordaining men to this ministry without adequate training."

The head of the Committee on Voluntary and Part-Time Ministries, Bryan of Barrackpore, told the Lambeth fathers that "in remote areas what we need is not supplementary ministers but supplementary priests." He said that "no single member of the committee was in favor of the permanent diaconate."

East Africa, vice-chairman of the Ministry Section, commented from the floor that "the supplementary ministry may become the norm in some of the newer churches."

While the prediction was well taken, Snow of Whitby, Suffragan to York, objected to the use of the word *supplementary,* because as a schoolmaster for many years "I nonetheless considered myself a priest, not a supplementary priest." He suggested that the title should be assistant priest, not auxiliary, supplementary, or nonstipendiary.

In Resolution No. 33 the bishops reaffirmed Lambeth IX "on the supplementary ministry and recommend [ed] a wider and more confident use of that ministry." In so doing it combined the thinking of three Lambeths on the subject, since the 1958 Resolution had in turn referred back to Lambeth VII: "The Conference considers that while the fully trained and full-time priesthood is essential to the continuing life of the Church, there is no theological principle which forbids a suitable man from being ordained priest while continuing in his secular occupation. While calling attention to Resolution 65 of the Lambeth Conference of 1930, the Conference now wishes to go further and to encourage provinces to make provision on these lines in cases where conditions make it desirable. Such provision is not to be regarded as a substitute for the full-time ministry of the Church, but as an addition to it."

THE DIACONATE

The unauthorized addition of two words, *and women,* in the bound proceedings of Lambeth X made it appear that the bishops recommended the ordination of women to the diaconate—thus implying that they would be in line for advancement to the priesthood.

That was decidedly not the case and subsequent investigation brought to light one of the greatest ironies of all Lambeth Conferences—that the Archbishop of York, who as head of the Ministry Section had suggested that the misleading words be removed at the time the Resolution was on the floor, was, by his own admission, responsible for later reinserting them when the approved Resolution was put in the hands of the printers.

The discovery came to light nearly six weeks after the Conference had adjourned, when the Bishop of Springfield (Illinois),[8] the Rt. Rev. Albert A. Chambers, made Lambeth X the subject of his address to his diocesan synod. He reported the bishops' recommendation in Resolution No. 32 "that the diaconate, combining service of others with liturgical functions, should be opened to men remain-

---

[8] The Diocese of Illinois, organized in 1835, was divided into three parts in 1877—Springfield, Quincy, and Chicago (which continued until 1884 to be known as the Diocese of Illinois). Ohio-born, GTS educated Albert Chambers had been Rector of the Church of the Resurrection in New York City for twelve years when he became the diocesan on October 1, 1962. In the fall of 1968 he was elected president of the American Church Union.

ing in secular occupations." In an aside, Bishop Chambers explained that the original Resolution had read "men and women" but that the Archbishop of York, Donald Coggan, had realized that the phrase "and women" was confusing the thrust of the Resolution, which was to dignify the ancient office of deacon with a potentiality of greater service. It had nothing to do with another clause of Resolution No. 32, which recommended that women already ordered deaconesses be declared within the diaconate—a recommendation that was in itself of questionable retroactive legality.

When Bishop Chambers had completed his address he was approached by a priest of the diocese who had just received by air mail from London one of the first copies of the newly bound *Lambeth Conference 1968 Resolutions and Reports*. Turning to page 38, he pointed out to the Bishop that the bound report said of Resolution No. 32, "The Conference recommends: (a) That the diaconate, combining service of others with liturgical functions, be open to (1) men and women remaining in secular occupations. . . ." The words *and women* were not included in what the Bishop had just reported to the synod, nor were they, as Bishop Chambers readily agreed, what the Conference had approved in London.

On returning to his office at Springfield, Bishop Chambers immediately fired off complaints to SPCK and to the Archbishop of York with copies to Canterbury, Cariboo, Exeter, and Bishop Hines. Three weeks later, in a letter dictated from Bishopthorpe, the archiepiscopal palace, Archbishop Coggan replied:

My dear Bishop,
   Thank you very much for your letter about the wording of Resolution 32 of the Lambeth Conference. Mr. R. J. Brookes, Editorial Manager of SPCK, has also been in touch with me about the correspondence that you have kindly had with him.
   I find it a little difficult to remember exactly what happened in the pressure of Lambeth, but I think it was something like this: The Resolution was in galley before it was considered by the Conference. The words "and women" were deleted, as you say in your letter. The question then arose whether they should be restored when the Conference had recommended that "those made deaconesses by laying on of hands with appropriate prayers be

declared to be within the Diaconate." I believe that both the Bishop of Warrington [Laurence Ambrose Brown, Suffragan to Liverpool and secretary of the Ministry Section] and I talked this over with SPCK and were of the opinion that for the purpose of clarification the words "and women" should be inserted to a (i). We took it that the deletion of the words in Plenary Session was a procedural matter so as not to prejudice discussion of Clause C.

I hope that I have made this point clear. I understand that Bishop Dean [the Bishop of Cariboo, Episcopal Secretary] may have seen you earlier this month, and I hope he may have had a word with you about the matter.

It was good seeing so many friends at Lambeth, including a splendid deputation from the United States of America.

With my warmest good wishes,
Yours very sincerely,
Donald Ebor:

The reaction of Bishop Chambers was that "the Archbishop's logic seems illogical" and, refusing to accept the explanation, he pressed the matter further in a longer letter to York on November 14:

Dear Archbishop:

Thank you for your letter. . . . I am still very concerned that a resolution adopted by any body of the Church should be subject to "clarification" and change after the resolution has been adopted. Only the body itself has the authority to make any change.

The problem is further complicated by the title page of the resolutions (page 27) which says: "Resolutions—formally adopted by the Conference." In fact the *edited resolution was not* formally adopted. And further, the "note" on page 51 of the Report emphasizes—"The Conference as a whole is responsible only for the formal resolutions agreed to after discussion. . . ."

Beyond this, I question your assumption that the deletion of the words "and women" in Plenary Session was a "procedural matter so as not to prejudice discussion of Clause C." Nothing was said to this effect and I believe this is a non-sequitur. The first resolution offered by Section II, sub-committee 20 (which, incidentally, was not in galley form, but on yellow mimeographed paper) was "That the order of deacons be reformed in accordance with the recommendations of this Report." This was "not put," the objection being that in the Report one of the recommendations was for a "renewed diaconate, open to men and women." This was further underscored with the deletion of "and women" in Resolution A (1) which was later voted by voice vote. There was no call for division since obviously the majority of the bishops wanted the deletion.

Clause C, in regard to deaconesses is a different matter. 1. Deaconesses do not remain in secular work as a rule. 2. The intention of this resolution was to clarify the ambiguity in the statements of previous Lambeth Conferences about the status of deaconesses. 3. This was voted by division (221 ayes, 183 noes and 19 abstentions.)

I am most anxious to have this matter corrected and will appreciate word from you as to how this can be done. I will gladly poll the bishops who attended the Conference if this is necessary. The record should be corrected, not only in the official files, but through a news release of some sort.

With thanks for your assistance in what I think is a most important matter.

Sincerely yours,
† *Albert A. Chambers*

The same day Bishop Chambers wrote the Archbishop of Canterbury and from Lambeth Palace received the following reply dated November 25:

My dear Bishop Chambers,

Thank you for your letter. . . . I have looked into the matter and compared notes with Bishop Dean . . . and it is clear to me that in the proper form of the resolution as passed by the Conference the words "and women" were not part of the text. It is desirable that the official text should be the resolution as actually passed by the Conference. I propose therefore to take some steps to make this known in the various Anglican Churches and Provinces and to give the matter some necessary publicity. It may be a week or two before I am able to take these steps, but I will let you know what steps I am taking. I think it would be undesirable to deal with the matter by an individual polling of the bishops as you have suggested.

With my warmest good wishes,
Yours ever,
† *Michael Cantuar:*

There the troublesome matter was allowed to rest for several months. Misinformation had been spread and the correction was lamentably delayed—first by the weeks that elapsed while the doctored resolution got into print, secondly by the exchange of correspondence, and finally by Canterbury's delay in taking the action he promised. Whatever the correction, it could have the effect of magnifying the Resolution out of all proportion, of seeming to stress a prejudice against women, of making the Church appear overly concerned with irrelevant internal technicalities, and of exposing the Church to public conjecture that a few bishops had broken trust with their brother bishops.[9]

When at last Canterbury did move on the matter (it was not until the week after Easter when he was back at Lambeth from a tour of eight dioceses in the West Indies) his action took the form of a letter to the Metropolitans.

"Having had a long tour abroad I delayed in dealing with the matter about which we were in correspondence in November," he explained in an attached note to Bishop Chambers. "I now enclose a copy of a letter which I have sent to the Metropolitans of the Anglican Communion so that there may be no doubt as to the text as actually passed by the Conference."

In the letter to the 25 Metropolitans (a list headed by York), Canterbury began by expressing his regret "that there has been some dispute about the text" of Resolution 32.

"It was the duty of the Episcopal Secretary and his staff to record accurately the Resolutions exactly as they were passed and to transmit the text to SPCK for printing," Canterbury wrote. "There is no reason to doubt that in this case as in every other these officers accurately carried out their task. Nor is there any doubt that in

---

[9] A much less important change, but one indicating more liberties in making "adjustments," was a line that spoke of "the continuing element of *diakonia*," whereas the Resolution approved by the bishops had spoken simply of "the continuing nature of the diaconate."

Resolution 32 the words passed by the Conference under 32(a) (i) were 'men remaining in secular occupation.' Subsequently it was put to SPCK, though not by the Episcopal Secretary and his staff, that the words 'and women' should be inserted into 32(a) (i) as an inference from 32(c) "That those made deaconesses by laying on of hands with appropriate prayers be declared to be within the diaconate."

Canterbury's letter continued: "Whether the inference is correct has been a matter for some argument, and as I am appealed to in the matter I can only say with the concurrence of the Episcopal Secretary that the text passed by the Conference under 32(a) (i) is 'men remaining in secular occupations' and that this is the text which is valid for official purposes. I am asking SPCK to correct the text on any occasion for reprinting."

In conclusion, Canterbury wrote that "the words of Resolution 32(c) with their recommendation about the status of deaconesses stand."

So the dispute was dismissed, if not resolved, in a letter of three paragraphs that brought the Resolution back to its original wording before York and Warrington had changed it "for the purpose of clarification."

Although Canterbury made no reference to what had transpired, it was apparent that he was absolving the Episcopal Secretary from any blame in the matter.

Typically, Canterbury was careful to refrain from suggesting how the Metropolitans might transmit the information to diocesans —either directly or through the heads of provinces. In that respect he was exercising his customary restraint and respect in working with Anglican Churches over which he has no real jurisdiction. Yet his letter was notably lacking in suggesting how the Metropolitans might make the "news release" which Bishop Chambers had requested and to which Canterbury seemed to agree when he wrote about "necessary publicity." A mere correction of the text by SPCK would not do the job if, indeed, there was to be any additional reprinting of the Conference Report. Most regrettable of all was the lack of any sort of concurrent explanation from the Archbishop of

York.

The preparatory paper on the diaconate was the only one written by a bishop—John William Alexander Howe of St. Andrews, a mountain-climbing bachelor consecrated in 1955 at the age of thirty-five and still at forty-eight the youngest of the Scottish diocesans.[9a] He pointed out that "history does not provide any adequate warrant for our present use of the diaconate as the final year or so before priesthood."

Three courses of possible action were cited—to continue the current status, to allow the order to lapse, or to promote a new image of the diaconate more closely related to the serving office portrayed in the early Church.

During the floor discussions, a fourth alternative was added—that no more men should be ordained to the diaconate until the office was fully clarified.

The final Report took the view that the office needed reform to bring it into line with "the importance which we attribute to it in our formularies" and the clarity needed for ecumenical conversation.

"We do not recommend that the diaconate should be allowed to lapse," the Report said. "To do so would be to reject our firmly established tradition; it would produce stresses in our relationships with those Churches which retain the three-fold order of ministry; and it would deprive the Church of the witness of service which was an essential element in the ministry of Christ, and which is reflected in the over-all ministry of his Church to the world."

The final Lambeth Report saw several advantages in a "renewed diaconate open to men [and women] . . . persons professionally

---

[9a] Shortly after Lambeth X it was announced that Bishop Howe would succeed the Bishop of Cariboo as Anglican Executive Officer. A student at St. Chad's College, Durham University, during the years when Michael Ramsey was teaching there, he was ordained by York in 1944. After serving a curacy in Scarborough in Yorkshire he was chaplain at Adisadel College in Accra, 1946–50, and vice principal of Edinburgh Theological College, 1950–55. He was consecrated in St. Ninian's Cathedral, Perth, October 18, 1955.

employed by the Church, and persons who believe themselves called to an office in the ministry while remaining in secular life."

The advantages, said the Report, "would lie, first, in a re-establishment of the relationship of the secular world to the will of God, through the liturgical action of the deacon; secondly, in the opportunity offered to persons in secular occupation to offer their work to God in the ministry of his Church; and, thirdly, in relating more closely the vocation of those in full or part-time Church work to the worshiping life of the Church."

In a practical aside, the Report observed that "it might well be possible to dispense with the use of distinctive clerical titles and dress" for permanent deacons. (It made no attempt to deal with the picture it conjured of women deacons momentarily leaving their regular work to undertake what the Report called "the liturgical action of the deacon.")

As for men with the intended goal of priesthood, the Report said "it would be desirable that candidates for the priesthood should pass through and be part of the diaconate." Thus, while expanding and upgrading the office in one sense, the Conference did nothing to change the diaconate as a stepping-stone to priesthood.

In conclusion the Report stated that "the fact that a deacon would be in some sense a minister of religion would be a matter for canonical resolution and negotiation in different parts of the world."

Ironically, the author of the preparatory paper, Howe of St. Andrews, found himself in disagreement with the Report. "The attempts in most places with perpetual deacons is not successful," he told the Conference. "I suggest that the scheme recommended could do a great deal of harm. The duties are precisely the same as those that lay people are doing. We should suspend the ordination of deacons altogether for a time—do nothing with it, or we risk bringing this ministry into complete confusion." Further, he said, the Conference was failing to think of deacons in the "current conception of what members of the clergy are and are about, and we are not considering for the diaconate the idea of indelibility—taking it on for life."

Luxton of Huron also commented that, while he had hoped Lambeth X would clarify the position of the diaconate, it seemed that the Draft merely confused the situation, blurred the lines still further, and "makes some of us despair of a clear lead from the Conference."

Huron also said that he believed there was no doubt in the minds of the men concerned "that they are 'parsons.' They have left the ranks of the laity, joined the ranks of the clergy and hold the conviction that they are not perpetual but look forward to the priesthood at the earliest possible date. They present as many problems as they help us solve."

Disagreeing with Huron, Ellison of Chester declared that the Church should "extend it or abolish it altogether, acknowledging that we have just two orders of ministry. Or we revolutionize the whole idea of what the diaconate should be, and make it an order of ministry of service open to those in the Church called to it. . . . As things are, we seem to have only deacons who are preparing for the priesthood, yet we really have a diaconate which is composed of workers, readers, and others. Why not bring them into a reformed order of the ministry? I believe there are a large number of people who do not aspire to the priesthood, but who would welcome a special order."

In the discussion, one well-told incident lingered with many of the bishops. It was related by Allison of Winchester whose diocese, one of the most ancient in England (it was founded in 676), had 150 lay readers and 349 clergymen in 334 parishes. He told of a conversation on a crowded commuter train that morning with a businessman who was an enthusiastic and devoted lay reader. "Whatever the Report says about the diaconate," cautioned Winchester, "it must not discourage these men who are doing their work as straightforward Christians."

The most thoughtful speech of all, one of the most memorable of the Conference, came from Lambeth's woman consultant, Mollie Batten.[10] Wise, humorous, and ranging over wide experience as an

---

[10] Born in 1905 and christened Edith Mary Batten, she studied at Liverpool University, the London School of Economics, and St. Anne's College, Ox-

active laywoman and educator, the address came to be known as "Mollie's leave-us-as-we-are talk." She was given far more than the usual time allotted a speaker and it was worth it.

"I am one of two of the genuine laity here," she said from the railing of the gallery. (The other half of the "genuine laity" apparently was Peter Day, Ecumenical Officer of the American Church.) "First I want to mention our confusion about the word *diakonia* as total ministry. Applying it to one part of the ministry seems to me to be as acute as our problem in applying the word 'priest' in the total concept of priesthood."

In business and government, she said, one man of twenty-three faces approximately seven years of training before he heads up a department. "I would like to suggest that there might be some useful thinking to be done about a prolongation of the period of the diaconate and that we should think more seriously as to whether young men should be promoted to be in charge of a parish before the age at which, in civil service, they would even become a principal officer, and if we were to think of the career structure, and I use this phrase not as a bad word but as a good concept, of the longer-term education of a man between leaving a theological college and going into the responsibility of a parish and seeing that he has a diversity of ministry. And we've not said very much about the several bits of education he might receive: for a time going to a specialized ministry rather than the parochial ministry and back again. If we had that sort of concept then there is, indeed, something to be made of this specialization of *diakonia* at this point as a preparation for the ministry."

Miss Batten then turned to the second portion of her address, the area that earned her the "leave-us-as-we-are" label.

"I have never understood why anybody should want to ordain me

---

ford. In the 1930s Miss Batten worked in settlement houses in Birmingham and London; from 1940 to 1947 she was associated with the Ministry of Labor, and the following year was made a member of the Order of the British Empire. After sixteen years as principal of William Temple Theological College at Rugby in Warwickshire (1950–1966), she became research officer of the Board for Social Responsibility of the Church Assembly.

further for my job in the world," she said with an exaggerated puzzlement. "I was baptized. I have been confirmed. What more do you wish to do to me?"

There was prolonged laughter and then applause from the bishops before she continued. "I am inclined to think you might like to do something else to me and I would like to know very clearly what it is. And, secondly, what you think I would do as a result of it which, by the grace of God, I have not been able to do for the Church as I am? What I have been able to do has been extremely odd in many ways and I've always thought that it lacked something when I was asked to preach the Word of God in cathedrals. But for the ordinary run of my lay work, I haven't thought that was the condition. I would like to see in this document spelled out very clearly what it is you are going to do to lay people in relation to their work in the world if you propose to make them into some sort of order in the Church.

"Now if on the other hand your real purpose in this is to do something to people like myself in order to be able to minister in the liturgical life of the Church—which we might or might not like to do— I hope again you will not see that in terms of our wanting to do it. The Bishop of Chester used the phrase, 'people who like to be ordained.' Now I have been suspicious about people who want to be ordained to do anything unless they know what it is they want to be ordained to do. And this is one of my worries about the young men. So many of them whom I know quite well and who come to see me . . . I try to encourage them in terms of what I think they are ordained to do, Your Grace. They are ordained to minister Word and Sacrament in the priesthood of the Church. Now if you want some of us to help—and I do go to services where the priest is greatly lacking in help—then say to us that this is what you want us to be around for so that we can help to administer the chalice and preach the Gospel when you wish us to do so. And if you are going to do that, are you going to make us into deacons or are you going to ask us to exercise some supplementary ministry or are you going to let us do that on the strength of our confirmation?

"Now there are these three possibilities that seem to me, Your

Grace, that we should be a little clearer about. May I further and finally say this, as one who has been principal of a theological college for over sixteen years—of which you, Your Grace, were President—I have talked to lots of men and women, old and young, from the world and from the Church, about all sorts of things, and they have done me the honor of consulting me. Now there have been occasions in my college when I was exceedingly well served by my chaplains, both senior and junior, but there have been occasions on which people who have consulted me have in fact made their confessions, and there have been occasions on which a particular group of persons ought to have been able to have had Eucharist together. I am not at the moment arguing for the admission of women to the priesthood, but what I am saying to you is this: Will you have a look at the man or woman who is ordained a permanent deacon in the context of their ministry? Can you in the long run separate the total ministries of persons in the Church? . . . I believe that the permanent diaconate will always fail if the person concerned has enough theological competence and ability to be a priest.

"Now if you are then to say you can have a diaconate of people who will in fact [be inferior]—and this sounds an impossible thing to say—but we have got to face the fact of a breach in our society. I have seen people who are competent to preach the Word and others who are not. They ought not to be allowed to get themselves ordained, however much they want it! And there are some people in our society who are competent to preside over the sacraments and there are some people who are not. No business undertaking mistakes the level of competence of the people it employs. Now if we go on—if you in your wisdom decide to have a permanent diaconate—and I have the greatest respect for the work that lay readers do, I suggest to you that this is not apart from the problem of lay readers. The permanent diaconate will, in my view, always tend to become a less well-qualified and a less well-organized and a less understanding group of rather clerical people. I do just wonder whether [we] are wise to do that at this moment in the life of the Church? The serious person who wants to minister in the life of the Church will, I suggest to you, if they are competent, always want to move into the priesthood. If the diaconate is made permanent, it will tend to become a group of second-class ministers. Why not leave us laity?"

When the Draft was returned in the form of a final Report, many of the bishops still voiced their reservations.

Wickham of Middleton, Suffragan to Manchester, warned of the "danger of trying to solve the problem of the diaconate by imposing it upon the laity." He added that "diaconate in secular employment is neither fish nor fowl. Secular society does not see the difference between priest and deacon."

Thomas of Swansea & Brecon (Wales) also opposed the Resolution, on the grounds that the study "gives no way for reforming our present diaconate."

Throughout the final discussions the bishops often fell into discussion of deaconesses and diaconate, losing sight of their essential task of restructuring the traditional third order of ministry. Numerous bishops spoke pro and con:

Clements of Canberra & Goulburn (Australia) praised perpetual deacons for being "able to reach areas of life that regular clergymen cannot."

Kellogg of Minnesota boasted that one of his perpetual deacons was "a surgeon who frequently wears his collar when he operates."

Putnam, Suffragan of Oklahoma, declared that "the perpetual diaconate does not diminish the ministry of the laity, but serves to encourage and inspire it."

Reed of Ottawa took issue with a reference in the Report that "the diaconate must by its nature remain a Holy Order"; however, if the secular were admitted, "it could be a lay Holy Order." He asked what it meant. There was no reply, but the bound volume of reports and resolutions omitted the reference.

Another awkward phrase appended in the original Resolution —a reference describing the diaconate "as an order of accredited ministry"—was spotted by Maguire of Montreal, who pointed out that the phrase implied that the diaconate had not previously been an accredited order. It was omitted in the abridged Resolution.

Canterbury had some thoughts to add when asked about the perpetual diaconate at his last news conference. "In my view there are countries where the perpetual diaconate works very well," he said. "There are other countries where I think it won't develop because the emphasis will be far more upon laymen serving God and the Church as laymen. I think that in this country there is likely to be some development of the permanent diaconate but I don't think that we are going to be cluttered up with men who are serving the Church in a sort of minor order. Because one of the great things in England in our Church life is the revival of the role of the laity who serve the Church by virtue of the laying on of hands which he received when he was confirmed. And I don't want to interpose another kind of laying on of hands. . . . I think that in England that will rather be the emphasis, but nonetheless, there is a role for the perpetual diaconate."

DEACONESSES

Next the bishops turned to a consideration of deaconesses, a subject toward which they had veered throughout the discussion of the diaconate. Their tendency to bring the topic into their initial talks was indicative of their mixed feelings about it; in the end, the decision to recognize deaconesses as being within the diaconate produced the most divided vote of Lambeth X—221 to 183—on section c of Resolution No. 32.

The sharp and rather recent memory of an attempt to ordain a deaconess to the office of deacon—an unsuccessful effort in 1965 by James A. Pike, then Bishop of California—also increased interest in the question.[11]

"If the order of deacon needs clarifying, how much more does the

---

[11] The last had not been heard of the much discussed Deaconess Phyllis Edwards. Long after Bishop Pike's retirement to the more serene vistas of the Center for Democratic Studies at Santa Barbara (where he remained a controversial figure after taking as his third wife the co-author of a book on his "talks" with his deceased son) Deaconess Edwards again burst into the news during Lent, 1969, when she solemnized a marriage while serving as Acting Vicar of St. Aidan's Parish, San Francisco, Diocese of California.

order of deaconess!" cried the Archbishop of York in his address to the opening plenary session. "We surely must get this straight! And is there not every reason to state plainly that a deaconess shall be allowed to fulfill all the functions which a deacon at present is entitled to do, including preaching at the Eucharist and administering the chalice?"

The need to define the status of deaconess had been pressed several times since the revival of the order in the nineteenth century. Lambeth's opinions appeared ambiguous until the issue of women's ordination to the priesthood suddenly gave the matter new importance. (Simultaneously, the renewal of the religious life and the lifting of many of its traditional restrictions signified that the future might see more vocations to the order of deaconess and that the order could be clearly defined.)

In 1920 the Lambeth fathers had referred to deaconesses in the Conference Report and ten years later they had gone a step further and made them the subject of a Resolution. Lambeth X studied the statements side by side:

> Lambeth 1920, from the Report: "In our judgment, the Ordination of a Deaconess confers on her Holy Orders. In Ordination she receives the 'character' of a Deaconess in the Church of God; and, therefore, the status of a woman ordained to the Diaconate has the permanence which belongs to Holy Orders. She dedicates herself to a life-long service."
> Lambeth 1930, a Resolution: "The Order of Deaconess is for women the one and only Order of the Ministry which we can recommend our branch of the Catholic Church to recognize and use." [Other resolutions of 1930 outlined the duties of deaconess as more restricted than those of the diaconate.]

The Ministry Report of Lambeth X said that "we have been asked to clarify the ambiguity in the statements of previous Lambeth Conferences about the status of deaconesses." It then declared its belief that "we are justified by Scripture and tradition [and] we reaffirm the statement of the Committee on the Position of Women in the Councils and Ministrations of the Church [Lambeth Conferences 1920]. . . ."

After quoting the 1920 statement the Ministry Report concluded "that those who are made deaconesses by the laying on of hands with the appropriate prayer should be regarded as within the order of deacons." It added, "We appreciate that, in view of this reaffirmation, canonical regulations will have to be made by each province or regional Church to regularize the status of deaconesses ordained in the past."

In presenting the Report, York added his personal opinion, "that women deacons can perform all functions a man deacon can—in and outside the church building."

Consistent with the Report, Resolution No. 32(c) presented to the bishops read, "The Conference recommends . . . that those made deaconesses by laying on of hands with appropriate prayers be declared to be within the diaconate." [12]

Its presentation (which York managed to have voted on separately from the parts of the Resolution designed to strengthen the diaconate) brought forth a wave of discussion from the floor.

Loane of Sydney immediately protested, "I am strongly in favor of strengthening the deaconess order, but I am not in favor of identifying it with the order of deacons."

Ellison of Chester spoke for the Resolution, pointing out that it called for a reaffirmation of 1920 whereas, he said, "Lambeth 1930 went back on its opinion. For many of the deaconesses it was a painful thing to be told that what they had believed was denied."

Canterbury interjected the opinion that he did not read 1920 as "admitting women to the order of deacons. They are an order of deaconesses."

Eley of Gibralter said, "I do not believe previous Lambeth Conferences intended to include deaconesses in the threefold holy orders. To include women in the third order of deacons is nearly the same as admitting them to the priesthood and episcopate. We must concern ourselves with the reaction from Rome and the Orthodox."

Masaba of Mbale (Uganda), who had only 106 clergymen for 693 congregations, poignantly reflected his need for deaconesses

---

[12] The Resolution, as originally worded, erred in saying that the 1920 statement was a Resolution. Canterbury pointed out the mistake and it was reworded.

when he pleaded that "the women of Uganda should be given hope."

The possible redundancy of the Resolution was pointed out by Garnsey of Gippsland (Australia), who said, "In my diocese they have been considered as being in Holy Orders."

An Irish bishop, Stanistreet of Killaloe, Kiefenora, Clonfert, & Kilmacduagh, questioned if the Conference had the right to declare such a Resolution, whereas Schuster of St. John's (a South African diocese with 1400 lay catechists) thought that a decision of ordination of women to the priesthood should take precedence over a Resolution on deaconesses.

Right down to the call for voting, Oxford and Chester as well as other bishops continued to disagree on what 1920 really said.

So the scene was set for the closest vote of the Conference: through the door marked "Ayes" passed 221 bishops and through the opposite exit, labeled "Noes," passed 183; nineteen abstentions were counted (Trevor Huddleston among them), but observers in the gallery thought there were even more.

After the victory in favor of declaring deaconesses within the diaconate there did not seem much point in discussing a further Resolution recommending that provinces pass legislation canonically placing women already deaconesses within the diaconate. A few, including the Bishop of Exeter, tried to continue the discussion, but Resolution No. 32(d) was put to a vote and passed by show of hands in about the same proportion as the previous vote.[13] Then the Conference prepared to move on to the far greater controversy on women in the priesthood.

WOMEN AND THE PRIESTHOOD

If Lambeth X did not open the door for women to be admitted to the priesthood, it surely unfastened the latch.

Feelings ran high, long before the bishops assembled, about

---

[13] It became the last clause of Resolution No. 32: "(d) That appropriate canonical legislation be enacted by provinces and regional Churches to provide for those already ordained deaconesses."

ordination of women and resultant theological, pastoral, and socio-logical considerations. Caution prevailed and the resolutions as they finally appeared were mild and low-key.

Of the five resolutions (Nos. 34–38), the first was of basic importance because in a single sentence it swept away a longtime barrier: the belief that since Christ chose only male apostles those who followed in apostolic succession should be male. The Archbishop of York and his party constantly sought to downgrade the argument as "silly" and "insulting." Even so, the wording of the Resolution was a delicate matter. As originally presented for approval, it read "there are, in principle, no conclusive theological reasons for withholding priesthood from women." But as the bishops mulled it over thoroughly and amended it, Resolution No. 34 in the end was entirely different: "The Conference affirms its opinion that the theological arguments as at present presented for and against the ordination of women to the priesthood are inconclusive."

The next three resolutions made the Anglican Consultative Council (or Lambeth Consultative Body) a clearing house of information and advice so that, hopefully, no Church would move too hastily.

The final Resolution, No. 35, let down the gates by recommending that the several Churches make canonical provision where necessary "for duly qualified women to share in the conduct of liturgical worship, to preach, to baptize, to read the Epistle and Gospel at the Holy Communion, and to help in the distribution of the elements."

The week after Lambeth ended, Canterbury told the press that he was "glad of what has been said about women in the priesthood" although, he added, "I would have preferred the original Resolution which just said plainly there are no overwhelming theological objections to admission of women to the priesthood; what it did say was not quite so strong an affirmation as that."

More candidly, during the question period of the news conference, Canterbury said, "It was impossible for the Lambeth Conference to tell the Churches what to do. It could only make some affirmation about the principle and leave it to Anglican Churches to make their decisions in consultation with one another. That in fact is what has happened: the Resolution passed is rather milder than the Resolution originally offered."

For those who wanted more positive action (there were charges that the bishops were "holding back" or indulging an attitude of "wait and see"), Lambeth X still could point out a decided change since 1948 when the Conference said "that the time has not come for its further formal consideration." [14]

The other eleven members of the Committee on Women and the Priesthood were obviously chosen with care for one of the most sensitive tasks of the Conference. They included suffragans of both Canterbury and York, Tremlett of Dover (the only unmarried committeeman), and Sargent of Selby; another member was Barrett of Rochester, N.Y., chairman of a similar committee in the American House of Bishops; also included was Andrew Tsu, Assistant Bishop of Pennsylvania, who in 1948, as Assistant Bishop of Hong Kong, had been among the eleven Chinese bishops who brought in a plan for women's ordination for an experimental twenty-year period.[15]

Since York's was the strongest voice for the cause, it was not surprising to note that the preparatory paper for the committee was from the Dean of York, Allen Richardson. Contrary to the committee's verdict, he wrote: "There are serious theological arguments for and against the ordination of women to the priesthood. The most important of them concern the nature of priesthood itself."

After demolishing some of the standard arguments, Dean Rich-

---

[14] Lambeth VIII was confronted with a *fait accompli:* the ordination of a woman in 1944 by one of its members, R. O. Hall, Bishop of Hong Kong & South China. When the archbishops of Canterbury and York repudiated the bishop's actions the woman's ministry ceased immediately.

[15] The proposal, which originated in what was then the Diocese of Hong Kong & South China, asked Lambeth VIII to concur with a plan by which "for an experimental period of twenty years a deaconess might (subject to certain conditions) be ordained to the priesthood." The answer was that "the Conference feels bound to reply that in its opinion such an experiment would be against the tradition and order [within the Anglican Communion] and would gravely affect the internal and external relations of the Anglican Communion."

ardson said that the question remained "whether such a decision taken by a single separate branch of the Church (for example, the Anglican Communion) could possess such authority; it would not be reverting to an ancient practice (as, for example, restoring the Cup to the laity), but would be making an innovation for which there was no ancient or ecumenical precedent. This is the crucial question which underlies the debate whether the Anglican Communion should proceed to the ordination of women to the priesthood now. It is a profoundly theological question, since it raises the issue of authority in the separated branches of the universal Church of Christ. . . . The fundamental question concerns the theological propriety of an innovation within one branch of the historic Church, lacking the consensus of the whole Church."

Further, Dean Richardson said, "To ordain women as priests merely because the parochial ministry cannot be kept going as a result of the shortage of manpower would be the worst of all possible reasons for the innovation."

The first Resolution, in draft form, asked outright for the ordination of women. (Obviously its authors knew that compromises would have to be made but, as one of the bishops put it, "Their rule seems to be that it is better to ask a lot and be given some of it than to ask meekly for little and be cut off with even less.") Halfway down the long galley of the Draft Report, it stood out prominently: "*Resolution:* That this Conference approves the ordination of women to the priesthood and asks national and regional Churches or provinces to consider making appropriate provision [for the same] within their own spheres."

The recommendations, York told the bishops, came from "a group that began with very different views and ended with a unanimous resolution."

Again, as he had in his address to the opening plenary session, York said the Conference was not to be insulted "with silly arguments about our Lord having no women in the Apostolic Twelve." He also pointed out a recent development that he evidently felt was germane: the action of the Church of Scotland [Presbyterian] a few months earlier in opening its ministry to women.

There was an ominous quiet while some other topics in the

Draft Report were routinely discussed. The only direct reference to the controversial resolution was made by Metropolitan Parthenios, Orthodox Patriarch of Alexandria and Metropolitan of Carthage. "I will not speak about the priesthood of women," he declared. "You understand my position!"

The sides were being chosen and soon came one of the most memorable Lambeth addresses, both applauded and bitterly denounced, and when he resumed his seat, Loane of Sydney had become a chief spokesman against women's ordination.

Slender and vigorous at fifty-seven, Marcus Lawrence Loane, Archbishop of Sydney, began mildly ("I must express my complete inability to accept the proposals the Draft contains.") but quickly built up to a strong denunciation of the Resolution. "It *is* significant that there is no New Testament precedent for the ordination of women," he shouted in flat defiance of York's position.

Referring to Lambeth IX's Resolution that "the idea of the Christian family is rooted in the Godhead," Sydney declared his belief that "there is a distinction in the functions which the Persons of the Godhead fulfill." Further, he said, "equality and subordination exist in the Trinity side by side. There is a distinction in function as there is in human life. To do what the Report proposes would be in conflict with the doctrine of the Godhead. As God has made men and God has made women, there is a function for each —and I believe in order!"

In a practical aside that gained him newspaper headlines the following day, Sydney said, "I believe that if the ministry of the Church is to be thrown open to women it will be the death knell of the appeal of the Church for men." Uneasy laughter went dead in midair as he continued: "Already men are saying that the Church is the concern of women and children, and if we ordain women, will not ordinary man be convinced that it is so?"

Swift support came from one of Sydney's countrymen, Shevill of North Queensland. He had just begun, with a passing reference to York's plea for ordination of women, when York leaped to his feet in interruption, shouting, "I had only *one* sentence about women! Only one!"

After the interruption, North Queensland continued, "This

question arises, whether women are capable of receiving the indelible character of Holy Orders, and the fact remains that our Lord did choose twelve men. One fourth of the members of the World Council of Churches have opened their ministeries to women, but it is important to note that they are mostly smaller groups. With the larger groups, the picture is very different. Besides, would not some action such as is proposed destroy the degree of unity already achieved with Old Catholics and interrupt the dialogue with Roman Catholics and the Orthodox?"

Almost as though North Queensland had given them a cue, the observers began entering more fully into the discussion; but as tempers neared fever pitch on the floor as well as in the gallery, the Conference managed to proceed within a certain tongue-in-cheek manner. There were humorous references, such as when one of the Jesuit observers, John Coventry, said, "I must apologize for breaking away for a moment from this fascinating debate about women, to which I am sure you will return forthwith. . . ."

From the gallery, John Huxtable, Minister-Secretary of the Congregational Church in England and Wales, posed the question, "Is God masculine?"

Huxtable posed a second question, "Are women people?" then continued, ". . . The Lambeth Conference needs to determine that sexual discrimination shall have no part in the life and ministry of the Anglican Communion . . . in St. Paul's statement of Christian freedom 'there is neither male nor female, for ye are all one in Christ Jesus.' "

Turning to personal experience, Huxtable said, "I belong to a church that has had ordination of women for fifty-one years. I think the Congregationalists whom I represent would want me to tell you that since 1917 we have never thought that we have made a mistake. . . . There has never been the flood of women clamoring to be ordained, which, I gather, is a prospect that terrifies some of you. . . . Some eighty have been ordained and not all are alive today. . . . It hasn't cut into church attendance!"

The next speaker could not have been in more contrast to the Congregationalist: he was Athenagoras, perhaps the most orthodox of the Orthodox. His comments were the same that he always made when the Conference veered from Cathoic norms, reminding the bishops that "when we depart from the apostolic experience we do not contribute to the unity of Christianity." (Embracing two priests of the American church on a London street late the following Sunday afternoon, Athenagoras cried in mock astonishment, "I thought yours was a *Catholic* church!") From the gallery he told the bishops, "Our poor Lord did not include in his cabinet of twelve any of those women who contributed with their substance for his sustinence."

Except for a speech by Barrett of Rochester, N.Y. (who said that if the bishops opposed women's ordination they would have to be "very, very careful" what they said about racism), heavy support continued for Sydney's thumbs-down position. It came from Hand of New Guinea ("A woman's priesthood is as mother and homemaker."), and from the Archpriest Ignatiew of the Russian Church in Exile ("We are happy to hear a very Orthodox proclamation from an Anglican archbishop such as Sydney!")

Ellison of Chester came nearest to expressing the Conference's mind, if applause was any indication, when he observed that "there is nothing in Holy Scriptures that is definitive one way or the other whether women may be ordained. I think we should say that there is no theological reason why the representative priesthood should be withheld from women, but we should be cautious beyond that point."

From a seat in the back row, Brady of Fond du Lac (USA), asked the Conference "to imagine going to a woman priest and saying, Bless me, Mother, for I have sinned."

The Dutch Old Catholic Van Kleef warned that women's ordination would, indeed, interfere with reunion. "We would receive it with great regret and embarrassment," he said.

Since no Conference session seemed complete without some profundity or wit from Welles of West Missouri, the bishops had been more or less waiting for an opinion from the most talkative of the Americans. What he had to say was as appealing as it was amusing in its tone of folksy resignation.

"Your Grace, I'm just an old fashioned Anglo-Catholic," he began, "and I've always thought women were wonderful . . ."

As the laughter died down, he continued, "I'm not happy to see the Christian Church appear to deny women the respect of persons equal in the full gamut of Christian experience. I'm conscious that this is a discrimination that with the passing of the years I feel more uncomfortable about, but I think I'm coming to the place where —although I would be extremely uncomfortable to have women priests in the Diocese of West Missouri . . . I am not impressed by the majority argument that is being used—that most churches do not have women priests—for since when has the Anglican Communion been concerned with necessarily being on the side of the majority? After all, thirty-eight years ago it was painful for the Lambeth Conference to make a ruling on birth control and nearly four hundred years before that we certainly went against the majority in translating the Mass into the vernacular. So I'm not worried about the Anglican Communion being a majority, I'm worried about the Anglican Communion being right in God's eyes and if God wants women to have at least the right to be priests, whether they exercise it or not, I think maybe we'd better do a little thinking here. Perhaps the reason the world has been so slow to be converted is that we have not spared our manpower but our womanpower."

As speeches continued, opposition built up, both on and off the Conference floor, until it appeared, at the close of the plenary session, that Lambeth X might refrain from any resolution or go a step further and recommend against it. The rumor was widespread that there would be something less strong than outright endorsement of ordination of women to the priesthood.

When York presented the final Report, with the five rather mild resolutions on ordination of women, his address roamed widely over many arguments: the Church had in the past "been ungracious in the place it accorded women in its ministry [and] the New Testament does not encourage Christians to think that nothing should be done for the first time. . . . The Resolution for women in the priesthood has been recast and a large number of bishops are eager to see it go forward while others feel that prejudice and ignorance need breaking down first. We as bishops are slowest to face change even though we know that the Church of Rome is giving serious consideration to the matter. . . . Whatever our decision, the

Resolution strikes a blow at outdated theological arguments and outdated thinking."

The vice-chairman of the Ministry Section, Beecher of East Africa, added his support. "Before the next Lambeth we will see in Africa a need for women to take their place beside men in the total ministry of the Church. Those who do not need those offices should not deny them to those in other parts of the world whose needs are different. We must bear one another's burdens."

Sydney, reiterating his own stand, refuted the Congregationalist observer. "What is right in the Congregational church has no bearing on the matter," he said. "The doctrine of the ministry in the Catholic Church is totally different. . . . Those who want to have women priests are acting from sentiment. . . . My view is based on Scriptures and what we hold as the historic ministry." [16]

Finally, the redrafted resolutions were proposed by the committee chairman, Davis of Nova Scotia (who quoted an Englishwoman who had written "It is not women's problem, but a problem of the Church."), and was seconded by the vice-chairman, Roberts of Ely.

As the time drew near for voting, the bishops hurried to register their objections. One complaint was that a serious matter was being treated hastily. "I am still totally open to conviction of theological argument on the question," said Trevor Huddleston, "but I want time to consider it, and I am not prepared to apologize for not having considered it fully before, because in the diocese where I have worked up to now [Masasi] we have more important things to think about and to do!"

Russell, Assistant Bishop of Zanzibar & Tanga, also protested the pressure: "I am altogether in favor of the Resolution, but I must protest again the 'loaded' speech given this morning by the Archbishop of York. It seems to me that some of the bishops are pushing us along in the direction *they* want us to go."

Much of the dissension was summed up by Goodman of Calgary

---

[16] "There was a sad aspect in the fact that only two women sat among the bishops," wrote Ann Cheetham, churchwoman, feminist, and newspaper columnist. "One took down every male word of wisdom uttered, the other rushed forward with a glass of water to slake the dry male throat that had uttered them!"

[Canada]: "I have reacted against what seems to be 'loaded' statements and the tendency to label as reactionaries anyone who is opposed. . . . If one can judge them by their speeches, some bishops rather want to steam-roller us into approving ordination of women without a proper consideration. I have reacted to such words as 'stupid,' used by a speaker in the last hour; 'prejudiced'; and 'the whole world is watching us' as well as 'young people are concerned about what we are going to do.' I don't know why they should be considered logical arguments. . . . I feel personally that we haven't gotten into the deep heart of the matter."

Eastaugh of Peterborough also spoke for a goodly number when he said, "I will not vote against the Resolutions, but we have not been told the theological reasons for passing them."

The Bishop of Chester, the Bishop in Iran, and the Bishop of Birmingham added a trio of endorsements. The latter, Leonard Wilson, said wearily that he "could not see why women should not have their place in the ministry of Christ as deacons, priests, or bishops. . . . I can't help but think of the time when the early Church had to decide whether to let in the Gentiles!"

An objection from Guy of Gloucester that "the Report's theological argument is inconclusive" took the form of an amendment to change the Resolution to state "no theological arguments for or against." His point was taken up by Bennison of Western Michigan and the change was made. The reworded Resolution No. 34 read: "The Conference affirms its opinion that the theological arguments as at present presented for and against the ordination of women to the priesthood are inconclusive."

The other Resolutions (Nos. 35–37) referring to women were approved without delay. Later some of the bishops expressed surprise that no opposition had been voiced to Resolution No. 38, which called for canonical provision for "duly qualified women to share in the conduct of liturgical worship." [17] Montgomery, Coad-

---

[17] Two months later the House of Bishops of the Anglican Church of Canada followed Lambeth's recommendation by granting permission for "lay persons, either men or women," to administer consecrated bread and

jutor of Chicago, was noted as one of a handful who voted against it. Some may have voted for it, not out of frank approval but out of belief that the issue was redundant: the Archbishop of Perth, and perhaps individual bishops, had already licensed deaconesses to administer the chalice. Moreover, as was pointed out by one of the bishops from New Zealand, the whole Resolution sounded like a job description of the diaconate, and perhaps was consistent with the Conference's decision to regard deaconesses as being within the diaconate.

The "great debate" of Lambeth X ended, as T. S. Eliot, himself a lay adviser for Lambeth VIII, might have described it, "not with a bang but a whimper." As with so many matters at Lambeth, whatever success was achieved by any faction tended to be obscured in a forest of details. Nonetheless, at least for the moment, the door to the holy priesthood remained closed to women, but the latch was off.

THE EPISCOPATE

After their evasive evaluation and definition of the diaconate and the priesthood, the Lambeth fathers took a close look at the nature of their own functions in the office of bishop.

"Anglican churches have inherited episcopacy by the providence of God," R. P. C. Hanson, Professor of Christian Theology at the University of Nottingham, reminded the bishops in his preparatory paper, "The Nature of the Anglican Episcopate."

"Though they do not unchurch those Christians who do not possess it, they are bound to try to persuade them to adopt this form of government, and they have no authority to abandon it themselves, even for the sake of Christian unity," he wrote. "Episcopacy has in Anglican hands shown itself remarkably flexible and has manifested a surprising power of survival."

---

wine at Holy Communion. The Canadian bishops justified their action on the belief that much of the original meaning of receiving the Sacrament had been lost by the "various regulations, restrictions and taboos" developed through the centuries.

Canon Hanson's thinking about the relevance of a bishop's work and its centrality to the life of the Church was reflected in the Report of the Ministry Section and in two of the Conference's three Resolutions (Nos. 39–41) on the episcopate. The first recommended special training for bishops while the second emphasized "that all coadjutor, suffragan, and full-time assistant bishops should exercise every kind of episcopal function and have their place as bishops in the councils of the Church." The latter philosophy was already borne out in Lambeth X, in which coadjutors, suffragans, and assistant bishops were participating alongside diocesans for the first time.

It was the third Resolution that made headlines after it was proposed by a bearded, ascetic missionary bishop with the eyes of a mystic. From his seat near the back of the meeting hall, the Assistant Bishop of Zanzibar & Tanga, Scottish-born Robert Neil Russell, voiced the hope that the bishops would consider a Resolution for a more simplified style of life and form of address.

He began by recalling the worldliness and poor taste of the much discussed guidebook, *Lambeth '68*. Widely denounced and condemned at the start of Lambeth X, the booklet had been so forgotten as the Conference continued that Bishop Russell's mention of it during the final week made some bishops restless to get on with other business; yet more than a few felt the Conference needed to officially dissociate itself from the tenor of the booklet.

"Many of us were embarrassed," Bishop Russell said, ". . . and while I do not intend to speak on it, I do want to ask how was it that that last page—which gave details of where meals could be obtained, some of them at enormous expense—ever came into being unless bishops do give the kind of impression that this is the life we live. I think one of the troubles is that in many churches influential laity are of the upper strata and they take it for granted that the bishops should appear to be also in the upper strata. There is a necessary dignity and splendor of Church worship, but we should distinguish between what is glory to God and that which is glory to us as bishops.

"Quite a lot of honors that we get conjure up the idea of Princes of the Church which makes the idea of servants of God an object of public incredulity," he continued. "Some among us say that such honors are necessary to witness to the lordship of Christ, but I think we will find little support for that in the Gospels. 'Master' is forbidden and I think 'My Lord' [or Lordship] would be also."

With that introduction, Bishop Russell proposed his Resolution: "The Conference recommends that the bishops, as leaders and representatives of a servant Church, should radically examine the honors paid to them in the course of divine worship, in titles and customary address, and in style of living, while having the necessary facilities for the efficient carrying on of their work."

Seconding the motion, Trevor Huddleston said that "as the one who is on the cover of the booklet, I support the Resolution with all the strength I have."

Arden of Malawi, who had labored in Africa for nearly twenty-five years, also spoke in favor of Resolution No. 41, saying that diocesans should be known as "The Bishop in" rather than the more inclusive and presumptuous title "The Bishop of. . . ."

With Mortimer of Exeter and perhaps one other bishop dissenting, the Lambeth fathers approved the Resolution.

Despite the almost unanimous approval of Resolution No. 41, many bishops felt it represented a bit of righteous breast-beating. "A mild revolt," the *Church Times* called it. They could no more openly argue a motion for simplicity of life than they could vote against aid for the hungry—although it was significant that the very next motion, proposing that the bishops contribute a percentage of their stipends to world relief, was voted down partly on the grounds that they should not be publicly coerced in their giving.

Bishop Russell's reference to forms of address was somewhat academic in that Anglicans almost never use such terms as "Your Excellency" and similar forms popular in Roman circles; moreover, only the British occasionally murmur "Milord," and even then it is more a matter of politeness than obligation. Indeed, almost everyone's relish in addressing Canterbury as "Your Grace" indicated its uniqueness and the pleasure that many overseas bishops took in using it for the first time.

In a rather mischievous reaction to the Resolution, the bishops laughed aloud when Bishop Russell near the end of his talk addressed the chair as "Your Grace" and, catching himself, added, "That may be the last time I call you that!" Later the bishops pointedly addressed the Archbishop as "Sir" and Welles of West Missouri provoked more laughter when he directed a statement to the chair with the words, "Beloved First Among Equals." [18]

It was doubtful if the Resolution would have any more effect than a proposal made at Vatican II that all the bishops should leave their pectoral crosses in a heap at the High Altar of St. Peter's. Also, the traditional titles reserved for the episcopate—"Right Reverend" for all bishops and "Most Reverend" for archbishops and metropolitans—served to distinguish them from their fellows more than honor them.

"I don't allow my people in Canada to call me 'My Lord,' " Cariboo said at a noontime press conference at which he was commenting on the proceedings of the morning. "If I walk down the street and people want to say, 'Hi, Bish,' that's all right with me. I just want to be the father to all. The point is that bishops should have a style of life as simple as is consistent with efficiency. It doesn't mean we have to be hermits. Obviously there are times when it is necessary to give dinner parties and everyone knows that things are settled over a pleasant meal that wouldn't be worked out so well in a committee meeting. The point is that the episcopal style of life should be simple." [19]

---

[18] Canterbury appeared to sidestep the issue of how he preferred to be addressed by saying simply at his final press conference that the "correct" thing was to say "Good morning, Bishop" or "Good morning, Archbishop"—and, he added laughingly, he had especially liked the publication "that referred to me simply as Michael Ramsey." He nonetheless politely acknowledged a question a few moments later from reporter John Redfern who continued to address the Archbishop, as he had at the first press conference, as "Most Reverend Father."

[19] Referring in an editorial the following day to Cariboo's statement, the Manchester *Guardian* ["No Cause for Irreverence," August 21, 1968] said: "What to call a bishop is a deep and complex problem [but] bishops' precedence is a more certain matter. No one, presumably, would challenge Debrett's *Peerage.* Canterbury follows the Sovereign's Great Uncles, York

John Redfern of the London *Daily Telegraph* pointed out that the resolution called for a radical examination and asked who was "going to examine radically." Cariboo replied simply, "Each bishop with his own conscience."

In implementing the Conference's resolutions on the episcopate, a bishop's conscience would be, as Cariboo said, the guiding factor in deciding what to relinquish or retain. The final words of the Ministry Report might well serve as a touchstone for the 462 Bishops of Lambeth X and all who follow them in apostolic succession: "Simplicity in life, humility in manner, and joy in serving should be the marks of a bishop's life."

---

comes after the Lord High Chancellor, and the Prime Minister and the Lord High Treasurer follow York. The procession winds on a long way before there is another mitre, the Bishop of London's. *He* follows the younger sons of Marquis."

CHAPTER 8

LAMBETH AND UNITY

$$\mathbf{L}_{\text{IKE A GIANT CORPORATION CON-}}$$
templating an international merger, Lambeth X sought to get its
house in order about its principles (the Faith) and about its personnel (the ministry) so that it could move happily toward the
renewal in unity for which Christ prayed.

The Archbishop of Canterbury told his first news conference that
"the Unity Section will be surveying the whole field of Christian
unity . . . and will assess the role of the Anglican Communion
within the whole ecumenical task."

More specifically, on Anglicanism, Canterbury said that the
unity committees would "be asking what sort of organization do we
need." At the present, he said, "it has very little central structure.
The first Anglican Executive Officer was, uh, what's his name, uh,
Steve Bayne, Jr., he was the first, and now Bishop Dean.[1] The Sec-

[1] "Those who know the Archbishop of Canterbury will be aware that he
has a quite remarkable memory," wrote a columnist in *New Christian* on
Canterbury's momentary forgetfulness. "Shake his hand at a confirmation in

tion on Unity will have to be considering if we've got the right ways for the Anglican Communion to be working together. It might insist on more organization or less."

At his concluding news conference, Canterbury found it possible to commend the Unity Section's work, expressing gratefulness "that it has done what I hoped it would do in a comprehensive manner . . . in relation to Christian unity in every direction."

"We stand on holy ground, for unity is the will of the Lord and Saviour who has called us to shepherd his flock," declared Lakdasa de Mel, Bishop of Calcutta and Metropolitan of India, in his address to the opening plenary session. "The situation is more promising today than it has been for five hundred years."

With fresh vigor, the tenth Lambeth Conference turned to a subject that had held a prominent place on each of its agendas since 1888, when it adopted the now-famous Lambeth Quadrilateral. More than a third of the 462 bishops who listened to Archbishop de Mel were members of committees of the Unity Section which he headed. They constituted the largest group ever assigned to study unity and, in the ensuing weeks, they produced nearly half (twenty-six out of sixty-nine) of the Conference resolutions.

Hiyanirindu Lakdasa Jacob de Mel (who signed himself *Lakdasa: Calcutta*) was already well known to many of the bishops as an indefatigable worker and witty speaker. He felt at home on a London podium. After all, he had been coming to England for nearly fifty years, first as a student at Oxford, and then many times since World War II as one of the most active and widely traveled bishops in the Anglican Communion.

The eldest son of a family of wealthy landowners (Christians

Croydon and he will surely recognize your face and remember your name when you bump into him at an Icelandic airport a decade later. Underneath that medieval exterior is a mind as highly disciplined and retentive as a computer. . . . [When he recalled Bishop Bayne's name] I liked the 'Steve'—a fine recovery which indicated in a flash that the Archbishop was after all on intimate terms with the man whose name had slipped through the computer."

since 1534 and Anglicans since 1810), he studied at Keble College, Oxford. Influenced by two Anglican religious (first a Cowley father and later an American priest of the Order of the Holy Cross) Lakdasa de Mel went on to Cuddeston Seminary near Oxford, was ordained in 1926 in the Diocese of Southwark, served as curate of St. John the Divine, Kennington, and returned home in 1927. After eleven years as a vicar and an Indian Army chaplain, he was consecrated in 1945 as Assistant Bishop of Colombo. He became first Bishop of Kurunagala in 1950, Bishop of Calcutta (and Metropolitan of India) in 1962.

His appointment to head the Unity Section seemed a natural choice because of his active participation in the Third Assembly of the World Council of Churches in India in 1961 (his genial explanations of the proceedings at New Delhi earned him the affectionate esteem of the press corps) and his leadership in guarding his own province in the North-India Pakistan Plan and the Ceylon Scheme for unity.

Obviously, de Mel knew whereof he spoke when he reminded the Lambeth fathers that "there has to be flexibility when dealing with differing traditions," and that "it is desirable to agree on the absolute fundamentals of doctrine with diversity in many things and marginal differences charitably accepted by all concerned."

De Mel warned that "careful examination has to be made for discovering nontheological factors which often weigh far more heavily than one would think. . . . It is advisable to make clear to a great many people, including the clergy, that when they reach the frontiers of the promised land of Church unity, denominational baggage will not be too vigorously searched at the customs!"

The remark was typical of the de Mel wit, which easily turned to sarcasm and by the end of the Conference annoyed rather than amused the bishops. At the first plenary session, the bishops good-humoredly responded to his description of Uppsala's verbosity as "Uppsalalia," and to his chiding that too frequent upheaval of the roots for inspection of ecumenical growth was poor practice "of ecclesiastical horticulture."

Sometimes chiding, sometimes scolding, de Mel prodded the

Unity committees as well as whole plenary sessions on to a Report many were to consider the most radical ever produced by an Anglican body.

When the bishops assembled for the first plenary session on unity, they heard again, briefly, from Archbishop de Mel. He began by recalling that in interfaith discussions people sometimes ask for a precedent; but, he said, "you cannot have precedents for an unprecedented situation. There are times when there are pressures of the Holy Spirit—younger bishops who come to us and press for unity, and who am I to stand in the way of people obviously under the pressures of the Holy Spirit,[2] even though change does not come easily for a man of my upbringing and, I think, advancing years. . . . Anglican balance and temper is something very valuable in the history of the Holy Catholic Church [but] there are some persons imprisoned in the Middle Ages! We must set those captives free!"

Unexpectedly, de Mel left the podium after he had been speaking only a few minutes: he deferred to Winchester, the vice-chairman of the Unity Section, for presentation of the Draft Report. "I would like some of the British experts to report on that," de Mel said. "I'm only a bewildered Asian!"

The first objection to the Draft came from a consultant, A. M. Allchin, and pertained to the Introduction's statement "that the Church is called into being to serve the world." He thought it better to say that the Church is "to serve and please God" because, he said, "the Church has a destiny higher than just the service of the world." Allchin also noted the Draft's failure to mention other faiths and their leaders, "especially Martin Buber, the great Jewish thinker. Is it not time to think of unity with them?"

A second objection came from another consultant, Jarrett-Kerr, who thought there should be a sharper note of penitence at the outset of the Draft. Other objections were made by not only con-

---

[2] Leonard of Willesden, Suffragan to London, later the same day spoke against "pressures other than that of the Holy Spirit, which we assume that we must not resist . . . and that we must be swept along with them and not stop and say, 'Have we an obedience to Christ which makes us demand that we should stand firm?' . . . There is all the difference between saying we must stand firm and saying that we must be swept along."

sultants and observers but also by bishop after bishop arising to score the Report for failure to give more prominent attention to the Holy Spirit, technology, the unity of the spiritual and material, racism, illiteracy, civil disobedience, greed, want, immigrants, hunger, and other issues. For all differences of opinion, the Draft was to remain in substance less changed than the Faith Report but somewhat more than the Ministry Report.[3]

[3] "I am not so sure the Kingdom of Heaven can be brought about by a multiplication of general secretaries," said one of the American bishops who had observed most of the unity meetings since World War II. "One of the problems is that if two units merge, three may result—the new group and the holdouts on each side. Also, there is inadequate attention to the legal aspects. There are cases in the American courts holding that the group adhering to the original doctrine has the right to the property. Of course, England would not have this [since] Parliament would legislate it into legality. Take COCU, if it should come into existence I think I should go into the practice of law, when I retire, because a fortune can be made if COCU happens: there will certainly be dioceses who will not go along."

Speakers from the floor at the plenary sessions on the Draft Report on Unity, August 9, and Monday, August 12, included Uganda, Chichester, Georgia, Long Island, Singapore, Lagos, York, Virgin Islands, Masasi, Hines (USA), Lichfield, Arkansas, Ottawa, Willesden, Chicago, Oxford, Edinburgh, Woolwich, London, Colombo, Kootenay, Central Africa, Peterborough, Newark, Iran, Stockport, Corrigan (USA), Dublin, Salisbury, Gippsland, Dunedin, Wangaratta, Bristol, Armidale, Milwaukee, Ripon, Ossory, Columbia, Mbale, Argyll, Fulham, Nova Scotia, Gibraltar, Western New York, Norwich, Winchester, Guatemala, Grafton, Mauritius, Durham, Hong Kong, Kurunagala, Barrackpore, Rochester (UK), Colombia, Perth, Mbale, Melbourne, Connecticut, Colchester, Croydon, Algoma, Leicester, Seoul, Armidale, California, West Missouri, Matabeleland, Bayne (USA), and Burnett of Christian Council of South Africa; suffragans of Toronto, Melbourne, West Indies, and Venezuela; and assistants of London, Johannesburg, St. Edmundsbury, Birmingham, and Sheffield. *Consultants:* Allchin, Jarrett-Kerr, Mbiti, Paton, Taylor, Carpenter, Fairweather, Roseveare, Root, Anderson. *Observers:* Sarkissian, Stewart, Payne, Solomon, Athenagoras, MacArthur, Van Kleef, Beazley, Newbigin, Ignatiew, Parthenios.

Speakers from the floor at the plenary session on Unity, August 20, included Dublin, Hines (USA), Rupert's Land, Brisbane, Melbourne, Wales, Waikato, Stockport, Saskatoon, St. John's Mbale, Northern Uganda, Huron, Bristol, Wellington, London, Newcastle (Australia), Corrigan (USA), Singapore, Mombasa, Jerusalem, Calgary, Clogher, Grimsby, Georgia, Peterborough, West Missouri, St. Edmundsbury, Sudan, Gibraltar, Karachi, Argentina, Kensington, Birmingham, Cape Town, Nova Scotia, Gambia,

THE ANGLICAN QUEST FOR UNITY

"If a rough-and-ready working definition of unity is sought, it must be in terms of harmonious cooperation towards a common goal under the guidance of a common vision," wrote C. F. D. Moule, Lady Margaret's Professor of Divinity at Cambridge, in a preparatory paper for the Committee on Christian Unity and Human Unity. "Unity of such a quality is not uniformity but harmony —the harmony of an advanced organism in which a diversity of functions is coordinated into a single system."

Professor Moule declared that the Church derives unity from the

---

George, Iran, Winchester, Gippsland, Masasi, Canal Zone, South Florida, Guatemala, Bloemfontein, Sodor & Man, Malawi, Lincoln, Bristol, Sierra Leone, St. Arnaud, and Cuba; coadjutor of Melbourne; suffragans of Oklahoma and South Florida; and assistants of Zanzibar, Sheffield, and Guildford (Pike).

Speakers from the floor on Unity, August 21, included York, Rupert's Land, Wales, Algoma, New Westminster, Hines (USA), Melbourne, Perth, Central Africa, Uganda, Chile, Iran, Pretoria, British Honduras, Nuku-alofa, Nelson, Polynesia, Dunedin, Wellington, Ballarat, Wangaratta, Adelaide, Colombo, Nagpur, Ottawa, Ontario, Saskatoon, Zululand, Campbell (USA), California, West Missouri, Rochester (UK), Albany, Newark, Exeter, Bristol, Oxford, Leicester, Lincoln, Peterborough, Rochester (USA), Birmingham, London, Winchester, Fond du Lac, Long Island, Bangor, Connecticut, Sherwood, Warrington, Ripon, Manchester, Durham, Willesden, Woolwich, Southwark; suffragan of Oregon, Dallas, and Oklahoma; assistants of London and Wakefield.

Speakers from the floor on Unity, August 22, included Dublin, York, North Queensland, Olympia, Chicago, Jarrow, Peterborough, Western Michigan, Virginia, Huron, Norwich, Sodor & Man, Cape Town, and assistant Bishop of Birmingham.

Speakers at the final plenary session, August 24, included Canterbury, York, Cariboo, Hines (USA), Rupert's Land, Perth, New Westminster, Cape Town, Jerusalem, Chile, Singapore, Masasi, Nakuru, Iran, Sierra Leone, Colombo, British Honduras, Chota Nagpur, Karachi, Nagpur, Barrackpore, Quebec, Ottawa, Huron, Guatemala, California, Mississippi, South Carolina, Newark, Erie, Milwaukee, West Missouri, Western New York, Connecticut, Ossory, London, Stockport, Middleton, Sodor & Man, Ripon, Durham, Ely, Hereford, Leicester, Norwich, Chichester, Winchester, Bayne (USA), the Suffragan of the Philippines, and the assistants of London and Guildford (Usher-Wilson).

unity already existing in Christ. "If, each time this is formulated, it sounds unrealistic and Utopian, if the MRI program has remained little implemented, if there is no guarantee that the Church will ever completely reach the end of its commission, it is nonetheless true that the Church can never know its possibilities until it has entered more fully into the unity existing in Christ," he wrote. "The Christian failure in the world is undoubtedly due, in large measure, to its disunity. Once the unity of the Body of Christ begins to be shared by Christian congregations, who can set limits to the possibilities?"

In the torrent of special studies and papers that flooded the Unity Section, swelled by literally tons of material from Uppsala, Professor Moule's thoughtful approach to the complexities of unity exerted a subtle influence, even though the committee for which it was prepared did not submit a resolution.

In order to implement "the Anglican quest for union" (the title given to one of the major parts of the Unity Section), the bishops laid down the longest of their resolutions on unity, presented by Tomkins of Bristol. Resolution No. 44 urged that "each bishop of the Anglican Communion should ask himself how seriously he takes the suggestion of the Lund Conference on Faith and Order that we should do together everything which conscience does not compel us to do separately. To do so immediately raises the need to review Church structures (conduct of synods, budgets, areas of jurisdiction, etc.) to see where they can be altered to foster rather than hinder cooperation."

Secondly, the Resolution recommended that ecumenical life at the local level should be given priority.

Thirdly, it endorsed Uppsala's hope that the Church would "work for the time when a genuinely universal council may once more speak for all Christians."

Finally, it expressed the hope that "areas in which little ecumenical activity is at present possible" would be given encouragement and support from the more strongly established areas.

All that was easily accepted and passed in a routine manner, a calm prelude to the cry that arose when the bishops discovered that the Lambeth Quadrilateral had been rewritten by the Committee on Principles of Union. The bishops scanning the Report saw immediately that there were the customary four points, but they seemed drastically watered down from the statement orginated by the 1886 Chicago Convention of the American Church and adopted by Lambeth two years later as "Articles [which] supply a basis on which approach may be by God's blessing made towards Home Reunion." Further study showed that they could be compared thusly:

1888	*1968*
1. The Holy Scriptures of the Old and New Testament, as "containing all things necessary to salvation," and as being the rule and ultimate standard of faith.	1. Common submission to Scripture as the Word of God, the uniquely authoritative record of God's revelation of himself to man.
2. The Apostles' Creed, as the Baptismal Symbol; and the Nicene Creed, as the sufficient statement of the Christian faith.	2. Common profession of the faith derived from that revelation, especially as witnessed to in the primitive Creeds.
3. The two Sacraments ordained by Christ Himself— Baptism and the Supper of the Lord—ministered with unfailing use of Christ's words of institution, and of the elements ordained by Him.	3. Common acceptance of the divinely instituted sacraments of baptism and the Holy Communion.
4. The Historic Episcopate, locally adapted in the methods of its administration to the varying needs of the nations and peoples called of God into the unity of His Church.	4. Common acknowledgment of a ministry through which the grace of God is given to his people.

Williams of Leicester was the first to call the Conference's attention to the changes. He said the rewriting made it impossible to see four objective points, only "common acknowledgment" of them. "There is a subtle difference between presenting them as subjective statements rather than objective statements," he said. "Point Four has been rewritten so that it seems to exclude the historic epis- copacy. No one has ever denied that all ministers are channels of the grace of God, but——"

Stark of Newark, a member of the committee that had made the changes, was ready with an answer. "It is true that the Quadrilat- eral has been rewritten and it is about time," he said. "It was rewrit- ten in 1920 and has appeared to other Churches in Christ as if it is a standard which they themselves must meet before talking to us. The purpose of rewriting was to recognize that we haven't gotten very far in eighty years."

Newark continued sharply. "We have been talking and smiling unity but with our eyes and not our hearts. I would hope Christians in the future would hark back to the rewriting of the Lambeth Quadrilateral in 1968 and refer to it as the Lambeth Quadrilateral of 1968 because there is, indeed, as one of the opponents of this rewriting has pointed out, a subtle difference. The air of patroniza- tion has been taken out; the spirit that we are somehow 'up here' and the others are 'down there below' has been taken out, and the Lambeth Quadrilateral has been rewritten with the purpose of deal- ing in equal fellowship with our brothers in Christ. I don't find any place in the New Testament where our Lord asked us to feel superior to other disciples of his, and if there is such a place, I'd like to hear about it. It seems to me it's just the other way around, and so the Lambeth Quadrilateral has, indeed, been rewritten, and I am thankful to God that it has been rewritten. When we heard from some of our observers the first day it came up, you may well re- member the joy with which it was received upstairs [the con- sultants' and observers' sections of the gallery] because its air of superiority has at last been taken out."

(Bishop Stark evidently referred to remarks by a Scottish Presby- terian observer, William Stewart, who had objected to the Quadri- lateral's inclusion in the Draft because, as Stewart put it, "it had its function in 1888 and should not be used now as a measuring rod."

He said it was theologically unjustified. Ironically, Dr. Stewart's remarks immediately preceded Canterbury's address, which chided
Anglicans for regarding "Church unity in a rather static way, looking back to the norms of the Catholic tradition, and conserving
those norms, and spreading those norms to unfortunate people who
are without them!")

Despite Newark's hard-hitting defense, Leonard of Willesden,
Suffragan to London, registered further objection, harking back to
Leicester's observation that much was being sacrificed in substitut-
ing subjective statements for objective.

The first support outside the group which had drafted the new
statement came from Kenneth Howell, English-born Bishop of
Chile, Bolivia, and Peru. "I believe that when the Lambeth Report
is received overseas, the change in the wording of the Lambeth
Quadrilateral will be of interest and encouragement to our brethren," he said. "It will be welcomed in my diocese."

Most of the objections centered on the fourth point. Sherman of
Long Island requested a footnote to the intercommunion Resolution to convey the idea that the rewording was "not intended to represent a revision of the Quadrilateral." Putnam, Suffragan of Oklahoma, agreed; he said that the thinking on intercommunion appeared to sweep the fourth point under the rug, whereas "one of the
important things we Anglicans bring to ecumenical meetings is the historic episcopacy."

Finally, it was Tomkins of Bristol, chairman of Principles on
Union, who did the most to soothe the situation. First, he told the
bishops that the redrafting was an attempt "to paraphrase the
Quadrilateral rather than quote it with its changes from later Conferences." Then he suggested that the final Report might carry a
footnote setting forth the Quadrilateral in the familiar language of
1888.

Newark contended that the Unity Section would object because
"we intended it to be the 1968 version," but Canterbury picked up
Bristol's suggestion: "The fourth point in the Report is not in
agreement with what is stated in the Quadrilateral," Canterbury
said, and endorsed the idea of a footnote.

Eventually there was fuller agreement on the need for a footnote repeating the Quadrilateral but, despite the urging of Canterbury and others, accord was not reached on expanding the reference to "agreement on faith and order" in the intercommunion Resolution (No. 47) to explain that it meant agreement with the Quadrilateral. The result was that many of the bishops could conclude from the resolutions and the Unity Report only that the Church was inclined to relinquish the traditional Anglican concept of the historic episcopacy.

Toward noon, when the last of some two dozen speakers had resumed his seat, Canterbury surprised the bishops by rising to address them.

"I wish to say some things with a glance forward into the next Section," he said, hooking his thumbs in the pockets of his purple cassock. Then followed a brief but brilliant address that dramatically lifted the Conference out of its quibbling mood and cleared the way for a more objective discussion of the complexities of unity.[4]

INTERCOMMUNION

The most intense and prolonged debate of Lambeth X centered around liberalization of the ancient restrictions concerning the Eucharist. After presentation of the Resolutions by Johnston of Dunedin (New Zealand), chairman of the Committee on Intercommunion in a Divided Church, the recommendations were seen as threefold: that all baptized persons be permitted to receive at Anglican altars, that Anglicans be allowed to receive at altars of other churches, and that intercommunion be considered acceptable between churches where unity negotiations were progressing amicably.

Resolutions Nos. 45–47 were a radical departure from the thinking of previous Lambeths, but they reflected the approach that the Archbishop of Canterbury had suggested.

---

[4] See Appendix for text.

"There is a world of difference between intercommunion on the old liberal Protestant get-together lines with no intention of organic unity and intercommunion in a serious ecclesiastical situation with agreement upon the goal in faith and order," Canterbury said. "Where that situation exists, I believe it is possible for there to be Eucharistic intercommunion, not with a sense of doing something surreptitious, but with a sense of doing something that does belong to a true understanding of the Eucharist in relation to the Catholic Church."

The minority opposition, somewhat fewer than a hundred bishops, was concerned about lessening the importance of the Eucharistic doctrine as well as the prospect of Anglicans receiving the Sacrament from ministers not episcopally ordained. Opinions were generally unpredictable, however, since the bishops of some traditionally Catholic dioceses indicated that events of recent years had changed their minds

"My brethren, I stand before you to tell you that I have come to a very great change in my thinking," declared Francis Burrill, Suffragan of Dallas 1950–1953 and Bishop of Chicago since that time. "There are those in the world who cannot wait for deliberations and very fine distinctions of theological import. . . . There have been many clandestine, unofficial gatherings of Christian people in the dark night in some apartment house on the South Side of Chicago. They are Christian people feeling the hunger and necessity of sharing the Lord's Sacrament . . . and I feel basically that there is nothing wrong when spiritually hungry people are able to share the Bread of Life with each other."

Carey of Edinburgh said he had been "moved to tears" by the Draft. "I live in a country where our Lord's mission is daily frustrated, inhibited, and crippled by our divisions," said the bachelor Englishman whose see city is the capital of Scotland. "I am not suggesting that reciprocal intercommunion will bring unity at once in Scotland, but it will make unity possible in a situation where at present it seems unlikely."

Woolwich, Suffragan to Southwark, agreed and said of the area of greater London in which he worked, "There are many local situations in which it is becoming more difficult to break bread separately than together."

Opinions from the observers were more predictable—Athenagoras, the ranking Greek Orthodox, registered his unhappiness with the Resolutions while Arthur MacArthur, General Secretary of the Presbyterian Church in England, called them "effective steps toward reunion."

One of the Canadian consultants, Eugene Fairweather of Trinity College, Toronto, obviously nervous on taking the floor for the first time, asked, "If intercommunion is all right in some places, why isn't it in all places?" He warned that "some will hear the Conference saying to them that it does not matter greatly whether they continue to walk in the Anglican fellowship."

Eastaugh of Peterborough set off a mild furor when he used an analogy of intercommunion and premarital sex. "Integrity demands," he said, "that you do not have sex before you are married and that you do not participate in intercommunion until union is effected." Newark was loudly applauded when he replied, "I don't think the analogy of comparing the Sacrament with sexual relations should go unchallenged!"

The overseas bishops, particularly those from remote areas, were generally in favor of intercommunion. Dehqani-Tafti of Iran, for one, soulfully but rather sentimentally asked the Conference what he could say when he had to take a stand against intercommunion in a town, for instance, where forty Presbyterians and a dozen Anglicans were unable to have communion together. Corrigan of the Executive Council of the American Church spoke strongly for it, and unexpected support came from a bishop of the Old Catholic Church in Holland, G. A. Van Kleef, who said that Christians working together in his country felt impelled toward intercommunion. Simms of Dublin saw it as an aid "toward the goal of unity without examination of orders."

More analogies were used. "It's like a marriage when the parents think the couple are not suited to each other," observed Fison of Salisbury. "Then they realize that the couple love each other. Some of my congregation are Methodists, and we love one another. How long must we go on saying 'No'?" A more striking analogy, which compared lack of intercommunion with *apartheid,* was suggested by the only bishop among the consultants, Richard Roseveare, S.S.M., who had valiantly fought *apartheid* during a dozen years as Bishop of Accra [South Africa]. "There is a danger of *apartheid* creeping into the Church," he said, "an *apartheid* of doctrine and order rather than color."

For all the vocal acclaim for the liberal resolutions, some bishops shook their heads and others remained uncommitted. McCall of Wangaratta [Australia] said he had the feeling that those who did not agree were being pressured, but he later wrote that intercommunion provided "the only first-rate debate of the plenary session."

Feeling still ran high about the resolutions twelve days later when Johnston of Dunedin again brought them in along with the final Report. "We feel the Report is a fairly conservative document," he said, "and none of the resolutions [Nos. 45–47] advocate open communion."

The first and most effective speaker that morning was Mortimer of Exeter, who thought the resolutions revealed "a trend away from the principles of episcopacy that amounts almost to advice to surrender."

"It is clear and true that when we talk to the Roman Catholic and the Greek Orthodox Churches, we make our proud boast of unbroken continuity from the pre-Reformation Church, of being at once Catholic and Reformed, with unfailing loyalty to the teaching and structure of the undivided Church," he said. "But when we talk to nonepiscopal churches we say and do things quite differently. . . . I want Christian unity. I pray for Christian unity. But I have been brought up to believe that it does take time. That unity will come and it will be based on the Lambeth Quadrilateral. I do not think these resolutions are in accordance with that Quadrilateral."

Riches of Lincoln rebutted that "until five years ago I would have found myself following the Bishop of Exeter in defense of the episcopacy as a principle of Anglicanism. I can no longer feel that way.

You will recall that the love of Romeo and Juliet was killed by the ridiculous vendettas of their families. I think we are in grave danger in Christendom of killing the loveliness around us by continuing the vendettas which come out of past ages." [5]

Lincoln's metaphor of "vendettas" was taken up by the newspapers almost as swiftly as it earned the displeasure of the Lambeth fathers. The Archbishop of Wales, Simon of Llandaff, said at once that reference to "vendettas" was unfortunate. "When I was ordained forty years ago I believed that I was ordained not into the Protestant ministry but into that of One Holy Catholic Church," he said. "I deeply respected the former but I did not believe then, nor now, that it was part of the historic ministry of the Holy Catholic Church, as it has been understood for twelve centuries and still accepted as such by a great majority. The Church of England has for centuries carried on an ecumenical experiment . . . that ecumenical experiment has rested upon the Book of Common Prayer and episcopal ordination. After many years of erosion, the Prayer Book has disappeared from the ecumenism of the Church . . . and the process of erosion is being applied to episcopal ordination. I do not think that intercommunion would be a good thing for Anglicanism or for the Church of England as a whole."

More support for Exeter came from Barnds, Suffragan of Dallas, Leonard of Willesden, and Williams of Leicester. Lincoln's position was backed by Stark of Newark, Williams of Bangor [Wales], and Sadiq of Nagpur.

The latter, born of Indian parents converted from Islam, likened provisions against intercommunion to the caste system. "Where the caste system exists, people do not eat together," he said. "We all

---

[5] The Bishops of Exeter and of Lincoln, rapidly following each other on the floor, offered a contrast in the extemporaneous speaking in which the English excelled. "Lincoln's sentences were beautifully rounded; the fresh and appropriate word seemed to fall readily into place, yet the speech was not without passion and moving power," wrote a Canadian bishop. "Exeter, in his several scholarly interventions, gave us, in a lower key, the same polished phrase and rounded sentence. There was a calm deliberation in his speeches, and the assurance of one who had long pondered the subject and explored its every avenue."

seem to be taking the food of the Holy Communion from different tables."

Clark of Rupert's Land, Primate of All Canada, where a large United Church exists side by side with the Anglican Church, lent his support to the unity Resolution. "What does it mean when I say I recognize the ministry of one of the free churches?" he asked. "I do not mean it is good—the threefold ministry seems the best way for the Church to carry forth its ministry—but when a Christian seeks some means to find the grace of God in his worship, he finds a way. . . . The Lord's Supper is the one place where pretense is unthinkable. If otherwise, it is blasphemy."

De Soysa of Colombo, recalling Peterborough's analogy to premarital sex, said: "This is different. They are people who have been married, are divorced and are being reconciled. They should just be allowed to live together before they can find a house."

As the laughter subsided, Sabiti of Uganda recalled the bishops to serious thinking. "To me, renewal means the facing up to the fact that we have been sinners and need repentance," he said. "In Africa, I have Communion with others and we are one at the Cross— those who love the Lord."

It was Wright, Archbishop of Algoma [Ontario], who suggested that the final Resolution, on intercommunion between churches, No. 47, be rounded off with a sentence that might protect negotiators from difficult pressures. His point was well taken, and words were added to the effect that each province should "determine when the negotiations for union have reached the stage which allows for intercommunion."

Others who spoke for the resolutions were Zulu of Zululand, Barrett of Rochester, N.Y., and Appleton of Perth. "In the Eucharist the effective celebrant is the Lord himself," Perth said. "I believe the ministry of other churches is as valid and effective in their situations as mine is in my own situations."

With typical propensity for seizing the moment when the bishops might be unusually attentive, the first speaker after lunch was the Presiding Bishop of the American Church. He began by recalling from the Manchester *Guardian* a statement that "the Church has lost its place not so much by its indiscretion, but by the obduracy of its discretions."

"Too often, the Church *has* lost its place because of the obduracy of its discretions, because it has continued more to look back over its shoulder at the stance which it previously has taken than to look forward to the position which perhaps, under God, it ought to take," said John Hines. "I am convinced, in my own mind at least, that God is calling the Church to renewal in these days and that one aspect of the call to renewal is openness and courage to do the things which may be indeed considered indiscreet by some. . . . In my opinion . . . these resolutions . . . would be a minimal kind of overture on the part of this Church toward our Christian brethren whoever they are in the interest of the unity of the Church of Christ."

For all that had been said, there were bishops who had other points to make. Among them, Knapp-Fisher of Pretoria [South Africa] said that "there seems to me to be an assumption here that to receive Communion is the only experience of mutual love, concern and respect for one another. . . . The act of communicating is only one of the many elements in the many-sided parts of Holy Communion. Participation is praising without communicating. . . . It is the experience of a great many of us that real constructive participating without communicating is a true means forward. This is possible without any sacrifice of principle."

While supporting the Resolution, Reed of Ottawa said that the reference to intercommunion "under general direction of the Bishop" was a cautious one. (Later an American bishop said that was exactly why he opposed the resolution, "I do not trust the direction of most bishops!")

The speeches continued through the long afternoon. Brown of Albany was against the proposals for "denying the high doctrine of the Eucharist." Welles of West Missouri was for them because "the Holy Communion is not the only goal of reunion but Holy Communion is a means—the grateful means by which God grants us reunion."

Steer of Saskatoon suggested that the phrases "under the direction of the Bishop" should be replaced by a wider area of authority such as "under Provincial regulations." The suggestion enlisted the interest of Robinson of Woolwich, Suffragan to Southwark, which in turn brought forth the opposition of Southwark himself, Mervyn Stockwood. "Sorry to oppose my Suffragan, but I would not like to see the proposed amendment," he said. "If a suffragan gets permission of his bishop to publish books (such as *Honest to God*) it is highly unlikely he would get that permission of the Province!"

After six hours of debate, the first of the three Resolutions (No. 45) on intercommunion was put to a vote. It recommended that all baptized persons could, "to meet special pastoral needs," be communicated at Anglican altars; it passed with only a few dissents.

The second Resolution (No. 46), which recommended that Anglicans may on occasion receive at other altars, passed 351 to 75, with seven abstentions.

The passage of the third Resolution, No. 47, on intercommunion of churches where unity talks are in progress, was complicated with a last-moment amendment from Wright of Algoma, who took up Ottawa's suggestion that the stage allowing intercommunion should be a decision of a province. Dunedin said he objected "in the interest of brevity," but the motion was seconded by another Canadian, Gower of New Westminster, and passed by a close vote, 182 to 151.

The amended Resolution received slightly less approval than the accompanying resolutions. It was passed 341 to 87. Abstentions were not counted.

No specific mention was made of Roman Catholic churches, but some bishops later expressed belief that the freedom to receive Holy Communion in non-Anglican churches would presumably apply there as well.

CHURCH OF SOUTH INDIA

"The Church of South India is no longer on trial, we are on trial," said Allison of Winchester in proposing Resolution No. 48 for full communion. "It is no longer an experiment."

Twenty years earlier the same bishop (then Principal of Ridley Hall, Cambridge) had spoken of the Church of South India—or CSI, as it had quickly become known—in his first address at Church House. In the ensuing years CSI had taken on its own character from its heterogeneous background of Anglicans, Methodists, and the South India United Church.

Once decried, it gradually had come into partial communion with some Anglican bodies—including the Church of England and the American Church. In these Churches CSI members were allowed to receive Holy Communion, and any bishop or episcopally ordained presbyter of CSI was free (with the diocesan's permission) to celebrate at Anglican altars, although there were some restrictions: e.g., any bishop or priest of CSI who desired to officiate in Anglican provinces could not officiate at other than Anglican altars.

Lambeth X urged that those restrictions be dropped and it asked that every province take steps to establish full CSI communion.

Resolution No. 48 was passed as the CSI Moderator, Dr. Pereji Solomon, and two other CSI observers watched from the gallery. A small group of Lambeth bishops dissented, withholding their approval apparently because some CSI ministers (about 10 per cent) still lacked episcopal ordination.

In two additional resolutions, Lambeth X recommended full communion with churches whose inaugurations were approaching.

The first, Resolution No. 49, called for full communion with the new body to be known as the Churches of North India and Pakistan. In its formation, eleven of the fourteen dioceses of the Anglican Church of India, Pakistan, Ceylon, and Burma had voted unanimously to merge with the Methodist Church, the United Church of North India, and the Baptist churches in Northern India.

In the second, No. 50, full communion was proposed with the Church of Lanka (pronounced Lan*kah,* Archbishop de Mel reminded the Conference), which would, on completion of the merger, consist of the Anglican dioceses of Colombo and Kurunagala, the Methodist Church of Ceylon, the Presbyterian Church of Ceylon, the Baptist Church, and the Jaffna Diocese of CSI.

ANGLICAN-METHODIST TALKS

Ever since Archbishop Fisher's 1946 Cambridge sermon, in which he said intercommunion might be achieved if a way could be found for other churches to "take episcopacy into their systems," the possibility of Anglican and Methodist union in Britain had grown increasingly strong.

The Unity Section's Report for Lambeth X approached the subject thoughtfully. "We draw the attention of the Conference to the vital significance of the proposed coming together of these two churches in Great Britain," it said. "Their separation has had far-reaching consequences for the development of the Church in other lands. The healing of this breach in Great Britain is likely to be influential for the relations of Anglicans and Methodists in many other parts of the world." [6]

After more than two decades of talks, many thought that the endorsement of the Lambeth Conference might be a decisive factor in effecting intercommunion and eventual reunion. Others feared that a thrashing-out on the Conference floor might permanently damage the negotiations. Whatever the outlook, there was always the poignant reminder that the Methodists were a body who had sprung directly from the Church of England in a movement led by an Anglican cleric, John Wesley, who remained a priest all his days.

The outcome of the spirited and prolonged debate on the Anglican-Methodist talks was again a typically Anglican compromise: the bishops neither gave full approval nor withheld partial favor. The object of contention was the proposed Service of Reconciliation: because of the intense feelings about it, Resolution No. 51 could only state cautiously that "the Conference notes was satisfaction"

---

[6] The merger failed to gain the required approval of 75 percent, on the Anglican side, when it came up for a vote July 8, 1969. Meeting in Birmingham, the Methodist Conference voted 77.4 in favor. At the same hour, in London, the bishops of the Convocation of Canterbury voted 93 percent in favor, and the bishops of York Convocation, 78 percent in favor. However, the lower houses (priests) of both Convocations fell short of the necessary majority—Canterbury was only 67 percent in favor, and York only 68 percent.

the view of the Service of Reconciliation expressed in the Report of the Unity Section. Viewing with satisfaction and outrightly endorsing the service were two different matters: the Unity Report said only that the service was "theologically adequate," a phrase that combined faint praise with careful tolerance; by the time the bishops viewed with "satisfaction" what was only "adequate," the whole thing became a bland brew of caution added to conservatism.

Ten years earlier, Lambeth IX had found it possible to pass a wordy resolution encouraging "continuance of the conversations with a view to the making of concrete proposals, as offering a possible first step on the way to reunion in the particular historic understanding that organic union is definitely acceptable as the final goal, and that any plans for the interim stage of intercommunion are definitely linked with provisions for the steady growing together of the Churches concerned."

Since Lambeth IX the Church of England, acting through Canterbury and York, had appointed a commission and early in 1968 had received its final report. It called for Anglicans and Methodists to vote in 1970 on a plan which offered, first, full communion with the two Churches existing side by side, and second, organic unity at a later date after Parliament had given permission for the established body, the Church of England, to proceed.

That plan figured prominently in Resolution No. 51, proposed by Carpenter of Oxford, although he admitted that the whole subject was so debatable that "anything we say or do not say will be controversial."

Harry James Carpenter, Bishop of Oxford since 1955, had been fully exposed to all sides of the Anglican-Methodist talks: he had been chairman of the Church of England representatives in the conversations with the Methodists that led to the original report and more recently he had been a member of the Anglican-Methodist Unity Commission.[7]

---

[7] While holding his appointments in the Anglican-Methodist talks, Bishop Carpenter also administered a diocese with more parishes than any other in England, a family of clergymen (682 parishes, 741 priests) second only to London and an area so large (Oxfordshire, Berkshire, Buckinghamshire) that

The Service of Reconciliation was at once both a gate to unity and a stumbling block. Like many Anglicans before them, the Lambeth bishops asked what would be the intention of the nonepiscopally ordained Methodists when they received the laying on of hands (by Canterbury and four priests of the Church of England) and would they accept it as episcopal ordination, which they could then transmit in subsequent ceremonies throughout Britain? The second part of the Service of Reconciliation raised more questions of integrity when it called for the president of the Methodist Conference and other ministers to lay hands in silence on Anglican clergy.

There were objections from both the Catholic and evangelical wings within the Church of England.

The evangelical party rejected the mutual laying on of hands because, it said, "both bodies of ministers are already ordained, and hence the service is a concealed ordination of Methodist ministers."

The Catholic faction pointed out that "the service does not require Methodist ministers to intend to receive ordination as priests, and at the same time it seems to question the adequacy of the earlier ordinations of the Anglicans."

The strongest Catholic voice was that of Leonard of Willesden, Suffragan to London. Young (forty-seven) and well-informed, Graham Douglas Leonard said that he believed that opposition to the Anglican-Methodist scheme was not confined to Anglo-Catholics or extreme evangelicals. "There are many that fall in between these categories and you can't ignore us," he said, pointedly raising the left forefinger on which he wore his episcopal ring. "If I could endorse the scheme, now at this very moment, and with a clear conscience face my Lord in prayer, I should do so with the greatest of joy. Nothing would give me greater relief at this present time.

"I don't want to be unduly personal, but I think some speak as if we were wicked people, dragging our feet, unwilling to go forward

a report on diocesan boundaries recommended it be separated into three dioceses, with new bishops appointed to Aylesbury in Buckinghamshire and Reading in Berkshire.

prompted by the Holy Spirit," he continued. "If you knew what it is like to live day by day with the ache of knowing that you can't see your way to go through with it, I think they would perhaps understand us a little better."

Willesden pointed to a reference in the Unity Report which contended that " [reunion] is not fitting together of damaged parts into a makeshift whole"—a phrase, he said, which could be applied to the Anglican-Methodist plan.

"We are concerned here with a formal act between two churches that will have permanent significance," he declared. "We are concerned because we believe that the Catholic norms . . . are not antiques to be preserved for their own sakes but given by Christ so the Church may grow in obedience to that increased fullness." Further, he said, the Service of Reconciliation was misleading, unclear, lacking in integrity, and tinged with "historic Pelagianism."

Vaughan of British Honduras, a Welshman who had been active in Anglican-Methodist talks in the West Indies, defended the Service of Reconciliation as "theologically adequate to achieve its declared intentions." As for conscience, he reminded the bishops that "conscience is not the monopoly of one group and those members of the Anglican Communion whose consciences keep them from communion with Methodists fail to remember that Methodists and others, too, have consciences."

Back and forth it went, with the next speech of opposition coming from Moorman of Ripon. Without citing Archbishop de Mel by name, he recalled the remark ("There are still those who are dwelling in the Middle Ages and must be set free.") that the Indian Metropolitan had made in his keynote address on unity.

"I may be regarded as a medievalist, yet it is the present and the future which must engage our attention," he said in obvious effort to shake off his reputation as a historian. "Much in the proposal is sound, good, and hopeful, but I am concerned about the number of our clergy and laity who are bothered by the proposals. For some clergymen it will mean the end of the road—giving up their ministry. There will be few ordinations. There will be successions and resignations. Can it be right to speak with such self-confidence when the lives of so many are involved? There are many ways in which union can be advanced. Some of us dare to think that perhaps this is not the right way. Instead of unity, it will have disastrous effects."

In reply, Stopford of London, speaking as the Anglican chairman of the Anglican-Methodist Commission, said that his group had examined all ways and had concluded that the plan was the only one to be followed and added that the Service of Reconciliation should not be considered apart from the over-all scheme of unity.

It was McCall of Wangaratta [Australia] [7a] who first pointed out that many of the bishops had not seen copies of the plan before arriving in England and therefore were not prepared to pass judgment.

Eastaugh of Peterborough took up the point, adding that "other churches here are being asked to make judgments on a plan they haven't read. It is improper to vote on it, either for or against."

In a quick exchange Wangaratta proposed an amendment asking that "the Service of Reconciliation be considered separately and apart from the conflicting interpretation given in the scheme and that it be declared theologically adequate."

The motion was seconded and voted on; it lost, but the vote appeared so close that it concerned those bishops who wanted the Conference to say something positive on the Anglican-Methodist plan.

Immediately, Peterborough moved that the whole Resolution be "not put."

Brown of Warrington, Suffragan to Liverpool, asked the Chair what effect the Resolution might have on the progress of Anglican-Methodist negotiations and Canterbury replied, "The English con-

---

[7a] Theodore Bruce McCall, a merchant marine before ordination to the priesthood, made his journey to Lambeth X a round-the-world trip in what turned out to be the last year of his life. En route to London he visited the Soviet Union, realizing a longtime desire to see the Russian Orthodox Church at work in its own country. After Lambeth he visited the U.S., addressing the ACU annual Council Dinner at Raleigh, North Carolina. Consecrated Bishop of Rockhampton (Province of Queensland) in 1959, he was translated to Wangaratta (Province of Victoria) in 1963. He died January 16, 1969.

vocations have not passed at any time resolutions asking the advice of the Lambeth Conference."

Vockler of Polynesia reiterated the previously made point that it would be "highly improper for bishops who have not read or studied the proposals to vote on them."

Once again came a reply from Canterbury: "I could suppose then that our study of the Church of England is improper, while our study of India, Ceylon, and other areas is competent."

By then, the hour was late and the Resolution was obviously in trouble. Wilson of Birmingham asked for and was granted a postponement of the discussion until the following day.

Fortunately, the strained atmosphere was relieved the next morning when Shevill of North Queensland, supporting Peterborough's suggestion that the Resolution be "not put," said that the situation reminded him of a conversation between Big Ben and the Leaning Tower of Pisa.

"Big Ben is reported to have said to Pisa, 'You haven't the time, and I haven't the inclination,' " he said. "We from Australia have the inclination to pass the Resolution, but we don't have the time to study it properly."

North Queensland's suggestion did not please an American, Curtis of Olympia. "We cannot turn our backs on this," he said. "We must debate and advise. Although the Church of England will decide for itself, it is our apostolic duty to preserve the faith, and it is none the less our duty to reconcile the Church."

He was supported by Sinker, Assistant Bishop of Birmingham: "At least let us be courteous enough to welcome that which the Church of England, through its representatives, has produced."

The evident stalemate had been studied overnight by the Steering Committee. One of its members, Simms of Dublin, spoke for the group: "It does seem that there are many provinces outside the Church of England which cannot at this time act on a Resolution like this one." He suggested a Resolution that would not ask Lambeth to pass on details but would simply read "The Conference welcomes proposals made since 1958 toward unity between the Methodists and the Church of England along lines recommended in

1958, and hopes the churches will be able to proceed toward inter-communion and eventually organic unity."

The compromise suggestion immediately brought objections—among them from Burrill of Chicago, who said that he did not understand how the Conference could seek substitutes for what one-third of the bishops present [the Unity Section] had by a very large majority recommended. He asked approval of the original Resolution.

Thereupon Peterborough decided to withdraw his motion from the preceding day in favor of Dublin's substitute.

At that point, Archbishop de Mel, who had been watching in silence, sharply rebuked the bishops for discussing the measure for so long and for trying to water it down in various ways.

"I hope the Conference realizes what we are about to do," he began. "People who are troubled by their conscience should not prevent other people from unity. Some bishops have not increased their reputations with their views."

De Mel criticized the "easy way of trying to dispose of our Methodist brothers whom we have kept dangling for ten years and put in this bloodless substitute Resolution. It would be a grevious thing and I would beg the elder brethren here who really have had some experience and who are not so confused as some others here, to try to bring to bear upon this distinguished assembly the fact that we cannot act in a hasty and irresponsible way," he said. "I feel a little more of this behavior will mean that Anglicanism will get such a reputation for double-talk in ecumenical circles and will become utterly disreputable . . . that we will never be believed. We are very good at talking and then backing out. Church union is like another issue—peace. If you want peace, you must pay the price. If you want Church union, you must pay the price also."

Agreeing with Canterbury's remark of the day before about Lambeth's proclivity for commenting on unity plans in other countries, de Mel put the case even more plainly: "We are perfectly ready to advise North India or Lanka, but when it comes to this, we say we haven't had time to study it."

Finally, de Mel said, "It would be a menial thing if we did not

bring forward something like the Bishop of Jarrow has proposed
—at least to say that we 'note with satisfaction' if we cannot more
strongly say that 'we believe' the Service of Reconciliation is theologically adequate. Above all, don't behave as did one of the best
English bishops of his day with John Wesley. 'Mr. Wesley,' he
asked, 'what is this enthusiasm? It is a very horrid thing, a very horrid thing!' " [8]

Archbishop de Mel's speech quieted the opposition and the Resolution proceeded toward adoption. Gibson of Virginia, who had
often been the Episcopal representative in unity talks in the U.S.,
added his support to the measure. York then capped the long proceedings by asking Hamilton of Jarrow to read his amendment,
which slightly but significantly changed the Resolution. It passed
with some dissents.

The controversial resolution, less than five lines long, became
No. 51 of the sixty-nine resolutions adopted by Lambeth X, but it
did not pass into the record without bitterness. Trevor Huddleston
called de Mel's actions "utterly un-Christian," and they were
also condemned by Russell, Assistant of Zanzibar & Tanga.

During the next few days feelings against de Mel ran so high that
several bishops sent their regrets to Canterbury, saying that they
could not be present at the closing Eucharist at St. Paul's, at which
de Mel was to be the preacher. In the end, almost all of them were
persuaded to attend, but, even so, the man who once had been regarded as the most jovial of bishops came to the end of his last
Lambeth under a heavy cloud of disapproval.

Five days later, Peterborough said in a letter to the *Church
Times* that de Mel's speech was far from "a personal triumph," as it
had been described editorially, but "was in fact not a speech which
should be heard in any civilized assembly, let alone an assembly of
Christians. It was a torrent of abuse, insult and hysteria—a rabble-

---

[8] Archbishop de Mel quoted incorrectly. The conversation occurred August 18, 1739, between Wesley and Joseph Butler, twenty-eighth Bishop of
Bristol (1738–1750), who said to Wesley, "Sir, the pretending to extraordinary revelations and gifts of the Holy Ghost is a horrid thing—a very horrid thing!"

rouser ... [but] it certainly succeeded, and, if there could have been anything more sickening than the speech itself, it was the tumult of applause with which it was received. This classic instance of mass-reaction and non-thought was utterly disillusioning about the judgment of the Conference.

"It is important that these facts should be widely known," Peterborough concluded. "The resolution on this matter passed by the Lambeth Conference must not be taken as a considered and responsible decision of the bishops."

Canterbury's reaction, expressed in his final press conference, was that even though the Conference hadn't read the whole of the Anglican-Methodist document or studied closely the Service of Reconciliation, it still "was glad" to endorse the Unity Section's commendation of the Service. "The Unity Section is a third of the membership," he observed. "That, I say, is a pretty good commendation."

For all the equanimity of Canterbury's statement, it was soon overshadowed by the wide reprinting and discussion of Peterborough's strongly worded letter of protest.

RELATIONS WITH ROME

"The Vatican Council has changed the ecumenical situation in the world," wrote Gregory Baum, OSA, in the greatest masterpiece of understatement to come out of Lambeth X.

"While the Church in communion with Rome regards herself as in essential continuity with the Church of the New Testament, she also acknowledges that other churches are communities in which Christ is alive and in which the Spirit acts to save and sanctify men," continued the Canadian priest, the only Roman Catholic invited to write a preparatory paper for Lambeth X.

Father Baum pleaded for the churches to strive for "a common involvement that touches the people as well as their leaders." He said forthrightly that "the sociological separation of the Vatican from the rest of the Christian Church presents an enormous obstacle to the renewal of the Church and the ecumenical movement."

Could Anglican churches, he asked, "through closer association and occasional invitations do anything to bring the members of
the Vatican into closer contact with contemporary life?"

Despite his frank appeal, Father Baum disclaimed any right for
Rome to be given priority treatment in ecumenical advancement.
Instead, he wrote, "the ecumenical relations between the Anglican
Church and the Protestant churches is, according to my view, of
greatest importance for the future reconciliation of all Christians
[and] it is those relations which have a certain priority over the
ecumenical link with the Roman Catholic Church."

Sixty years earlier, the Lambeth Conference of 1908 had declared ". . . there can be no fulfillment of the Divine purpose in any
scheme of reunion which does not ultimately include the great Latin
Church of the West, with which our history has been so closely
associated in the past and to which we are still bound by many ties
of common faith and tradition." The statement was repeated by the
Conferences of 1920 and 1930.

Lambeth X in its Unity Report went further, adding that it
recognized the Papacy "as a historic reality whose developing role
requires deep reflection and joint study by all concerned for the
unity of the whole body of Christ."

Liberal as the words may have sounded, they were considerably
toned down from those of the preliminary Draft. There it had
stated that "Although as we understand them at present we are
unable to accept the claims of the Papacy to infallibility and immediate and universal jurisdiction, we believe that a considerable
majority of Anglicans would be prepared to accept the Pope as
having a primacy of love, implying both honor and service, in a
renewed and reunited Church, as would seem right on both historical and pragmatic grounds."

The statement was prepared by the Unity Section's Committee
on the Papacy and the Episcopate, headed by Hallock of Milwaukee. Lodging the first objection, the Metropolitan of Carthage,
the Orthodox Patriarch of Alexandria, said he was "not happy to
see [that] the Bishop of Rome has the power to settle the affairs of

the whole Church. . . . I believe that every bishop has the duty and the right for the affairs of the whole Church."

The second speaker, also an objector, was Moorman of Ripon, an Anglican observer at Vatican II and himself the chairman of the Unity Section's Committee on Relations with the Roman Catholic Church. "The statement on the Papacy does not add a great deal that is realistic at the present time," he said drily.

More objections came from McAdoo of Ossory [Ireland]: "These paragraphs speak in the nature of prophecy; they presume too much, and they stand to do more harm than good." Reed of Colombia & Ecuador said that "they sound like we stand on the side of Rome . . . [and therefore] could do danger to our relationships with the evangelicals."

At that point, Canterbury intervened with the comment that the statements were "a mixture of prophecy and guess . . . they would show the frivolity of Anglicans and they are very careless."

Canterbury suggested that the Draft be scrapped—and it was, but not before Masaba of Mbale [Uganda] told Canterbury, "Our people have heard of you, Sir, but when we speak of Rome, they ask, 'Where?'."

Eventually the Draft was molded into a shape the Conference felt it could recommend in a formal Resolution, No. 52.

"Conversations between Anglicans and Roman Catholics should be conducted with due regard to the multiplicity of conversations also in progress with other churches," the Report said. "In them all we propose to hold fast the principles of Catholic truth as we have been given to understand them, though we realize that, in renewed obedience to the Holy Spirit, we must at all times be willing to go forward adventurously."

In a separate Resolution, No. 53, the bishops recommended the setting up of a permanent joint commission for which the Anglican delegation should be chosen by the Lambeth Consultative Body (or its successor) and be representative of the Anglican Communion as a whole.

Toward the establishment of a joint commission for Anglican-

Roman talks Archbishop de Mel had paved the way early in his keynote address on unity. "Let us remember with deep veneration and affection that servant of the servants of God, John XXIII, who gave himself so obediently to the promptings of the Holy Spirit," he had said. "How far are we in this Conference going to follow with a like obedience?"

Myers of California added his voice in urging the Conference not to allow talks with Roman Catholics to be impeded by the Pope's speech of late June (mentioning infallibility and the Immaculate Conception) nor by the encyclical on the Pill. "We must encourage them to resume the view of the Papacy held by John XXIII," he said. "We must offer at this time whatever encouragement we can to Roman Catholics in our dioceses."

Even Canterbury applauded California's speech—a rare indulgence by the Chair.

In addition to the issues ordinarily mentioned, the subject of mixed marriages was also recognized as a major point of difference. Consequently, the Conference adopted still another Resolution, No. 54, noting "the urgent pastoral questions" raised by mixed marriages. It urged the "speedy continuance" of the work of the Joint Commission on the Theology of Marriage and its Application to Mixed Marriages.

"We welcome a suggestion from the [Roman Catholic] Third World Congress for the Lay Apostolate that Anglican priests should be acceptable as the official ministerial witnesses required by the Roman Catholic Church," the Unity Report said. "We note that the same Congress has asked that the responsibility for the Christian education of the children of a mixed marriage should be regarded as the responsibility of both parents who share in the grace of the marriage sacrament, and note that this is endorsed by the Declaration on Religious Liberty of Vatican II, which states: 'Parents ... have the right to determine, in accordance with their own religious beliefs, the kind of religious education that their children are to receive.' "

The over-all picture of relations with Rome was affected, Canterbury acknowledged to the press, by the encyclical on birth control that started off the Conference "in an atmosphere of sky a bit darkened," but "there are many friends within the Church of Rome, and the Roman Catholic observers to the conference were immensely helpful . . . and I'm glad that the Report and the Resolution call for continuing theological discussion with the Church of Rome and are able to lift already points of agreement as a basis for that discussion, at the same time asking that the Commission on Mixed Marriages shall continue."

THE ANGLICAN CENTER IN ROME

The most tangible expression of the advance in ecumenical relationships—an Anglican study center and library in the city of Rome—gained unanimous support and approval from Lambeth X.

A nonagenda item, the project came up for consideration in a plenary session at the start of the Conference. Ironically, it coincided with discussion of the Papal encyclical on birth control, but that controversy had little or no effect on Lambeth's support for what was already officially called the Anglican Center in Rome.

The development of the Anglican Center began in 1960, when Archbishop Fisher established permanent representation in Rome following his visit to John XXIII. (The first appointee was the Rev. Bernard Pawley, followed by the Rev. John Findlow.[8a]) In 1966, a library for public use was set up in the quarters occupied by Canon Findlow in the Via del Corso, not far from the Piazza Venezia.

[8a] A graduate of Worcester College, Oxford, Canon Findlow was Michael Ramsey's student at Lincoln Theological College in the mid 1930s, later was curate at Little St. Mary's, the Anglo-Catholic Cambridge parish. After the war he became Anglican Secretary of the Fellowship of St. Alban and St. Sergius and for three years was Assistant General Secretary of the Church of England Council on Foreign Relations (in whose quarters at Lambeth he has an office when he is visiting from Rome). He was chaplain of All Saints', Rome, and for the British Embassy, 1949–56, and later served chaplaincies in Switzerland and Greece. Fluent in Russian, he has twice been Canterbury's interpreter on trips to the Soviet Union and is Associate Secretary of the Archbishop's Commission on Roman Catholic Relations. He has a flat at Centro Anglicano in Rome and another at Lambeth Palace.

"The Anglican student is often a debtor to writers within the Roman Catholic Church," said Archbishop Ramsey when he solemnly blessed the premises on March 22, 1966, during his visit to Paul VI. "This center is an attempt to repay that debt by making available the resources of Anglican learning to any who will come and enjoy them."

Acting on Resolution No. 61, proposed by Moorman of Ripon and seconded by Hallock of Milwaukee, Lambeth X heartily endorsed the venture.

"We hope that our library will eventually have at least ten thousand volumes," Ripon said. "It has nearly four thousand now and is constantly being used by Roman seminarians and others, and it exists so that people can find out exactly what is the Anglican view on matters which concern both the Roman Church and our own."

In a news conference later, Cariboo described the lecture center and library as "the growing edge of dialogue with the Roman Catholic Church." He said that the Church of England supported Canon Findlow's expenses but that £4000 had been allocated from the Anglican Communion's budget in 1968 and plans were being made to spend £8574 in 1969 to allow for a larger staff.

THE ORTHODOX CHURCHES

"Long before ecumenism became a household word, strong ties of love and mutual respect had already bound us closely to our Orthodox brothers," said the Unity Report of Lambeth X. "Now in a changed and changing ecumenical climate we still cherish that intimacy and the shared appreciation of the glorious experience of being in Christ."

In acknowledging the long friendship with the Orthodox, Lambeth X also rejoiced in the lively evidence of it during the primacy of Michael Ramsey. His unprecedented exchange of visits with the Orthodox patriarchs had been warm and extraordinarily successful.

The ties between Anglicanism and Orthodoxy had been further strengthened by the active participation of the Orthodox observers at Lambeth X. Scaife of Western New York paid tribute to their work, especially their contributions to subcommittees, in proposing Resolutions Nos. 56–57 that urged continued talks and study.[9] The Conference welcomed especially the proposed resumption of the pan-Orthodox and pan-Anglican discussions which began in 1931.

In Resolution No. 57, the Conference encouraged continuing discussions with the ancient Oriental churches: a total of 15 million persons belong to the Armenian, Coptic, and Ethiopian Orthodox, as well as the Syrian Orthodox (Jacobite), Assyrian Church of the East, and the Mar Thoma Syrian Church.

The Lambeth Report noted that the pan-Orthodox conference at Belgrade in 1966 had compiled a list of theological subjects for discussion with Anglicans, one of them being the consideration of "the restoration of the Nicene Creed in a form omitting the Filoque" especially "by Anglican provinces engaged in liturgical reform."

The Report asked that the matter of "comprehensiveness" be more totally explored. "Comprehensiveness is an attitude of mind which Anglicans have learned from the thought-provoking controversies of their history," it said. "Comprehensiveness demands agreement on fundamentals, while tolerating disagreement on matters in which Christians may differ without feeling the necessity of breaking communion. In the mind of an Anglican, comprehensiveness is not compromise. Nor is it to bargain one truth for another. It is not a sophisticated word for syncretism. Rather it implies that the apprehension of truth is a growing thing: we only gradually succeed in 'knowing the truth.' It has been the tradition of Anglicanism to contain within one body both Protestant and Catholic elements. But there is a continuing search for the whole truth in which these elements will find complete reconciliation. Comprehensiveness im-

[9] Lauriston Livingston Scaife, consecrated in 1948, has been the recipient of the Cross of the Patriarch of Moscow; the Engolpion of the Catholicos and Patriarch of all Armenians, Vasken I; the Panigia of the Ecumenical Patriarch of Constantinople, and the Red Cross of the Polish Orthodox Church in Exile. After Lambeth X, he visited Ethiopia to receive still another decoration from Emperor Haile Selassie for aid given to nine Deacons of the Ethiopian Orthodox Church who have studied at the State University College at Buffalo, New York, in his See City.

plies a willingness to allow liberty of interpretation, with a certain slowness in arresting or restraining exploratory thinking. . . ."

Acting on a suggestion for consultation made by the Lutheran World Federation in 1963 (and after a meeting early in 1968 of a joint committee appointed by Canterbury and the General Secretary of the World Federation), Lambeth X passed a brief Resolution, No. 59, recommending "the initiation of Anglican-Lutheran· conversations on a world-wide basis as soon as possible."

THE ANGLICAN PRESENCE IN EUROPE

In Europe and some other areas of the world (West Africa, the Caribbean, and Latin America) Anglican priests and parishes of various Anglican churches have existed in close proximity. The situation had become known, in ecclesiastical parlance, as "parallel jurisdiction," and Lambeth X took steps to remedy it.

The prime movers, a year earlier, were the general secretaries of the Church of England missionary societies, who had asked, in the words of the Unity Report, "that the Lambeth Conference give guidance about the direction in which Anglican activity in Europe should move."

"Over several centuries this work has grown naturally to meet the needs of Anglicans permanently or temporarily resident on the Continent," said the Lambeth Report in an excellent summary of the situation. "It includes the outstanding work of the Missions to Seamen. It involves ministry among the armed forces. There is a continuing need to minister to short-term visitors. These activities have been partly under the jurisdiction of the Bishops of Gibraltar and Fulham, partly under Bishops of the Episcopal Church of the U.S. To some extent the work has reflected national loyalties rather than the Anglican Communion as a whole."

While shunning any intention to deprecate past or present Anglican work in Europe, the Report was forthright in stating that "we have a continuing duty to minister to Anglicans in Europe, but it is not our policy to develop Anglicanism as a separate confessional body on the Continent."

For all the clear thinking reflected in the Report, differences were evident during the floor discussion. Rogers of Fulham, Suffragan to London, spoke at length of his jurisdiction over North and Central Europe. He good-naturedly admitted that Bishop Bayne, whose jurisdiction was the American churches in Europe, had referred to him as "the last surviving ray of the sun of English imperialism." His defense of his work, however, was overshadowed by his long-windedness.

The mild censure of it from the Chair occurred near the end of a long afternoon of speeches. The day's proceedings ended on a note of futility when the tiny Bishop of Gibralter, Stanley Eley, gave a brief, rather negative reply. As a member of the Steering Committee, Bishop Eley had a seat behind the podium but was almost always obscured by the solid ranks of primates as well as by Canterbury and Cariboo and their secretaries and chaplains. Hence it was a surprise when he popped up at the end of Fulham's speech and made his way forward. The comments of the Bishop of Fulham, he said tersely, did not necessarily reflect his own opinions as head of a diocese responsible for chaplaincies throughout Southern Europe and parts of North Africa.

When the resolutions were brought in some weeks later, Gordon of Sodor & Man [10] demanded plainly that "the Church that would recommend unity to others must start with itself." He thereupon proposed Resolution No. 63, which put the Conference on record as deploring parallel jurisdiction. Strutt of Stockport thought a moral judgment was implied and asked that the words "take notes of" be substituted for "deplored." Canterbury got into the exchange, suggesting that "regrets" be used instead—and adding, to the bishops' amusement, a wry comment: "We've been 'taking note of' for decades. . . . It is a mixture of the scandalous and ludicrous."

---

[10] Eric Gordon, consecrated Bishop of Sodor & Man in 1966, spoke as chairman of Lambeth's Committee on the Role of the Anglican Communion in the Families of Christendom and also out of his experience as ordinary of a diocese which has traditionally had a large measure of administrative autonomy. Founded in 447, its original name was Sodor (meaning Southern Isles, as distinct from the Northern Isles of Orkney and Shetland) and at one time it included the Hebrides and other islands off Scotland's western coast. The diocese was designated Sodor & Man in the seventeenth century.

In the end, the Conference stuck to the wording of the original Resolution. It also recommended, in a statement with obvious ecumenical overtones, that "in any such area where there exists a Church with which we are in full communion, that Church should participate in the consultations."

In a separate action, entirely ecumenical, Lambeth X sanctioned the need for an Anglican Center and a permanent representative in Geneva, the headquarters city of the World Council of Churches. The Anglican Executive Office plans to add a second deputy in 1969 (in addition to Cariboo and his assistant) who probably will be assigned to Geneva. The cost will be shared by the provinces of the Anglican Communion, but in the meanwhile, the existing American and English chaplaincies will continue in Geneva.

THE ANGLICAN PRESENCE IN LATIN AMERICA

In an open letter to the archbishops and bishops of the Anglican Communion, the South American bishops pleaded for Lambeth X to address itself to what it called "the continuing ambiguity about the Church in Latin America." [11]

"It consists, on the one hand, of the view that questions seriously whether such tightly structured churches such as the Roman Catholic and Anglican really should be in Latin America at all," wrote the Rev. Charles Moya, liaison officer of the Conference of Anglican Bishops in South America. "On the other hand, there are those who affirm that there is a 'special Anglican vocation' in Latin America, and that it is here that Anglicans, by virtue of their tradition, are most called by God to be the *via media* between the extremes of Rome and Pentecostalism."

The Lambeth fathers might well have passed a Resolution of encouragement on the basis of the open letter, but they acted with considerably more understanding and compassion after an address by Gooden of Panama & the Canal Zone.

---

[11] The letter was signed by the three Anglican bishops in Brazil and by the Bishops of Argentina and Eastern South America; Chile, Bolivia, and Peru; and Colombia.

"I have been in Latin America longer than most Latin Americans —ten years as a priest in Cuba and twenty-three years as a bishop in Panama with jurisdiction at one time over as many as eight republics and nine monetary systems with never enough of any one system," began Bishop Gooden with the insight and humor that characterized his discourse.

After describing Latin America (Brazil alone is larger than the U.S.) and the progress of Anglicanism,[12] Reginald Gooden discounted the persistent report that 97 per cent of Latin America was Roman Catholic.

"Just where they get this percentage is a mystery to me," he exclaimed. "Would God that Latin America were ninety-seven per cent Roman Catholic! My friends in the hierarchy there say that not more than ten to fifteen per cent could be considered 'good Catholics.' Indeed, one might claim that the United States and England are more Roman Catholic than Latin America."

On Anglicanism's appeal in Latin America, Bishop Gooden was unusually candid. "There are Anglicans, devout and intelligent people, who visit Latin America for two or three weeks and return home to express opinions that are quite contrary to those of us who have spent ten, twenty or thirty or more years there," he said. "Some of them say that Anglicanism is not suited to the Latin temperament, whatever that is. . . . I have visited England for the past five weeks, and I sometimes wonder if Anglicanism is really at home here among the allegedly stolid, unemotional, sober, Anglo-Saxons who inhabit the land in which my father was born.[13] I have

---

[12] "In the thirty-three years I have worked in Latin America, I have seen the Anglican expression of Christianity somewhat modified in a Latin-Americanized form—growing and becoming increasingly indigenous," said Bishop Gooden. "Brazil with its three Anglican dioceses has become an autonomous church, Cuba is also, and Mexico may soon follow. Already half of our bishops there are nationals and probably within the next twenty years all of them will be natives of Latin America."

[13] A native of Lancashire, Robert Burton Gooden migrated to California as a child and was Suffragan of Los Angeles, 1930–1947. His son was consecrated Missionary Bishop of Panama and the Canal Zone in 1945 at the age of thirty-five.

met Englishmen who are not stolid, not unemotional, but very Anglo-Saxon and sometimes not even sober!

"We do not claim that Anglicanism will be warmly embraced by all Latin Americans any more than it is welcomed by all Englishmen or all Americans, or all Africans, for that matter," he continued, "but we do find that Anglicanism is welcomed by many Latin Americans and by an even greater number who recognize it as a means of bringing together, ecumenically, Pentecostal and other Protestants with Roman Catholics and Orthodox." [14]

There were, he said, "thousands of people south of the United States who are unchurched, who are estranged from their mother Church, who are seeking a spiritual home. They seek a home which is both Catholic and Protestant, Evangelical, Apostolic and Reformed, where the whole Bible is read, where all the Sacraments are administered, and where there is political and intellectual liberty, where married couples can raise a family in responsible freedom under God, where the worship is dignified and beautiful in accordance with that treasury of public praise and liturgy known as the Book of Common Prayer."

In conclusion, Bishop Gooden said, "We have not gone there to proselyte but to enrich, to supplement, to strengthen the total Christian witness in those vast lands where there is a great spiritual vacuum that urgently needs to be filled."

Bishop Gooden's Resolution was seconded by Reed of Colombia & Ecuador with the single comment: "I don't think there is anything I need to add—I don't think I could."

There was, of course, no arguing with the long address that had been delivered out of deep conviction and intimate knowledge of Latin America. Resolution No. 64, which the bishops approved,

---

[14] In a similar vein, the Primate of Igreja Episcopal do Brasil, Egmont Krischke, wrote in the Lambeth issue of *Pan-Anglican,* "The Church in the developing countries needs the full assurance that it truly belongs in the worldwide Anglican Communion, the assurance clearly stated that Anglicanism is not just an Anglo-Saxon episode, but a living branch of the Church Universal, with vital characteristics that transcend the British vein and the British historical incidents."

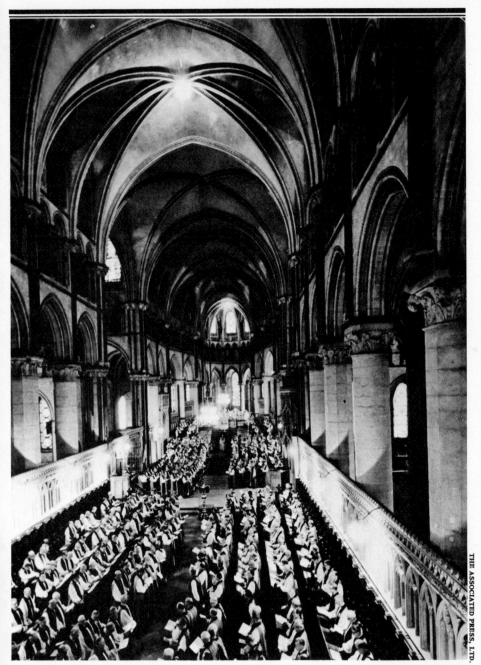

A total of 462 bishops from throughout the world fill the choir of the Cathedral Church of Christ, Canterbury, moments before the opening prayers of Lambeth X. In the distance the Archbishop of Canterbury ascends the steps of the High Altar where the great stone Chair of St. Augustine awaits him.

(Top) Led by a priest of the Diocese of Canterbury, as was each group of bishops, the tiny delegation of the Episcopal Church of Brazil winds its way into Canterbury Cathedral. (Bottom) In sharp contrast, the American episcopate forms the largest group at Lambeth X. Directly behind the standard-bearer is Andrew Tsu (left), formerly Assistant Bishop of Hong Kong, now an assistant in the Diocese of Pennsylvania; and, with him, Donald Campbell, formerly Suffragan of Los Angeles, now an assistant in the Diocese of Massachusetts. They are followed by other Assistants, Suffragans, Coadjutors, and Diocesans.

Black bishops predominate in two more groups approaching the Cathedral—the episcopates of the Church of the Province of Uganda, Rwanda, and Burundi and of the Church of the Province of East Africa. Both were inaugurated as independent Churches of the Anglican Communion by Archbishop Fisher. Forming a background for the processions were the lush green hedges of Kent in midsummer and, rising above them, the gables and tower of the Old Palace, the Archbishop's residence, standing on the foundations of the house from which Thomas Becket fled to the Cathedral, and his martyrdom, in 1170.

(Top) Their snowy surplices topped by convocation robes of brilliant red, the bishops move slowly across the playing field of White City Stadium for an outdoor Eucharist "in thanksgiving for the progress of the Gospel." (Bottom left) At the Offertory, the mitred Archbishop in Jerusalem presides as chief celebrant at the free-standing altar. Behind him are the assisting deacons and, in the stands, massed choirs of London parish churches.

Actor Alec McCowen, who played the title role in the London and New York productions of *Hadrian VII,* shakes hands with Trevor Huddleston, C.R., during intermission of special matinee for Lambeth Conference. The monk-bishop, head of an East African diocese since 1960, was preparing to take up his duties as Bishop of Stepney.

(Top) The Bishop of Quincy (Illinois) meets Queen Elizabeth, accompanied by Canterbury, during reception at Buckingham Palace. At center, the Bishop of Tokyo awaits introduction. (Bottom) In front row of pilgrimage to Holy Island of Lisdisfarne during Lambeth's traditional Missionary Weekend is the host, the Bishop of Newcastle (pointing), and, in biretta, the Bishop of Springfield (Illinois).

Taking time out from deliberations on papal encyclical, Canterbury confronts self-styled "radical Christians" at main entrance to Lambeth Palace. They asked for and received a brief conference with the Primate. The bearded leader of the group was the curate of St. Michael's, Highgate, the Rev. David Hart. In picket lines, speeches, and letters, they urged the bishops to dispose of cathedrals and official residences, sever links with the Establishment, and require the clergy to live as Christ lived.

In Westminster Abbey, where a month earlier he had celebrated the initial Eucharist of Lambeth X, Canterbury pauses amid the memorials of a side aisle of the nave. On the final morning of the Conference he led the fathers in special intercessory prayer for a peaceful outcome of Russia's invasion of Czechoslovakia.

spoke of the "urgent need for an increasing Christian witness and involvement in which the Anglican churches must make their unique and full contribution." They also summoned the Anglican Communion to give Latin America "prominent emphasis" in missionary education, prayer, and commitment to the world mission.

A WIDER EPISCOPAL FELLOWSHIP

The idea of a fellowship of bishops from other episcopally governed churches and from united churches with which Anglican bodies have merged was frankly evaluated for Lambeth X by the Rev. David M. Paton, one of the Church of England's most knowledgeable men in ecumenical and missionary work.

In a preparatory essay, "The Positive Idea of A Wider Episcopal Fellowship," Paton clearly spelled out his belief that if a wider episcopal fellowship was thought of as a group existing in addition to the Anglican Communion, it would run into one of two alternatives—"too many meetings to go to and pay for" or, failing that, "it will not be of very great significance."

Further, Paton wrote, a larger fellowship of bishops would run the risk of appearing to be a "takeover bid by Anglicans for the united churches." (The appearance of such a takeover would be the result, he wrote, of people thinking that the Anglican Communion had been succeeded by a fellowship that embraced bodies that have not been Anglican—such as the Old Catholic or the Philippine Independent—as well as united churches, part of whose members were once Anglican.)

"A wider episcopal fellowship of *churches* such as might first supplement and later replace the Anglican Communion is not a practical possibility," Paton said. Then, bringing the discussion into a sharper focus, he declared that a "wider episcopal fellowship of *bishops* which might take the place of the Lambeth Conference probably is a practical possibility."

In addition to Paton, the committee had the advice of another seasoned expert in ecclesiastical and interchurch relations, Gray of Connecticut.

In its Report, which fell at the end of the long commentary pre-pared by the Unity Section, the committee expressed the hope that "new churches will be formed which can no longer be described in a limiting sense as Anglican but which will belong with us in a wider fellowship, sharing both the integrity of the faith and the historic episcopate in its various forms."

Two ancient and basic concepts—episcopacy and collegiality—were wisely defined in the Unity Report.

"The Anglican tradition has always regarded *episcopacy* as an essential part of its Catholic inheritance," it said. "We would regard it as an extension of the apostolic office and function both in time and space, and, moreover, we regard the transmission of apostolic power and responsibility as an activity of the college of bishops and never as a result of isolated action by an individual bishop. . . . Tra-ditionally, the bishop is father in God to the clergy and laity of a territorial diocese, and part of his vocation is to represent the Cath-olic Church in his diocese and, conversely, to represent his diocese within the councils of the wider Church."

The Report spoke of *collegiality* as an underlying principle "that the apostolic calling, responsibility, and authority are an inher-itance given to the whole body or college of bishops." Therefore "every individual bishop has a responsibility both as a member of this college and as chief pastor in his diocese."

After discussing the Anglican and Roman uses of collegiality, the Report concluded that "although the declaration and guardian-ship of the faith has traditionally been regarded as belonging fun-damentally to the episcopal office, the collegiality of the episcopate must always be seen in the context of the conciliar character of the Church, involving the *consensus fidelium,* in which the episcopate has its place."

In Resolution No. 55, approved by all the fathers, Lambeth X recommended "that the principle of collegiality should be a guiding principle in the growth of the relationships between the provinces of the Anglican Communion and those churches with which we are, or shall be, in full communion."

The mood of Lambeth seemed to anticipate in the near future a much longer list of "those churches." Consequently it viewed as realistic the prospect of new churches that can no longer be considered Anglican but with bishops recognized by Anglicans, although outside the Communion. Such meetings had been envisioned as long ago as Lambeth VIII. In 1964 Canterbury had met with thirty-nine archbishops and bishops representing Anglican churches, the Church of Finland, Spanish Reformed Episcopal, Lusitanian Church of Portugal, Mar Thoma Syrian Church, Old Catholic, Philippine Independent Catholic, Polish National Catholic Church of America, Church of South India, and Church of Sweden.

Lambeth adopted Resolution No. 65, urging that another such meeting, "a General Episcopal Consultation (drawn from many countries) be held in the near future." It apparently favored that name to replace the old references to wider episcopal fellowship. In so doing, the Conference affirmed Paton's contention that the phrase "has by now attracted sufficient misunderstanding that it may have to be abandoned."

Also in Resolution No. 65, Lambeth X recommended regional episcopal consultations on a basis of representation wider than that suggested for the General Episcopal Consultation.[15] Such meetings would set forth Canterbury's hope for "a community of bishops in the Church of God, both from ancient and from 'younger' churches, who find their sharing in the bishop's office to be a ground of present partnerships and an anticipation of future collegial unity in the one universal Church."

Although cloaked in ecclesiastical parlance and buried deep in the bundle of resolutions, such a recommendation could be vital if no more Lambeth Conferences were to be convened.

In the trend to include the laity in everything, Chiu Ban It of

---

[15] In October 1968 the Canadian bishops were guests for five days of the American bishops meeting at Augusta, Georgia. One of the major decisions was the establishment of a regional council of the Western Hemisphere under which the Canadian church, the American church, and the Church of the Province of the West Indies would coordinate many of their activities.

Singapore & Malaya said on the day the Resolution was presented that he hoped "wider" would include laity as well as clergy. He was one of several who said that meetings should be spaced to avoid following on an assembly of the World Council of Churches. "It's too much at one time," he warned. "But I also have a feeling of isolationism growing because of disengagement of Britain among the nations and of churches going into other bodies. Insularism may return to the Church of England. Regional conferences give rise to regionalism and continentalism."

Another warning came from Allison of Winchester, who said that inclusion of anyone besides bishops would be a duplication of the World Council of Churches.

Confident that the Resolution would pass, Cariboo was ready with the announcement that the recommended meeting would take place in the autumn of 1969.

At his final press conference, Canterbury said, "I was glad of the Resolution about the Wider Episcopal Fellowship to be convened by the Archbishop of Canterbury and its ecumenical significance that the Archbishop of Canterbury is given a free hand to invite to the episcopal conference not only Anglican bishops, but bishops of churches in communion and also other bishops who are willing to come. That flexibility and fluidity means that Anglicanism's future in relation to other churches isn't predefined. Perhaps one was disappointed that there wasn't more discussion and definition about the boundaries of Anglicanism in the ecumenical scene, but I daresay that such definitions were really impossible. But personally I am rather glad of this vagueness. The impression upon me is that there is a great Anglican solidarity in these pursuits, but that Anglican solidarity sees that it is great to have two roles—the role of being an Anglican Communion until the reintegration of Christendom has gone further, but also of being in a rather undefined way a faithful witness about Christian traditions. I tried to give a glimpse of that twofold idea in my sermon at Canterbury, and I think that quite unself-consciously the Conference has affirmed the same kind of idea."

ANGLICAN CONSULTATIVE COUNCIL

More than a year before Lambeth X convened, George Luxton, Bishop of Huron since 1948, began a personal campaign for "an organized and planned unity within our Anglican Communion." In addresses throughout the United States and Canada he repeated his conviction that the infrequency of Lambeth Conferences and the even fewer Anglican Congresses (three since 1908) made it imperative for the bishops to take some action toward strengthening Anglican unity.

Huron's greatest inspiration appeared to be the late Rector of New York City's Trinity Parish, the Rev. John Heuss, who had written that "there are few sins today so damaging to the cause of Christ as haphazard, individualistic planning which, in fact, is both the sin of pride and sloth." [16]

The role of the Church of England as the established Church, Huron felt, had delayed the Anglican Communion's development as a world-wide force in Christendom. He sought to transcend the difficulty with a drastic remodeling of the Anglican Communion from its traditional existence as a loose collection of national provinces held together only by the Lambeth Conference, the Lambeth Consultative Body, and the Council on Missionary Strategy.

Huron won much support in dioceses where he spoke, and, although he did not get all the backing he wanted, his efforts did force

---

[16] Much of Dr. Heuss' contempt for the lack of cooperation that resulted in wastes of manpower, money, and effort was seen in the statement to which Huron often referred: "It is my belief that we will be just about what we are—a self-centered, self-righteous, self-satisfied caricature of what the One, Holy, Catholic, and Apostolic Church should be—unless we take some bold action to form an authoritative governing body. This is not to say that there are no great bishops, other clergymen, and outstanding lay people in the Anglican Communion. Nor is it to say that devotion to Christ and the Gospel, self-sacrificial living, and inspired work do not exist among us. It is to say that the average diocese and the average parish are a pale image of what God intended His Church to be."

Lambeth X to decide on what sort of centralized organization Anglicanism should have.

The Huron plan called for a revised Anglican congress with approximately 500 representatives (bishops, priests, laymen) from throughout the Anglican Communion who would have definite legislative powers and would meet at least every five years.

With numerous references to the *aggiornamento* of the Church —a term admittedly borrowed from Pope John—Huron offered his plan "to promote further discussion, and to draw forth alternatives that will better serve Christ's mission for the Church today."

An alternative was proposed almost immediately. That it came from the Bishop of Cariboo surprised some who thought he was preoccupied with details of administering Lambeth X. It was pointed out, however, that few had observed the governmental needs of Anglicanism as closely as Cariboo while Anglican Executive Officer.

In presenting his plan, Cariboo did not forego the opportunity to criticize Huron's and to say, "It is interesting that just as the Roman Catholic Church is beginning to decentralize, we Anglicans seem to be moving toward centralization."

Cariboo called for a central committee of only fifty persons— far smaller than Huron's group and little more than an enlargement of the present Lambeth Consultative Body of twenty-six members. The increase was to make it possible for priests and laymen to join the bishops in consultation.

Cariboo never publicly spelled out what authority his plan might have, but it was obviously less than Huron's proposal. Cariboo himself predicted that "the plan adopted will be neither mine nor the Bishop of Huron's." He was right, as the course of events revealed, although the final plan was far closer to Cariboo's proposals than to Huron's.

In discussion it was brought out that Huron had sent his plan to every bishop of the Anglican Communion during the year before Lambeth X, and that McCall of Wangaratta had drafted a reply and sent copies of it to all the bishops.

"An executive body with power to act would be very dangerous and would surely turn us into a 'denomination,'" Wangaratta wrote. "Our whole position as Anglicans has surely always been that we are members of the Christian Church in communion with the See of Canterbury—a connection of historical accident that has certainly not been without its blessings. . . . In Australia we are quite aware that the Archbishop of Canterbury has no jurisdiction, and has not had for many years, nor has he sought it but, because he occupies the see that he does, he remains the focal point of the Anglican Communion. The suggestion that certain clear powers, including that of ecumenical dialogue, should be transferred to an executive officer and his advisers is extremely dangerous."

The upshot of the matter was, predictably, compromise. Lambeth X adopted a plan subject to ratification by two-thirds of the member Churches before October 31, 1969; if approved, it would establish an Anglican Consultative Council that would still not have legislative power but would permit a wider scope in the task of informing, advising, and encouraging churches of the Anglican Communion.

As outlined in the Resolution, No. 69 (the longest approved by Lambeth X), the Council would have a minimum membership of fifty-two bishops, priests, deacons, and laymen. It would meet every two years and its standing committee annually. A unique feature of the Council is the provision for two women members and two laymen not over age twenty-eight at the time of their appointment.

Taylor of Cape Town proposed the Resolution from the podium rather than the floor. Its seconding by Huron indicated that he felt he could approve it even though the much-hoped-for legislative powers were omitted.

Cape Town said that the most controversial part of the Resolution was a section calling for Canterbury to be president instead of chairman, for him to be consulted before the Council is convened, and for him to preside at the inaugural session. It had run into opposition because some feared it did not insure the historic role of the Archbishop of Canterbury. It was felt that a presidency rather than a chairmanship still insured his historicity but at the same time prevented the primate from having to deal with details which might better be dealt with by another chairman. The presidency stayed, and the Council is to elect a chairman and vice-chairman.

A further amendment covered the placement of deacons on the Council—an innovation that could allow members of the Council even younger than the twenty-eight-year-olds. The provision for women and for laymen under twenty-eight was instigated by the Presiding Bishop of the American Church, who felt that the membership was otherwise "heavily weighted on the side of the ordained."

Again a Lambeth resolution suffered somewhat by lack of time for proper changes. When it was presented it was noted that there was no specific provision for representatives from the Church of Brazil, and an amendment was passed to include it and to change the provision for representatives from Latin America to "Council of Anglican Bishops in South America." Neither change was made in the final Report, although Brazil could well be included by the reference to "any province of the Anglican Communion not at present represented," but, as one bishop said, the newest member of the Anglican Communion might well have wished to see its name spelled out in print.

THE COST OF THE ANGLICAN
COMMUNION PROGRAM

To many of the churches of the Anglican Communion, the first question about the proposed Anglican Consultative Council had to be "How much is it going to cost?"

Woods of Melbourne mentioned expense early in the Conference and asked that a price tag be made known before a vote was called on the new consultative body. An *ad hoc* finance committee was appointed with Huron as chairman and the Presiding Bishop of the American Church as one of the members.

When the report was submitted to the Conference, the cost of the Anglican Communion's joint projects and Executive Officer became public knowledge for the first time. The 1968 budget was £31,045 ($75,000). When asked what it included, Cariboo replied,

"My salary, the Deputy Executive Officer, my secretary and two girls in my office. Also the office and office maintenance and rent—in fact, considerable rent, for the house in Belgravia [the embassy area of central London]."

The budget also includes support for the Jerusalem archbishopric and the Anglican Center in Rome.

It had been found impractical to prorate the budget among the member churches on the basis of baptized or communicant members; instead, the deciding factor had been the church's ability to pay. Consequently, more than 80 per cent of the budget had been raised from among the "better established Churches"—England, Wales, Ireland, Scotland, the United States, Canada, Australia, and New Zealand. Of the contributors, England and the U.S. shared about 60 per cent. (The American Church's portion in 1968 amounted to £9,887 [$24,000].)

With the formation of the Anglican Consultative Council to meet every two years (standing committee annually), and also with the addition of another deputy officer to be stationed in Geneva, and an expansion of the Center in Rome, 1970's budget was set at £53,410 or $129,000, with the U.S. and English portions roughly $40,000 each. Tentative arrangements call for "economy travel plans" for the 1970 kick-off meeting of the Anglican Consultative Council, with funds supplied from a central budget. In addition, board and lodging for the ten-day meeting would be at the Council's expense with the recommendation that members "if possible should live in community during the meetings."

MRI

For all the enthusiasm with which the MRI program [17] had been launched less than five years earlier at the Anglican Congress in Toronto, there was only slight discussion of it at Lambeth X.

---

[17] Anglicanism has rarely been more eloquent than in the manifesto entitled *Mutual Responsibility and Interdependence in the Body of Christ,* for which MRI quickly became the abbreviation. Issued at Toronto, August 17, 1963, it paired off "companion dioceses" in widely scattered parts of the

MRI had long ago faced up to the charge that it was a program handed down from on high with the intent to produce material results only, but some bishops felt that such criticism had to be made a part of the Lambeth record. Among them, Arthur of Grafton [Australia] believed that MRI efforts should not be confined to Anglicans.

There were, however, some moving testimonies from bishops, especially those of the "third world," about great benefits received; on the Conference floor and in the lounges it was obvious that MRI had succeeded in bringing together in close friendship many bishops and dioceses who might have remained strangers.

Early in the Conference, Allison, Bishop in the Sudan, praised MRI but asked for a sharper definition.

Shelton of Matabeleland said it showed that "the American Church is beginning to face the world situation with more than words—and MRI is a good example."

With little other discussion, the Conference adopted Resolution No. 67, expressing "gratitude for the concept of MRI" and summoning "our churches to a deeper commitment to Christ's mission through a wider partnership of prayer and by sharing sacrificially and effectively their manpower and money, and by a readiness to learn from each other."

Indicating some dissatisfaction in approach, the Resolution added that "the Conference believes that the time has come for a reappraisal of the policies, methods, and areas of responsibility of the Anglican Communion in discharging its share of the mission of Christ and that there is a need for a renewed sense of urgency."

The Lambeth Report gave some practical advice: each church should be free to decide to what extent MRI is appropriate to its own needs; project programs should be realistic in scale, flexible in

---

Anglican Communion, declaring "Mission is not the kindness of the lucky to the unlucky; it is mutual, united obedience to the one God Whose mission it is." Discussing it in a newspaper interview two days later, Bishop Bayne said, "Some Church members will have to cease thinking of the Church as a kind of memorial association for a deceased clergyman named Christ."

operation, and in harmony with accepted criteria; in building projects, account should be taken of the continuing cost of maintenance as well as original cost; support of the local ministry should be a first charge of the local church and not usually included in MRI projects; and competent advice should be sought either from regional churches or the Secretary General's office in deciding on priorities.

WORLD ANGLICAN CONGRESSES

The nearest thing to a world-wide synod of the Anglican Communion has been the Anglican Congresses in which bishops, priests, and laymen came together for discussions of the problems and the programs of member Churches. Like Lambeth, it never had legislative powers and met even less frequently (London, 1908; Minneapolis, 1954; Toronto, 1963). Long before Lambeth X opened, there was a consensus that there would never be another congress on so large a scale as Toronto.

Its doom was formally sealed by the Committee on Inter-Anglican Structures, which stated that the world-wide Anglican Congresses should be replaced by *"a joint meeting* at the time of an Assembly of the World Council of Churches, of the Consultative Council and of Anglican participants in the Assembly; and, secondly, regional meetings of representatives of Anglican churches, if possible in association with meetings of area councils of churches."

The Archbishop of York told Lambeth X that "they have become increasingly expensive, and I suppose the holding of them laid us open to the charge of conducting jamborees," but he added that he had an open mind on the matter and hoped "the Consultative Council would keep the situation under review."

Infrequency of regional meetings, he said, lessened the opportunity to meet others or, as he put it, "We need to see to it, however we do it, that East meets West and West meets East."

Further, said York, "We do not need to meet at the exalted level, if I may use that word, of the Lambeth Conference or at the level of

the Consultative Council. We need to meet at the ordinary level of
the man who is doing a parish job in Lambeth or a parish job in
Lesotho."

Cariboo frequently stated that one of the problems of an Anglican congress was where to meet. "Who else can afford to be host,"
he asked, "after you have met in England, the U.S., and Canada?"

Gray of Connecticut was one of those who felt unhappy about the
decision. "I think one of the things that would be lost, if we should
never decide to have a meeting again, would be the fuller aspect of
our fellowship," he said. "If there were only regional groups, then
we would lose that contact that I personally feel has been valuable
—in having laity from all sections of the world, and bishops and
priests from all sections of the world, meet one another."

Such pleas had no effect on the Conference: the recommendation
of the committee held.

FUTURE LAMBETH CONFERENCES

Having discussed numerous facets of ecumenism, intercommunion, plans for unity, and Anglicanism's own organizational
structure, the bishops came finally to an examination of prospects
for future Lambeth Conferences.

"Many persons have been deeply troubled by the oft-repeated
idea that the mission of the Anglican Communion is to die in order
that it may be reborn in a larger sphere of usefulness by absorption
into a numerically greater Church," Gray of Connecticut acknowledged in a paper published a few months before Lambeth X convened. "Whatever the future may hold in the way of Church unity,
certainly the Anglican Communion has values which cannot be ignored and which should not be depreciated."

When questioned by Dorothy Mills Parker of the Washington
Post about the possibility that 1968 would see the last Lambeth, the
Archbishop of Canterbury said simply that it was premature to predict and that "how this Lambeth Conference sees the future will be
more clear at the end."

Pessimistic comments about "the last Lambeth" rapidly decreased once the bishops were worshiping and meeting together, realizing anew the stimulation and strong ties the Conference produced.

A long, rambling, and sentimental but highly sensitive address supporting future Lambeths was made by Stephen Bayne, who was applauded by his fellow bishops as he strode to the platform, stoop-shouldered but tan.

"Your Grace, I had hoped to get through this Lambeth Conference without opening my yap," he said.

After touching briefly on organizational structure and ideas about unity, Bishop Bayne took up the matter of future Lambeths. "I'm not sure that we really need to say anything to Your Grace about when you ask this large houseparty to come together, it's your party, and you would call us at your will, but I have a rather deep feeling about Lambeth that I wish somehow might find expression. I wish that we could say to every church in the Anglican Communion, if you go into a locally united church, we bid you well, we support you, we want to say to you that we hope that you will feel free to join any kind of world association that you choose to belong to. We hope that you will want to play your part in the World Council of Churches. We hope that you will want to relate yourself to any confessional body but we want you to know that should you choose to maintain some kind of relationship with the Lambeth Conference that we want you to do that, too.

"I would hope that we would say this and mean it," Bishop Bayne continued. "I would hope that we would say to those churches which are not in any sense Anglican churches, but with which we are in communion, I would hope that we would want to say to them, if you wish to join with us in our brotherly conference as bishops, we are glad to have you and we want you to take your place among us."

Turning to the Draft Report's efforts "to describe that mysterious thing known as Anglicanism or the Anglican tradition," Bishop Bayne confided, "I've tried my hand at it, God knows, enough times, and I still don't believe fully everything I've ever written about it. What I do believe about the Anglican Communion is that it is a thing and a process. A Lambeth Conference has meant for me since I was first a bishop quite a few years ago . . . a living relationship, constantly changing, a bringing together of bishops of many different backgrounds and traditions, and nationalities, a meeting sometimes abrasive, sometimes exalting, sometimes wisely teaching and leading, sometimes shaping. It has been a living meeting of men who are sharing one apostolate everywhere in the world, under radically different conditions. I do not know how to describe the spiritual quality of these meetings. I am not happy trying to describe the spiritual contribution, regardless of whether we have a contribution to make. The only thing I'm sure of is the meeting. The only way that I would be sure that the Anglican Communion was playing its part . . . would be by meeting, by sharing our common problems, by joining as we have joined in time past, in seeking together new insights and improvising new improvisations. And that's why I believe in the Lambeth Conference. I would long to see us say to this great President, the Archbishop of Canterbury, that if he chooses to call us once a year, we would like to come, but we believe the invitation to share in it should be expanded as widely and freely as possible and that we believe that whatever gift our tradition is going to make to the united Christendom will come because we are faithful to it, not because we abandon it."

Again applauded as he finished, Bishop Bayne resumed his seat only briefly before leaving the hall. He slipped out quietly, but those who saw him go felt that they had heard a moving tribute to the whole spirit of Anglicanism delivered by one who perhaps had embraced it as thoroughly and who knew it as deeply as anyone present.

Later in the day the Archbishop of York, whose sentiments were not always predictable, also went on record as approving future Lambeths. "I am very glad the door has been left open for the possibility or probability of holding future Lambeth Conferences," he said of the Draft of the Unity Report. "There has been a good deal of talk, here and there, about this being the last Conference . . . but these Conferences are, I think, precious things, and I think it is well that we should not think of this Lambeth as necessarily the last, but that the door is left open, if Your Grace in consultation with the Consultative Committee should think it right to call us."

The next speaker, Wright of Algoma [Canada], spoke mainly of the Anglican Cycle of Prayer, an innovation of Lambeth VIII. While his subject did not directly pertain to future Lambeths, his comments could not help but remind the bishops of the support by prayer which they had received from all the dioceses represented around the room.

"The main personal thing I want to speak of is the deep spiritual relationship between bishops and the upholding of one another in prayer," said Archbishop Wright, who was also Metropolitan for the Province of Ontario. "How many of you, this morning, remembered the Bishop of Newark over there? I won't ask for an open vote . . . but oh, the times I have been in a railroad station, traveling, in some waiting room at four-thirty in the morning, reading my daily office. There, on some railroad siding in Canada, I am upholding in prayer some diocese such as Carlisle in England. 'It is not things for the sake of places' [a reference to Pope Gregory's words so recently quoted from the Chair of St. Augustine]. We speak also of the 'revival of the priestly spirit.' I wish to thank you, my brother bishops, for that and the personal relationship, upheld in prayer. 'O Lord revive Thy Church, beginning with me.' "

Another valuable endorsement for future Lambeths came from Ramsey of Durham. "We are still very provincial and one would not suspect, except for Lambeth, that we are an international communion," he pointed out. "There is no business or commercial organization worth its salt that does not count international contacts as its lifeblood. Only study and inquiry on that basis can give us that breadth of vision which is so much needed. Of course it will cost money and time and manpower, but nothing that is worth doing can be done 'on the cheap.' "

Then, poignantly, one of the missionary bishops was heard—Curtis of Mauritius, a French-speaking, multiracial, extraprovincial diocese under Canterbury's jurisdiction, embracing the islands of Mauritius, Rodrigues, and the Seychelles. Bishop Curtis, an Englishman who worked on Mauritius from 1937 to 1944 and returned there as bishop in 1967, said: "It is likely we will have a Council of the Dioceses of the Indian Ocean, but still our isolation is great. It might be a year before I see another bishop unless one is flying from Australia to Africa, and, as sometimes happens, changes planes in Mauritius. I hope we shall not lose touch with the mainstream of Anglicanism."

Within the hour, following hard on the affirmations of support for Lambeth, the young, native Bishop of Kurunagala, Ceylon, Cyril Wickremesinghe, took the floor to criticize the bishops who "speak sentimentally" of the Lambeth Conferences. "When we are given money by the West to come here, it is a stigma among our people," he declared. "Those of us in Asia, away from the west, feel that far too much time is spent in conferences of this sort. What we need is Anglican participation in inter-Church affairs." [18]

Kurunagala said that bishops in Asia could not afford to leave their countries to discuss subjects they had already mulled over at the World Council of Churches, in some cases at deeper and more relevant levels. He was criticizing not only Lambeth but regional conferences, he said, such as what was recommended to replace worldwide Anglican Congresses. He thought it would be far better if those from the West came to Asia.[19]

---

[18] Another bishop from a distant diocese, Bryan of Barrackpore, disagreed with Kurunagala's approach. Speaking later in the same session, Barrackpore chided his colleague for making "such a large point about the expenses of attending the Conference."

[19] By then, the tide had turned so definitely in favor of future Lambeths that Kurunagala found himself in a difficult position when London newspapers the following morning headlined LAMBETH CONFERENCE COSTLY AND FUTILE, BISHOP SAYS (*The Times*) and BISHOPS SAY CONFERENCE A WASTE OF TIME (*Telegraph*). Seeking to make his position clear, he appeared at the Bishop of Cariboo's news briefings to say, not too convincingly, that he had been misunderstood. He had not, he said, intended to mean that Lambeth was a waste of time but rather the scheduling of additional meetings that would mean "a multiplication of Conferences within the Anglican Communion." Also, he said, the bishops should not plan large meetings that duplicated others or obscured the value of regional ecumenical gatherings in which the Anglican presence should be felt. Cariboo commented philosophically, "You can't win. You are either accused of talking about the same things as the World Council of Churches at Uppsala or you are asked why you are not talking about the same things as Uppsala."

With Kurunagala's comments, the Conference veered momentarily toward discussion of the more negative aspects of future Lambeths.

The Assistant Bishop of St. Edmundsbury and Ipswich, Arthur Michael Hollis (originally consecrated Bishop of Madras in 1942, and from 1948 to 1952 a moderator of the Church of South India) looking directly at Kurunagala, spoke of Lambeth as a denominational Conference. "Every organization has in some way a vested interest against change," he said in a high-pitched voice. "We can't be a part of a united Church and of the Anglican Communion at the same time. My experience with South India shows that. Most of the world is not so rich as the West. . . . Anglicans as much as other bodies do engage in doubletalk, speaking of unity and the Anglican Communion at the same time."

The former Bishop of Accra, Richard Roseveare, SSM, easily identified in his monk's habit of purple, addressed the Conference from the gallery railing, the only consultant to speak out on future Lambeths. "I usually find it impossible to disagree with what Stephen Bayne says, but he is mistaken when he says that we should ask Anglican bishops who go into united churches to come to Lambeth Conferences," he declared. "If such invitations are given, they are given to the church where the Anglican bishops are and not to the bishops. It would encourage Anglican bishops to go into other churches and continue to look back over their shoulder at their Anglican homes when they should be applying themselves to their new jobs."

Welles of West Missouri said he was moved by Kurunagala's comments but added, "I would say to him and myself that while indeed the Lord said it was more blessed to give than to receive, the greatest single 'hangup'—or hindrance, to use a less American term—is that none of us seem sufficiently ready to receive. We are ready to give and to share, but we seem increasingly lacking in humility and holiness in receiving of others that which we happen sorely to need."

The Bishop of Iran, Dehqani-Tafti, near the end of the afternoon wondered aloud about the position of his distant diocese, and his successors, without a Lambeth Conference. "Dioceses such as ours may fall into isolation," he warned. "We are not so developed as the Church of India, Pakistan, Burma, and Ceylon. I am beginning to feel lonely already. What is going to happen to us if we are not members of the World Council of Churches? People probably have it in mind but it is vital to our life. We want to be independent and have our own national Church but we can't do it alone."

Both apathy toward and enthusiasm for future Lambeths had held sway, but the recommendation of the Draft remained substantially the same in the Report: "In view of the historic importance of the Lambeth Conference over the past hundred years and the undoubted value of the present meeting, the Archbishop of Canterbury should be asked to decide, on the advice of the Anglican Consultative Council, upon the calling of future Conferences and on their time, place, and agenda."

Thus the right and privilege that was the prerogative of Canterbury in the first place was handed back to him with the approval and blessing of the tenth Lambeth Conference. The discussion came full circle when the same American reporter who had questioned Canterbury at the first press conference asked him at the last one: "Your Grace . . . do you think there will be another conference of Anglican bishops, whether at Lambeth or not?"

Canterbury replied that he did, indeed, believe there would be another Conference. "I think it's likely that it won't be here but will be in some other part of the world, and I think it likely that there will be bishops not defined as Anglican, but bishops with us," he said. "That is my guess."

CHAPTER 9

LAMBETH'S MESSAGE

O_N THE CLOSING DAY OF LAM-
beth X, the Conference approved a short paper called simply "A
Message from the Bishops at the Lambeth Conference to the Clergy
and Laity of the Anglican Communion." It replaced the Encyclical
Letter to the Faithful in Jesus Christ, that grandly worded but
self-conscious and rambling document with which the Lambeth
fathers had traditionally concluded their talks.

Issued at the close of Lambeth I, the rolling cadences of the first
encyclical had established a pattern for the pastoral letters written
by the next eight Conferences.

"We, the Bishops of Christ's Holy Catholic Church, as based on
Scripture, and defined by the first four General Councils, now
assembled by the good providence of God at the Archiepiscopal
Palace of Lambeth under the presidency of the Primate of All England," wrote the Bishops in 1867, "desire first to give thanks to
Almighty God for having thus brought us together for common
counsels."

259

The colorful sweep of words (the prefaces thereafter varied only slightly) caught the imagination of several generations of Anglicans. True to form, Lambeth IX echoed the same splendor, perhaps more eloquently than ever, in what was to be the last of the letters.

"We, Archbishops and Bishops of the Holy Catholic and Apostolic Church in communion with the See of Canterbury, three hundred and ten in number, assembled from forty-six countries, under the Presidency of Geoffrey, Archbishop of Canterbury, in the year of our Lord one thousand nine hundred and fifty-eight, send you greeting in the name of our Lord and Saviour Jesus Christ," it said. "In his Name we desire to set before you the outcome of the deliberation to which, with earnest prayer and Eucharist, we have for five weeks devoted ourselves day by day."

The flowery language of the first encyclical and some subsequent ones had been translated into several languages, for Orthodox patriarchs and other dignitaries. The letters had been signed with a flourish by all the bishops and were read from pulpits throughout the Anglican Communion. At later Conferences, they were signed only by the Archbishop of Canterbury and the Episcopal Secretary; fewer bishops were involved in the drafts, and these were rarely read in their entirety, if at all, from pulpits. As the Church sought a more vital image in the 1960s, it was suggested that the encyclical as traditionally framed was a custom cherished by some but regarded as sanctimonious, or simply ignored, by many others.

"Those things are pious, ponderous, presumptuous, and persnickety," complained a Canadian seminarian in a paper on Church history. "Besides, who reads them?"

As Lambeth X approached, there was more talk that the letters were outmoded, overly long, and ineffective. And with the publication of *Humanae Vitae* the word "encyclical" took on added disfavor. In his news briefings, the Bishop of Cariboo repeatedly warned that the Conference might not issue an encyclical.

It was less than astonishing then, that the Steering Committee of Lambeth X submitted a "message" of fewer than a thousand words (the 1958 encyclical had run to approximately 4400) which gave the briefest introduction and only the most cursory treatment to the

Conference themes. It was presented apologetically and approved reluctantly.

"The Steering Committee was charged with the responsibility of producing a message," the Bishop of London told the Conference when he came to the podium toward the middle of the last morning. "It was not clear until last night how we stood on certain issues. We are sorry we could not give it to you to read in advance. It was only dictated onto the typewriter and came from the typewriter in final form about twenty minutes ago."

As he spoke, the men from the Church Information Office distributed Xeroxed copies of the text that showed it had indeed been swiftly pieced together.

"In the judgment of the Steering Committee, this is not an encyclical letter," London continued. "We did not feel that the old-style letter addressed to the peoples of the world was quite in keeping with our Conference together."

For the next few minutes, London read aloud the message—the only document thus presented, in its entirety, to an open plenary session.

"At the end of our Conference we thank God for the renewal of fellowship and vision which he has given us as we have worked and prayed together," said the opening paragraph.

As background, it sketched the conditions that had surrounded Lambeth X—"a background of grim events in Vietnam, West Africa, and Czechoslovakia, and of mounting protest against social injustice."

It took sure but fleeting notice of change in the world—"a world which will no longer accept widespread want and poverty; a world in which inherited institutions and traditional ways of thought are increasingly questioned. Even in the realm of theology, their faith is being re-examined and in part rejected by some theologians."

Without pause, London went on to report what the message said on faith: "To those bewildered by all this we say: *God is.*"

London's voice came down hard on the acclamation *"God is"* as it did with the other assurances that were the burden of the message —*"God is. . . . God reigns. . . . God loves. . . . God speaks."*

In the Ministry Section, the message saw the role of the Church allied with its Lord as "the suffering servant." It emphasized its awareness of the insistence of youth, and of men and women throughout the world, that "the Church will be renewed only insofar as she pursues that role."

Finally, in Unity, the message returned to the theme that had also been present in the encyclicals—the waste and scandal of divisions within the Body of Christ. "Renewal demands unity: unity cannot come without renewal," it declared.

The message reached its conclusion with reaffirmation of its belief in hope and in God as an active force in the world. "It is no time for either despair or doubt," it said. "Rather it is a time to remember the Lord's saying, 'Be of good cheer, I have overcome the world.' "

The applause that greeted the message was perfunctory at best. Even Canterbury publicly indicated his disappointment by asking, "What would the Conference like to do with the message?"

He suggested several courses. "It can be sent out in the name of the Conference, or of the Steering Committee, or it can be torn up."

Although Canterbury had observed that there would not be time to discuss the message, there nonetheless was spirited discussion from the floor for the next few minutes. Only one bishop, Crittenden of Erie, dealt with the phrasing of the message by objecting to a reference to "worldly entanglements." The rest of the talk was on whether to release it.

For a moment the choice lay between following Gray of Connecticut, who asked that it be issued in the name of the Conference, or Clark, Primate of Canada, who said it should come from the Steering Committee. At that point it was suggested that the message should be issued by Canterbury.

A murmur of voices broke out on the floor as Canterbury shifted restlessly in his chair, obviously wanting nothing to do with putting out the message over his signature. Then London spoke again, saying that a message from a Steering Committee would not be well received by the world and that Canterbury should not be asked to give his sole, personal endorsement.

The Archbishop of York spoke next, acknowledging that Canterbury was in a difficult position and perhaps the message should go out with a footnote saying it was only "generally approved." The Presiding Bishop of the American Church sought to break the deadlock. "Do we agree generally on the message?" he asked. "If not, say 'no' and junk it. If 'yes,' say so and send it out."

The bishops voted their approval more to speed the dispatch of business than to endorse the message. In any case, it was merely a token of last-minute unity rather than real agreement or affirmation. (Only the Bishop of Southwark was seen to raise a hand in objection.) In its mildness and superficiality, nobody could be proud of the message, nor was it worthy of the 462 bishops. Even so, no one appeared to miss the traditional encyclical: it was gone, and an attempt at a corporate message did not fill the void.

Moving into its final hour, the Conference could not stop to consider its near-abandonment of the Thirty-nine Articles and the reluctant approval of the message. Instead, the Conference pressed on to make several acknowledgments to groups and individuals.

"We don't want the gallery to end in silence," Canterbury said, calling on Ernest Payne of the Baptist World Alliance for a word from the observers. Dr. Payne thanked the Conference, and was in turn thanked by Canterbury, who said that "the vigorous contributions from the observers were the most worthwhile parts of all."

Bishop Bayne came forward once again, identifying himself as "President and only member of the Alumni Society of Anglican Executive Officers—the 'Old Axe-onians.' " Turning to Cariboo, Bishop Bayne said, "I direct my remarks to the next prospective member of the Society. He has won his way into our hearts. He has vexed, encouraged, led, guided, and accused us."

Bishop Bayne's motion of gratitude to Cariboo was seconded by the Bishop of London, who as Bishop of Peterborough had been Episcopal Secretary of Lambeth IX and recalled that the duties of the office were "sometimes of a soul-shattering nature." Cariboo and his staff had worked with "great skill, great understanding, great charm," London said, and Cariboo had "found a way of keeping more bishops in order and of doing it with a graciousness and a humor that has made us all quite willingly his slaves."

In reply, Cariboo made only the briefest reference to himself, then turned to present a gift to Canterbury.

"I am only the figurehead of a vast amount of work we have done together," Cariboo told the bishop. "As I thank you, as your servant, I now do a task on your behalf and wish to present to you, Your Grace, a Prayer Book containing the signature of over 400 bishops with a short inscription composed by 309—Welles of West Missouri."

There was laughter as the bishops heard again the identifying number, name, and diocese of the American bishop who had amused and delighted them in his frequent addresses. Cariboo held aloft the scarlet-and-gold Prayer Book, and then read its inscription: "To our dearly beloved Michael Ramsey, Archbishop of Canterbury, who with grace and truth presided over his brothers assembled in the 1968 Lambeth Conference."

Far more than West Missouri might have imagined as he browsed in the SPCK Bookshop in Tufton Street, selecting the Prayer Book, the gift had a symbolic value for the Lambeth fathers. At least they had signed their names in a Prayer Book, whereas in the last hour a message from the Lambeth Conference had been released for the first time in history without the names of Canterbury or the Episcopal Secretary or any of the bishops. It had been a negative action not in keeping with the documents of Anglicanism—the honored testimonials of consecrations, institutions, ordinations, and other certifications—which have traditionally carried the inky signatures of bishops and often their episcopal heraldry deeply stamped in wax or embossed on golden seals. As their gift to the Primate, and in signing their names and dioceses therein, they could not have picked a better document than the Book of Common Prayer. Nor was Canterbury himself unaware of the emotions of the moment.

"I am overwhelmed at this gesture and symbolic gift and the significance of it—significance that will mean a great deal to me for the rest of my life," he said. "I approached the Conference with a kind of trepidation but very soon it was replaced by a feeling of great happiness as for a whole month we worked together. . . . I hope and believe that this Lambeth Conference has done a little something in the service of God in our Anglican Communion as a part of the One Holy Catholic Church of Christ."

CHAPTER 10

LAMBETH IN RETROSPECT

THE TENTH LAMBETH CONFERENCE cast long shadows across the Anglican world. Those who knew and loved the Church found the life and work of the Conference interesting, enlightening—and utterly frightening, both in what the bishops said and did and what they failed to say and do.

As the months passed, it became increasingly clear that too many liberal bishops had been encouraged in their readiness to water down or sell out the essence of Anglicanism, that "ordered liberty and scriptural catholicity" to which the Archbishop of Canterbury referred at the outset of the Conference.

The fears and dismay of many were cogently summarized with the publication on December 12 of a new edition of *Crockford's Clerical Directory*.[1] Its traditionally well informed, sagacious,

---

[1] First published in 1858 by John Crockford, the unofficial *Who's Who* of Anglicanism (oriented to the Commonwealth, it omits the American and Japanese churches) has been owned by Oxford University Press since 1921, published biennially since 1948. The identity of the author of the preface is

anonymously written preface warned that the Conference's apparent "move away from the balance of previous Conferences to a more Protestant position," if not checked, might "well presage the breakup of the Anglican Communion and indeed of the Church of England itself."

Crockford's also commented: "There are those who hold that the redrawing of denominational boundaries along the lines of theological opinion would be no bad thing, but it would spell the failure of one of the chief aims of Anglicanism and of the whole concept of the bridge Church. The tenth Lambeth Conference may well have begun to do that."

On the official consultants, the preface commented sharply that "the presence of a selected number of Anglicans, not in episcopal orders, [was] no doubt to remedy the present theological deficiencies of the episcopate." How consultants were chosen was not clear, it said, "but it is notable that the traditional Catholic position within the Anglican Communion was very thinly represented among them. . . ."

Another innovation, the invitation extended to suffragan bishops, was written off by *Crockford's* as an effort to use the large number of English suffragans "to repair by voting power at Lambeth the loss of influence which the Church of England has sustained in the Anglican Communion since the end of the war."

As for the post of Anglican Executive Officer, *Crockford's* said that its existence had not been able to save the proceedings of Lambeth X from bearing "all the marks of great pressure of time and of quite inadequate consideration of serious topics."

Faced with damning evaluations of Lambeth X, there was a ten-

---

always a closely guarded secret. The publisher says only that he is "a person of distinction in the Church of England" or, as a Lambeth Palace chaplain once put it, "somebody near the center of things but not quite inside." Speculating about him, the *Church Times* ventured to guess that the man behind the latest preface was more likely "a priest rather than a bishop; of academic background and inclinations; with special admiration for the Church in Wales, if not with some actual connection with it; in a moderate Catholic tradition of Churchmanship; a product, perhaps of Westcott House or Cuddesdon; and almost certainly an Oxbridge man."

dency to turn back to the Archbishop's speech from the Chair of St. Augustine to savor the comfort and encouragement it had seemed to hold as the Conference opened. It too was found lacking. When reconsidered in the gloomy light of Lambeth X, Ramsey's reference to Anglicanism's future role as "less like a separate encampment and more like a color in the spectrum of a rainbow" could be construed as a disposition toward amalgamations in which much would be sacrificed. In the end, not even the Archbishop of Canterbury was above suspicion as being among those who would abandon the Anglican Communion.

It was toward such a dreaded abandonment that the resolutions and reports, on the whole, seemed to point instead of developing the Conference's stated theme of renewal in faith, ministry, and unity. "The only renewal at Lambeth was the renewal of friendships," said one observer; that was perhaps the only positive aspect on which the bishops could agree. Renewal as a theme was a cliché and a tired misnomer from Vatican II as well as the World Council of Churches.

In its first task, renewal in faith, the bishops failed to grasp the opportunity to denounce the ridiculousness of the whole "death of God" philosophy. Instead, it managed at best to express concern for the relationship of faith to the problems of the times and the Church's waning influence.

On renewal in ministry, it was in the consideration of their own roles that the bishops seemed most perplexed. They appeared to have somehow lost confidence in their own ability to lead and to be recognized as leaders. Almost all talk of future meetings was not in terms of bishops alone, but of priests, deacons, and laity as well. The principles of collegiality appeared to be giving way to the desire for a more congregational type of international assembly.

In an era when Rome was doing its own soul-searching about how best to use deacons, the Anglican bishops had a distinct opportunity to lead in modernizing the diaconate without compromising its ancient role in the Church. Instead, it diluted its uniqueness by merging more of its functions with those ordinarily reserved for priests—and by opening its doors to women. The latter move was an attempt at conferring retroactive authority that was neither legal nor logical since many women had become deaconesses without any desire or thought of being considered a deacon and many bishops had ordered them deaconesses with no awareness that someday their action would be considered synonymous with that of ordaining deacons.

The priesthood, too, was given a superficial assessment that did not add to its dignity. For instance, there was the trend toward ordaining men who would not serve as full-time priests; there was also the tendency to share freely most of the priestly functions with the laity. Finally, there was the matter of ordaining women to the priesthood; on that score, the conservative forces won almost their only victory at Lambeth X. But their valiant efforts may have been little more than a holding action, overshadowed as they were by the recommendation that deaconesses should be considered within the diaconate.

After it was learned that the wording of the first part of that controversial Resolution had been changed before being put in the printers' hands, the other resolutions and reports were accepted with something less than complete trust. The reaction was one of disgust, anger, fear that the bishops had been selfishly manipulated, and a new awareness of the need for vigilance—even in the highest council of the Church.

The discussions on renewal in unity were potentially the most disastrous of all. It was as if the "notes of the Church," its ancient marks of being One, Holy, Catholic and Apostolic—scripturally substantiated, traditionally held, and deeply cherished—were placed figuratively on the windowsills of Church House and left teetering above the pavement.

In a head-first plunge toward ecumenism and unity with non-Catholic bodies, many of the bishops overlooked, ignored, or downgraded what the Church already held in common with the rest of the Catholic world. Time and again the bishops promoting one of the unity schemes imperiled if not outrightly abandoned the idea of the Church as one Body under one Head and suggested instead that it cast its lot with denominationalism. Any hope of the continued indwelling of the Holy Spirit was usually regarded as a fringe benefit. There was scant assurance that many of the Catholic Sacraments would continue to be dispensed and defended.

It took an Eastern Orthodox prelate, Athenagoras, to set straight the priorities as he saw them from his many years of representing Constantinople in the U.S., Canada, and England. "Intercommunion ought first to be practiced within churches that adhere to the Orthodox-Catholic tradition—the Roman Catholic, the Anglican and the Orthodox," he said. "I feel that the Orthodox mind will have difficulty in accepting the proposal that all Christians baptized in the name of the Holy Trinity may be admitted to the Anglican Eucharist."

Another warning, more significant than was realized at the time, came from a relatively obscure English bishop, John Howard Cruse of Knaresborough, Suffragan to Ripon. "Reformers often succeed in destroying what they are trying to renew," he said.

Destruction rather than renewal may, indeed, characterize the place of Lambeth X in history. It was not what many hoped it would be, but regrettably it was what many feared it might be—muddled, noncommittal where it should have spoken out, overly liberal where it should have held firm. The concept of Lambeth Conferences as low-key, conservative, and quiet was at odds with a time when no less a personage than Canterbury himself urged careful discernment "in order that what cannot be shaken may remain."

Perhaps Lambeth X did not rise to its potential simply because no meeting, at the summit or elsewhere, is any better than its participants. One veteran commentator, Trevor Beeson, spared almost no one in sizing up the Conference. "Very ordinary men," he wrote in New Christian, "few of them with outstanding talent, most of them weary with the burden which the episcopal office lays upon them, many of them genuinely perplexed about the future work of their dioceses, hardly any of them (apparently) with the opportunity to undertake sustained reading and thinking about the major theological and social issues of the day. Given this, it would have been a miracle of a considerable order if the Conference had produced massive new insights and set the Anglican Communion aflame with new zeal. Such a miracle was denied us."

Another who looked back thoughtfully, consultant John Mac-quarrie, thought the trouble was that the bishops spent "too much time on the wrong things." Of the day the Draft Report on Faith was presented, he recalled, "the bishops ran out of steam by noon and cancelled for the rest of the day, then the next day they spent too long talking about ordination of women. When it came to unity, Canterbury could sum it up very well, theologically, but then in about five minutes what he said was forgotten as people spoke sentimentally about union pro and con, or made snap judgments. On intercommunion, a Canadian bishop might say that instead of regretting that he could send a priest to some people only once a month, he could now tell them to go along to the Methodists. Then there would be men like Peterborough saying that intercommunion before union was like premarital sex—a more counter-productive comparison I never heard of. On the whole, I would say the bishops didn't sufficiently consider what the Church was and were moving toward a great non-Church!"

The week after Lambeth X adjourned, the BBC, itself as thrifty as the Old Lady of Threadneedle Street, the Bank of England, used the last of its taped interviews with the bishops. One of them was with Wyatt of Spokane, who said that the Church was irrelevant to 90 per cent of Americans, that only half the population was on the rolls, and only 10 to 20 per cent of them was active.

His British listeners, accustomed to sparsely filled churches, may have wondered how so many bishops could be concerned for so few, and they may well have asked why the Lambeth fathers had not stayed home with their dwindling flocks and concentrated on massive membership drives.

Such questions were being asked by the bishops themselves, as well as one often expressed in a holdover phrase from the gas-rationing days of World War II, "Is this trip necessary?"

A total of 462 bishops had been away from home for at least five weeks. The cost of assembling them in London approached a half-million dollars for transportation alone. More than a month of even the most economical living added at least another half-million.

Some of the expense was footed by national churches or dioceses and the more personal expenses were out-of-pocket, but the point was: what did the bishops get for their million dollars?

Near the end of Lambeth X, Stradling of Johannesburg spoke for many when he said, "We must consult with our brother bishops and move forward together, and it is quite impossible to do that unless bishops actually meet. My only question about the Lambeth Conference is whether it meets often enough."

Doubtless the fellowship of the bishops was stimulating for them as individuals and, through them, for their dioceses, but what did the national churches gain by sending their chief shepherds to Lambeth? More important, what did the cause of Christ gain? And in the final analysis, could the man in the pew, in the next few years or so, expect to be influenced in any appreciable way by what happened in London in the summer of 1968?

The tangible result of the bishops' work was the slim volume of 158 pages—the Conference Message, sixty-nine formal resolutions, the three Section Reports, and the lists of participants. Placed alongside the 1958 Report (which had 131 Resolutions and much longer commentaries), the work of Lambeth X stood in obvious obedience to the Archbishop of Canterbury's desire that it produce disciplined, concentrated work. For the national churches which wish to be guided by what the bishops think as a body, it is of some lasting value.

Canterbury's hope for more solid thought and less episcopal verbosity was taken up by Clark of Rupert's Land, Primate of All Canada. "There is a great difference between a man who has something to say and a man who has to say something," he reminded the first plenary session. "There have been times when a Lambeth Conference has given the impression of men who, having nothing to say, still felt that they had to say something. The result is pious platitudes." [2]

---

[2] Archbishop Clark quoted George Malcolm Thomson's question on the 1930 Conference: "Was it really necessary, one wonders, to bring hard-working bishops from the outposts of Christendom in order to assist at the birth of a compilation of debating-society platitudes, genial emptiness, fine

Although Lambeth X may have successfully avoided long-windedness, it held fast to two positive virtues—the ability to differ and the ability to reach compromises of the type that have often been the essence of Anglicanism.[3]

Influenced by the recent world conference at Uppsala, the bishops struggled with the issues of world hunger, racism, war, and violence and, in the short period of weeks, had little to add. The magnitude of world problems on which the bishops thought they should comment sometimes left them fanning the air with such vague statements as "The Use of Power," Resolution No. 17: "The Conference, profoundly aware of the effect on human life of the responsible and irresponsible use of power at all levels of human society, considers that the Church should address itself energetically to the range of problems arising in this area."

Perhaps such resolutions would, in Conference terminology, have been better "not put." One that was not accepted from the overburdened Faith committees was almost artful: "The Conference calls the attention of those concerned with liturgical revision to the need, in public worship, to balance emphasis upon the dignity of work with recognition of the creative use of man's energies apart from gainful employment."

Lambeth X was, all agreed, a great meeting ground, but it was not without negative aspects that, sooner or later, were felt by almost every group: the liberals believed that not enough was said or done; the catholics were frankly discouraged. The English and Australian evangelicals were alarmed. Indian and African bishops remained for the most part on the sidelines despite many efforts to bring them forward and seemed convinced that the Western bishops didn't understand their problems. Each of the groups had mem-

---

but flabby sentiments, wishy-washy thinking, blustering potvaliance, and jejune English prose?"

[3] The fine art of Anglican compromise came in for some light-hearted treatment in a letter that climaxed an exchange of correspondence in *The Times* of London about the advisability of special stickers for automobiles of English clergymen. Such insignia "would be an extremely bad idea and dangerous to highway safety," wrote a rural dean, "since the traditional Anglican position is unfailingly middle-of-the-road."

bers who loved the Church and felt that it was slowly being closed down and nothing being done to replace it.

At least, the press reaction of disappointment was predictable. Because of Lambeth's function as consultative rather than legislative—a distinction that had to be reiterated many times—it was not the Conference's nature to make headlines or even much news at all; indeed, it was astonishing that the Conference was as newsworthy as it turned out to be and it was to its credit that it did not sensationalize itself to accommodate the press or gain the world spotlight.

The London newspapers and *The New York Times* gave it almost daily coverage, although Lambeth X was rarely front-page news. The Associated Press and other wire services and correspondents also filed stories several times a week to newspapers and broadcasters around the world. The custom was an expansion of what had been attempted at Lambeth VIII, and to a greater extent at Lambeth IX, and was greatly facilitated by the plenary sessions being opened to the press. It was, however, an operation marked by what some of the bishops had feared—that on days when little else was newsworthy some rather unimportant matter would be played up disproportionately. An example was the motion to dispense with some honors traditionally accorded bishops; it was an innocent, well-intended suggestion and was received as such, but when it was placed next to headlines on starvation and warfare it made the bishops seem like an irrelevant, self-centered group.

If Lambeth X appeared dull or ponderously massive, nobody was more aware of the fact than the bishops themselves. The simple truth was that they were conferring—and that wasn't always interesting news. "Rome wasn't built in a day," one of them said. "Neither was a Lambeth Report."

The pessimism that marked the start of Lambeth X ("Is it the last Lambeth?") overshadowed the reports carried in such internationally circulated magazines as *Time* and *Newsweek,* publications that unfortunately gave little attention to the Conference once they had reported its questionable future. On the whole, Lambeth X had a friendly press, as evidenced by such comprehensive reports as the one that appeared in *The National Catholic Reporter,* a Roman weekly published in the U.S., under the headline "A Trimmer Ship Heads for Open Sea."

In its final fumble, the Church Information Office failed to make any post-Lambeth plans for explaining the work of the Conference. It offered no summary articles or round-up pieces, no interpretative interviews, no commentaries on the resolutions and reports. It also missed the opportunity to provide the bishops with outlines of suggested speeches that would have helped immeasurably in reviewing the Conference for their priests and people.[3a] Only Michael De-la-Noy's rudeness remained consistent as he refused to parry even politely questions about where the Archbishop might go on holiday, then publicly boasted at the final news conference, "No journalist, Your Grace, will ever learn from me anything about your private plans!"

With Lambeth's adjournment the bishops prepared to return to the more routine work of their dioceses, the unending rounds of visitations and confirmations, and, for most, a heavy backlog of correspondence. "Back to the care of souls and the raising of money," one of them said. Could they do their jobs more effectively after a month's consultation with other bishops? Did they realize more clearly the role of the Church? Were they better pastors and leaders than when they came to Lambeth? The answers to such questions would come, if ever, only over a period of years and would never be entirely discernible.

Lambeth's effect on the American Church was viewed realistically by Bishop Bayne in a television interview a few weeks later. "It depends a good deal on our seriousness in taking up the recommendations," he said. "The first steps will be a regional relationship with the Anglican Church of Canada . . . and encouragement in ecumenical experiment."

Amid the assessments the question persisted—will there be an-

---

[3a] In the U.S., follow-up commentaries on Lambeth X were televised on Sunday mornings—hardly prime time and, unfortunately, at the same hours when the people who would have been most interested were themselves at worship.

other Lambeth? It was asked before Lambeth X convened and was still being asked after the Conference ended.

The concept of large united national churches, so much discussed at Lambeth, may in time lessen the number of purely Anglican churches throughout the world. If that happens to an appreciable extent, then any meetings of bishops would have to be in the concept of the "wider episcopal fellowship." In such a case, it would be impossible to predict whether the See of Canterbury would continue to command its traditional loyalty and respect.

Most of the talked about reunion schemes were still only schemes. Projected mergers involving the Anglican Church of India, Burma, Pakistan, and Ceylon seemed the nearest at hand. Other unions lie in the more distant future. It seems highly unlikely that anything even approaching stage two of the Anglican-Methodist Union in England could occur with much swiftness, even if the two churches gave formal approval.

There will be, then, almost all of the Anglican churches still in existence in 1978 and, hopefully, a few more. Among the fertile fields for growth, with support from other churches, are Latin America and South-East Asia.

Why not, therefore, a Lambeth XI—a continuation of the tradition begun in 1867? The answer will of course depend to a great extent upon the occupant of the Chair of Augustine during the next decade. Lambeth Conferences are called at his pleasure but his decision will reflect the thinking of the bishops, all over the world, with whom he is in consultation.

At Lambeth X there was a pessimistic feeling about future meetings, polite utterances to the contrary. Some voiced doubts because of their enthusiasm for united churches and the death of the Anglican Communion. Others frowned on future Conferences exclusively for bishops because of a belief that the laity must henceforth be included. Still others felt that the only answer was regional conferences with agendas limited to more relevant local problems. Finally, there was the group that believed that the World Council of Churches—in its assemblies and regional meetings—should have a priority over other conferences.

All these facts placed an enormous responsibility on the Anglican Consultative Council. It will be the strongest factor in deciding on future Lambeths. Hence it is a cause for prayerful concern that the representatives elected to it—from the episcopate and the other orders of the ministry as well as laity—will still believe in the office of bishop.

If there is to be another Lambeth, is strong leadership being developed? Certainly in the person of Michael Ramsey the Conference had an example of a man equal to the task. He was by far the star of Lambeth X. As its president he should have been, but his spirituality and inspiration was above all expectations. With humor, compassion, and the ability to speak clearly to all issues, he entered the Conference and left it as a great leader of Anglicanism and Christendom. All of the factions in Anglicanism—catholics, liberals, evangelicals—respected him and regarded his speeches as high points in the Conference.

"Pre-eminently Lambeth 1968 was Archbishop Ramsey's Conference," said a special supplement published by *Church Illustrated*. "He showed an infinite capacity to grasp the heart of opposites. . . . He was able to understand the speaker who insisted that open altars at once were the Church's only hope and the man who followed with a speech that seemed to have come directly from the Anglo-Catholic Congress of 1933. The opinion that women priests should be ordained tomorrow and the opinion that women have their rightful place but should never be admitted to the priesthood reached his Chair and somehow bounded back transmuted."

What about leaders for 1978 should Archbishop Ramsey not be alive or not wish to continue in office? Those most readily mentioned as his successors were York, Durham, and London. The suggestion of those names set off more hopeful speculation and so the unofficial nominations went on and on, but it was likely that the next Archbishop of Canterbury was somewhere among the Englishmen already consecrated and present at Lambeth X.

As for other leadership that evidenced itself, the Bishop of Cariboo's demonstrated the same administrative abilities that had marked his work in the Anglican Congress at Toronto and as Anglican Executive Officer. With an efficiency that was comforting and a blandness that made him unthreatening, he seemed a prime choice for translation to a prominent see in England, Canada, or Australia.

Of the three Section chairmen, Clark of Rupert's Land was a gentle and much respected figure, but the others, Coggan of York and de Mel of India, were not well liked. Both were resented by the other bishops for their efforts to push through the programs they personally favored.

The strong catholic voices were Mortimer of Exeter; Leonard of Willesden, Suffragan to London; and Trevor Huddleston. In his dignity a true Lord Bishop, Exeter was revered for the strength of his catholic appeals. Willesden's zeal and sincerity would long be remembered and admired, even by those who did not agree with him. Trevor Huddleston always made sense and showed a great Christian stability rooted in the religious life.

In an assessment of Lambeth's outstanding personalities from "an overseas point of view," Luxton of Huron also singled out the bishops of Lincoln, Leicester, London, Winchester, Manchester, Southwark, Chester, Bristol, Coventry, Ripon, Peterborough, and Salisbury.[4]

In addition, the Bishop of Durham was definitely a leader in his theological grasp and ability to articulate his thoughts.

Among the Americans, many looked closely at Kim Myers of California to see what manner of man had succeeded James A. Pike, who since the last Lambeth had come near a heresy trial and finally had retired. They found the tall, graying Bishop of California—once a vicar in the slums of New York—a man who soon distinguished himself as a young liberal.

---

[4] "By comparison, we of the New World handle our tongue in a ponderous fashion, without the light touch, the rapier-like thrust, the devastating irony, the polished finesse of the British debater," said the Bishop of Huron in the *Church Times*, November 28, 1968. "There was improvement in overseas debating recorded in the latest Lambeth, but we are still far behind the doughty sword-swingers on the English scene."

A black American, John Burgess, Suffragan of Massachusetts, was much admired for his moving and eloquent address. Among his countrymen, those who made significant contributions were the Presiding Bishop, Burrill of Chicago, Stark of Newark, Gooden of the Canal Zone, Crittenden of Erie, and Frey of Guatemala. Two Americans who distinguished themselves in committee work were Gray of Connecticut and Hallock of Milwaukee.

Few would forget Welles of Missouri, "No. 309," the best-known number at Lambeth, who frequently injected a sense of humor—sometimes a showoff politician or a sage Will Rogers, but always a warm-hearted, conscientious father in God.

Anybody who sat down with pencil and paper the day Lambeth X ended would also be likely to list several other outstanding men—Iran, Zululand, Huron, Ottawa, Sydney, Wales, Uganda, and Middleton.

The bishop who spoke most often at Lambeth X was Wilson of Chichester, a cousin of Archbishop Ramsey.[5]

---

[5] The Bishop of West Missouri kept a running tally of speakers. The final count "through Friday, August 23, at 5:15" was captioned "Intervention Score at Plenary Sessions—Utterly Unofficial." It indicated that Ottawa was in the lead, having spoken fourteen times with Chichester and York ranking next. On the final morning of Lambeth X, Chichester spoke three more times, bringing to sixteen the number of times he was recognized by the Chair. He was followed by Ottawa, recognized fifteen times, and the American Presiding Bishop and York fourteen each. Others were readily recalled as frequent speakers—West Missouri, Iran, Rupert's Land, and the Assistant of London, thirteen; Bristol, twelve; Exeter, Peterborough, Newark, and Willesden, eleven; Huron, Barrackpore, and Newcastle (Australia), ten; Central Africa, Melbourne, Dublin, Sodor & Man, and Norwich, nine; Leicester, Southwark, Chester, Chicago, Gippsland, Durham, London, and Hong Kong, eight; St. Edmunsbury & Ipswich, Polynesia, Uganda, Canterbury, Singapore & Malaya, Winchester, Perth, Karachi, Guatemala, Barking, the Metropolitan of India, and Pike, Assistant Bishop of Guildford, seven; Manchester, California, British Honduras, Dunedin, Nelson, Middleton, the Suffragan of the Philippines, and the Assistant of St. Edmunsbury, six. Those who had spoken at least five times by the end of the last full day included Algoma, Mbale, St. John's, Calgary, Nova Scotia, Colombia, Virgin Islands, North Carolina, Oxford, Lichfield, Derby, Birmingham, and the Coadjutor of Melbourne; the suffragans of Toronto and Woolwich; and the assistant bishops of Zanzibar and of Sheffield. The final full day saw the largest number of speakers in a single session—a

When the final speaker had been heard and the last blessing pronounced, only the bishops could fairly judge the worth of Lambeth X because it was by, of, and for the bishops themselves, yet the reports and resolutions were for the study and benefit of the whole Church.

At Lambeth X, bishops with small flocks and meager resources found new strength and direction in personal associations with men of large and prosperous sees, who in turn, were humbled and inspired by the lesser fry.

Among Anglican priests, some would be indifferent to Lambeth and others would feel that at best it was all distant and remote, but there were many more priests—in remote mission outposts, in city parishes, in small towns, slums, suburbs—for whom news of the Lambeth Conference brought a lift to the heart and a renewed sense of identification with a world-wide Communion.

Clergy and laity alike, in sending off the bishops to Lambeth and in welcoming them home again, could feel that, through the Conference, their future work together was in touch with the life and thought of the Church far beyond the confines of their own dioceses.

"At its best it sends forth a fresh, spontaneous response to the problems facing the Church and the world," said the Primate of All Canada, Archbishop Clark of Rupert's Land, in his address to the first plenary session. "Its words are not the Church's final decrees, but messages from the pilgrim Church sent out as she journeys."

The talk of basic changes for future Lambeths—of having a chairman other than Canterbury and of meeting elsewhere than in England with a wider group of participants—misses the point that efficiency might not be served so much by a different president, location, and membership as by simply removing the Conference to an atmosphere of less distraction.

One of the best suggestions was that expanded accommodations be made available at one of the large religious houses, or an Ox-

---

total of 106. During the morning the Chair recognized 59 bishops, and in the afternoon 102 bishops addressed the Conference.

bridge college, where seclusion and greater quiet would encourage uninterrupted concentration and regular worship.

Such an arrangement would drastically curtail the social events so roundly criticized at previous Conferences; it would decrease the expenses of hotels and meals and taxis and would offer the participants greater opportunity for personal visits.

Should all that seem too reminiscent of seminary days or gloomy retreats—or leave the Conference members open to charges of cloistering themselves—it could be embellished with a few sessions amid the lights of London with wives freshly arrived instead of having become increasingly bored by five weeks in London hotels.

As for the Conference program, longer meetings and some evening discussions would not make it necessary for the bishops and others to be away from their posts for so long a time. Most important of all, there would unquestionably be greater spirituality in a setting that provided for Holy Communion each day (privately, as concelebrants, or as communicants) as well as corporate observances of the Prayer Book offices.

When Michael Ramsey was enthroned at Canterbury, one of Britain's more astute journalists observed that "under him the Church of England may not obviously become a greater force in the land, but is quite likely to become more religious—with possible consequences which no one can predict."

Nobody can fail to hope that the Church of England, or any of its daughter churches, would become "more religious," but the Conference of 1968 made it obvious that the Anglican Communion of Catholic Churches is fast forgetting what it once was, uncertain of what it now is, and doubtful of what it should be.

APPENDIX

ARCHBISHOP OF CANTERBURY'S SERMON
OPENING 1968 LAMBETH CONFERENCE

Hebrews xii: 27–29. *The phrase "yet once more" indicates the removal of what is shaken . . . in order that what cannot be shaken may remain. Therefore let us be grateful for receiving a kingdom which cannot be shaken, and thus let us offer to God acceptable worship with reverence and awe, for our God is a consuming fire.*

Today we have all come to Canterbury with hearts full of thankfulness for a place, a man and a history. This place means very much to us as we think of St. Augustine and his monks coming here from Thanet with the Cross borne before them, preaching the Gospel to king and people, and inaugurating a history which includes not only the English Church in its continuity through the centuries but a family of Churches of many countries and races which still see in Canterbury a symbol and a bond. Today we thank God for all this, and for the witness within Christendom of a tradition of ordered liberty and scriptural Catholicity which the name Anglican has been used to describe. Thanks be to God for his great goodness.

No part of the early history is more moving than the questions which St. Augustine sent to Pope Gregory about some of his perplexities and the answers which the Pope gave to him. One of the matters which bothered St. Augustine was the variety of customs in different Churches, and Pope Gregory told him that if he found anything in the Gallican or the Roman or in any other Church acceptable to Almighty God he should adopt it in England, because—and here comes the great principle—because "things are not to be loved for the sake of places, but places for the sake of good things." *"Non pro locis res, sed pro bonis rebus loca amanda sunt."* How suggestive, how far-reaching, is this principle, how applicable to other issues and to other times. *"Non pro locis res, sed pro bonis rebus loca."* The local, the limited, the particular is to be cherished by Christian people not for any nostalgic attachment to it for its own sake, but always for the *real thing* which it represents and conveys, the thing which is catholic, essential, lasting. So our love for Canterbury melts into our love for Christ whose shrine Canterbury is; our love for what is Anglican is a little piece of our love for One, Holy, Catholic, Apostolic Church; the love of any of us for our own heritage in country, culture, religious experience or theological insight, all subserves the supreme thing—the reality of God who draws men and women and children into union with himself in the fellowship of his Son. Not things for the sake of places, but places for the sake of good things: let that be a guiding principle, and the good things which concern us are what the apostolic writer calls the things which are not shaken.

Today the words of the Epistle to the Hebrews come home to us, in cadences which seem to roll like thunder. Follow the thought of this tremendous passage. The voice of God shook the earth when the divine law was given on Mount Sinai, a divine law which, reinterpreted by our Lord, still stands and still must be proclaimed. Then, in the new covenant, the voice of God shakes heaven as well as earth, since the Incarnation at Bethlehem and the resurrection from the tomb belong to both earth and heaven. Today the earth is being shaken, many things are cracking, melting, disappearing; and it is for us who are Christians to distinguish the things which are shaken and to receive gratefully a kingdom which is not shaken, the kingdom of our crucified Lord. Within this kingdom, the writer goes on, we offer to God the worship that God can accept—but as we do so we are never in cosy security, we have awe in our hearts, for we are near to our God, and our God is blazing fire.

Today the earth is being shaken, and there can be few or none who do not feel the shaking: the rapid onrush of the age of technology with the new secularity which comes with it, the terrible contrast between the world of affluence and the world of hunger, the explosions of racial conflict, the amassing of destructive weapons, the persistence in some countries of war and killing. And Man, they say, has come of age. Indeed he has, in the height of the powers the Creator gave him, in the fulfilment of the Psalmist's words "thou hast put all things under his feet," but without, alas, Man learning to say also with the Psalmist "O Lord, our Governor, how excellent is thy name." That is the nature of Man's triumph, and of Man's utter frustration.

Amidst a shaken earth we who are Christians receive a kingdom which cannot be shaken, and we are called so to enjoy it that others are led to find it and receive it with us. How is God today calling us to do this? God calls us to faith, to ministry, to unity.

FAITH. The faith to which we are called will always be folly and scandal to the world, it cannot be in the usual sense of the word popular; it is a supernatural faith and it cannot adapt itself to every passing fashion of human thought. But it will be a faith alert to distinguish what is shaken, and meant to go, and what is not shaken and is meant to remain. When men today tell us that they revere Jesus but find God or theism without meaning it sometimes is that the image of God as we Christians in our practice present it is the image of a God of religious concerns but not of compassion for all human life, and it is just not recognizable as the God and Father of Jesus Christ. So too when men reject theism it sometimes means that they cannot accept in this shaken world any easy, facile assumption that the universe anywhere has a plan, a center, a purpose. It is for us Christians to be sure that our faith is no facile assumption but a costly conviction that in Christ crucified and risen, in suffering and victorious love and in no other way, there may be found a plan, a center, a purpose. In dying to live, in losing life so as to find it—there is the place where divine sovereignty is found, the place where theism has meaning and vindication. The bishops who will be leading our thinking about faith at this Lambeth Conference will help us to see that faith means standing near the Cross in the heart of the contemporary world, and not only standing but acting. Our faith will be tested in our actions, not least in our actions concerning peace, concerning race, concerning poverty. Faith is a costly certainty, but no easy security, for our God is blazing fire.

MINISTRY. The ministry to which we are called is described in our text. It is "to offer to God acceptable worship," the God who created us. We know that the only worship which God accepts is the expression of lives which reflect God's own righteousness and compassion. Yet amidst all the energies of serving humanity which so rightly concern Christian people let there be a deep revival of the priestly spirit, the spirit of loving God for God's own sake who made us for himself. The bishops who will lead our thinking about ministry will help us to recapture this priestly spirit while they show the way to new forms of practical service in every community where Christian people are. That service must not only inspire individuals, it must go on to affect states and nations in their policies, rich and poor, developed and undeveloped, one towards another. But while Christians try to serve every human need they can serve, the greatest is the need to serve the love of God Himself.

UNITY. Here Christendom is feeling the first tremors of a shaking which would have seemed incredible a few years ago. What has been shaken? Much of the old complacency, much of the old contentment with our divided condition, much of the sheer ignorance of one another in theology and in practice, and above all much of the self-consciousness which gave absurdity to the dealings of Christians with Christians. But the shaking has gone deeper still. Christendom has begun to learn that unity comes not by combining this church with that church much as they are now, but by the radical altering of churches in reformation and renewal. It is here that the Vatican Council has had influence far beyond the boundaries of the Roman Catholic Church. We all are stirred to ask God to show us what are things rightly shaken and the things not shaken which must remain.

As Anglicans we ask ourselves: *"Quo tendimus?"* This Lambeth Conference faces big questions about our relations with one another as a world-wide Anglican family and about our role within a Christendom which is being called to unity in the truth. Can we do better than take to heart and apply to our tasks the counsel which Pope Gregory gave to St. Augustine—*"non pro locis res, sed loca pro bonis rebus,"* "not things for the sake of places, but places for the sake of good things." We shall love our own Anglican family not as something ultimate but because in it and through it we and others have our place in the one Church of Christ. The former, your Anglican family, is a lovely special loyalty: the latter is the Church against which our Lord predicted that the gates of death would not prevail. Now, as the work of unity advances there will come into existence united churches not describably Anglican but in communion with us and sharing with us what we hold to be the unshaken essence of catholicity. What then of the future boundaries of our Anglican Communion? We shall face that question without fear, without anxiety, because of our faith in the things which are not shaken. Perhaps the Anglican role in Christendom may come to be less like a separate encampment and more like a color in the spectrum of a rainbow, a color bright and unself-conscious.

"See that you do not refuse him who speaks." The writer to the Hebrews has, indeed, his urgent message for us, telling us of the removal of what is shaken in order that what is not shaken may remain. Therefore let us be grateful in receiving a kingdom which cannot be shaken. It is the kingdom of Christ crucified, our king who was crowned with thorns. And his Cross is the secret of our faith, the heart of our ministry, and the source of our unity as we live not to ourselves but to one another and to him. Each of us at this time will want to say from his heart:

> Thanks be to thee, O Lord Jesus Christ
> for all the benefits thou hast won for me,
> for all the pains and insults thou hast borne for me.

O most merciful redeemer, friend and brother,
may I know thee more clearly,
love thee more dearly
and follow thee more nearly."

"REGARDING PRINCIPLES OF UNION," ADDRESS BY ARCHBISHOP OF CANTERBURY, LAMBETH CONFERENCE, AUGUST 9, 1968

I wish to say some things with a glance forward into the next Section:

In my reading on the doctrine of the Church in the last few years, I have got the impression that the most valuable and creative trend in the study of the doctrine of the Church has been what some writers call the eschatological aspect of the Church. I understand it means this: the Church of God is something once for all given to the world—and also (guided by the Spirit of God) moving towards fullness . . . plenitude . . . final realization—and that applies to every note of the Church.

Holiness is given once for all in the holiness of Christ. The Church grows into the perfect realization of that holiness through all the struggles of the centuries.

Truth is given once for all—in a perfect revelation through the centuries. The Church, guided by the Spirit through the centuries, grows into the complete understanding of that truth.

So, too, unity is once for all given in the incorporation of Christians into Christ, but the Church grows into the full realization of unity through centuries of time.

Now that may sound so obvious and platitudinous, but in fact it has not always been apparent in our thoughts and action about Christian unity. And if we have an eye upon this double polarity of the Church once given and awaiting plenitude, it does affect things a good deal. I think that it is this eschatological view of this thinking of the Church that in recent years has greatly helped the Roman Catholic theologians during and after the Vatican Council to hold together, as they seem to do, the upholding of the claims of their own church with a positive valuing of other Christian communions whose life is giving something to the Church's growth to plenitude. I think that for us Anglicans a similar theological grasp can help us in our attitudes towards intercommunion and the Eucharist in relation to Christian unity as a present fact and as a future realization. As Anglicans we have always been accustomed to think of church unity in a rather static way—looking back to the norms of the catholic tradition, and conserving those norms, and spreading those norms to unfortunate people who are without them!

Now it is perfectly right to do that, but that is only half of our duty and understanding. The other half is, while doing that, we ought also to be looking ahead to the plenitude of the Church, and where we and other Christians are really set upon that plenitude, where we have a common understanding of it and a commitment to it in our minds, we can already be doing things in anticipation of that plenitude. The Eucharist in its essential theology has always had its anticipatory trend in which the looking forward as well as looking backward has played its part.

There is a world of difference between intercommunion on the old liberal Protestant get-together lines with no intention of organic unity and intercommunion in a serious ecclesiastical situation with agreement upon the goal in faith and order. Where that situation exists, I believe it is possible for there to be eucharistic intercommunion, not with a sense of doing something surreptitious, but with a sense of doing something that does belong to a true understanding of the Eucharist in relation to the Catholic Church. We bear in mind firmly both the Church as already given with those catholic norms to which we are pledged to be faithful, and looking ahead to the Church in its plenitude towards which we are moving. There is identity between the Church once given and the Church in its coming plenitude.

MESSAGE FROM HIS HOLINESS POPE PAUL VI

The following is the text of the message to the Lambeth Conference from His Holiness Pope Paul VI (dated at the Vatican on July 21), read by the Most Rev. Msgr. J. G. Willebrands, Bishop of Mauriana, of the Secretariat for Promoting Christian Unity, at the opening plenary session at Church House, Westminster, Saturday morning, July 27, 1968:

The Lambeth Conference of 1968 meets at a critical moment in the history of Christendom. Its overriding theme may be expressed, like that of the great assembly just concluded at Uppsala, in the words of Rev. xxi, 5: "Behold I make all things new"; it is in the forefront of all Christian thinking today.

We rejoice that Roman Catholic interest will, through the hospitality of the Anglican Communion, find expression in the presence of seven official Roman Catholic observers and some other guests. Their diligent presence will reflect the interest and be supported by the prayers of Roman Catholics everywhere.

Our interest is sharpened by the fact that the Conference follows close on the profitable deliberations of the Joint Preparatory Commission between the Roman Catholic Church and the Anglican Communion. All that the Conference can do to advance further the cause of Christian unity will be blessed by God.

REPLY TO *HUMANAE VITAE:*
LAMBETH CONFERENCE, AUGUST 6, 1968

This Conference has taken note of the Papal Encyclical Letter *Humanae Vitae* recently issued by His Holiness Pope Paul VI. The Conference records its appreciation of the Pope's deep concern for the institution of marriage and the integrity of marriage life.

Nevertheless, the Conference finds itself unable to agree with the Pope's conclusion that all methods of conception control other than abstinence from sexual intercourse or its confinement to the periods of infecundity are contrary to the "order established by God." It reaffirms the finds of the Lambeth Conference of 1958 contained in resolutions 112, 113, and 115, which are as follows:

> 112. The Conference records its profound conviction that the idea of the human family is rooted in the Godhead and that consequently all problems of sex relations, the procreation of children, and the organization of family life must be related, consciously and directly, to the creative, redemptive and sanctifying power of God.

113. The Conference affirms that marriage is a voca
through which men and women may share in th
ative purpose of God. The sins of self-indulgenc
ity, born of selfishness and a refusal to accept
divine vocation, destroy its true nature and depth
fullness and balance of the relationship betwe
women. Christians need always to remember that s
not an end in itself nor a means to self-gratificatic   ...at
self-discipline and restraint are essential conditions of the responsible freedom of marriage and family planning.

115. The Conference believes that the responsibility for deciding
upon the number and frequency of children has been laid by
God upon the consciences of parents everywhere: that this
planning, in such ways as are mutually acceptable to husband
and wife in Christian conscience, is a right and important factor
in Christian family life and should be the result of positive
choice before God. Such responsible parenthood, built on
obedience to all the duties of marriage, requires a wise stewardship of the resources and abilities of the family as well as a
thoughtful consideration of the varying population needs and
problems of society and the claims of future generations.

The Conference commends the report of Committee 5 of the Lambeth
Conference 1958 together with the study called "The Family in Contemporary Society," which formed the basis of its work of that Committee, to the attention of all men of good will for further study in the light
of the continuing sociological and scientific developments of the past
decade.

MEMBER CHURCHES OF
THE ANGLICAN COMMUNION

The Church of England

The Mother Church of Anglicanism is the sole member of the Anglican Communion which is established by law (as the official religion of the land) and whose membership is a majority (61.6 per cent) of its national population. As such, it enjoys a voice in government (its bishops are allotted 26 seats in the House of Lords) and a prominent role in the nation's ceremonial life (the primate crowns the sovereign and ranks in precedence just after the royal family). The dearest price of Establishment, however, is that the Church is not free to order its worship without consulting Parliament, nor does it have the last word, or sometimes the first, in the appointment of bishops. The principal bodies are the Convocations of Canterbury and York (which meet separately in the spring and fall, usually at the same time) and the Church Assembly, which convenes three times a year and includes the bishops and priests of the Convocations as well as large lay representation. The Church Commissioners constitute another important body, controlling the considerable investments and land holdings of the "C of E." Its statistics are impressive: 110 bishops at work in 43 dioceses, nearly 18,000 active clergymen; 14,351 parish churches, and over 27 million baptized members. The prevalence of "nominal Anglicans," however, is no secret; only 9.7 million are confirmed, only 2.1 million make their Easter Communions. The emptiness of English churches, almost legendary, is often decried. Also, with some decline in ordinations, the number of seminaries has been reduced to 27. At the same time, the flourishing life of the religious communities (11 for men, 49 for women) continues to inspire and strengthen the revival of the religious life throughout the Anglican world.

The Church in Wales

"Without question the Church in Wales is the oldest branch of the Anglican Communion, and to any impartial reader of history it can make good its claims to being, in terms of the historic past, *the* Catholic Church in Wales," wrote Canon Howard Johnson in his book *Global Odyssey*. It traces its founding to Roman missionaries of the fourth century. Some 800 years later it submitted to Canterbury but in 1920 won disestablishment and became an independent province. "We are a small province but our history lays on us responsibilities which we want to accept," said the Bishop of St. Asaph shortly before Lambeth X. He was one of six Welsh bishops who formed the Lambeth delegation led by the newly enthroned Archbishop of Llandaff, the Most Rev. William Glyn Hughes Simon, formerly Bishop of Swansea & Brecon. It is his Cathedral Church of SS. Peter & Paul, one of the most ancient in a land of ancient churches, that has become famous in recent years for its starkly modern *Christ in Majesty* sculpted by Sir Jacob Epstein for a center arch of the nave. Another contemporary project, undertaken in 1957, has been the revision of the Prayer Book in English and Welsh. Its approval is expected to coincide with union with the Methodist Church in Wales. To such a union, the Church in Wales would bring 1,300,000 baptized members (roughly half the population). Of that group, only 165,000 made their Easter communions in 1967. The clergy numbers 1013. Distinctly Welsh saints—Asaph, David, Deiniol, and Woolos—are perpetuated in the dedication of cathedrals and parish churches in towns that bear such names as Cwmffrwdoer (Diocese of Monmouth) and Llanymawddwy (Diocese of Bangor).

The Church of Ireland

The Celtic Church, which with the Welsh Church dates from the fourth century, retained much of its character when it came for a time under the jurisdiction of Canterbury. The same tendency to individuality was reinforced by the Reformation, which left Ireland still a predominantly Roman Catholic country, and by the Irish Church Act of 1869, which dissolved the statutory union between the Churches of England and Ireland. Consequently, the Church of Ireland emerged as a body overly occupied with being austerely different from Rome and Canterbury. For years it forbade the placing of a Cross on an altar and it permitted candles only with the understanding that they would not be used except in near-darkness or a power failure. Conversely, it has rejoiced in colorful altar frontals, stained glass, statuary, and chanted Psalms. To its great credit it has escaped being split by the conflicts that have divided the Emerald Isle between the Northern Counties and the Irish Free State. The Archbishop of Armagh heads a diocese that straddles the border, thus fully realizing his ancient title, Primate of All Ireland. (Armagh's first bishop in 444 was St. Patrick.) The other province, dating from 790, is headed by the Archbishop of Dublin who has the title Primate of Ireland. (His see city, Dublin, boasts St. Patrick's, the national cathedral, as well as Christ Church, the diocesan cathedral.) Names of the dioceses —such as Meath, Clogher and Connor—are evocative of the romance of Ireland. Among them are several known as united dioceses—Dublin & Glendalough & Kildare; Cork, Cloyne, & Ross; Killaloe & Kilfenora and Clonfert & Kilmacduah; Limerick, Ardfert, & Aghadoe; Cashel & Emly, Waterford & Lismore. Nor are the Irish saints forgotten in the dedication of the Anglican cathedrals: five bear the name of Patrick and others are under the patronage of Macartan, Columb, Eunan, Fethlimidh, Bridgit, Fin Barr, Colman, Fachtna, Flannan, Brendan, Canice, and Laserian. The Church of Ireland is small (its 469,000 members represent less than 11 per cent of the population), poor in funds and priests (about 650), timid still in claiming its Catholic heritage, and slow in liturgical experimentation. At the same time it is caught up in numerous national problems that plague Ireland, especially the depletion of rural areas by emigration to other countries.

The Episcopal Church In Scotland

Dourly persevering through years of persecution, the Scottish Church is not quite the "shadow of a shade" that Sir Walter Scott called it after the severe suppression of 1746 92. It is small (98,000 members, 55,000 communicants) but is still a vital force in the land where Presbyterianism 280 years ago replaced it as the established church. Something of its indomitable spirit is seen in the actions of three of its bishops who passed on the episcopacy to the American church at a time when episcopal functions in Scotland were narrowly restricted and the English bishops did not feel they could come to the aid of the U.S., so recently in rebellion against the crown. ("The Scottish bishops are more willing to follow the Acts of the Apostles than they are the Acts of the British Parliament," cried the Bishop of Aberdeen, "and therefore we proceed to the consecration of this Godly man!") Today some 320 priests serve under the seven Scottish bishops, of whom the Bishop of Glasgow is Primus. Two of the Cathedral Churches (at Aberdeen and Inverness) are dedicated to the Scottish patron, St. Andrew, while the Perth Cathedral proudly bears the name of St. Ninian, first occupant of the ancient See of Galloway. After the fashion of united dioceses that predominate in the Church of Ireland, Galloway is now combined with Glasgow; other united dioceses are Aberdeen & Orkney; Argyll & The Isles; Moray, Ross

& Caithness; and St. Andrews, Dunkeld & Dunblane. (It was from the latter diocese that John Howe resigned his jurisdiction of thirteen years to succeed the Bishop of Cariboo as Anglican Executive Officer.) As many of the diocesan names suggest, parishes are scattered over lowlands, highlands, and coastal islands. It makes for a highly pastoral ministry exercised by itinerant clergy constantly on the move in the wide, bleak areas committed to their care.

The Episcopal Church in the United States of America

The 1967 General Convention (which was the sixty-second since 1785) was described by a leading American layman as "perhaps the most constructive and harmonious convention in the recent history of the Church," even though some went home in dismay. At least it gave some bishops new heart for large meetings. They came 125 strong to Lambeth X, the biggest contingent, exuding American confidence and assurance despite reports of substantial decreases in baptisms, confirmations, and attendance at church school. If it was static, it still was secure in the knowledge that it had three and a half million members, more than 11,000 priests (only 258 are black), total annual receipts in excess of $268 million, and a budget of over $13 million for its Executive Council. In its 79 dioceses and 23 missionary districts (in nine provinces) it was, in the best tradition of American clichés, striving to "project an image" of "being relevant." To that end, it encouraged continued dialogue in a controversial set-up called COCU (Consultation On Church Union), authorized use of a trial liturgy, sanctioned greater participation of laity, expressed deeper concern for its dozen seminaries, and at long last declared officially that "The Episcopal Church" was a name equally as acceptable as the cumbersome and offensive title "The Protestant Episcopal Church in the United States of America." (Oblivious to change, the Executive Council's men at Lambeth X, and some bishops, continued to use the hackneyed term PECUSA.) Further, it had decided to admit women delegates to the House of Deputies (under most diocesan canons, women also are permitted on vestries), but the right to elect a Presiding Bishop is still reserved for the episcopate. The office of "P.B." gradually evolved, varying between seniority and rotation until 1804, when the latter method was adopted. Rotation continued in effect until 1925, when a Presiding Bishop was elected for the first time. The seventh Bishop of Maryland was chosen, and in accordance with the new canon, resigned his see and became, literally, a bishop without a diocese. Of the seven named since that time, only four have been in office at the time of a Lambeth Conference. The twenty-second to hold the post, John El-

bridge Hines, was Bishop of Texas at the time of his election in 1964. His
official seat is the Cathedral Church of St. Peter & St. Paul in Washington, his office is in New York, and his residence is Dover House, Greenwich, Connecticut.

The Anglican Church of Canada

Nova Scotia became the first Anglican diocese in Canada in 1787, but
not until well after World War II did the Canadians definitely set themselves apart from the Church of England. First they produced their own
Prayer Book and then in 1955 they dropped the name "The Church of
England in Canada" in favor of the present title. Thus it became the first
member of the Anglican Communion to incorporate *Anglican* as part of
its legal name and, more important, it formally recognized that its growing numbers were no longer confined to emigrants from England. It has
1,292,762 members (12 per cent of the population) in 28 dioceses (four
provinces) spread over an area (3,851,000 square miles) larger than the
U.S. or Australia. Eleven of the dioceses have a commissary in England,
as do many churches of the Anglican Communion, reflecting a traditional dependence on the mother country. Diocesan names are rich in
Canadian history—Saskatchewan, Saskatoon, Moosonee, Kootenay
—and one of them, Edmonton, preserves its original cathedral of logs.
Most of the Canadian dioceses cover vast areas, including the Diocese of
the Arctic, which is the largest (2,750,000 square miles) in the Anglican
Communion. There is a special concern in ministering to the mining industry as well as to Indians and Eskimos. The Primate of All Canada
may be elected from any of the dioceses and is allowed to continue as
diocesan.

The Church of England in Australia

The largest Anglican body outside England, the Australian Church's
4,150,000 members are a third of the population of the continent "down
under." Once an archdeaconry of the Diocese of Calcutta, Australia
gained its first bishop in 1836, added a second diocese in 1842, five more
in 1847, and convened its initial synod in 1872. In 1905 it formed its
four provinces, which now embrace 26 dioceses, including one, the
Diocese of the Northern Territory (see city: Darwin), which was formed
the year Lambeth X convened. Australia is characterized by its vastness
(the air route from Perth to Brisbane is slightly longer than that from
London to Cairo) and the concentration of 40 per cent of its people in
the cities of Sydney and Melbourne. Yet the Australian Church is keenly

conscious of its responsibility to the people in the far reaches of the country known as the Outback, to the aborigines ("the first Australians"), and to the huge Asiatic population on its northwestern perimeter. Helping to meet the demands for mission work are several native orders (including the Bush Brotherhood of St. Barnabas) and branch houses of the Anglican Franciscans and the Society of the Sacred Mission. Twenty-one of its 36 bishops were born in Australia.

The Church of the Province of New Zealand

From the time of his consecration in 1841 as first Missionary Bishop of New Zealand, George Augustus Selwyn guided the New Zealand Church through sixteen eventful years to the signing of a constitution that established it as the Empire's first autonomous body in communion with the See of Canterbury. In 1867, the year he took a leading role in the first Lambeth Conference, he accepted translation to be Bishop of Lichfield. The small white frame church that he built on a hill overlooking Auckland Bay still stands, revered as the birthplace of the New Zealand Church, which has grown to nine dioceses and a membership of 900,000—a third of the population. All nine of its diocesans attended Lambeth X, including John Vockler of Polynesia, who shortly afterward resigned as diocesan to enter the Anglican Franciscans. Also present was one of the assistant bishops—Fine Tenga'ila Halapua, a native of Tonga, a Polynesian island that has its own monarchy. The Church was not able to send its two native-born Melanesian suffragans or the Bishop of Aotearoa, Suffragan to Waiapu, who traditionally is a member of the Maori race—a tribe largely resident on the North Island of New Zealand. The Bishop of Waiapu, Norman Alfred Lesser, automatically assumed the rank of archbishop on being elected primate in 1961. His diocese recently completed its new Cathedral Church and both Auckland and Wellington are at work also on new cathedrals. Seeking to express the ethos of Anglicanism, *Time* magazine in a major article on the Anglican Communion in 1963 observed that "it is grand and symbolic that as a typical consequence, there should be in the South Pacific a Bishop who follows the ancient Church of England custom by styling himself Norman New Zealand. Empire is gone; the Church remains."

The Church of the Province of South Africa

Founded in 1853, it is the largest and oldest of the African churches. There are 1,579,400 baptized members in fourteen dioceses. Of the seventeen bishops (elected by the clergy with assent of a house of laity) nine

were born in England and six in South Africa. One, the Bishop of
Lebombo, is a native of Portugal (appropriately, his diocese covers the
whole of Portuguese East Africa) and was originally a priest of the
Lusitanian Church. Another, Robert Mize, an American, consecrated
Bishop of Damaraland in 1960, departed for Lambeth X knowing that
the South African government was not going to renew a residence permit that would enable him to return. Prominent names in the early history of the South African Church are Robert Gray, first Bishop of Cape
Town, and John Colenso, Bishop of Natal, around whom centered the
great controversy of Lambeth I. (Colenso, consecrated in 1853, was deposed for heresy in 1863 and a majority of the Lambeth fathers upheld
the ruling.) In recent years the history of the Church in South Africa has
been distinguished by the names of such men as Scott, Huddleston,
Reeves, and de Blank. For all of them, *apartheid* has been a crucial issue.
Archbishop de Blank faced it dramatically by erecting on the grounds of
St. George's Cathedral Church, Cape Town, a large sign that proclaimed
*This Church is open to welcome men and women of all races to all ser-
vices at all times.* Along with Mize, Reeves, and de Blank, Edward
Crowther, Bishop of Kimberley & Kuruman was eventually forced to
give up his see. Their suffering and compassion for South Africa was
well expressed in some poignantly simple lines with which Trevor Huddleston responded to a request of elderly people who wrote that they
would like to pray for Africa: "God bless Africa/ Guide her leaders/
Guard her people/ And give her peace."

The Church of the Province of West Africa

The stamp of recent change and growth is fresh on the West African
Church, founded in 1951. Only three of its 17 bishops are white and a
dozen of them have been consecrated since 1961. Its diocesan boundaries
have been altered frequently since 1952, when the Diocese of Lagos was
divided into four dioceses. Since that time the Ekiti diocese has been
formed out of the northern parts of the dioceses of Ondo and Benin,
while both Niger Delta and Owerri were carved from the Diocese of
Niger. More changes, drastic ones, were in store under a unification plan
in which seven dioceses (Lagos, Ibadan, Ondo, Benin, Niger, Owerri,
and Niger Delta) were to have merged with Methodist and Presbyterian
bodies. Had the Nigeria-Biafra conflict not interrupted the plan, there
would have been far fewer West African bishops at Lambeth X.

The Church of the Province of Central Africa

Inaugurated in 1955, the smallest of the African churches, it covers the
territories of Rhodesia, Zambia, and Malawi together with part of

Bechunanaland and the Katanga province of the Congo Republic. The 241,000 Anglicans are less than 2 per cent of the population. The Archbishop, Francis Oliver Green-Wilkinson (consecrated when the name of the diocese was changed from Northern Rhodesia to Zambia), and three of the other five bishops were born in England. The most recently consecrated, John Paul Burrough, is a former missionary to Korea and chaplain to immigrants in the Diocese of Birmingham. He was named to the episcopate in June 1968, and had to wait until the adjournment of Lambeth X to visit his new diocese for the first time.

The Church of the Province of East Africa

The union of 13 dioceses and over 439,000 Anglicans in the East African Church represents years of missionary work stretching back to the 1880s and the arrival of James Hannington, martyred first Bishop of Eastern Equatorial Africa. It also illustrates the Anglican tolerance for different degrees of churchmanship stemming directly from the influence of the determinedly low Church Missionary Society and the ultra-high University Mission to Central Africa. Hence there was a great deal to be accepted in Christian charity when at last the dioceses (most of them had been under the jurisdiction of Canterbury) inaugurated the East African Church in 1960. Its constitution provides for autonomy similar to that of other Anglican provinces, with a special provision on the doctrine of man as related to the life of the new Africa: "In conformity with Christian doctrine, the Church of this Province proclaims that all men are of equal value and dignity in the sight of God and, while careful to provide for the special needs of different peoples committed to its charge, allows no discrimination in the membership and government of the Church based solely on grounds of racial difference." The East African Church began with five dioceses (Mombasa, Zanzibar, Masasi, Central Tanganyika, and South-West Tanganyika) and a few months later created three new ones—Maseno, Kakuru, and Fort Hall (later called Mount Kenya). In 1968 two of the English-born bishops—William Scott Baker, who had headed the Diocese of Zanzibar (more recently Zanzibar & Tanga) for nearly twenty-five years, and Trevor Huddleston, who had been Bishop of Masasi for eight—relinquished their posts in favor of indigenous clergy. The native bishops now outnumber the British eleven to seven. Of them all, the man most intimately associated with the development of the East African Church is its archbishop, Leonard James Beecher, who went out to Kenya as a teacher in 1927 and was ordained to the priesthood there in 1929. He successfully interspersed his work as a translater and legislator with his parochial duties for more than two decades before being elevated to the episcopate.

The Church of Uganda, Rwanda, and Burundi

Four of the five African churches were inaugurated by Geoffrey Fisher
during his years at Canterbury, the last being the Church of Uganda,
Rwanda, and Burundi. Its membership totals 1,500,000 in ten dioceses,
seven of which formerly comprised the old Diocese of Uganda and three
of which made up the Diocese of the Upper Nile. The church came into
being in April 1961 and could claim with satisfaction that eleven of the
twelve bishops it sent to Lambeth X were Africans. (The exception was
the Bishop of Kigezi, an Englishman who spent years in the Sudan as a
lay missionary and civil commissioner before being ordained priest in
the Diocese of Carlisle in 1956.) The primate, Erica Sabiti, once was a
lay reader. A member of the Ankole tribe and a one-time schoolteacher,
he called himself the "new boy" among the Anglican metropolitans but
soon dispelled any impression of shyness by managing to speak at almost
every plenary session of Lambeth X. His own diocese, Ruwenzori, has
been recovering from the disastrous earthquake of 1966. Like several
other dioceses, it also works with refugees from Rwanda and the Sudan.
Other special areas of work are among pagans and Muslims, establishment of centers for training lay readers, and translation of the Holy
Scriptures into six languages and twelve dialects.

The Church of India, Pakistan, Burma, and Ceylon

Begun in 1814 with the founding of the Diocese of Calcutta, the church
has experienced almost continual growth and change. Calcutta became
the metropolitan see when the Indian church was established as an independent Anglican body in 1835. In the ensuing decades the Church's life
paralleled India's development as one of the proudest possessions of the
Empire. After World War II, it weathered a stormy period in which it
reluctantly gave permission for four dioceses (Madras, Travancore, Tin-
nevelly, and Dornakal) to become a part of the newly formed Church of
South India. In the late 1960s it faced further change in unity plans that,
if brought to fruition, will leave Burma alone to be reorganized as an
independent province of the Anglican Communion. (The Diocese of
Rangoon, dating from 1877, comprises the whole of Burma; the military-
socialistic government expelled all missionaries in 1966 and with other
Christian bodies it has achieved an entirely indigenous leadership.)
Headed by the ebullient Lakdasa de Mel, fifteenth Bishop of Calcutta,
seventeen of the twenty IPBC bishops attended Lambeth X. They are

fathers in God to some 746,000 Anglicans. Three of them (Amritsar, Bombay, Nandyal) are members of the Brotherhood of the Ascended Christ and one, the Bishop of Dacca, is a member of the Oxford Mission to Calcutta. Their dioceses, as much as any in Anglicanism, are deeply involved with "all sorts and conditions of men"—with aboriginal tribesmen, with militant Hindus as well as members of passive sects, with starving hordes of poor and homeless, and with refugees from the Chinese Communists—among them the Dalai Lama and his loyal followers.

Nippon Sei Ko Kai (The Holy Catholic Church in Japan)

St. Francis Xavier brought Christianity to Japan in 1549, but more than three centuries passed before Admiral Perry opened the islands to the West. Then, in 1859, two missionaries of the American church were the forerunners of a small group later enlarged by the Church of England. By 1887, the Japanese church was able to hold its first general synod. At the time of Pearl Harbor it had ten dioceses (two self-supporting sees with native bishops and eight missionary jurisdictions) and the war years forced the church to stand on its own feet. In 1947, the Bishop of Kobe (Michael Yashiro, consecrated in 1940, himself the son of an Anglican priest) became presiding bishop and the following year set out for Lambeth VIII as one of the first Japanese allowed to travel abroad after the war. He returned again for Lambeth IX. An apparent prejudice against elevating younger men to the episcopate is only gradually being overcome, as evidenced by the twenty-two ballots necessary in 1959 to elect fifty-year-old David Goto as Bishop of Tokyo. Since the recent retirement of the Suffragan of Tokyo, Kenneth Viall, SSJE, an American, the entire episcopate is Japanese and there are 317 Japanese priests. Major Anglican institutions include St. Paul's University, St. Luke's Hospital, and the Central Theological College, all in Tokyo. Christianity accounts for only 1 per cent of the 95 million Japanese. Of that number, Rome has some 250,000; Kyodan, a Protestant amalgamation, 180,000; and the Anglican Church, 48,000—hence its description as "a minority within a minority." (It was an American Episcopalian, General Douglas MacArthur, who decided that Shintoism should no longer be the state religion.) "Japan is not lost for Christ," wrote an American priest on returning home. "Though it knows it not, it awaits him, but when he comes, as assuredly he will, he must not resemble too closely an American tourist."

Chung Hua Sheng Kung Hui (The Holy Catholic
Church in China)

"The Chinese church is truly catholic in its origins," declared the 1968 edition of the *Church of England Yearbook* as it outlined the work begun by the American Church in 1844 and later strengthened by more missionaries from England, Canada, Ireland, Australia, and New Zealand. Nonetheless, the noble heritage of the Chinese Church serves only to underline the tragic suppression and isolation it has suffered under Communist rule. What it once was, however, supplies a vision of what it may be again. It began to achieve its own identity in 1912 when eleven Chinese dioceses held their first general synod. A constitution was approved in 1915 and three years later the first Chinese bishop was consecrated. By 1947 the majority of its House of Bishops was Chinese, a situation that prepared the Church for the exodus of missionaries and all foreign clergy after the advent of the Peoples' Government in 1949. Since that time there has been little contact with the rest of the world except for the years between 1955 and 1963, when a limited number of visitors were allowed and when the Bishop of Chekiang was permitted a trip to London. With the onslaught of the "great proletarian cultural revolution" in 1966 the Chinese Church was completely cut off from the rest of the world. Most of its leaders are believed to have been imprisoned and the public observance of Christmas and Easter was forbidden. Although fifteen Chinese dioceses are still listed in directories of the Anglican Communion, the membership figure of 20,000 persons is only for the Diocese of Hong Kong & Macao. Formerly known as the Diocese of Victoria, Hong Kong (in Chinese, "Kong-O") it has been headed since 1966 by a tall, athletic Englishman, Gilbert Baker, who was ordained priest in Canton in 1934 and has spent most of his life in the Far East.

The Church of the Province of the West Indies

Touching on two continents and embracing many of the intervening islands, the Church of the West Indies has eight dioceses and 1,146,000 members. Even though it has been self-governing since 1883 and is to a great extent self-supporting, it has always had a serious shortage of clergy. Its 315 priests are hard-pressed to cope with large congregations (urban parishes with registered communicants totaling 2000 are not unusual) which are scattered and often difficult to reach. A further complication is considerable illegitimacy and devotion to voodoism: both are ever-present in an otherwise seemingly peaceful region of sunny days, cloudless skies, and diocesan heraldry emblazoned with sailing ships, mahogany leaves, and even a pineapple. The West Indies sent ten bishops to Lambeth X. Its metropolitan, the Archbishop of Guyana, is British-born, as are five other members of the episcopate. In his area and in the Diocese of Trinidad, about half the population is non-Christian—mainly Hindu and Muslim—but the rest of the West Indies, nominally Christian, counts five out of ten as Anglicans.

Igreja Episcopal do Brasil (Episcopal Church of Brazil)

In the largest country in South America (over 3 million square miles with more than 66 million people) Anglicanism seeks to make a significant contribution, as much as anywhere in Latin America, as a Church both catholic and reformed. It became an independent province on April 25, 1965, but still is extremely small, with only 18,928 members and a tiny band of clergy augmented by British chaplaincies in central and northern Brazil. The primate elected by the synod is Egmont M. Krischke, who is also Bishop of Southern Brazil. On his translation to his present see he was succeeded as Bishop of Southwestern Brazil by Plinio Lauer Simoes. Both are Brazilians, but the third bishop, Edmund Knox Sherrill, is an American. He was consecrated in 1959 by his father, Henry Knox Sherrill, Presiding Bishop of the American Church from 1947 to 1958.

The Jerusalem Archbishopric

Good Friday offerings and other contributions from throughout the world support Anglican witness and work in Jerusalem and four other dioceses in the Middle East. Begun in 1841, the work lapsed for a few years in the early 1880s but was revived by the Church of England in 1886. The Archbishopric in Jerusalem was created by the Archbishop of Canterbury in 1957 with the enthronement of Angus Campbell Mac-Innes, whose father was Bishop in Jerusalem from 1914 to 1932. ("People used to say to us, 'One day you will wake up and find yourselves in Israel.' We did," he observed drily of the invasion of June 1967.) After Lambeth X, Archbishop MacInnes retired to his native England to be Assistant Bishop of Sheffield and was succeeded by George Appleton, Archbishop of Perth, 1963–68, as the tenth diocesan. The Archbishop in Jerusalem is especially charged with representing the Anglican Communion in the Holy City and with "the promotion of good relations with all other Christian authorities and communities in the area of his archbishopric." As metropolitan, he has oversight for the Diocese of Egypt with Libya and North Africa (dating from 1920), the Sudan (held with Egypt until 1945), Iran (founded in 1912), and Jordan, Lebanon, and Syria (1956). Anglicans total 158,000. Governed by an episcopal synod responsible to Canterbury as chairman of the Lambeth Consultative Body, the archbishopric looks forward to provincial status when larger numbers of clergy and laity permit it to extend its synod beyond a House of Bishops. St. George's College, in the cathedral close at Jerusalem, was founded in 1962 as a center for special study in the Holy Land.

Iglesia Episcopal de Cuba (Episcopal Church of Cuba)

For more than six decades (1901–1966) a missionary district of the American Church, the Cuban Church still awaits full realization of its independence. For some years it has been "treading water," as one bishop put it, and has somehow managed to stay alive despite the Communistic regime of Fidel Castro. It is a single diocese with 74,000 members and is the only body in the Anglican Communion governed by a metropolitan council. The ex-officio members of the council are the Metropolitan of Canada (with whose country Cuba maintained diplomatic relations after breaking off with the U.S.), the Archbishop of the West Indies, and the bishop who is president of the Caribbean Province of the American church. The Cuban-born, American-trained Bishop of Cuba is José Agustín González Martínez, who was Dean of Holy Trinity Cathedral, Havana, at the time of his appointment as executive overseer of the Cuban Church in 1966. He was elected bishop on February 4, 1967, and was consecrated the following day.

The Council of the Church of South-East Asia

Nine bishops of South-East Asian dioceses marched together at Lambeth X, members of a council that since 1954 has provided a fellowship of common action and a quasi-provincial structure. They represented the dioceses of Seoul, Taejon, Singapore & Malaya, Kuching, and Sabah (formerly called Jesselton), all under Canterbury's jurisdiction; Hong Kong & Macao, temporarily separated from the Church in China; Rangoon, still a part of the Church of India, Burma, and Ceylon; and the Philippine Episcopal Church and the Missionary District of Taiwan, both associated with the American Church. (The Philippine Independent Catholic Church is also a member of the Council.) J. C. L. Wong, third Bishop of Taiwan (the Formosan diocese was transferred from the jurisdiction of the Japanese Church in 1960), as chairman of the Council was given the rank of metropolitan in the processions at Lambeth.

Extra-Provincial Dioceses to the See of Canterbury

The name seems rather grand when borne aloft on a banner, but actually it is a catch-all for all missionary dioceses not attached to member churches of the Anglican Communion or to the South-East Asian Council. At Lambeth X, the group included six dioceses scattered across the map from the Mediterranean to South America. The latter area includes two dioceses of gigantic proportions—Argentina & Eastern South America with the Falkland Islands (founded 1869, divided into two dioceses in 1910, reunited in 1946) and Chile, Bolivia and Peru (founded in 1963). Another member from the Western Hemisphere is the Diocese of Bermuda, which dates from 1839. The other extraprovincial dioceses are Gibraltar (which is responsible for Church of England chaplaincies throughout southern Europe and parts of North Africa), Madagascar, and Mauritius.

THE LAMBETH CONFERENCES

Lambeth I, 1867

President: Charles Thomas Longley   *Bishops present:* 76

The carefully disciplined but rather leisurely meeting that was the first of the Lambeth Conferences, a forerunner of one of the great institutions of Anglicanism that now has spanned more than a century, came about through a combination of factors:

> The rapid overseas growth of the Church of England, an expansion that raised many problems and made closer ties with the mother church of vital importance.
>
> The desire of independent Anglican bodies—especially the American Church, then in its seventy-fifth year, and the Canadian Church, which had just organized its own convocation—to obtain guidance and consultation with the primatial see of Canterbury and the English episcopate.
>
> The isolation of distance and infrequent contact, felt keenly by many colonial dioceses.
>
> The hope that an international meeting of bishops could negotiate reconciliation with other communions.
>
> Theological reaction to a liberalism that appeared to be sweeping the Church in the mid-1860s.

The latter situation, of which the Bishop of Natal came to be a symbol, did the most to underline the need for the bishops to meet. It added an urgency, although the other topics were more important in the long run. The dispute began rather academically after John William Colenso, who had been consecrated as first Bishop of Natal in 1853, wrote a book questioning the historical accuracy of the Pentateuch: consequently he fell into disfavor with his metropolitan, the Bishop of Cape Town, and was deposed for heresy. The deposition was not upheld by the Judicial Committee of the Privy Council, and eventually the need to unravel all the claims of jurisdiction pointed up the need for an international meeting of all the bishops.

304

At the same time other rumblings and discontent contributed to the case for a conference—the general growth of rationalism, the continuing witch-hunts in ritualism, and the onslaught of publications that questioned the traditional beliefs of Christianity.

As the varying situations became known to the Archbishop of Canterbury, Charles Thomas Longley, along with repeated requests for a meeting, he reacted cautiously but admitted that the idea was "not by any means foreign to my own feeling."

The Convocation of Canterbury cautiously approved the meeting only after the Archbishop assured them that "no declaration of faith shall be made and no decision come to which shall effect generally the interests of the Church, but that we shall meet together for brotherly counsel and encouragement."

Thus the consultative nature of all Lambeths, as opposed to any legislative powers, was cast long before the first Conference was called to order. What was the reason for the great reluctance to summon the bishops? There were many factors, ranging from aloofness ("Are they really bishops in the same sense that we are?") to fear that such a meeting would jeopardize the relationship with the Crown. Finally, on February 22, 1867, the invitations went out to assemble in London the following September.

Of the 144 bishops invited, it was somewhat disappointing to find that only slightly more than half were present. The entire Convocation of York, excepting the Bishop of Chester, stayed away for fear of weakening the link between Church and state. Matters of expense and great distance kept many overseas bishops at home.

Lambeth I began with a celebration of Holy Communion by Archbishop Longley in Lambeth Palace Chapel. The Bishop of Illinois, John Henry Whitehouse, was the preacher. Others taking part in the service were the Archbishop of Armagh, the Primus of Scotland, and the metropolitans of Canada, New Zealand, and South Africa. The bread was made from corn grown at Bethlehem and the wine was from Jerusalem, both especially sent for the bishops' Eucharist.

Meeting in the Guard Room of Lambeth Palace (except for Lambeth IV, which also used the Guard Room, all of the other Conferences until 1968 were in the Lambeth Library), the bishops spent only four days in deliberations, but some of the committees continued until December.

Archbishop Longley handled the Colenso affair with great skill. The Bishop of Cape Town lost out on his desire for a full and formal censure when Longley ruled out of order a motion for a Resolution of condemnation made by the Presiding Bishop of the American Church; the Conference ended with no formal criticism of either the Bishop of Natal or the authors of the controversial *Essays and Reviews*.[1]

Most of the discussions were on purely family affairs of intercommunion between the churches of the Anglican Communion, problems of the colonial churches, and cooperation in missionary activities. The closing service was at St. Mary at Lambeth, the parish church just outside the grounds of Lambeth Palace.

Lambeth I was both stimulating and placid, but the *Pall Mall Gazette,* among other newspapers, saw only the latter aspect: "If the members of the Pan-Anglican Synod have not a single word to say upon any of the great questions, theoretical or practical, which concern the very existence of the Church of England, their impotent caution and misplaced decency will do more to endanger it than any external attack with which it is at present threatened."

The bishops did prove, however, that they could meet together for mutual advice and encouragement without being a threat to the authority of Church or state. Instead of becoming a general council they were satisfied to be a fellowship of bishops, and despite its disclaimers, the Lambeth Conferences had from the start an authority uniquely their own, no less real for being undefined. "The immediate result of the Conference is two-fold," observed the *Church Times* of October 19, 1867. "It has dealt a heavy blow to the Erastian spirit by showing the spiritual equality of the unestablished prelates of a Republic with the mitred peers of a Kingdom. It has struck more heavily still at the insular narrowness which limits all interest within the compass of England and Wales."

Lambeth II, 1878

President: Archibald Campbell Tait   *Bishops present:* 100

Again the Canadian Church took the first official step toward an international meeting of Anglican bishops. In December 1872 the bishops of

---

[1] In a sermon at Lambeth Parish Church marking the centenary of the Lambeth I service there, Eric James, director of the Parish and People Program and Precentor of Southwark Cathedral, compared the Bishop of Natal with the Bishop of Woolwich, John Robinson, and the former Bishop of California, James Pike. "Anyone who reflects on the fact that not one of the bishops (at Lambeth I) defended *Essays and Reviews,* and on the condemnation of Colenso, and on what has happened in more recent years over *Honest to God,* and over Bishop Pike, will see the force of the assertion that the way we most often kill our prophets in the Church these days is not by stoning them but by consecrating them."

the ecclesiastical province of Canada sent a formal appeal to the Convocation of Canterbury to join with them in a request addressed to Archbishop Tait, the former Bishop of London who had been translated to Canterbury later in the year that Lambeth I convened. The Bishop of Lichfield, George Augustus Selwyn, endorsed and expanded the appeal in an address to Convocation. (Selwyn, Bishop of New Zealand, 1841–1868, died in 1878 before Lambeth II met; Selwyn College, Cambridge, is named in his memory.) In 1873 the West Indian bishops and in 1874 the American Church (in a letter signed by forty-two bishops) also urged another Conference, and the Bishop of Pittsburgh engaged Archbishop Tait in a prolonged correspondence about it.

Efforts to reconvene within a few years after Lambeth I were unsuccessful and Archbishop Tait, who had been skeptical about the first Conference, remained cautious in addressing the Convocation in April 1875, pointing out that it was "a serious matter to gather the bishops together from all parts of the globe unless there is some distinct object for their so gathering."

He was, however, greatly encouraged by the approval of the Northern Convocation [York], which had held aloof in 1867. On March 28, 1876, he wrote all bishops of the Anglican Communion that a future Conference should be much longer than the four-day meeting of 1867 and stressed his readiness to call them together "if it shall seem expedient after the opinions of all our brethren have been ascertained."

The official invitations were sent July 10, 1877, and for the first time the schedule that was to set the pattern for future Conferences was outlined—a general meeting during the first week, followed by two weeks of committee work and concluding with a fourth week of general sessions. Subjects proposed for consideration were "the best mode of maintaining Union among the various Churches of the Anglican Communion," voluntary boards of arbitration for churches to which such an arrangement would be applicable, the relationship of missionary bishops and missionaries from various Anglican churches working in the same country, the position of Anglican chaplains and chaplaincies on the Continent and elsewhere, and "modern forms of infidelity and the best means of dealing with them."

A total of 108 bishops accepted, but at the last moment some canceled their plans, leaving a hundred bishops to compose the membership of Lambeth II.[2] On St. Peter's Day, June 29, 1878, the custom of journeying to Canterbury for the initial meeting was inaugurated with a morn-

---

[2] The group included thirty-five English, thirty colonial and missionary, nine Irish, seven Scottish, and nineteen American bishops.

ing service at St. Augustine's College (with sermon by the Bishop of Western New York, Cleveland Coxe) and an afternoon service of welcome in the Cathedral Church. For the first time, the Archbishop was seated in the Chair of St. Augustine as he welcomed the bishops. In London, the first meeting of Lambeth II was preceded by a celebration of Holy Communion in Lambeth Palace Chapel and thereafter the litany was recited every morning in the chapel.

The success of Lambeth II, as vital as the first in shaping future Lambeths, owed much to the wisdom and leadership of Archbishop Tait. Brought up a Scottish Presbyterian, he was confirmed while at Oxford and in English history has been called "the most remarkable prelate that has sat on the throne of Canterbury since the Reformation." More of a statesman than a churchman, he was an evangelical who failed to some extent to understand the Tractarians but still was noted for his profound understanding of the layman's point of view. His personal life was marked by deep personal tragedy: five of his six daughters succumbed to scarlet fever in five weeks' time, a son died a month before Lambeth II convened, and his wife died the following winter.

The agenda of Lambeth II was concerned mainly with domestic interests of the Anglican Communion and some discussion of mutual problems of missionary work—a limited range of interests, admittedly, but the value of the meetings had been established.

At the close of Lambeth II, eighty-five of the bishops met Archbishop Tait at the west door of St. Paul's Cathedral to form a procession that moved up the nave as the congregation sang the hymn "The Church's One Foundation." The Primate was the celebrant and the Bishop of Pennsylvania, William Bacon Stevens, was the preacher.

Lambeth III, 1888

President: Edward White Benson   *Bishops present:* 145

"Brethren most dear, and to me most Reverend, few privileges of my office can surpass that which, though unworthy, I exercise today," said Archbishop Benson from the Chair of St. Augustine to the bishops assembled for Lambeth III. "It is to bid you welcome in the Name of the Lord. . . . Welcome from all continents, and seas, and shores, where the English tongue is spoken. Welcome, bearers of the great commission to be His Witnesses unto the ends of the earth. Welcome, disciples of the great determination to 'refuse fables,' and seek the inspiration of the Church at the fountain-head of inspired reason. Welcome to the Chair, which, when filled least worthily, most takes up its own parable, and speaks of unbroken lines of government, and law, and faith. . . ."

The Conference soon settled into the schedule established by Lambeth II—general sessions interspersed with a fortnight of committee work. Of the 145 bishops present (a total of 211 had been invited) the Americans numbered twenty-nine, a sizable increase over the nineteen who attended Lambeths I and II. (The first Bishop of Fond du Lac, John Henry Hobart Brown, died shortly before the Conference opened.)

Its greatest accomplishment was adoption of the Lambeth Quadrilateral that briefly set forth the essentials of Anglicanism. It was based on the statement of belief approved at Chicago two years earlier by the General Convention of the American Church.

Social questions were much in evidence on the agenda: temperance, divorce, Socialism, polygamy, unemployment, and industrial cooperation. The Church's concern beyond its domestic life was also indicated by resolutions pertaining to the Old Catholics, Eastern churches, and Scandinavian bodies. (One Resolution noted friendly communications among Anglican bishops and the Eastern Orthodox, with the hope that "the barriers to fuller communion may be, in course of time, removed by further intercourse and extended enlightenment.") Other topics were the bishops' relation to religious communities and the conferring of degrees in divinity.

A committee dealing with the subject of purity praised the standard of a high and pure morality and called for continued support. It asked the Church to deliberate on "how best to purify art and literature, and to repress all that is immodest in language, manners, and dress." (Meanwhile the newspapers reflected London's shock over Oscar Wilde and Jack the Ripper.)

Besides the service at Canterbury, the opening week of Lambeth III also saw the bishops worshiping in Westminster Abbey for the first time and some of the committees meeting nearby in Church House.

"This, the third Conference of bishops of the Anglican Communion, proved with striking force the marvellous vitality and growth of that branch of the Catholic Church which, at this moment, is undeniably the most active, the most influential, and in the judgment of many, the one that approximates most nearly to the primitive Apostolic ideal," wrote one of Benson's biographers a few years later. "It brought home to the minds of all Churchmen, and of all English-speaking nations, the strength, the unity, and the zeal of the Anglican Church."

Lambeth IV, 1897

President: Frederick Temple   *Bishops present:* 194

A total of 194 bishops (out of about 240 eligible) assembled in England in the summer of 1897 for a corporate observance of St. Augustine's arrival on the same shores 1300 years earlier.[3]

Some eleven months before they were to meet, Archbishop Benson wrote to the bishops about discussion topics that "have reached me from my Episcopal brethren in all parts of the world"—suggestions for critical study of Holy Scripture, organization of the Anglican Communion (a central consultative body, a tribunal of reference, the relation of primates and metropolitans in colonies and elsewhere to the See of Canterbury) and the position and function of the Lambeth Conference.

His letter was still fresh in the hands of many of the bishops when, in September 1896, Leo XIII issued the Papal Bull *Apostolicae Curae,* in which Anglican orders were condemned as invalid through defect both of form and intention. Work began almost immediately on the *Responsio* to be sent to the Pope over the signatures of the Archbishops of Canterbury and York. It was prepared by the Bishops of Oxford, Peterborough, and Salisbury. The latter bishop drafted the reply in Latin and it was dispatched to reach Archbishop Benson at Hawarden in Wales, the estate of Prime Minister Gladstone, but it was never opened by the Archbishop who, on the day the papers arrived, was stricken with a fatal heart attack as the celebrant was pronouncing the Absolution during Holy Communion.

Consequently, two great responsibilities—the reply to the Vatican and final preparation for Lambeth IV—awaited Frederick Temple, already quite old and nearly blind when he came to the Chair of St. Augustine. Nonetheless, as his biographer later noted, "he threw himself with the force of his character and all the vigor of his scholarship into the consideration of the *Responsio* [and] made it his business to 'cut out all the thunder.'"[4]

In June 1897, Britain and its Empire marked the sixtieth year of Victoria's reign. Some weeks later, with the opening of Lambeth IV, another

---

[3] Because Lambeth III had adjourned in 1888, the nine-year period before the convening of Lambeth IV is the shortest period that has elapsed between Lambeths; the longest was the eighteen-year interlude, from 1930 to 1948, caused by World War II.

[4] Made public in March 1897, it declared in part, "For the difference and debate between us and him Pope Leo arises from a diverse interpretation of the self-same Gospel, which we all believe and honor as the only true one. We also gladly declare that there is much in his own person that is worthy of love

festive occasion was the bishops' pilgrimage by special train to Ebbs Fleet, on the Kentish coast, for a solemn service on the spot where Augustine and his band of monks landed in the year 597.

In the business sessions, the Papal view of the last year failed to dampen Lambeth's zeal. For one thing, it had become an established institution and with confidence it set up a permanent Consultative Continuation Committee. It also gave closer attention to matters of unity, and requested Canterbury, York, and London to act as a committee to confer personally or by correspondence with the Orthodox Eastern patriarchs "with a view to considering the possibility of securing a clearer understanding and of establishing closer relations between the Churches of the East and the Anglican Communion."

Benson's death almost on the eve of Lambeth IV could have been a staggering blow, but that was not the judgment of history. "To Archbishop Benson the distant bishops throughout the world had for years turned for sympathy and advice," his biographer wrote. "He knew their needs, their hopes, their fears. To the American bishops he was a *persona gratissima,* and there can be no doubt that they came to the Conference with a sense that its highest personal attraction had passed away. They went back to America full not only of the greatest reverence for Dr. Temple but also of the warmest personal affection for him."

At the final service at St. Paul's, Archbishop Temple preached on Acts 1:8, "Ye shall receive power from on high." The following week, despite his infirmities, he joined more than a hundred of the bishops aboard a special train to Glastonbury, "the cradle of British Christianity," the site most intimately associated with the earliest traces of pre-Augustinian Christianity in Britain.

Lambeth V, 1908

President: Randall Thomas Davidson   *Bishops present:* 242

In the years immediately after the turn of the century, Bishop Montgomery, Secretary of SPG and father of Field Marshal Montgomery, began planning a great Pan Anglican Congress. It materialized in an

---

and reverence. But that error, which is inveterate in the Roman Communion, of substituting the visible head for the invisible Christ, will rob his good works of any fruit of peace. Join with us then, we entreat you, most reverend brethren, in weighing patiently what Christ intended when he established the ministry of His Gospel. When this has been done, more will follow, as God wills in his own good time. God grant that even from this controversy may grow fuller knowledge of the truth, greater patience and a broader desire for peace in the Church of Christ, the Saviour of the world."

eight-day meeting at Albert Hall in London that drew a total of 17,000 persons, both clerical and lay, from throughout the Anglican world. Mainly a conference of speeches, it accomplished little except to implant a consciousness of membership in the widespread, growing Anglican Communion—a feeling that carried over with marked influence to Lambeth V as it convened in London the following month.

The Pan Anglican Congress, followed by Lambeth V, made Anglican-ism much in evidence in London in the summer of 1908. "There was a Canadian bishop who relieved the tedium of the Lambeth Conference by dropping in, during lunch-time, at a rifle-range to indulge his favorite tastes, by shooting at tin bears down a tube and hitting at every shot," recalled Scott Holland in his book *A Bundle of Memories.* "Probably, at certain hours of the day, all those gentlemen who were in the habit of taking sliding headers down the chutes in Westminster Baths were mem-bers of the American Episcopal Bench!"

Paradoxically, for whatever distractions its bishops found, Lambeth V was relevent and realistic about its work. Archbishop Davidson, then in his fifth year at Canterbury,[5] and the bishops themselves, were far more aware of their participation in an international Communion: in turn, they were eager to convince their own people that in a world-wide Church the dioceses of China or South Africa were as important as the Church of England. At Lambeth V, they encouraged independence and autonomy, choosing of native bishops, and the adaptation of services, discipline, and diocesan organization to accommodate local needs.

(In the U.S., during the same month, the Episcopal Church was shaken by the defection to Rome of several prominent Anglo-Catholics and some of their followers—including the Mother General of the oldest American order, the Community of St. Mary—but this was little felt at Lambeth.)

The first Lambeth of the twentieth century, shaking off the brooding presence of Victoria and all that her era symbolized, discussed faith and modern thought as well as marital problems, moral witness, abortion, racism, and intercommunion. On the latter subject, the bishops agreed to allow communicant members of any church of the Orthodox Eastern Communion to receive the sacraments in Anglican Churches if deprived of the ministration of a priest of their own communion.

---

[5] Archbishop Davidson worked at the center of five Lambeths: in 1878, he was Chaplain to Archbishop Tait; in 1888, as Dean of Windsor, he was Gen-eral Secretary; in 1897, as Bishop of Winchester, he was Episcopal Secretary; in 1908 and 1920 he was President. Although he was the first Archbishop of Canterbury to retire from office (in 1928), he accepted an invitation to address Lambeth VII and died only shortly before it convened.

Lambeth VI, 1920

President: Randall Thomas Davidson   *Bishops present:* 252

The sixth Lambeth, called as soon as possible after "the Great War," really stirred the imagination of Christendom. Its "Appeal to All Christian People" caused it to be reckoned by many the most important Conference to date and had a profound effect upon ecumenical discussions already given a hearty impetus by the pioneering Edinburgh Conference of 1910. (Nearly fifty years later at Lambeth X, in his keynote address on unity, the Metropolitan of India, Archbishop de Mel, referred to the 1920 appeal as "the most significant document ever issued by a Lambeth Conference: it had a great effect, and now the day of reckoning is come.")

The framing of the appeal resulted from an informal conversation on July 18, 1920, while a group was sitting on the lawn of Lambeth Palace: the Archbishop of York, Cosmo Gordon Lang; the Bishop of Peterborough, Frank Theodore Woods; the Bishop of Western New York, Charles Henry Brent; and the Bishop of Pennsylvania, Philip Mercer Rhinelander. They were joined by Archbishop Davidson, the first primate to preside over two Lambeths, and from their talk on that midsummer afternoon came the idea for the appeal. It eloquently acknowledged "all those who believe in our Lord Jesus Christ and have been baptised into the name of the Holy Trinity as sharing with us membership of the Universal Church which is His Body."

The bishops also acknowledged the guilt of their own communion in the disunity and called for a wider vision of a United Catholic Church within which "Christian communions now separated from one another would retain much that has long been distinctive in their methods of worship and service." Acceptance of Holy Scripture, the Nicene Creed, baptism, and Holy Communion would be involved, it said, together with "a ministry acknowledged by every part of the Church as possessing not only the inward call of the Spirit but also the commission of Christ and the authority of the whole body."

The 252 bishops of Lambeth VI put forth their appeal for fellowship (the official theme of the Conference) with hope for a truer unity of Christians "that the world might believe."

In addition, the Lambeth fathers said that they were willing to receive from other communions "a form of recognition or commission," and they hoped that ministers of non-Episcopal churches would accept "a commission through episcopal ordination, as obtaining for them a ministry throughout the whole fellowship." There were resolutions justifying bishops in giving permission for clergymen to preach in churches of ministers not episcopally ordained; also the Conference recommended that baptized Christians should, in certain circumstances, be admitted to the Holy Communion.

There were other items of discussion at Lambeth VI more directly related to the postwar world of the early 1920s, but the far-reaching effect of the appeal overshadowed all else. It was a manifestation that was, in a sense, an ironic reply to Bishop Lawrence of Massachusetts, who earlier in the year had expressed doubt that "not a hundred persons in the United States [would] attach the smallest importance to the decisions of Lambeth."

Besides the men concerned directly with the appeal, some of the other prominent figures in Lambeth VI were Henson of Durham, Weston of Zanzibar, Gibson of Gloucester, and Matheson of Rupert's Land.

Lambeth VII, 1930

President: Cosmo Gordon Lang   *Bishops present:* 307

The world was in the grip of a great economic depression when the bishops again came to London in 1930. During the opening week they marched in procession down Canon Street to St. Paul's, where William Temple, Archbishop of York, was the preacher of the day. His frequently quoted sermon ended on a note of triumphant assurance: "While we deliberate, He reigns; when we decide wisely, He reigns; when we decide foolishly, He reigns; when we serve Him in humble loyalty, He reigns; when we serve Him self-assertively, He reigns; when we rebel and seek to withhold our service, He reigns—the Alpha and the Omega, which is, and which was, and which is to come, the Almighty!"

The Conference that began on such a positive note came to be regarded as the least successful of Lambeths. The Americans and most of the Canadians did not find it a very happy experience, feeling that it was managed too exclusively by English bishops.

Among the Conference reports, the long paper on the Christian doctrine of man was widely hailed for its attempt to reconcile religion and science.

Another outstanding report was on the unity of the Church. It came from a seventy-two-member committee headed by Archbishop Temple. Representatives of the free churches and the Orthodox were on hand to be consulted.

When the South India scheme was presented to the Conference for the first time it was decided that the proposed church would not be a member of the Anglican Communion but would be regarded as a province of the Universal Church with only a restricted relationship with Anglicanism. Temple's report on the scheme was credited with dispersing what serious opposition there might have been at that critical moment.

On birth control, the Conference gave answers more thoughtful than it had in 1920, but it still seemed to be offering only the most reluctant approval. Even so, such approval was regarded nearly forty years later as a landmark decision when Lambeth X sought to show some of the historical background of its thinking in rejecting the Pope's condemnation of artificial birth control.

Lambeth VIII, 1948

President: Geoffrey Fisher   *Bishops present:* 326

Eighteen years passed before another Lambeth could be convened. The intervening period saw the Roosevelt era, the brief reign of Edward VIII, Hitler, concentration camps, Dunkirk and the Battle of Britain, Pearl Harbor, Hiroshima and the atomic bomb, the United Nations and postwar recovery from the greatest of all wars. William Temple had come to Canterbury for a brief primacy before his death in 1944; he was perhaps the greatest Archbishop of Canterbury since Longley but he was the only one destined not to preside over a Lambeth Conference.

In many ways, the first Lambeth after World War II was the most successful of all the Conferences. Three bishops came from Japan, their presence a symbol of the task of reconciliation facing the Church in a world that had been torn apart by hatred and warfare. Missing were the bishops of four dioceses of South India who had become part of a new church to which the Conference spoke with cautious warmth.

The theme of Lambeth VIII was "The Christian Doctrine of Man" and the forty-nine resolutions it passed were concerned with man as an individual and as a member of society.

Lambeth VIII spoke boldly on race relations. "All men, irrespective of race or color, are equally the objects of God's love," it declared. "All men are made in His image; for all, Christ died and to all there is made the offer of eternal life." Further, it said, the rights of every individual "should be declared by the Church, recognized by the State, and safeguarded by international law."

The Conference reaffirmed its 1930 stand "that war as a method of settling international disputes is incompatible with the teaching and example of our Lord Jesus Christ" and it requested governments to work on reduction of armaments.

Looking to the future, the Conference recommended an Advisory Council on Missionary Structure and a central college for graduate study for priests from throughout the Anglican Communion. The

ACMS came about but the college (housed at St. Augustine's, Canterbury) eventually foundered. A happier achievement was the establishment of the Anglican Cycle of Prayer, a carefully planned calendar which in 365 days embraces all of the dioceses and is in wide use in personal devotions and in Anglican churches throughout the world.

Another recommendation was for the second Anglican Congress of the century. By 1954 it had been arranged, with the American Church acting as hosts for laymen and clergymen from many dioceses gathered in Minneapolis in the Diocese of Minnesota. Bishop Gray of Connecticut saw in it "a new era in the history of the Anglican Communion in that it is the first representative gathering of the Church held outside the British Isles." Besides its own work of mutual encouragement and sharing, it provided opportunity for friendships that were to flourish in the two successive Lambeths as well as the Anglican Congress at Toronto in 1963.

Lambeth IX, 1958

President: Geoffrey Fisher   *Bishops present:* 310
For the first time, the bishops present were fewer than at the previous Conference, perhaps because in 1948 many of the bishops had been able to tie in the trip to Lambeth with the World Council of Churches' first assembly at Amsterdam.

The theme of Lambeth X was reconciliation; it was a successful Conference despite the observation of an elder statesman of the Church of England, George Bell, Bishop of Chichester, of "too little of supernatural or spiritual or (if preferred) too little of theological approach anywhere."

The reports of two of the committees were outstanding—"The Holy Bible: Its Authority and Message," from the group headed by Michael Ramsey, then Archbishop of York; and "The Family in Contemporary Society," produced by a group of which Stephen Bayne, Bishop of Olympia, was chairman. For a decade after Lambeth IX the latter paper remained one of the finest treatises available on the ideals of Christian family life and, in the first days of Lambeth X, it served as the backbone for the bishops' reply to the Papal encyclical on birth control. ("It is utterly wrong to urge that, unless children are specifically desired, that sexual intercourse is of the nature of sin," said the 1958 paper. "It is also wrong to say that such intercourse ought not to be engaged in except with the willing intention to procreate children.")

One of the far-reaching resolutions of Lambeth IX, on the "Progress of the Anglican Communion," created the post of Executive Officer of the Anglican Communion, and within the next year Bishop Bayne was named to the position.

There were many memorable features of Lambeth IX and numerous sidelights. One was the absence of any bishops of China. Another was the intrusion of a young man dressed as an Orthodox bishop who proceeded to harangue the bewildered bishops until he was ousted.

"We set ourselves to consider not only domestic problems concerning the Anglican Communion and Christendom, but also some of the fundamental issues which confront the whole of mankind," said the encyclical letter. "What we have tried to do is to think out again the principles, as we find them in God's Word and revelation, by which we believe nations, Churches, and individual men and women will be judged, and on which their conduct and policies should be based."

Reflecting on Lambeth IX in his York Diocesan Leaflet a few months later, Archbishop Ramsey wrote that "the nature of our fellowship in the Anglican Communion is as hard to describe and to explain as it is inescapable to see and to feel. . . . It is indeed a unity which includes Sacramental Communion, Creed, the bond everywhere of the bishop exercising the same pastoral office, a worship whose character has been moulded by the Prayer Book, a devotion to the Bible, and a sense of ancient tradition blending with a spirit of experiment."

It is possible, he added, "to say that here is a portion of the One, Holy, Catholic and Apostolic Church of Christ, not claiming any unique excellence, but living by the principles of a non-papal and scriptural catholicity."

LAMBETH CONFERENCE 1968

CONSULTANTS

The Rev. A. M. Allchin
Dr. Paul B. Anderson
Miss E. M. Batten, O.B.E.
The Ven. E. F. Carpenter
The Rev. Professor Henry Chadwick
The Rev. Canon A. K. Cragg
The Rev. H. F. J. Daniel
Dr. Peter Day
The Rev. Professor E. Fairweather
The Rev. Canon John Findlow
Dr. W. C. Fletcher
The Rev. E. M. B. Green
The Rev. Father M. Jarrett-Kerr
The Rev. Canon D. E. Jenkins

The Rev. John Luwum
The Rev. Professor John MacQuarrie
The Rev. J. Mbiti
The Rev. Canon B. S. Moss
The Rev. Professor D. E. Nineham
The Rev. Canon D. M. Paton
The Rev. C. Powles
The Rev. Professor H. E. Root
The Rt. Rev. R. R. Roseveare, S.S.M.
The Rev. Canon J. R. Satterthwaite
The Rev. Canon J. V. Taylor
The Rev. Canon D. Webster

OBSERVERS

ARMENIAN CHURCH
Catholicossate of Etchmiadzin, The Most Rev. Archbishop Bessak Toumayan

Catholicossate of Cilicia, The Rt. Rev. Bishop Karekin Sarkissian

ASSEMBLIES OF GOD
Dr. Thomas F. Zimmerman

BAPTIST WORLD ALLIANCE
The Rev. Dr. C. Ronald Goulding, The Rev. Dr. Ernest A. Payne

CHURCH OF SOUTH INDIA
The Rev. Dr. Russell Chandran, The Rt. Rev. Dr. Leslie Newbigin, The Most Rev. Pereji Solomon

COPTIC CHURCH
The Rt. Rev. Bishop Athanasius

EVANGELICAL CHURCH IN GERMANY
The Rt. Rev. Dr. Hanns Lilje, *Oberkonsistorialrat Rev. Dr. F. Schlingensiepen

INTERNATIONAL CONGREGATIONAL COUNCIL
The Rev. Dr. Norman Goodall, The Rev. John Huxtable

LUSITANIAN CHURCH
The Rt. Rev. Dr. Luís C. R. Pereira

LUTHERAN WORLD FEDERATION
The Rt. Rev. Dr. Fridtjov Birkeli, The Rev. Dr. Keith R. Bridston, The Most Rev. Dr. Gunnar A. E. Hultgren, The Rev. Dr. Harding Meyer, The Most Rev. Dr. Martti Simojoki, *The Rev. Dr. Åke Andrén, *The Rev. Dr. Martin L. Kretzmann, *The Rev. Dr. Jacob Kumaresan, *The Rev. Dr. Einar Molland, *The Rev. Dr. Martti Parvio, *The Rev. Dr. Regin Prenter, **The Rt. Rev. Bengt Sundkler

MAR THOMA CHURCH
The Rt. Rev. Philipose Mar Chrysostom

OLD CATHOLIC CHURCH
The Most Rev. Dr. Andreas Rinkel, *The Rt. Rev. Josef Brinkhues, *The Rt. Rev. Gerhardus A. van Kleef

ORTHODOX CHURCH
Constantinople, The Most Rev. Archbishop Athenagoras of Thyateira, **Professor Basil Anagnostopoulos
Alexandria, The Most Rev. Metropolitan Parthenios of Carthage
Jerusalem, The Very Rev. Archimandrite Cornelios Rodoussakis
Moscow, The Most Rev. Archbishop Antony of Minsk and Byelorussia
Serbia, The Rt. Rev. Bishop Firmilian
Romania, The Rt. Rev. Bishop Antim of Tîrgoviste
Bulgaria, The Most Rev. Metropolitan Nicodim of Sliven
Cyprus, The Rt. Rev. Bishop Kallinicos of Amathus
Orthodox Church of France and Western Europe, The Very Rev. Archimandrite Alexandre Semenoff-Tian-Chansky
Russian Orthodox Church in Exile, The Very Rev. Archpriest Count Leonid Ignatiew

PHILIPPINE INDEPENDENT CATHOLIC CHURCH
The Most Rev. Isabelo de los Reyes, **The Rt. Rev. Camilo C. Diel,
**The Rt. Rev. Macario V. Ga

RELIGIOUS SOCIETY OF FRIENDS
Douglas V. Steere

ROMAN CATHOLIC CHURCH
The Rt. Rev. Msgr. Peter J. Butelezi, O.M.I., The Rt. Rev. Dom Christo-
pher Butler, O.S.B., The Rev. Fr. John Coventry, S.J., The Most Rev.
Remi J. De Roo, The Very Rev. Canon William Purdy, The Rev. Dr.
Herbert J. Ryan, S.J., The Rt. Rev. Msgr. J. G. M. Willebrands, *The
Most Rev. William Z. Gomes, *The Rt. Rev. Thomas Holland, **The
Rt. Rev. Msgr. Jean-François Arrighi, **The Very Rev. Canon Josef A.
Dessain, **The Very Rev. Dom Philibert Zobel, O.S.B.

SALVATION ARMY
Commissioner Herbert Westcott, *Brigadier William G. Brown

SPANISH REFORMED EPISCOPAL CHURCH
The Rt. Rev. Ramón Taibo

SYRIAN ORTHODOX CHURCH
The Most Rev. Mar Severius Zakka Iwas

WORLD CONVENTION OF CHURCHES OF CHRIST
The Rev. Dr. George G. Beazley Jr.

WORLD COUNCIL OF CHURCHES
The Rev. Dr. Eugene Carson Blake, Dr. Nikos A. Nissiotis, *The Very
Rev. Archpriest Vitaly M. Borovoi, *The Rev. Steven G. Mackie, *The
Rev. Dr. Lukas Vischer

WORLD METHODIST COUNCIL
The Rev. Bishop Fred P. Corson, The Rev. A. Raymond George, The
Rev. Bishop Odd Hagen, The Rev. Dr. Harold Roberts

WORLD PRESBYTERIAN ALLIANCE
The Rev. Arthur L. MacArthur, The Rev. Dr. James I. McCord, The
Rev. Dr. Wilhelm Niesel, The Rev. Dr. William Stewart

*Invitations were sent to the following Churches but Observers were not
present:*
CHURCH OF THE EAST (ASSYRIAN)
ETHIOPIAN CHURCH
ORTHODOX PATRIARCHATES OF ANTIOCH AND GEORGIA AND THE
CHURCH OF GREECE

* Alternate Observers
** Special Guest Observers

BISHOPS ATTENDING LAMBETH X

The Church of England

Province of Canterbury

Name	See	Committee Assignment
Arthur Michael Ramsey	Primate of All England and Archbishop of Canterbury	President of Conference
Robert W. Stopford	Bishop of London	Steering Committee
S. Falkner Allison	Bishop of Winchester	*Vice-Chairman*, Unity Section
J. Leonard Wilson	Bishop of Birmingham	The Nature of Theological Language (*Vice-Chairman*)
E. M. Gresford Jones	Bishop of St. Albans	Oversight and Discipline (*Chairman*)
Geoffrey Francis Allen	Bishop of Derby	Intercommunion in a Divided Church (*Vice-Chairman*)
C. K. N. Bardsley	Bishop of Coventry	Laymen in Mission (*Chairman*)
J. Maurice Key	Bishop of Truro	The Nature of the Anglican Episcopate
Roger Plumpton Wilson	Bishop of Chichester	International Morality Today (*Chairman*)
Robert Cecil Mortimer	Bishop of Exeter	Steering Committee
W. L. Scott Fleming	Bishop of Norwich	Faith and Culture (*Chairman*)
Cyril Eastaugh	Bishop of Peterborough	Faith and Society

Name	See	Committee Assignment
Kenneth Riches	Bishop of Lincoln	Christian Appraisal of the Secular Society
A. Stretton Reeve	Bishop of Lichfield	Urbanization and the Metropolis
Ronald Ralph Williams	Bishop of Leicester	The Debate About God
Leslie Wilfrid Brown	Bishop of St. Edmundsbury & Ipswich	The Finality of Christ (*Chairman*)
Harry James Carpenter	Bishop of Oxford	Current Unity Schemes (*Chairman*)
Edward Barry Henderson	Bishop of Bath & Wells	Intercommunion in a Divided Church
Mark A. Hodson	Bishop of Hereford	The Diaconate
L. M. Charles-Edwards	Bishop of Worcester	Relations with the Eastern Orthodox Church
Edward James K. Roberts	Bishop of Ely	Women and the Priesthood (*Vice-Chairman*)
Basil Tudor Guy	Bishop of Gloucester	Voluntary and Part-Time Ministries
Oliver S. Tomkins	Bishop of Bristol	Principles of Union (*Chairman*)
A. Mervyn Stockwood	Bishop of Southwark	Laymen in Ministry (*Chairman*)
John H. L. Phillips	Bishop of Portsmouth	Laymen in Society
R. David Say	Bishop of Rochester	The Nature of the Anglican Episcopate (*Vice-Chairman*)
George Edward Reindorp	Bishop of Guildford	The Priesthood
John Gerhard Tiarks	Bishop of Chelmsford	Voluntary and Part-Time Ministries
Joseph Edward Fison	Bishop of Salisbury	Confessing the Faith Today (*Secretary*)

Name	See	Committee Assignment
Roderic Norman Coote	Bishop Suffragan of Colchester (Chelmsford)	The Nature of the Anglican Episcopate
Kenneth Edward N. Lamplugh	Bishop Suffragan of Southampton (Winchester)	Relations with the Eastern Orthodox Church
Wilfrid A. E. Westall	Bishop Suffragan of Crediton (Exeter)	Dialogue With Other Faiths
John Taylor Hughes	Bishop Suffragan of Croydon (Canterbury)	The Priesthood
David Goodwin Loveday	Bishop Suffragan of Dorchester (Oxford)	Varieties of Unbelief
Richard George Clitherow	Bishop Suffragan of Stafford (Lichfield)	The Psychology of Faith
William F. P. Chadwick	Bishop Suffragan of Barking (Chelmsford)	Spirituality and Faith (*Chairman*)
Alan F. B. Rogers	Bishop Suffragan of Fulham (London)	Christian Unity and Human Unity
John A. T. Robinson	Bishop Suffragan of Woolwich (Southwark)	Confessing the Faith Today
James H. L. Morrell	Bishop Suffragan of Lewes (Chichester)	The Papacy and the Episcopate
William A. Parker	Bishop Suffragan of Shrewsbury (Lichfield)	Laymen in Society
Victor Joseph Pike	Bishop Suffragan of Sherborne (Salisbury)	The Finality of Christ
Forbes Trevor Horan	Bishop Suffragan of Tewkesbury (Gloucester)	Christian Appraisal of the Secular Society
David B. Porter	Bishop Suffragan of Aston (Birmingham)	Laymen in Society

Name	*See*	*Committee Assignment*
Francis H. West	Bishop Suffragan of Tauton (Bath & Wells)	Varieties of Unbelief (*Vice-Chairman*)
Clifford L. P. Bishop	Bishop Suffragan of Malmesbury (Bristol)	Laymen in Mission
Wilfrid G. Sanderson	Bishop Suffragan of Plymouth (Exeter)	Spirituality and Faith
Albert J. Trillo	Bishop Suffragan of Hertford (St. Albans)	Urbanization and the Metropolis (*Secretary*)
William S. Llewellyn	Bishop Suffragan of Lynn (Norwich)	The Priesthood
Eric W. B. Cordingly	Bishop Suffragan of Thetford (Norwich)	Christian Appraisal of the Secular Society
George C. C. Pepys	Bishop Suffragan of Buckingham (Oxford)	The Priesthood
Ronald C. O. Goodchild	Bishop Suffragan of Kensington (London)	Laymen in Mission
Graham D. Leonard	Bishop Suffragan of Willesden (London)	The Priesthood
Anthony P. Tremlett	Bishop Suffragan of Dover (Canterbury)	Women and the Priesthood
Ross S. Hook	Bishop Suffragan of Grantham (Lincoln)	Voluntary and Part-Time Ministries
William W. Hunt	Bishop Suffragan of Repton (Derby)	Oversight and Discipline
Gerald F. Colin	Bishop Suffragan of Grimsby (Lincoln)	Principles of Union
Robert A. S. Martineau	Bishop Suffragan of Huntington (Ely)	The Nature of Theological Language
David R. Maddock	Bishop Suffragan of Dunwich (St. Edmundsbury & Ipswich)	Laymen in Ministry

Name	See	Committee Assignment
John T. H. Hare	Bishop Suffragan of Bedford (St. Albans)	The Finality of Christ
David H. Halsey	Bishop Suffragan of Tonbridge (Rochester)	Laymen in Society
William N. Welch	Bishop Suffragan of Bradwell (Chelmsford)	The Positive Idea of a Wider Episcopal Fellowship
Simon W. Phipps	Bishop Suffragan of Horsham (Chichester)	Urbanization and the Metropolis
L. C. Usher-Wilson	Assistant Bishop of Guildford	The Technological Society
Douglas J. Wilson	Assistant Bishop of Bath & Wells	Christian Appraisal of the Secular Society
Arthur M. Hollis	Assistant Bishop of St. Edmundsbury & Ipswich	Women and the Priesthood
John D. McKie	Assistant Bishop of Coventry	The Papacy and the Episcopate
William Q. Lash	Assistant Bishop of Truro	Inter-Anglican Structures
T. G. Stuart Smith	Assistant Bishop of Leicester	Intercommunion in a Divided Church
A. R. Graham-Campbell	Assistant Bishop of Peterborough	The Diaconate
George Sinker	Assistant Bishop of Birmingham	Current Unity Schemes
Richard A. Reeves	Assistant Bishop of Chichester	Confessing the Faith Today
Laurence H. Woomer	Assistant Bishop of Portsmouth	Current Unity Schemes
Nigel E. Cornwall	Assistant Bishop of Winchester	The Positive Idea of a Wider Episcopal Fellowship
Thomas R. Parfitt	Assistant Bishop of Derby	Confessing the Faith Today
William A. Partridge	Assistant Bishop of Hereford	Laymen in Ministry

Name	See	Committee Assignment
John K. Russell	Assistant Bishop of Rochester	The Nature of Theological Language
St. John S. Pike	Assistant Bishop of Guildford	Relations with the Roman Catholic Church
C. Kenneth Sansbury	Assistant Bishop of London	Inter-Anglican Structures (*Secretary*)
E. J. Trapp	General Secretary of the United Society for the Propagation of the Gospel	Inter-Anglican Structures
PROVINCE OF YORK		
F. Donald Coggan	Primate of England and Archbishop of York	*Chairman,* Ministry Section
Ian T. Ramsey	Bishop of Durham	*Vice-Chairman,* Faith Section
Charles R. Claxton	Bishop of Blackburn	Confessing the Faith Today
William D. L. Greer	Bishop of Manchester	The Nature of Theological Language
Gerald A. Ellison	Bishop of Chester	The Diaconate
C. G. St. M. Parker	Bishop of Bradford	The Debate About God
Hugh Edward Ashdown	Bishop of Newcastle	Christian Appraisal of the Secular Society
S. Cyril Bulley	Bishop of Carlisle	The Diaconate
John R. H. Moorman	Bishop of Ripon	Relations with the Roman Catholic Church (*Chairman*)
Gordon D. Savage	Bishop of Southwell	The Papacy and the Episcopate (*Vice-Chairman*)
Eric Treacy	Bishop of Wakefield	The Varieties of Unbelief
F. John Taylor	Bishop of Sheffield	Oversight and Discipline

Name	See	Committee Assignment
Stuart Y. Blanch	Bishop of Liverpool	Inter-Anglican Structures
G. Eric Gordon	Bishop of Sodor & Man	The Role of the Anglican Communion in the Families of Christendom (*Chairman*)
Kenneth V. Ramsey	Bishop Suffragan of Hulme (Manchester)	The Varieties of Unbelief
George E. Holderness	Bishop Suffragan of Burnley (Blackburn)	Laymen in Society
A. L. E. Hoskyns-Abrahall	Bishop Suffragan of Lancaster (Blackburn)	Spirituality and Faith
Edward R. Wickham	Bishop Suffragan of Middleton (Manchester)	The Technological Society (*Chairman*)
Laurence A. Brown	Bishop Suffragan of Warrington (Liverpool)	*Secretary*, Ministry Section
George d'Oyly Snow	Bishop Suffragan of Whitby (York)	The Technological Society
Douglas N. Sargent	Bishop Suffragan of Selby (York)	Women and the Priesthood
Alexander K. Hamilton	Bishop Suffragan of Jarrow (Durham)	Spirituality and Faith
Hubert L. Higgs	Bishop Suffragan of Hull (York)	Principles of Union
John H. Cruse	Bishop Suffragan of Knaresborough (Ripon)	The Priesthood
Kenneth G. Thompson	Bishop Suffragan of Sherwood (Southwell)	Relations with the Eastern Orthodox Church
Eric A. J. Mercer	Bishop Suffragan of Birkenhead (Chester)	Urbanization and the Metropolis

Name	See	Committee Assignment
R. Gordon Strutt	Bishop Suffragan of Stockport (Chester)	Laymen in Mission
Reginald Foskett	Bishop Suffragan of Penrith (Carlisle)	Intercommunion in a Divided Church
William G. Fallows	Bishop Suffragan of Pontefract (Wakefield)	The Role of the Anglican Communion in the Families of Christendom
George V. Gerard	Assistant Bishop of Sheffield	The Debate about God
Victor G. Shearburn	Assistant Bishop of Wakefield	Principles of Union (*Secretary*)

The Church in Wales

Name	See	Committee Assignment
William G. H. Simon	Archbishop of Wales and Bishop of Llandaff	*Secretary*, Faith Section
David D. Bartlett	Bishop of St. Asaph	Current Unity Schemes
John R. Richards	Bishop of St. Davids	Dialogue with Other Faiths
Gwilym O. Williams	Bishop of Bangor	Varieties of Unbelief (*Secretary*)
John J. A. Thomas	Bishop of Swansea & Brecon	Principles of Union
Eryl S. Thomas	Bishop of Monmouth	The Nature of the Anglican Episcopate

The Church in Ireland

Name	See	Committee Assignment
James McCann	Primate of All Ireland and Archbishop of Armagh	Relations with the Roman Catholic Church
George O. Simms	Primate of Ireland and Archbishop of Dublin	Steering Committee

Name	*See*	*Committee Assignment*
Robert B. Pike	Bishop of Meath	Women in the Priesthood
Frederick J. Mitchell	Bishop of Down & Dromore	Intercommunion in a Divided Church
Richard G. Perdue	Bishop of Cork, Cloyne, & Ross	The Diaconate (*Vice-Chairman*)
Charles J. Tyndall	Bishop of Derry & Raphoe	The Nature of the Anglican Episcopate
R. C. H. G. Elliott	Bishop of Connor	Urbanization and the Metropolis
Henry A. Stanistreet	Bishop of Killaloe & Kilfenora, Clonfert & Kilmacduagh	International Morality Today
Arthur H. Butler	Bishop of Tuam, Killala, & Achonry	Laymen in Mission
Alan A. Buchanan	Bishop of Clogher	Christian Unity and Human Unity
Edward F. B. Moore	Bishop of Kilmore & Elphin & Ardagh	The Psychology of Faith
Robert W. Jackson	Bishop of Limerick, Ardfert, & Aghadoe	Laymen in Ministry
Henry R. McAdoo	Bishop of Ossory, Ferns, & Leighlin	Confessing the Faith Today (*Chairman*)

The Episcopal Church in Scotland

Francis H. Moncreiff	Primus of the Scottish Episcopal Church and Bishop of Glasgow & Galloway	The Papacy and the Episcopate
Duncan Macinnes	Bishop of Moray, Ross, & Caithness	Confessing the Faith Today
John W. A. Howe	Bishop of St. Andrews, Dunkeld, & Dunblane	The Debate about God (*Secretary*)

Name	See	Committee Assignment
Edward F. Easson	Bishop of Aberdeen & Orkney	The Priesthood
John C. Sprott	Bishop of Brechin	Spirituality and Faith
Kenneth M. Carey	Bishop of Edinburgh	The Psychology of Faith (*Chairman*)
Richard K. Wimbush	Bishop of Argyll & the Isles	Relations with the Eastern Orthodox Church (*Secretary*)

The Episcopal Church in the United States of America

Name	See	Committee Assignment
John E. Hines	Presiding Bishop	Faith and Society
Stephen F. Bayne, Jr.	Vice-Chairman of the Executive Council and Director of Overseas Department	Steering Committee
Daniel Corrigan	Director of the Home Department of the Executive Council	Faith and Culture
Charles C. J. Carpenter	Bishop of Alabama	The Nature of Theological Language
Walter H. Gray	Bishop of Connecticut	The Positive Idea of a Wider Episcopal Fellowship (*Chairman*)
Charles A. Voegeli	Bishop of Haiti	The Positive Idea of a Wider Episcopal Fellowship
Harry S. Kennedy	Bishop of Honolulu	Urbanization and the Metropolis
Austin Pardue	Bishop of Pittsburgh	The Psychology of Faith
William W. Horstick	Bishop of Eau Claire	Oversight and Discipline
Conrad H. Gesner	Bishop of South Dakota	The Role of the Anglican Communion in the Families of Christendom

Name	See	Committee Assignment
Reginald H. Gooden	Bishop of Panama and the Canal Zone	The Debate about God
Henry I. Louttit	Bishop of South Florida	The Nature of Theological Language
Charles A. Mason	Bishop of Dallas	The Finality of Christ
Thomas H. Wright	Bishop of East Carolina	The Debate about God
William R. Moody	Bishop of Lexington	The Debate about God
Lane W. Barton	Bishop of Eastern Oregon	Laymen in Society
George H. Quarterman	Bishop of Northwest Texas	Oversight and Discipline
Horace W. B. Donegan	Bishop of New York	Urbanization and the Metropolis
James W. Hunter	Bishop of Wyoming	Spirituality and Faith
Francis E. I. Bloy	Bishop of Los Angeles	Christian Appraisal of the Secular Society
Lauriston L. Scaife	Bishop of Western New York	Relations with the Eastern Orthodox Church (*Chairman*)
William J. Gordon, Jr.	Bishop of Alaska	International Morality Today
Matthew G. Henry	Bishop of Western North Carolina	Principles of Union
Edward H. West	Bishop of Florida	Faith and Society
Walter M. Higley	Bishop of Central New York	Laymen in Society
Jonathan G. Sherman	Bishop of Long Island	The Nature of Theological Language
Girault M. Jones	Bishop of Louisiana	The Nature of the Anglican Episcopate
Randolph R. Claiborne, Jr.	Bishop of Atlanta	The Finality of Christ
Robert F. Gibson	Bishop of Virginia	The Positive Idea of a Wider Episcopal Fellowship

Name	See	Committee Assignment
Edward R. Welles	Bishop of West Missouri	Relations with the Roman Catholic Church
Gordon V. Smith	Bishop of Iowa	Current Unity Schemes
Wilburn C. Campbell	Bishop of West Virginia	Spirituality and Faith
Gerald F. Burrill	Bishop of Chicago	Current Unity Schemes
Richard S. Watson	Bishop of Utah	Dialogue with Other Faiths
W. R. Chilton Powell	Bishop of Oklahoma	Confessing the Faith Today (*Vice-Chairman*)
Donald H. V. Hallock	Bishop of Milwaukee	The Papacy and the Episcopate (*Chairman*)
Hamilton H. Kellogg	Bishop of Minnesota	Relations with the Roman Catholic Church
William Crittenden	Bishop of Erie	The Technological Society (*Secretary*)
John S. Higgins	Bishop of Rhode Island	Relations with the Roman Catholic Church
Frederick J. Warnecke	Bishop of Bethlehem	The Nature of the Anglican Episcopate
William H. Brady	Bishop of Fond du Lac	The Nature of the Anglican Episcopate
Leland Stark	Bishop of Newark	Principles of Union
C. J. Kinsolving III	Bishop of New Mexico & Southwest Texas	Laymen in Mission
John B. Mosley	Bishop of Delaware	Inter-Anglican Structures
Charles G. Marmion	Bishop of Kentucky	The Finality of Christ
William H. Marmion	Bishop of Southwestern Virginia	Faith and Society

Name	See	Committee Assignment
J. Joseph M. Harte	Bishop of Arizona	Relations with the Eastern Orthodox Church
Albert R. Stuart	Bishop of Georgia	Laymen in Ministry
John Vander Horst	Bishop of Tennessee	The Priesthood
Harry Lee Doll	Bishop of Maryland	Spirituality and Faith
Robert R. Brown	Bishop of Arkansas	The Positive Idea of a Wider Episcopal Fellowship
James W. F. Carman	Bishop of Oregon	The Technological Society
Edward C. Turner	Bishop of Kansas	Oversight and Discipline
Clarence R. Haden, Jr.	Bishop of Northern California	Dialogue with Other Faiths (*Vice-Chairman*)
Francis W. Lickfield	Bishop of Quincy	Relations with the Eastern Orthodox Church
Allen W. Brown	Bishop of Albany	Confessing the Faith Today
George L. Cadigan	Bishop of Missouri	The Debate about God
William F. Creighton	Bishop of Washington	The Debate about God (*Vice-Chairman*)
Charles E. Bennison	Bishop of Western Michigan	The Diaconate
Paul A. Kellogg	Bishop of the Dominican Republic	Voluntary and Part-Time Ministries
Ivol I. Curtis	Bishop of Olympia	Laymen in Mission (*Vice-Chairman*)
Thomas A. Fraser, Jr.	Bishop of North Carolina	The Priesthood (*Secretary*)
Gary Temple	Bishop of South Carolina	Faith and Culture
Harvey D. Butterfield	Bishop of Vermont	International Morality Today
Russell T. Rauscher	Bishop of Nebraska	Laymen in Ministry

Name	*See*	*Committee Assignment*
John M. Allin	Bishop of Mississippi	Oversight and Discipline
Albert A. Chambers	Bishop of Springfield	The Debate about God
Cedric E. Mills	Bishop of the Virgin Islands	Faith and Culture
George W. Barrett	Bishop of Rochester	Women and the Priesthood
Walter C. Klein	Bishop of Northern Indiana	The Nature of Theological Language
John A. Pinckney	Bishop of Upper South Carolina	Current Unity Schemes
David B. Reed	Bishop of Colombia & Ecuador	Principles of Union
C. Kilmer Myers	Bishop of California	Christian Unity and Human Unity (*Chairman*)
George R. Selway	Bishop of Northern Michigan	Voluntary and Part-Time Ministries (*Secretary*)
Francisco Reus-Froylan	Bishop of Puerto Rico	Christian Appraisal of the Secular Society
George T. Masuda	Bishop of North Dakota	The Debate about God
James M. Richardson	Bishop of Texas	Dialogue with Other Faiths
William Davidson	Bishop of Western Kansas	Christian Unity and Human Unity
George A. Taylor	Bishop of Easton	The Psychology of Faith
John H. Burt	Bishop of Ohio	Christian Appraisal of the Secular Society
John R. Wyatt	Bishop of Spokane	Faith and Culture
William C. Frey	Bishop of Guatemala and El Salvador	Christian Unity and Human Unity
Edmund L. Browning	Bishop of Okinawa	Oversight and Discipline

Name	See	Committee Assignment
Iveson B. Noland	Bishop Coadjutor of Louisiana	Oversight and Discipline (*Vice-Chairman*)
George M. Murray	Bishop Coadjutor of Alabama	Intercommunion in a Divided Church
David S. Rose	Bishop Coadjutor of Southern Virginia	Women and the Priesthood (*Secretary*)
William E. Sanders	Bishop Coadjutor of Tennessee	Laymen in Mission
James W. Montgomery	Bishop Coadjutor of Chicago	Intercommunion in a Divided Church
Robert B. Hall	Bishop Coadjutor of Virginia	Christian Unity and Human Unity
Christopher Keller	Bishop Coadjutor of Arkansas	Laymen in Society
Robert B. Appleyard	Bishop Coadjutor of Pittsburgh	Laymen in Society
Harold B. Robinson	Bishop Coadjutor of Western New York	Relations with the Roman Catholic Church
Archie N. Crowley	Bishop Suffragan of Michigan	The Diaconate (*Secretary*)
Richard E. Dicus	Bishop Suffragan of West Texas	Laymen in Mission
Frederick P. Goddard	Bishop Suffragan of Texas	The Psychology of Faith
Arnold M. Lewis	Bishop Suffragan of the Armed Forces	Laymen in Mission
Philip F. McNairy	Bishop Suffragan of Minnesota	Faith and Culture
James S. Wetmore	Bishop Suffragan of New York	Principles of Union
George R. Millard	Bishop Suffragan of California	The Technological Society
Samuel B. Chilton	Bishop Suffragan of Virginia	The Nature of the Anglican Episcopate
James L. Duncan	Bishop Suffragan of South Florida	Urbanization and the Metropolis

Name	See	Committee Assignment
William L. Hargrave	Bishop Suffragan of South Florida	Faith and Culture
Charles W. McLean	Bishop Suffragan of Long Island	Urbanization and the Metropolis
John M. Burgess	Bishop Suffragan of Massachusetts	The Diaconate
Charles B. Persell, Jr.	Bishop Suffragan of Albany	International Morality Today
Frederick W. Putnam, Jr.	Bishop Suffragan of Oklahoma	Laymen in Mission
Leonardo R. Romero	Bishop Suffragan of Mexico	Principles of Union
Melchor Saucedo	Bishop Suffragan of Mexico	The Nature of Theological Language
Scott F. Bailey	Bishop Suffragan of Texas	Varieties of Unbelief
Robert C. Rusack	Bishop Suffragan of Los Angeles	Laymen in Society
Hal R. Gross	Bishop Suffragan of Oregon	Intercommunion in a Divided Church
Albert W. Van Duzer	Bishop Suffragan of New Jersey	Confessing the Faith Today
William F. Gates, Jr.	Bishop Suffragan of Tennessee	Faith and Culture
William P. Barnds	Bishop Suffragan of Dallas	Confessing the Faith Today
Richard B. Martin	Bishop Suffragan of Long Island	The Debate about God
Robert R. Spears	Bishop Suffragan of West Missouri	Current Unity Schemes
Milton L. Wood	Bishop Suffragan of Atlanta	The Papacy and the Episcopate
Edward McNair	Bishop Suffragan of Northern California	Varieties of Unbelief
Edwin L. Hanchett	Bishop Suffragan of Honolulu	Oversight and Discipline
Albert E. Swift	Assistant Bishop in South Florida	The Psychology of Faith (*Secretary*)

Name	See	Committee Assignment
Andrew Tsu	Consultant Bishop in Pennsylvania	Women and the Priesthood
Donald J. Campbell	Formerly Suffragan Bishop of Los Angeles (attending for Massachusetts)	Role of the Anglican Communion in the Families of Christendom

The Anglican Church of Canada

Howard H. Clark	Primate of All Canada, Archbishop and Metropolitan of Rupert's Land	*Chairman,* Faith Section
William L. Wright	Archbishop of Algoma and Metropolitan of Ontario	Inter-Anglican Structures
Alexander H. O'Neil	Archbishop of Fredericton and Metropolitan of the Province of Canada	The Finality of Christ
Godfrey P. Gower	Archbishop of New Westminster and Metropolitan of British Columbia	Current Unity Schemes (*Vice-Chairman*)
Harold E. Sexton	Bishop of British Columbia	The Papacy and the Episcopate
George N. Luxton	Bishop of Huron	Inter-Anglican Structures
Walter E. Bagnall	Bishop of Niagara	Dialogue with Other Faiths
Ivor A. Norris	Bishop of Brandon	Faith and Society
Donald B. Marsh	Bishop of the Arctic	Confessing the Faith Today
Stanley C. Steer	Bishop of Saskatoon	The Debate about God (*Chairman*)

Name	See	Committee Assignment
Reginald J. Pierce	Bishop of Athabasca	Relations with the Roman Catholic Church
Kenneth C. Evans	Bishop of Ontario	The Nature of Theological Language (*Chairman*)
Harry E. Hives	Bishop of Keewatin	The Finality of Christ
Ernest S. Reed	Bishop of Ottawa	Christian Appraisal of the Secular Society (*Chairman*)
George B. Snell	Bishop of Toronto	International Morality Today (*Secretary*)
Ralph S. Dean	Bishop of Cariboo, Anglican Executive Officer	*Episcopal Secretary*, Steering Committee
William W. Davis	Bishop of Nova Scotia	Women and the Priesthood (*Chairman*)
Robert L. Seaborn	Bishop of Newfoundland	The Positive Idea of a Wider Episcopal Fellowship (*Secretary*)
Eric G. Munn	Bishop of Caledonia	The Psychology of Faith
William H. H. Crump	Bishop of Saskatchewan	Voluntary and Part-Time Ministries
William G. Burch	Bishop of Edmonton	Urbanization and the Metropolis
George F. C. Jackson	Bishop of Qu'Appelle	Relations with the Roman Catholic Church
Russell F. Brown	Bishop of Quebec	Laymen in Mission
Robert K. Maguire	Bishop of Montreal	Relations with the Eastern Orthodox Church (*Vice-Chairman*)
James A. Watton	Bishop of Moosonee	Faith and Culture
Edward W. Scott	Bishop of Kootenay	Christian Appraisal of the Secular Society

Name	See	Committee Assignment
Morse L. Goodman	Bishop of Calgary	Urbanization and the Metropolis
John T. Frame	Bishop of Yukon	Varieties of Unbelief
John O. Anderson	Bishop Coadjutor of Rupert's Land	Faith and Culture
Neville R. Clarke	Bishop Suffragan of James Bay (Moosonee)	Laymen in Ministry
Henry R. Hunt	Bishop Suffragan of Toronto	Urbanization and the Metropolis
H. F. G. Appleyard	Bishop Suffragan of Georgian Bay (Huron)	Intercommunion in a Divided Church
Henry G. Cook	Bishop Suffragan of Athabasca	Principles of Union
Carman J. Queen	Bishop Suffragan of St. Clair (Huron)	Spirituality and Faith
George F. Arnold	Bishop Suffragan of Nova Scotia	The Finality of Christ
William G. Legge	Bishop Suffragan of Newfoundland	Varieties of Unbelief
C. H. R. Wilkinson	Assistant Bishop of Niagara	The Priesthood
Tom Greenwood	Assistant Bishop of Cariboo	Current Unity Schemes

The Church of India, Pakistan, Burma, and Ceylon

H. Lakdasa J. de Mel	Metropolitan, Bishop of Calcutta	*Chairman,* Unity Section
C. J. G. Robinson	Bishop of Bombay	The Positive Idea of a Wider Episcopal Fellowship
Joseph Amritanand	Bishop of Lucknow	Faith and Society
Ronald W. Bryan	Bishop of Barrackpore	Voluntary and Part-Time Ministries (*Chairman*)
James D. Blair	Bishop of Dacca	Current Unity Schemes
Philip Parmar	Bishop of Delhi	The Diaconate

Name	See	Committee Assignment
Chandu Ray	Bishop of Karachi	The Finality of Christ (*Vice-Chairman*)
John W. Sadiq	Bishop of Nagpur	Laymen in Ministry (*Vice-Chairman*)
Arthur W. Luther	Bishop of Nasik	Voluntary and Part-Time Ministries
S. A. B. Dilbar Hans	Bishop of Chota Nag-pur	The Technological Society (*Vice-Chairman*)
Eric S. Nasir	Bishop of Amritsar	Spirituality and Faith (*Secretary*)
C. L. Wickremesinghe	Bishop of Kurunagala	Faith and Culture (*Vice-Chairman*)
C. H. W. de Soysa	Bishop of Colombo	Oversight and Discipline (*Secretary*)
M. D. Srinivasan	Bishop of Andaman and Nicobar Islands	Dialogue with Other Faiths
Ernest John	Bishop of Nandyal	Relations with the Eastern Orthodox Church
Avril V. Jonathan	Bishop of Assam	Laymen in Society
I. Masih	Bishop of Lahore	Intercommunion in a Divided Church

The Church of England in Australia

P. N. W. Strong	Primate of Australia, Archbishop of Brisbane and Metropolitan of Queensland	Spirituality and Faith
Frank Woods	Archbishop of Melbourne and Metropolitan of Victoria	*Secretary*, Unity Section
George Appleton	Archbishop of Perth, Metropolitan of West Australia	Dialogue with Other Faiths (*Chairman*)

Name	See	Committee Assignment
Marcus L. Loane	Archbishop of Sydney, Metropolitan of New South Wales	The Debate about God
J. A. G. Housden	Bishop of Newcastle	Urbanization and the Metropolis (*Chairman*)
Kenneth J. Clements	Bishop of Canberra & Goulburn	The Finality of Christ
Geoffrey D. Hand	Bishop of New Guinea	Christian Unity and Human Unity
Allen E. Winter	Bishop of St. Arnaud	Intercommunion in a Divided Church
Ian W. A. Shevill	Bishop of North Queensland	The Papacy and the Episcopate (*Secretary*)
Ronald C. Kerle	Bishop of Armidale	Confessing the Faith Today
Robert G. Arthur	Bishop of Grafton	The Positive Idea of a Wider Episcopal Fellowship (*Vice-Chairman*)
Ronald E. Richards	Bishop of Bendigo	The Nature of the Anglican Episcopate
Thomas T. Reed	Bishop of Adelaide	Laymen in Society (*Vice-Chairman*)
R. G. Hawkins	Bishop of Bunbury	The Priesthood
Thomas E. Jones	Bishop of Willochra	Laymen in Ministry
Ernest K. Leslie	Bishop of Bathurst	The Diaconate
David A. Garnsey	Bishop of Gippsland	The Nature of Theological Language (*Secretary*)
Theodore B. McCall	Bishop of Wangaratta	Relations with the Roman Catholic Church
Robert E. Davies	Bishop of Tasmania	Voluntary and Part-Time Ministries
W. A. Hardie	Bishop of Ballarat	The Technological Society
Donald N. Shearman	Bishop of Rockhampton	Laymen in Society

Name	See	Committee Assignment
H. A. J. Witt	Bishop of North West Australia	Urbanization and the Metropolis
J. B. R. Grindrod	Bishop of Riverina	Spirituality and Faith
Denis W. Bryant	Bishop of Kalgoorlie	International Morality Today
Kenneth B. Mason	Bishop of Northern Territory	International Morality Today
Ernest E. Hawkey	Bishop of Carpentaria	Faith and Culture
F. O. Hulme-Moir	Bishop Coadjutor of Sydney	Laymen in Mission
Geoffrey T. Sambell	Bishop Coadjutor of Melbourne	Faith and Society (*Secretary*)
George S. Ambo	Assistant Bishop of New Guinea	Current Unity Schemes

The Church of the Province of New Zealand

Norman A. Lesser	Primate and Archbishop of New Zealand and Bishop of Waiapu	Confessing the Faith Today
Henry W. Baines	Bishop of Wellington	Intercommunion in a Divided Church
J. T. Holland	Bishop of Waikato	International Morality Today
Allen H. Johnston	Bishop of Dunedin	Intercommunion in a Divided Church (*Chairman*)
John C. Vockler	Bishop in Polynesia	The Diaconate
Eric A. Gowing	Bishop of Auckland	Faith and Society (*Chairman*)
John W. Chisholm	Bishop of Melanesia	Faith and Culture
Peter E. Sutton	Bishop of Nelson	The Role of the Anglican Communion in the Families of Christendom (*Secretary*)
William A. Pyatt	Bishop of Christchurch	Laymen in Ministry (*Secretary*)

Name	See	Committee Assignment
F. Halapua	Bishop Suffragan of Nuku'alofa	Faith and Society

The Church of the Province of South Africa

Name	See	Committee Assignment
Robert S. Taylor	Metropolitan of South Africa and Archbishop of Cape Town	Inter-Anglican Structures (*Chairman*)
Leslie E. Stradling	Bishop of Johannesburg	The Nature of the Anglican Episcopate (*Secretary*)
J. A. A. Maund	Bishop of Lesotho	The Finality of Christ
Thomas G. V. Inman	Bishop of Natal	Laymen in Society (*Chairman*)
P. W. Wheeldon	Bishop of Kimberley & Kuruman	The Psychology of Faith
J. L. Schuster	Bishop of St. John's	Principles of Union
E. G. Knapp-Fisher	Bishop of Pretoria	The Priesthood (*Chairman*)
Robert H. Mize	Bishop of Damaraland	International Morality Today
Alphaeus H. Zulu	Bishop of Zululand & Swaziland	Laymen in Mission (*Co-Secretary*)
Gordon L. Tindall	Bishop of Grahamstown	Oversight and Discipline
P. H. F. Barron	Bishop of George	Faith and Culture
Daniel de P. Cabral	Bishop of Lebombo	The Papacy and the Episcopate
F. A. Amoore	Bishop of Bloemfontein	Current Unity Schemes
E. M. H. Capper	Bishop of St. Helena	The Nature of the Anglican Episcopate
P. W. R. Russell	Bishop Suffragan of Cape Town	Laymen in Ministry
Fortescue Makhetha	Bishop Suffragan of Lesotho	The Debate about God
B. B. Burnett	General Secretary of the Christian Council of South Africa	The Finality of Christ (*Secretary*)

Name	See	Committee Assignment
The Church in the Province of the West Indies		
Alan J. Knight	Archbishop of the West Indies and Bishop of Guyana	The Psychology of Faith
William J. Hughes	Bishop of Trinidad & Tobago	Faith and Society
Donald R. Knowles	Bishop of Antigua	Laymen in Ministry
Edward L. Evans	Bishop of Barbados	The Role of the Anglican Communion in the Families of Christendom
John C. E. Swaby	Bishop of Jamaica	Christian Unity and Human Unity (*Secretary*)
Benjamin N. Y. Vaughan	Bishop of British Honduras	The Technological Society
Bernard Markham	Bishop of Nassau & the Bahamas	The Diaconate (*Chairman*)
P. E. R. Elder	Bishop Suffragan of Stabroek	Current Unity Schemes
Guy Marshall	Bishop Suffragan in Venezuela (Trinidad & Tobago)	Christian Appraisal of the Secular Society
Nippon Sei Ko Kai (The Holy Catholic Church of Japan)		
David M. Goto	Bishop of Tokyo	Urbanization and the Metropolis (*Vice-Chairman*)
Mark T. Koike	Bishop of Osaka	The Nature of the Anglican Episcopate
K. Viall	Assistant Bishop of Tokyo	Intercommunion in a Divided Church

Name	See	Committee Assignment

The Church of the Province of West Africa

Name	See	Committee Assignment
Cecil J. Patterson	Archbishop of West Africa and Bishop on the Niger	Current Unity Schemes
S. O. Odutola	Bishop of Ibadan	Christian Unity and Human Unity (*Vice-Chairman*)
John E. L. Mort	Bishop of Northern Nigeria	Laymen in Society
G. E. I. Cockin	Bishop of Owerri	Current Unity Schemes (*Secretary*)
M. N. C. O. Scott	Bishop of Sierra Leone	Varieties of Unbelief
R. N. Bara-Hart	Bishop of the Niger Delta	Christian Unity and Human Unity
Agori Iwe	Bishop of Benin	Relations with the Roman Catholic Church
Seth I. Kale	Bishop of Lagos	The Nature of the Anglican Episcopate (*Chairman*)
I. O. S. Okunsanya	Bishop of Ondo	International Morality Today
T. O. Olufosoye	Bishop of The Gambia & The Rio Pongas	The Role of the Anglican Communion in the Families of Christendom (*Vice-Chairman*)
M. A. Osanyin	Bishop of Ekiti	The Debate about God
P. J. Jones	Assistant Bishop of Sierra Leone	Laymen in Ministry
H. I. A. Afonya	Assistant Bishop of the Niger Delta	Women and the Priesthood
L. M. Uzodike	Assistant Bishop on the Niger	The Finality of Christ

Name	See	Committee Assignment
I. S. M. Lemaire	Assistant Bishop of Accra	The Role of the Anglican Communion in Families of Christendom
I. G. A. Jadesimi	Assistant Bishop of Ibadan	Relations with Eastern Orthodox Church
J. B. Arthur	Assistant Bishop of Accra	Faith and Culture
A. K. Nelson	Assistant Bishop of Accra	Laymen in Ministry
B. C. Nwankiti	Assistant Bishop of Owerri	The Diaconate

The Church of the Province of Central Africa

Francis O. Green-Wilkinson	Archbishop of Central Africa and Bishop of Zambia	Relations with the Roman Catholic Church
Donald S. Arden	Bishop of Malawi	Laymen in Society (*Secretary*)
K. J. F. Skelton	Bishop of Matabeleland	Christian Appraisal of the Secular Society (*Secretary*)
John P. Burrough	Bishop of Mashonaland	Faith and Society
Filemon Mataka	Bishop Suffragan of Zambia	Voluntary and Part-Time Ministries
J. Mtekateka	Bishop Suffragan of Malawi	Intercommunion in a Divided Church

The Archbishopric in Jerusalem

Angus C. MacInnes	Archbishop in Jerusalem	Relations with the Eastern Orthodox Church
Oliver C. Allison	Bishop in The Sudan	Dialogue with Other Faiths
Najib A. Cuba'in	Bishop in Jordan, Lebanon, & Syria	Christian Appraisal of the Secular Society

Name	See	Committee Assignment
Hassan B. Dehqani-Tafti	Bishop in Iran	Dialogue with Other Faiths (*Secretary*)
Y. K. Dotiro	Assistant Bishop in The Sudan	Women and the Priesthood
E. J. Ngalamu	Assistant Bishop in The Sudan	Faith and Society

The Church of the Province of East Africa

Leonard J. Beecher	Archbishop of East Africa and Bishop of Nairobi	*Vice-Chairman*, Ministry Section
Alfred Stanway	Bishop of Central Tanganyika	Voluntary and Part-Time Ministries
Festo H. Olang	Bishop of Maseno	Spirituality and Faith (*Vice-Chairman*)
Obadiah Kariuki	Bishop of Mount Kenya	Principles of Union (*Vice-Chairman*)
Maxwell L. Wiggins	Bishop of Victoria Nyanza	Dialogue with Other Faiths
N. Langford-Smith	Bishop of Nakuru	The Diaconate
E. U. Trevor Huddleston	Bishop of Masasi	Varieties of Unbelief (*Chairman*)
J. R. W. Poole-Hughes	Bishop of Southwest Tanganyika	Intercommunion in a Divided Church (*Secretary*)
Musa Kahurananga	Bishop of Western Tanganyika	Varieties of Unbelief
John Sepeku	Bishop of Dar-es-Salaam	Christian Appraisal of the Secular Society (*Vice-Chairman*)
Peter Mwang'ombe	Bishop of Mombasa	The Positive Idea of a Wider Episcopal Fellowship
Gresford Chitemo	Bishop of Morogoro	Oversight and Discipline
Yohanna Jumaa	Bishop of Zanzibar & Tanga	Oversight and Discipline

Name	See	Committee Assign-ment
Robert Neil Russell	Assistant Bishop of Zanzibar & Tanga	The Priesthood (*Vice-Chairman*)
M. D. Soseleje	Assistant Bishop of Masasi	The Priesthood
Y. Madinda	Assistant Bishop of Central Tangan-yika	Spirituality and Faith
J. W. Mlele	Assistant Bishop of Southwest Tan-ganyika	Relations with the Roman Catholic Church
E. J. Agola	Assistant Bishop of Maseno	Christian Unity and Human Unity

The Church of Uganda, Rwanda, and Burundi

Erica Sabiti	Archbishop of Ugan-da, Rwanda, and Burundi and Bish-op of Ruwenzori	The Psychology of Faith (*Vice-Chair-man*)
S. S. Tomusange	Bishop of West Buganda	Faith and Culture
Kosiya Shalita	Bishop of Ankole	Faith and Society
Dunstan K. Nsubuga	Bishop of Namirembe	Faith and Society (*Vice-Chairman*)
Silvanus Wani	Bishop of Northern Uganda	Dialogue with Other Faiths
E. K. Masaba	Bishop of Mbale	Relations with the Roman Catholic Church (*Vice-Chairman*)
Y. Nkunzumwami	Bishop of Burundi	The Papacy and the Episcopate
A. Sebununguri	Bishop of Rwanda	Laymen in Ministry
A. Maraka	Bishop of Soroti	International Moral-ity Today
Richard E. Lyth	Bishop of Kigezi	Laymen in Mission
Y. K. Rwakaikara	Assistant Bishop of Ruwenzori	Spirituality and Faith

Name	See	Committee Assignment

Igreja Episcopal do Brasil (The Episcopal Church of Brazil)

Name	See	Committee Assignment
Egmont M. Krischke	Primate of the Episcopal Church of Brazil and Bishop of Southern Brazil	Faith and Society
Plinio L. Simoes	Bishop of Southwestern Brazil	Role of the Anglican Communion in the Families of Christendom
Edmund K. Sherrill	Bishop of Central Brazil	Relations with the Roman Catholic Church (*Secretary*)

The Council of the Church of South-East Asia

Name	See	Committee Assignment
J. C. L. Wong	Chairman of the Council and Bishop of Taiwan (PECUSA)	Voluntary and Part-Time Ministries (*Vice-Chairman*)
R. P. C. Koh	Bishop of Sabah (Canterbury)	Inter-Anglican Structures (*Vice-Chairman*)
B. C. Cabanban	Bishop of the Philippines (PECUSA)	Voluntary and Part-Time Ministries
D. H. N. Allenby	Bishop of Kuching (Canterbury)	Voluntary and Part-Time Ministries
Paul C. Lee	Bishop of Seoul (Canterbury)	Principles of Union
Cecil R. Rutt	Bishop of Taejon (Canterbury)	Faith and Culture (*Secretary*)
J. Chiu Ban It	Bishop of Singapore and Malaya (Canterbury)	Laymen in Mission (*Secretary*)
J. G. H. Baker	Bishop of Hong Kong and Macao	International Morality Today (*Vice-Chairman*)

Name	See	Committee Assignment
	(Chung Hua Sheng Kung Hui —The Holy Catholic Church of China)	
E. G. Longid	Bishop Suffragan of the Philippines (PECUSA)	The Role of the Anglican Communion in the Families of Christendom

The Church in Cuba

J. A. González	Bishop of Cuba	Confessing the Faith Today

Overseas Bishops in the Canterbury Jurisdiction

Jean Marcel	Bishop in Madagascar	The Papacy and the Episcopate
Stanley A. H. Eley	Bishop of Gilbraltar	Steering Committee
John Armstrong	Bishop of Bermuda	Spirituality and Faith
C. J. Tucker	Bishop in Argentina and Eastern South America with the Falkland Islands	Confessing the Faith Today
K. W. Howell	Bishop in Chile, Bolivia, & Peru	Relations with the Roman Catholic Church
Ernest E. Curtis	Bishop of Mauritius	The Finality of Christ
James Seth	Assistant Bishop in Madagascar	Laymen in Ministry

NOTES ON COATS OF ARMS

CHAPTER 1. Arms of the See of Canterbury, host to the opening service of Lambeth X: The Y-shaped length of white wool, edged and fringed with gold on an azure field, is the pallium or pall, the symbol of office bestowed by the Papacy on early Archbishops of Canterbury. The black crosses were used to pin the pallium to a primate's vestments in remembrance of Christ's passion. The fifty-fifth Archbishop of Canterbury, Simon Islip (1349–1366), was the first to have the arms engraved on his seal; all his successors have employed them as the arms of the metropolitan see of England. The arms of the dioceses of Dublin and Armagh are almost identical and the pall is incorporated in the arms of the dioceses of West Missouri, Saskatoon, Mexico, and the Sudan; the Roman Catholic dioceses of Westminster, Birmingham, and Cardiff also use the pall in their arms.

CHAPTER 2. Arms of the Diocese of Cariboo, British Columbia, Canada, whose bishop was episcopal secretary of Lambeth X: The "three rivers conjoined azure" are descriptive of the area as are the caribou heads. The ermine field and mitre, derived from the arms of New Westminster, recall that Cariboo was held with that see from 1914 to 1925.

CHAPTER 3. Arms of the Dean and Chapter of Westminster Abbey, in the precincts of which Lambeth X convened: A cross patonce between five gold martlets constitutes the arms of St. Edward the Confessor, founder of Westminster Abbey (the Collegiate Church of St. Peter) after acceding to the throne in 1042. Although designed long after his death, the shield is regarded as one of the best-known in English heraldry; the martlets are believed to have been suggested by the birds King Edward placed on his coins and at the top of his scepter. Between two Tudor roses is displayed the Royal Arms in the form used from 1405 to 1603.

CHAPTER 4. Arms of the Archbishop in Jerusalem, celebrant of the Lambeth X Eucharist in thanksgiving for the spread of the Gospel: The dove has for centuries been included in the Orthodox arms of the Holy City and, as the title of the see makes clear, the Anglican archbishop is *in* Jerusalem whereas the Archbishop *of* Jerusalem is the Orthodox patriarch. The multipointed mullets or stars, silver on the azure field, are from the arms of Jordan. The lion of England is found in the shields of four other dioceses: Leicester, Pretoria, Jamaica, and Guyana, and in all but one is bearing some Christian symbol.

CHAPTER 5. The Royal Arms, seen at the top of the Court Circular announcing Queen Elizabeth's reception for Lambeth X: In the first and fourth quarters of the shield are the lions of England; the lion of Scotland is seen in a double frame; and finally the Irish harp. The circular inscription ("Evil be to him who evil thinks") is the motto of the Order of the Garter, the ancient order of knighthood of which the Sovereign is head. The Sovereign's own motto, "God and my right," is proclaimed beneath the shield upheld by the English lion and Scotland's unicorn.

CHAPTER 6. Arms of the Anglican Church of Canada, whose primate headed the Faith Section of Lambeth X: A maple leaf, emblem of Canada, is in the four quarters formed by the Cross of St. George, traditional symbol of the Anglo-Saxon Christianity from which Anglicanism stems. In addition, there is the mitre and an open Bible. The inscription *Nisi Dominus* is from the opening words of Psalm 127, "Except the Lord build the House, their labor is but lost that build it." It was the motto of Charles Inglis who, as head of the Diocese of Nova Scotia (1787–1816), was the first bishop in the Empire overseas. Designed in 1910, the coat of arms was adopted for use by the General Synod in 1918.

CHAPTER 7. Arms of the Diocese of York, whose Archbishop headed the Ministry Section of Lambeth X: The "keys of the kingdom" on a red field (Matthew 16:19), the heraldic symbol of St. Peter, patron of Yorkminster, represent the divine authority to bind and to loose sins on earth and in heaven. The ancient Archbishops of York used a shield identical with that of the see of Canterbury, with which there was considerable rivalry; not until the enthronement of the fifty-first occupant of the see, Robert Waldby (1397–1398), were the present arms assumed. The crown, now seen in a modernized version, was earlier a peaked cap rising out of St. Peter's tiara. Behind the shield is the Primate's archiepiscopal crozier and pastoral staff.

CHAPTER 8. Arms of the Diocese of Calcutta impaled with the family arms of its ordinary, Lakdasa de Mel, also Metropolitan of India, who headed the Unity Section of Lambeth X: The diocesan shield on the left side includes palm branches surmounted by a mitre and a crozier surmounted by an open book. The de Mel arms is an excellent example of the incorporation of an ancient family's badges into the pattern of Western heraldry.

CHAPTER 9. Arms of the Diocese of London, whose bishop read aloud the Message of Lambeth X: The crossed swords of gold, symbols of the martyrdom of St. Paul, patron of the City of London and its cathedral church, were first displayed by the seventy-first Bishop of London, Ralph Stratford (1340–1354), although several of his predecessors had introduced into their seals a figure of the Blessed Apostle with his emblems of sword and book.

CHAPTER 10. Arms of the Anglican Communion: Radiating from the red Cross of St. George, the points of a compass in blue, green, and gold on a black field illustrate the world-wide spread of the apostolic and evangelical faith. In place of the usual decoration marking north, a mitre has been substituted as the time-honored symbol of the apostolic order essential to the churches that constitute the Anglican Communion. The inscription encircling the shield ("The truth shall make you free," the words of Jesus in John 8:32) is in the original New Testament Greek which, unlike Latin or English, is the only language studied in common by scholars throughout the Anglican Communion. Designed by the Reverend Canon Edward N. West, Canon and Sub-Dean of the Cathedral Church of St. John the Divine, New York City, for the 1954 Anglican Congress at Minneapolis, it was again used for the 1963 Congress at Toronto. It has also been the emblem of the Lambeth Conferences of 1958 and 1968 and, in the intervening years, inspired the cable address "Compasrose" for the London headquarters of the Anglican Communion's Executive Officer.

ABOUT THE AUTHORS

Like an increasing number of Episcopal priests, James B. Simpson and Edward M. Story had successful business careers of more than a decade before entering seminary to study for Holy Orders. Father Simpson was a writer and public relations executive (AP, NBC, BBDO) in New York and Father Story also was in communications and for several years was a chief financial officer of Cunningham & Walsh. They have worked together on *The Hundredth Archbishop of Canterbury* (Harper & Row, 1962) and on a large reference book, *Contemporary Quotations* (Crowell, 1964), now in its fourth printing. Father Simpson, Assistant Rector of Christ's Church, Rye, New York, is a graduate of Northwestern University, the University of Edinburgh, Scotland, and of Nashotah House. Father Story, who is Rector of Trinity Church, Lincoln, Illinois, holds degrees from the University of Tennessee, New York University, and Berkeley Divinity School.

INDEX